Web Content Delivery

Web Information Systems Engineering and Internet Technologies

Book Series

Series Editor: Yanchun Zhang, Victoria University, Australia

Other Books in the Series:

Semistructured Database Design by Tok Wang Ling, Mong Li Lee, Gillian Dobbie

Web Content Delivery

Edited by

Xueyan Tang
Nanyang Technological University, Singapore

Jianliang Xu
Hong Kong Baptist University

Samuel T. Chanson
Hong Kong University of Science and Technology

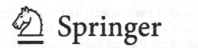 Springer

Xueyan Tang
Nanyang Technological University, SINGAPORE

Jianliang Xu
Hong Kong Baptist University

Samuel T. Chanson
Hong Kong University of Science and Technology

Library of Congress Cataloging-in-Publication Data

A C.I.P. Catalogue record for this book is available
From the Library of Congress

ISBN 978-1-4419-3726-1   e-ISBN 978-0-387-27727-1

Printed in the United States of America

9 8 7 6 5 4 3 2 1

springeronline.com

Contents

Preface

The concept of *content delivery* (also known as content distribution) is becoming increasingly important due to rapidly growing demands for efficient distribution and fast access of information in the Internet. Content delivery is very broad and comprehensive in that the contents for distribution cover a wide range of types with significantly different characteristics and performance concerns, including HTML documents, images, multimedia streams, database tables, and dynamically generated contents. Moreover, to facilitate ubiquitous information access, the network architectures and hardware devices also vary widely. They range from broadband wired/fixed networks to bandwidth-constrained wireless/mobile networks, and from powerful workstations/PCs to personal digital assistants (PDAs) and cellular phones with limited processing and display capabilities. All these levels of diversity are introducing numerous challenges on content delivery technologies. It is desirable to deliver contents in their best quality based on the nature of the contents, network connections and client devices.

This book aims at providing a snapshot of the state-of-the-art research and development activities on web content delivery and laying the foundations for future web applications. The book focuses on four main areas: (1) web content delivery; (2) dynamic web content; (3) streaming media delivery; and (4) ubiquitous web access. It consists of 17 chapters written by leading experts in the field. The book is designed for a professional audience including academic researchers and industrial practitioners who are interested in the most recent research and development activities on web content delivery. It is also suitable as a textbook or reference book for graduate-level students in computer science and engineering.

I

WEB CONTENT DELIVERY

Chapter 1

WEB WORKLOAD CHARACTERIZATION: TEN YEARS LATER

Adepele Williams, Martin Arlitt, Carey Williamson, and Ken Barker

Department of Computer Science, University of Calgary
2500 University Drive NW, Calgary, AB, Canada T2N 1N4
{awilliam,arlitt,carey,barker}@cpsc.ucalgary.ca

Abstract   In 1996, Arlitt and Williamson [Arlitt et al., 1997] conducted a comprehensive workload characterization study of Internet Web servers. By analyzing access logs from 6 Web sites (3 academic, 2 research, and 1 industrial) in 1994 and 1995, the authors identified 10 *invariants*: workload characteristics common to all the sites that are likely to persist over time. In this present work, we revisit the 1996 work by Arlitt and Williamson, repeating many of the same analyses on new data sets collected in 2004. In particular, we study access logs from the same 3 academic sites used in the 1996 paper. Despite a 30-fold increase in overall traffic volume from 1994 to 2004, our main conclusion is that there are no dramatic changes in Web server workload characteristics in the last 10 years. Although there have been many changes in Web technologies (e.g., new protocols, scripting languages, caching infrastructures), most of the 1996 invariants still hold true today. We postulate that these invariants will continue to hold in the future, because they represent fundamental characteristics of how humans organize, store, and access information on the Web.

Keywords: Web servers, workload characterization

1.   Introduction

Internet traffic volume continues to grow rapidly, having almost doubled every year since 1997 [Odlyzko, 2003]. This trend, dubbed "Moore's Law [Moore, 1965] for data traffic", is attributed to increased Web awareness and the advent of sophisticated Internet networking technology [Odlyzko, 2003]. Emerging technologies such as Voice-over-Internet Protocol (VoIP) telephony and Peer-to-Peer (P2P) applications (especially for music and video file sharing) further contribute to this growth trend, amplifying concerns about scalable Web performance.

Research on improving Web performance must be based on a solid understanding of Web workloads. The work described in this chapter is motivated generally by the need to characterize the current workloads of Internet Web servers, and specifically by the desire to see if the 1996 "invariants" identified by Arlitt and Williamson [Arlitt et al., 1997] still hold true today. The chapter addresses the question of whether Moore's Law for data traffic has affected the 1996 invariants or not, and if so, in what ways.

The current study involves the analysis of access logs from three Internet Web servers that were also used in the 1996 study. The selected Web servers (University of Waterloo, University of Calgary, and University of Saskatchewan) are all from academic environments, and thus we expect that changes in their workload characteristics will adequately reflect changes in the use of Web technology. Since the data sets used in the 1996 study were obtained between October 1994 and January 1996, comparison of the 2004 server workloads with the servers in the 1996 study represents a span of approximately ten years. This period provides a suitable vantage point for a retrospective look at the evolution of Web workload characteristics over time.

The most noticeable difference in the Web workload today is a dramatic increase in Web traffic volume. For example, the University of Saskatchewan Web server currently receives an average of 416,573 requests per day, about 32 times larger than the 11,255 requests per day observed in 1995. For this data set, the doubling effect of Moore's Law applies biennially rather than annually.

The goal of our research is to study the general impact of "Moore's Law" on the 1996 Web workload invariants. Our approach follows the methodology in [Arlitt et al., 1997]. In particular, we focus on the document size distribution, document type distribution, and document referencing behavior of Internet Web servers. Unfortunately, we are not able to analyze the geographic distribution of server requests, since the host names and IP addresses in the access logs were anonymized for privacy and security reasons. Therefore, this work revisits only 9 of the 10 invariants from the 1996 paper. While some invariants have changed slightly due to changes in Web technologies, we find that most of the invariants hold true today, despite the rapid growth in Internet traffic. The main observations from our study are summarized in Table 1.1.

The rest of this chapter is organized as follows. Section 2 provides some background on Moore's Law, Web server workload characterization, and related work tracking the evolution of Web workloads. Section 3 describes the data sets used in this study, the data analysis process, and initial findings from this research. Section 4 continues the workload characterization process, presenting the main results and observations from our study. Section 5 summarizes the chapter, presents conclusions, and provides suggestions for future work.

Table 1.1.　Summary of Web Server Workload Characteristics

Workload Characteristic	Description	Status
1. Successful Requests	About 65-70% of requests to a Web server result in the successful transfer of a document.	Lower than 1994 (Section 3.1)
2. Document Types	HTML and image documents together account for 70-85% of the documents transferred by Web servers.	Lower than 1994 (Section 3.2)
3. Transfer Size	The median transfer size is small (e.g., ≤ 5 KB).	Same (Section 3.2)
4. Distinct Requests	A small fraction (about 1%) of server requests are for distinct documents.	Same (Section 3.2)
5. One-time Referencing	A significant percentage of files (15-26%) and bytes (6-21%) accessed in the log are accessed only once in the log.	Same (Section 4.1)
6. File Size Distribution	The file size distribution and transfer size distribution are *heavy-tailed* (e.g., Pareto with $\alpha \approx 1$)	Same (Section 4.2)
7. Concentration	The busiest 10% of files account for approximately 80-90% of requests and 80-90% of bytes transferred.	Same (Section 4.2)
8. Inter-Reference Times	The times between successive requests to the same file are exponentially distributed and independent.	Same (Section 4.2)
9. Remote Requests	Remote sites account for 70% or more of the accesses to the server, and 80% or more of the bytes transferred.	Same (Section 4.2)
10. Wide-Area Usage	Web servers are accessed by hosts on many networks, with 10% of the networks generating 75% or more of the usage.	Not studied

2.　Background and Related Work

2.1　Moore's Law and the Web

In 1965, Gordon Moore, the co-founder of Intel, observed that new computer chips released each year contained roughly twice as many transistors as their predecessors [Moore, 1965]. He predicted that this trend would continue for at least the next decade, leading to a computing revolution. Ten years later, Moore revised his prediction, stating that the number of transistors on a chip would double every two years. This trend is referred to as Moore's Law. It is often generalized beyond the microchip industry to refer to any growth pattern that produces a doubling in a period of 12-24 months [Schaller, 1996].

Odlyzko [Odlyzko, 2003] observed that the growth of Internet traffic follows Moore's Law. This growth continues today, with P2P applications currently the most prominent contributors to growth. Press [Press, 2000] argues that the economy, sophistication of use, new applications, and improved infrastructure (e.g., high speed connectivity, mobile devices, affordable personal computers, wired and wireless technologies) have a significant impact on the Internet today. This observation suggests that the underlying trends in Internet usage could have changed over the past ten years.

The 1996 study of Web server workloads involved 6 Web sites with substantially different levels of server activity. Nevertheless, all of the Web sites exhibited similar workload characteristics. This observation implies that the sheer volume of traffic is not the major determining factor in Web server workload characteristics. Rather, it is the behavioral characteristics of the Web users that matters. However, the advent of new technology could change user behavior with time, affecting Web workload characteristics. It is this issue that we explore in this work.

2.2   Web Server Workload Characterization

Most Web servers are configured to record an *access log* of all client requests for Web site content. The typical syntax of an access log entry is:

`hostname - - [dd/mm/yyy:hh:mm:ss tz] document status size`

The hostname is the name or IP address of the machine that generated the request for a document. The following fields ("- -") are usually blank, but some servers record user name information here. The next field indicates the day and time that the request was made, including the timezone (tz). The URL requested is recorded in the document field. The status field indicates the response code (e.g., Successful, Not Found) for the request. The final field indicates the size in bytes of the document returned to the client.

Characterizing Web server workloads involves the statistical analysis of log entries and the identification of salient trends. The results of this analysis can provide useful insights for several tasks: enhancing Web server performance, network administration and maintenance, building workload models for network simulation, and capacity planning for future Web site growth. In our study, we characterize Web server workloads to assess how (or if) Web traffic characteristics have changed over time.

2.3   Related Work

Our study is not the first to provide a longitudinal analysis of Web workload characteristics. There are several prior studies providing a retrospective look at Web traffic evolution, four of which are summarized here.

Hernandez *et al.* discuss the evolution of Web traffic from 1995 to 2003 [Hernandez et al., 2003]. In their study, they observe that the sizes of HTTP requests have been increasing, while the sizes of HTTP responses have been decreasing. However, the sizes of the largest HTTP responses observed continue to increase. They observe that Web usage by both content providers and Web clients has significantly evolved. Technology improvements such as persistent connections, server load balancing, and content distribution networks all have an impact on this evolution. They provide a strong argument for continuous monitoring of Internet traffic to track its evolutionary patterns.

In 2001, Cherkasova and Karlsson [Cherkasova et al., 2001] revisited the 1996 invariants, showing several new trends in modern Web server workloads. Their work shows that 2-4% of files account for 90% of server requests. This level of skew (called *concentration*) is even more pronounced than claimed in 1996 [Arlitt et al., 1997], when 10% of the files accounted for 90% of the activity. The authors speculate that the differences arise from Web server side performance improvements, available Internet bandwidth, and a greater proportion of graphical content on Web pages. However, their comparison uses a completely different set of access logs than was used in the 1996 study, making direct comparisons difficult.

Barford *et al.* [Barford et al., 1999] study changes in Web client access patterns between 1995 and 1998. They compare measurements of Web client workloads obtained from the same server at Boston University, separated in time by three years. They conclude that document size distributions did not change over time, though the distribution of file popularity did. While the objective of the research in [Barford et al., 1999] is similar to ours, their analysis was only for Web client workloads rather than Web server workloads.

For more general workloads, Harel *et al.* [Harel et al., 1999] characterize a media-enhanced classroom server. They use the approach proposed in [Arlitt et al., 1997] to obtain 10 invariants, which they then compare with the 1996 invariants. They observe that the inter-reference times of documents requested from media-enhanced classroom servers are not exponentially distributed and independent. Harel *et al.* suggest the observed differences are due to the frame-based user interface of the Classroom 2000 system. The focus of their study is to highlight the characteristics of media-enhanced classroom servers, which are quite different from our study. However, their conclusions indicate that user applications can significantly impact Web server workloads.

A detailed survey of Web workload characterization for Web clients, servers, and proxies is provided in [Pitkow, 1998].

3. Data Collection and Analysis

Three data sets are used in this study. These access logs are from the same three academic sites used in the 1996 work by Arlitt and Williamson. The access logs are from:

1 A small research lab Web server at the University of Waterloo.

2 A department-level Web server from the Department of Computer Science at the University of Calgary.

3 A campus-level Web server at the University of Saskatchewan.

The access logs were all collected between May 2004 and August 2004. These logs were then sanitized, prior to being made available to us. In particular, the IP addresses/host names and URLs were anonymized in a manner that met the individual site's privacy/security concerns, while still allowing us to examine 9 of the 10 invariants. The following subsections provide an overview of these anonymized data sets.

We were unable to obtain access logs from the other three Web sites that were examined in the 1996 work. The ClarkNet site no longer exists, as the ISP was acquired by another company. Due to current security policies at NASA and NCSA, we could not obtain the access logs from those sites.

3.1   Comparison of Data Sets

Table 1.2 presents a statistical comparison of the three data sets studied in this chapter. In the table, the data sets are ordered from left to right based on average daily traffic volume, which varies by about an order of magnitude from one site to the next. The Waterloo data set represents the least loaded server studied. The Saskatchewan data set represents the busiest server studied. In some of the analyses that follow, we will use one data set as a representative example to illustrate selected Web server workload characteristics. Often, the Saskatchewan server is used as the example. Important differences among data sets are mentioned, when they occur.

Table 1.2.   Summary of Access Log Characteristics (Raw Data)

Item	Waterloo	Calgary	Saskatchewan
Access Log Duration	41 days	4 months	3 months
Access Log Start Date	July 18, 2004	May 1, 2004	June 1, 2004
Total Requests	176,492	6,046,663	38,325,644
Avg Requests/Day	4,294	51,243	416,572
Total Bytes Transferred (MB)	13,512	457,255	363,845
Avg Bytes/Day (MB)	328.7	3,875.0	3,954.7

3.2   Response Code Analysis

As in [Arlitt et al., 1997], we begin by analyzing the response codes of the log entries, categorizing the results into 4 distinct groups. The "Successful" category (code 200 and 206) represents requests for documents that were found and returned to the requesting host. The "Not Modified" category (code 304) represents the result from a GET If-Modified-Since request. This conditional GET request is used for validation of a cached document, for example between a Web browser cache and a Web server. The 304 Not Modified response means that the document has not changed since it was last retrieved, and so no document transfer is required. The "Found" category (code 301 and 302) represents requests for documents that reside in a different location from that specified in the request, so the server returns the new URL, rather than the document. The "Not Successful" category (code 4XX) represents error conditions, in which it is impossible for the server to return the requested document to the client (e.g., Not Found, No Permission).

Table 1.3 summarizes the results from the response code analysis for the Saskatchewan Web server. The main observation is that the Not Modified responses are far more prevalent in 2004 (22.9%) than they were in 1994 (6.3%). This change reflects an increase in the deployment (and effectiveness) of Web caching mechanisms, not only in browser caches, but also in the Internet. The percentage of Successful requests has correspondingly decreased from about 90% in 1994 to about 70% in 2004. This result is recorded in Table 1.1 as a change in the first invariant from the 1996 paper. The number of Found documents has increased somewhat from 1.7% to 4.2%, reflecting improved techniques for redirecting document requests.

Table 1.3. Server Response Code Analysis (U. Saskatchewan)

Response Group	Response Code	1995	2004
Successful	200,206	90.7%	68.7%
Not Modified	304	6.3%	22.9%
Found	301,302	1.7%	4.2%
Unsuccessful	4XX	1.3%	4.2%
Total	-	100%	100%

In the rest of our study, results from both the Successful and the Not Modified categories are analyzed, since both satisfy user requests. The Found and Unsuccessful categories are less prevalent, and thus are not analyzed further in the rest of the study.

Table 1.4 provides a statistical summary of the reduced data sets.

3.3 Document Types

The next step in our analysis was to classify documents by type. Classification was based on either the suffix in the file name (e.g., .html, .gif, and many more), or by the presence of special characters (e.g., a '?' in the URL,

Table 1.4. Summary of Access Log Characteristics (Reduced Data: 200, 206 and 304)

Item	Waterloo	Calgary	Saskatchewan
Access Log Duration	41 days	4 months	3 months
Access Log Start Date	July 18, 2004	May 1, 2004	June 1, 2004
Total Requests	155,021	5,038,976	35,116,868
Avg Requests/Day	3,772	42,703	381,695
Total Bytes Transfered (MB)	13,491	456,090	355,605
Avg Bytes/Day (MB)	328	3,865	3,865
Total Distinct Bytes (MB)	616	8,741	7,494
Distinct Bytes/Day (MB)	15.00	74.10	81.45
Mean Transfer Size (bytes)	91,257	94,909	10,618
Median Transfer Size (bytes)	3,717	1,385	2,162
Mean File Size (bytes)	257,789	397,458	28,313
Median File Size (bytes)	24,149	8,889	5,600
Maximum File Size (MB)	35.5	193.3	108.6

or a '/' at the end of the URL). We calculated statistics on the types of documents found in each reduced data set. The results of this analysis are shown in Table 1.5.

Table 1.5. Summary of Document Types (Reduced Data: 200, 206 and 304)

	Waterloo		Calgary		Saskatchewan	
Item	Reqs (%)	Bytes (%)	Reqs (%)	Bytes (%)	Reqs (%)	Bytes (%)
HTML	23.18	6.02	8.09	1.13	12.46	11.98
Images	63.02	10.77	78.76	33.36	57.64	33.75
Directory	4.67	0.19	3.12	0.65	13.35	19.37
CSS	0.93	0.03	2.48	0.07	6.54	0.84
Dynamic	1.96	0.09	3.63	0.55	5.78	8.46
Audio	0.00	0.00	0.01	0.16	0.01	0.29
Video	0.00	0.00	0.40	54.02	0.06	5.25
Formatted	5.13	82.32	1.02	8.30	1.30	17.25
Other	1.11	0.58	2.49	1.76	2.86	2.81
Total	100.0	100.0	100.0	100.0	100.0	100.0

Table 1.5 shows the percentage of each document type seen based on the percentage of requests or percentage of bytes transferred for each of the servers. In the 1996 study, HTML and Image documents accounted for 90-100% of the total requests to each server. In the current data, these two types account for only 70-86% of the total requests. This reflects changes in the underlying Web technologies, and differences in the way people use the Web.

Table 1.5 illustrates two aspects of these workload changes. First, the 'Directory' URLs are often used to shorten URLs, which makes it easier for people to remember them. Many 'Directory' URLs are actually for HTML documents (typically index.html), although they could be other types as well. Second, Cascading Style Sheets (CSS)[1] are a simple mechanism for adding fonts, colors, and spacing to a set of Web pages. If we collectively consider the HTML, Images, Directory, and CSS types, which are the components of most Web pages, we find that they account for over 90% of all references. In other words, browsing Web pages (rather than downloading papers or videos) is still the most common activity that Web servers support.

While browsing Web pages accounts for most of the requests to each of the servers, Formatted and Video types are responsible for a significant fraction of the total bytes transferred. These two types account for more than 50% of all bytes transferred on the Waterloo and Calgary servers, and over 20% of all bytes transferred on the Saskatchewan server, even though less than 5% of requests are to these types. The larger average size of Formatted and Video files, the increasing availability of these types, and the improvements in computing and networking capabilities over the last 10 years are all reasons that these types account for such a significant fraction of the bytes transferred.

3.4   Web Workload Evolution

Table 1.6 presents a comparison of the access log characteristics in 1994 and 2004 for the Saskatchewan Web server. The server has substantially higher load in 2004. For example, the total number of requests observed in 3 months in 2004 exceeds the total number of requests observed in 7 months in 1995, doing so by over an order of magnitude. The rest of our analysis focuses on understanding if this growth in traffic volume has altered the Web server's workload characteristics.

One observation is that the mean size of documents transferred is larger in 2004 (about 10 KB) than in 1994 (about 6 KB). However, the median size is only slightly larger than in 1994, and still consistent with the third invariant listed in Table 1.1.

Table 1.6 indicates that the maximum file sizes have grown over time. A similar observation was made by Hernandez *et al.* [Hernandez et al., 2003]. The increase in the maximum file sizes is responsible for the increase in the mean. The maximum file sizes will continue to grow over time, as increases in computing, networking, and storage capacities enable new capabilities for Web users and content providers.

Next, we analyze the access logs to obtain statistics on distinct documents. We observe that about 1% of the requests are for distinct documents. These requests account for 2% of the bytes transferred. Table 1.6 shows that the

Table 1.6.   Comparative Summary of Web Server Workloads (U. Saskatchewan)

Item	1995	2004
Access Log Duration	7 months	3 months
Access Log Start Date	June 1, 1995	June 1, 2004
Total Requests	2,408,625	35,116,868
Avg Requests/Day	11,255	381,695
Total Bytes Transfered (MB)	12,330	355,605
Avg Bytes/Day (MB)	57.6	3865.2
Total Distinct Bytes (MB)	249.2	7,494
Distinct Bytes/Day (MB)	1.16	81.46
Mean Transfer Size (bytes)	5,918	10,618
Median Transfer Size (bytes)	1,898	2,162
Mean File Size (bytes)	16,166	28,313
Median File Size (bytes)	1,442	5,600
Maximum File Size (MB)	28.8	108.6
Distinct Requests/Total Requests	0.9%	0.8%
Distinct Bytes/Total Bytes	2.0%	2.1%
Distinct Files Accessed Only Once	42.0%	26.1%
Distinct Bytes Accessed Only Once	39.1%	18.3%

percentage of distinct requests is similar to that in 1994. This fact is recorded in Table 1.1 as an unchanged invariant.

The next analysis studies "one-timer" documents: documents that are accessed exactly once in the log. One-timers are relevant because their presence limits the effectiveness of on-demand document caching policies [Arlitt et al., 1997].

For the Saskatchewan data set, the percentage of one-timer documents has decreased from 42.0% in 1994 to 26.1% in 2004. Similarly, the byte traffic volume of one-timer documents has decreased from 39.1% to 18.3%. While there are many one-timer files observed (26.2%), the lower value for one-timer bytes (18.3%) implies that they tend to be small in size. Across all three servers, 15-26% of files and 6-21% of distinct bytes were accessed only a single time. This is similar to the behavior observed in the 1994 data, so it is retained as an invariant in Table 1.1.

4.   Workload Characterization

4.1   File and Transfer Size Distributions

In the next stage of workload characterization, we analyze the file size distribution and the transfer size distribution.

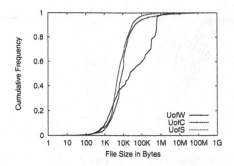

Figure 1.1. Cumulative Distribution (CDF) of File Sizes, by server

Figure 1.1 shows the cumulative distribution function (CDF) for the sizes of the distinct files observed in each server's workload. Similar to the CDF plotted in [Arlitt et al., 1997], most files range from 1 KB to 1 MB in size. Few files are smaller than 100 bytes in size, and few exceed 10 MB. However, we note that the size of the largest file observed has increased by an order of a magnitude from 28 MB in 1994 to 193 MB in 2004.

Similar to the approach used in the 1996 study, we further analyze the file and transfer size distributions to determine if they are heavy-tailed. In particular, we study the tail of the distribution, using the scaling estimator approach [Crovella et al., 1999] to estimate the tail index α.

Table 1.7 shows the α values obtained in our analysis. We find tail index values ranging from 1.02 to to 1.31. The tails of the file size distributions for our three data sets all fit well with the Pareto distribution, a relatively simple heavy-tailed distribution. Since the file size and transfer size distributions are heavy-tailed, we indicate this as an unchanged invariant in Table 1.1.

Table 1.7. Comparison of Heavy-Tailed File and Transfer Size Distributions

Item	Waterloo	Calgary	Saskatchewan
File Size Distribution	$\alpha = 1.10$	$\alpha = 1.31$	$\alpha = 1.02$
Transfer Size Distribution	$\alpha = 0.86$	$\alpha = 1.05$	$\alpha = 1.17$

Figure 1.2 provides a graphical illustration of the heavy-tailed file and transfer size distributions for the Saskatchewan workload, using a log-log complementary distribution (LLCD) plot. Recall that the cumulative distribution function $F(x)$ expresses the probability that a random variable X is less than x. By definition, the complementary distribution is $\bar{F} = 1 - F(x)$, which expresses the probability that a random variable X exceeds x [Montgomery et al., 2001].

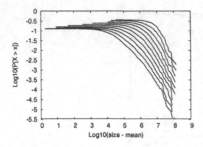

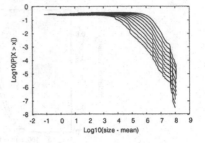

Figure 1.2.   File Size Distribution, UofS,
$\alpha = 1.02$

Figure 1.3.   Transfer Size Distribution,
UofS, $\alpha = 1.17$

An LLCD plot shows the value of $\bar{F}(x)$ versus x, using logarithmic scales on both axes.

In Figure 1.2, the bottom curve is the empirical data; each subsequent curve is aggregated by a factor of 2. This is the recommended default aggregation factor for use with the aest tool [Crovella et al., 1999].

On an LLCD plot, a heavy-tailed distribution typically manifests itself with straight-line behavior (with slope α). In Figure 1.3, the straight-line behavior is evident, starting from a (visually estimated) point at 10 KB that demarcates the tail of the distribution. This plot provides graphical evidence for the heavy-tailed distributions estimated previously.

4.2   File Referencing Behavior

In the next set of workload studies, we focus on the file referencing pattern for the Calgary Web server. In particular, we study the concentration of references, the temporal locality properties, and the document inter-reference times. We do not study the geographic distribution of references because this information cannot be determined from the sanitized access logs provided.

Concentration of References.   The term "concentration" of references refers to the non-uniform distribution of requests across the Web documents accessed in the log. Some Web documents receive hundreds or thousands of requests, while others receive relatively few requests.

Our first step is to assess the referencing pattern of documents using the approach described in [Arlitt et al., 1997]. Similar to the 1996 results, a few files account for most of the incoming requests, and most of the bytes transferred. Figure 1.4 shows a plot illustrating concentration of references. The vertical axis represents the cumulative proportion of requests accounted for by the cumulative fraction of files (sorted from most to least referenced) along the horizontal axis. High concentration is indicated by a line near the upper left

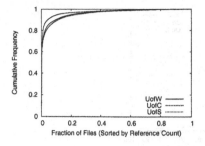

Figure 1.4. Cumulative Distribution for Concentration

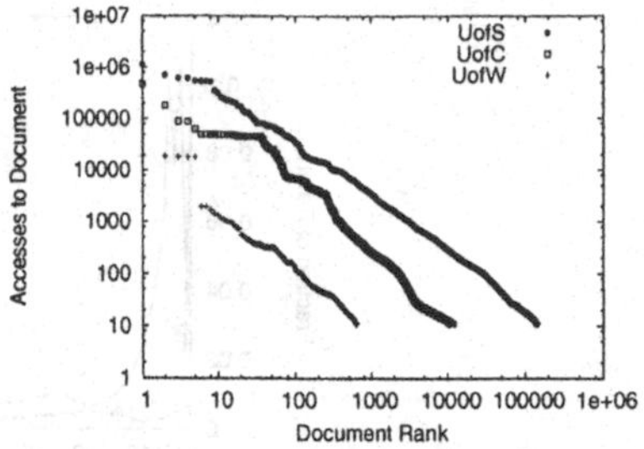

Figure 1.5. Reference Count Versus Rank

corner of the graph. As a comparison, an equal number of requests for each document would result in a diagonal line in this graph. Clearly, the data set in Figure 1.4 shows high concentration.

Another approach to assess non-uniformity of file referencing is with a popularity profile plot. Documents are ranked from most popular (1) to least popular (N), and then the number of requests to each document is plotted versus its rank, on a log-log scale. A straight-line behavior on such a graph is indicative of a power-law relationship in the distribution of references, commonly referred to as a Zipf (or Zipf-like) distribution [Zipf, 1949].

Figure 1.5 provides a popularity profile plot for each workload. The general trend across all three workloads is Zipf-like. There is some flattening in the popularity profile for the most popular documents. This flattening is attributable to Web caching effects [Williamson, 2002].

Temporal Locality. In the next set of experiments, we analyze the access logs to measure temporal locality. The term "temporal locality" refers to time-based correlations in document referencing behavior. Simply expressed, documents referenced in the recent past are likely to be referenced in the near future. More formally stated, the probability of a future request to a document is inversely related to the time since it was most recently referenced [Mahanti et al., 2000].

Note that temporal locality is not the same as concentration. High concentration does not necessarily imply high temporal locality, nor vice versa, though the two concepts are somewhat related. For example, in a data set with high concentration, it is likely that documents with many references are also referenced in the recent past.

One widely used measure for temporal locality is the Least Recently Used Stack Model (LRUSM). The LRUSM maintains a simple time-based relative ordering of all recently-referenced items using a stack. The top of the stack

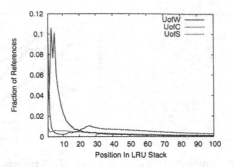

Figure 1.6.   Temporal Locality Characteristics

holds the most recently used document, while the bottom of the stack holds the
least recently used item. At any point in time, a re-referenced item D is pulled
out from its current position P, and placed on top of the stack, pushing other
items down as necessary. Statistics are recorded regarding which positions P
tend to be referenced (called the stack distance). An item being referenced for
the first time has an undefined stack distance, and is simply added to the top of
the stack. Thus the size of the stack increases only if a document that does not
exist already in the stack arrives.

Temporal locality is manifested by a tendency to reference documents at or
near the top of the stack. We perform an LRUSM analysis on the entire access
log and plot the reference probability versus the LRU stack distance.

Figure 1.6 is a plot of the relative referencing for the first 100 positions of
the LRUSM. In general, our analysis shows a low degree of temporal locality,
as was observed in the 1996 paper.

The temporal locality observed in 2004 is even weaker than that observed
in the 1994 data. We attribute this to two effects. The first effect is the increased level of load for the Web servers. As load increases, so does the level
of "multiprogramming" (i.e., concurrent requests from different users for unre-
lated documents), which tends to reduce temporal locality. The second effect is
due to Web caching [Williamson, 2002]. With effective Web caching, fewer requests propagate through to the Web server. More importantly, only the cache
misses in the request stream reach the server. Thus Web servers tend to see
lower temporal locality in the incoming request stream [Williamson, 2002].

Inter-reference Times.   Next, we analyze the access logs to study the inter-
reference times of documents. Our aim is to determine whether the arrival
process can be modeled with a fixed-rate Poisson process. That is, we need
to know if the inter-reference times for document requests are exponentially
distributed and independent, with a rate that does not vary with time of day.

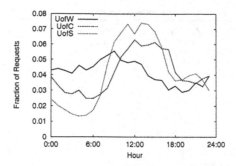

Figure 1.7. Distribution of Hourly Request Arrival Rate, by Server

Figure 1.7 shows a time series representation of the number of requests received by each server in each one hour period of their respective access logs. The aggregate request stream follows a diurnal pattern with peaks and dips, and thus cannot be modeled with a fixed-rate Poisson process. This observation is consistent with the 1996 study, and is easily explained by time of day effects. For instance, most people work between 9:00am and 6:00pm, and this is when the number of requests is highest.

Similar to the approach in [Arlitt et al., 1997], we study the request arrival process at a finer-grain time scale, namely within a one-hour period for which we assume the arrival rate is stationary. The intent is to determine if the distribution of request inter-arrival times is consistent with an exponential distribution, and if so, to assess the correlation (if any) between the inter-arrival times observed.

Figure 1.8 shows a log-log plot of the complementary distribution of observed inter-arrival times within a selected hour, along with an exponential distribution with the same mean inter-arrival time. The relative slopes suggest that the empirical distribution differs from the exponential distribution, similar to the 1996 findings.

Finally, using the approach proposed by Paxson and Floyd [Paxson et al., 1995], we study the inter-arrival times of individual busy documents in detail. We use the same threshold rules suggested in the 1996 study, namely that a "busy" document is one that is accessed at least 50 times in at least 25 different non-overlapping one-hour intervals.

We study if the inter-arrival times for these busy documents are exponentially-distributed and independent. The Anderson-Darling (A^2) test [Romeu, 2003] is a goodness-of-fit test suitable for this purpose. It compares the sampled distribution to standard distributions, like the exponential distribution. We express our results as the proportion of sampled intervals for which the distribution is statistically indistinguishable from an exponential distribution. The degree of

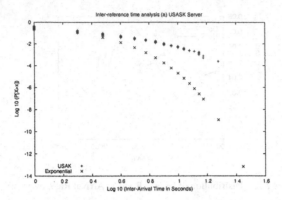

Figure 1.8.   Inter-Reference Time Analysis

independence is measured by the amount of autocorrelation among inter-arrival times.

Unfortunately, we do not have definitive results for this analysis. The difficulty is that Web access logs, as in 1996, record timestamps with 1-second resolution. This resolution is inadequate for testing exponential distributions, particularly when busy Web servers record multiple requests with the same arrival time (i.e., an inter-arrival of 0, which is impossible in an exponential distribution). We do not include our findings in this chapter because we could not ascertain our A^2 coefficient values for this test. However, since the document inter-arrival times closely follow the 1996 results for the two previous levels of analysis, we have no evidence to refute the invariant in Table 1.1. We believe that the inter-reference times for a busy document are exponentially distributed and independent.

Remote Requests.   While we do not have actual IP addresses or host names recorded in our logs, the sanitized host identifier included with each request indicates whether the host was "local" or "remote". For the Saskatchewan data set, 76% of requests and 83% of bytes transferred were to remote hosts. For the Calgary data set, remote hosts issued 88% of requests and received 99% of the bytes transferred.[2]

These proportions are even higher than in the 1994 workloads. We conclude that remote requests still account for a majority of requests and bytes transferred. This invariant is recorded Table 1.1.

Limitations.   We could not analyze the geographic distribution of clients as in [Arlitt et al., 1997] because of sanitized IP addresses in the access logs. Also, we do not analyze the impact of user aborts and file modifications in this study because we do not have the error logs associated with the Web access logs. The error logs are required to accurately differentiate between user abort and file modifications.

5.   Summary and Conclusions

This chapter presented a comparison of Web server workload characteristics across a time span of ten years. Recent research indicates that Web traffic volume is increasing rapidly. We seek to understand if the underlying Web server workload characteristics are changing or evolving as the volume of traffic increases. Our research repeats the workload characterization study described in a paper by Arlitt and Williamson, using 3 new data sets that represent a subset of the sites in the 1996 study.

Despite a 30-fold increase in overall traffic volume from 1994 to 2004, our main conclusion is that there are no dramatic changes in Web server work-load characteristics in the last 10 years. Improved Web caching mechanisms and other new technologies have changed some of the workload character-istics (e.g., Successful request percentage) observed in the 1996 study, and had subtle influences on others (e.g., mean file sizes, mean transfer sizes, and weaker temporal locality). However, most of the 1996 invariants still hold true today. These include one-time referencing behaviors, high concentration of references, heavy-tailed file size distributions, non-Poisson aggregate request streams, Poisson per-document request streams, and the dominance of remote requests. We speculate that these invariants will continue to hold in the future, because they represent fundamental characteristics of how humans organize, store, and access information on the Web.

In terms of future work, it would be useful to revisit the performance impli-cations of Web server workload characteristics. For example, one could extend this study to analyze caching design issues to understand if the changes ob-served in these invariants can be exploited to improve Web server performance. It will also be interesting to study other Web server access logs from commer-cial and research organizations to see if they experienced similar changes in Web server workloads. A final piece of future work is to formulate long-term models of Web traffic evolution so that accurate predictions of Web workloads can be made.

Acknowledgements

Financial support for this work was provided by iCORE (Informatics Circle of Research Excellence) in the Province of Alberta, as well as NSERC (Natural Sciences and Engineering Research Council) of Canada, and CFI (Canada Foun-dation for Innovation). The authors are grateful to Brad Arlt, Andrei Dragoi,

Earl Fogel, Darcy Grant, and Ben Groot for their assistance in the collection
and sanitization of the Web server access logs used in our study.

Notes

1. http://www.w3.org/Style/CSS
2. The Waterloo data set did not properly distinguish between local and remote users.

References

Arlitt, M. and Williamson, C. (1997) Internet Web Servers: Workload Characterization and Performance Implications. *IEEE/ACM Transactions on Networking*, Vol. 5, No. 5, pp. 631-645.

Barford, P., Bestavros, A., Bradley, A. and Crovella, M. (1999) Changes in
Web Client Access Patterns: Characteristics and Caching Implications. *World
Wide Web Journal*, Special Issue on Characterization and Performance Eval-
uation, pp. 15-28.

Cherkasova, L. and Karlsson, M. (2001) Dynamics and Evolution of Web Sites:
Analysis, Metrics and Design Issues. *Proceedings of the 6th IEEE Symposium
on Computers and Communications*, Hammamet, Tunisia, pp. 64-71.

Crovella, M. and Taqqu, M. (1999) Estimating the Heavy Tail Index from Scaling Properties. *Methodology and Computing in Applied Probability*, Vol. 1,
No. 1, pp. 55-79.

Harel, N., Vellanki, V., Chervenak, A., Abowd, G. and Ramachandran, U. (1999)
Workload of a Media-Enhanced Classroom Server. *Proceedings of the 2nd
IEEE Workshop on Workload Characterization*, Austin, TX.

Hernandez-Campos, F., Jeffay, K. and Donelson-Smith, F. (2003) Tracking
the Evolution of Web Traffic: 1995-2003. *Proceedings of 11th IEEE/ACM
International Symposium on Modeling, Analysis and Simulation of Computer
and Telecommunications Systems* (MASCOTS), Orlando, FL, pp. 16-25.

Mahanti, A., Eager, D. and Williamson, C. (2000) Temporal Locality and its
Impact on Web Proxy Cache Performance. *Performance Evaluation*, Special
Issue on Internet Performance Modeling, Vol. 42, No. 2/3, pp. 187-203.

Montgomery, D., Runger, G. and Hubele, N. (2001) *Engineering Statistics*.
John Wiley and Sons, New York.

Moore, G. (1965) Cramming More Components onto Integrated Circuits. *Electronics*, Vol. 38 No. 8, pp. 114-117.

Odlyzko, A. (2003) Internet Traffic Growth: Sources and Implications. *Proceedings of SPIE Optical Transmission Systems and Equipment for WDM
Networking II*, Vol. 5247, pp. 1-15.

Paxson, V. and Floyd, S. (1995) Wide-area Traffic: The Failure of Poisson
Modeling. *IEEE/ACM Transactions on Networking*, Vol. 3, No. 3, pp. 226-
244.

Pitkow, J. (1998) Summary of WWW Characterizations. *Proceedings of the Seventh International World Wide Web Conference*, Brisbane, Australia, pp. 551-558.

Press, L. (2000) The State of the Internet: Growth and Gaps. *Proceedings of INET 2000*, Japan. Available at http://www.isoc.org/inet2000/cdproceedings/8e/8e_4.htm\#s21.

Romeu, J. (2003) Anderson-Darling: A Goodness of Fit Test for Small Samples Assumptions. *Selected Topics in Assurance Related Technologies*, Vol. 10, No. 5, DoD Reliability Analysis Center.
Available at http://rac.alionscience.com/pdf/A_DTest.pdf.

Schaller, B. (1996) The Origin, Nature, and Implications of Moore's Law. Available at http://mason.gmu.edu/~rschalle/moorelaw.html.

Williamson, C. (2002) On Filter Effects in Web Caching Hierarchies. *ACM Transactions on Internet Technology*, Vol. 2, No. 1, pp. 47-77.

Zipf, G. (1949) *Human Behavior and the Principle of Least Effort*. Addison-Wesley Press, Inc., Cambridge, MA.

Chapter 2

REPLICA PLACEMENT
AND REQUEST ROUTING

Magnus Karlsson
HP Labs
1501 Page Mill Rd, 1134
Palo Alto, CA, U.S.A.

Abstract   All content delivery networks must decide where to place its content and how
to direct the clients to this content. This chapter provides an overview of state-
of-the-art solution approaches in both of these areas. But, instead of giving a
detailed description on each of the solutions, we provide a high-level overview
and compare the approaches by their impact on the client-perceived performance
and cost of the content delivery network. This way, we get a better understanding
of the practical implications of applying these algorithms in content delivery
networks. We end the chapter with a discussion on some open and interesting
research challenges in this area.

Keywords: Replica placement algorithms, request routing, content delivery networks, heuristics

1.   Replica Placement

Replica placement is the process of choosing where to place copies of web
sites or parts of web sites on web servers in the CDN infrastructure. Request
routing is the mechanism and policy of redirecting client requests to a suitable
web-server containing the requested content. The end goal of the CDN provider
is to provide "good enough" performance to keep the customers satisfied at a
minimum infrastructure cost to the provider, in order to maximize profit. This
chapter will focus on the impact of past and future replica placement and request
routing algorithms to the above system-level goal. Thus, it does not focus on
algorithmic details or tries to comprehensively survey all material in the field.
Instead, enough existing algorithms are discussed in order to explain the basic
properties of these algorithms that impact the system-level goal under various

situations (e.g., hotspots, network partitions) that a CDN experiences and is expected to handle.

The infrastructure costs that replica placement algorithms and request routing algorithms mainly affect are networking costs for fetching content and adjusting content placements, storage costs for storing content on the set servers, and computational costs for running the actual algorithms that make these two decisions. There are also management costs associated with these choices, but they are out of scope of this chapter. While the two policies interact in achieving the system-level goal, we will start by studying them both in isolation, then in the end discuss the combined effect.

1.1   Basic Problem and Properties

In the replica placement problem formulation, the system is represented as a number of interconnected *nodes*. The nodes store replicas of a set of data *objects*. These can be whole web sites, web pages, individual html files, etc. A number of *clients* access some or all of these objects located on the nodes. It is the system-level goal of a *replica placement algorithm (RPA)* to place the objects such as to provide the clients with "good enough" performance at the lowest possible infrastructure cost for the CDN provider. Both the definition of good enough performance (to keep and attract customers) and infrastructure cost are complicated in the general case and an active and heavily debated research topic.

But, even for some simple definition of good performance and infrastructure cost, this problem is NP-hard [Karlsson and Karamanolis, 2004]. Therefore, the problem is simplified by an RPA in order to reach some usually suboptimal solution within a feasible time frame. To understand what an RPA really is, we have identified a set of RPA properties that on a high-level capture the techniques and assumptions found in different RPAs. These properties will also help us in understanding the relationship between existing RPAs, the performance of the methods as measured by the system-level goal, and pin-point areas of research that might be interesting to explore in the future.

Most RPAs captures the performance of the CDN as a *cost function*. This cost function is usually an approximation of the overall performance of the system. E.g., it could be the sum of the number of read accesses that hit in a node, or the sum of the average latencies between clients and the closest replica of an object. This cost function is then minimized or maximized (depending on what makes sense for the actual cost function) subject to zero or more *constraints*. These constraints are usually approximations of the CDN providers costs for the system. The two most common ones are a constraint on the max storage space allocated for objects on each node (*storage constraint*), and a max number of replicas per object in the system (*replica constraint*). There are some RPAs that specifically express performance targets as constraints, such as a max latency between each client and object [Lu et al., 2004], but they are currently in minority.

The solution to this problem is usually also NP-hard [Vazirani, 2001], thus *heuristic methods* are used to find a solution that is hopefully not that far from optimal. One popular choice is the greedy ranking method [Karlsson et al., 2002]. It ranks the cost of all the possible placements of one more object according to the cost function and places the top ranked one; recomputes the ranking among the remaining possible placements and so on until no more objects can be placed. There are numerous others [Karlsson et al., 2002], but greedy ranking has been empirically found to be a good choice [Karlsson and Mahalingam, 2002] for many RPAs. While the cost function, constraints and the heuristic used are important properties of the RPA, they are just the means to achieve the system-level goal. They are themselves approximations of the real systems performance and costs. This means that a suboptimal solution might give as good and sometimes, if you are lucky, even better system-level performance as an optimal one.

To be able to minimize or maximize the cost function subject to the constraints, measurements are needed from the system to populate the variables found in the cost function and the constraints. If this was for free, most RPAs would perform better or at least as well as before if they had global information. But, many times the scale of CDNs are large and therefore global information might be prohibitively costly to obtain. To address this, measurements local to a node are used as in caching algorithms, or in a neighborhood around each node as in cooperative caching. We will refer to this property as *Knowledge*.

An often neglected but important property of an RPA is how often the algorithm is run. This is the *evaluation interval* (Δ). It represents the shortest interval between executions of the RPA on any node in the system. For example, a caching heuristic is run on a node upon every single object access initiated at that node (in order to be able to evict and store objects); a complex centralized placement heuristic may be run once a day as it takes a long time to execute. As we will see later, the choice of this parameter has a critical impact on system performance.

An RPA decides to place an object on the basis of the system's activity and measurements during some time interval. The *activity history* property captures the time interval considered when the RPA makes a decision. Any object referenced within that interval is a candidate for placement. We exemplify this with the two extreme cases. First, when the history is a single access, an RPA that makes a placement decision can only consider the object that was just referenced. Caching is an example of such an RPA. Second, when the history is all time from the time the systems was powered on, an RPA can consider any object referenced throughout the execution.

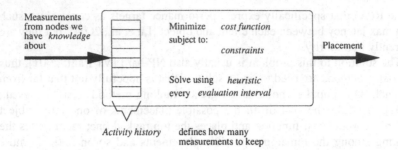

Figure 2.1.   An overview of what the RPA characteristics control in the execution of RPAs.

An overview of the various RPA characteristics and how they affect the execution of an RPA is shown in Figure 2.1. The RPA gets measurements from the nodes it has knowledge about and it stores these in a buffer. Measurements are discarded according to the activity history property. Once the measurements are collected, it uses these to minimize (or maximize) a cost function subject to some constraints. To solve this it uses a heuristic that produces a solution to the placement problem. This process is repeated every evaluation interval, e.g., once a second, once a day, or once every access.

Another property that we will only briefly mention here, is how to age measurement data that is stored on the node. Consider an RPA that maximizes the sum of read requests. One that keeps the data forever will be slow too react to changes while one that throws away data after just a few seconds might be too volatile. It is also possible to age the data using e.g., exponential forgetting. Cost function metrics based on access or load time does not have to bother about this, as they are explicitly aged.

In order to better understand the performance implications of using a specific RPA and how RPA's relate to each other, we have classified some existing RPA into heuristic classes that can be described by the properties in the previous section. Table 2.1 includes a list of RPA classes from the literature and shows how they are captured by various combinations of RPA properties.

A number of centralized RPAs that use global knowledge of the system to make placement decisions are constrained only by a storage constraint [Dowdy and Foster, 1982, Kangasharju et al., 2002] or a replica constraint [Dowdy and Foster, 1982, Qiu et al., 2001]. Other RPAs are run in a completely decentralized fashion, only having knowledge of activity on the local node where they run [Kangasharju et al., 2002, Rabinovich and Aggarwal, 1999]. The common caching protocols are sub-cases of those RPAs; they react only to the last access initiated on the local node and are run after every single access [Cao and Irani, 1997]. The only difference between cooperative caching [Korupolu et al., 2001] and local caching is the extended knowledge of the activity on other nodes in

Table 2.1. Examples of heuristic classes captured by combinations of heuristic properties. SC = storage constrained, RC = replica constrained, Δ = evaluation interval, "access" means only the object or node that was just accessed, and "all" means both past and future times.

Heuristic properties					Class of heuristics represented
SC	RC	Δ	*Know*	*Hist*	
×		any	global	past	storage constrained heuristics [Kangasharju et al., 2002]
	×	any	global	past	replica constrained heuristics [Qiu et al., 2001]
×		any	local	past	decentralized storage constrained heuristics [Rabinovich and Aggarwal, 1999]
×		1 access	local	access	local caching [Cao and Irani, 1997]
×		1 access	global	access	cooperative caching [Korupolu et al., 2001]
×		1 access	local	all	local caching with prefetching [Jiang et al., 2002]
×		1 access	global	all	cooperative caching with prefetching [Jiang et al., 2002]

the system that cooperative caching has. Last, performing proactive placement based on knowledge or speculation of accesses to happen in the the the future, captures variations of caching and cooperative caching, with prefetching [Jiang et al., 2002].

As we will see in Section 1.3, we can deduce many things about the performance and cost implications of an RPA from this high-level classification. But before we do that, the next section will discuss existing RPAs' cost functions and constraints in detail in order to get more depth and understanding of the problem. Note that most of the cost functions can be used in any of the heuristic classes in Table 2.1.

1.2 Existing Approaches in more Detail

Replica placement algorithms have in one form or the other been around for about 50 years. Some of the first incarnations were in operations research, NP-completeness theory [Garey and Johnson, 1979] and in the approximation algorithms used to solve these [Vazirani, 2001]. The focus of the latter have been to come up with theoretical bounds on how far from optimal an approximation algorithm is, not necessarily an algorithm that in most cases produce solutions that are close to optimal. A number of these problems of specific interest to the field of CDNs are facility location problems [Drezner and Hamacher, 2001] and file allocation problems [Dowdy and Foster, 1982]. The former deals with the problem of allocating facilities when there is a flow of resources that need to stored and/or consumed. The latter is the problem of optimally placing file or block data, given a storage system. These formulations are in many cases [Anderson et al., 2005] much more complicated and detailed than the ones used for CDNs.

The replica placement problem can be formally stated as follows. The system consists of a set of clients C (accessing objects), nodes N (storing objects) and objects K (e.g., whole sites or individual pages). Each client $i \in C$ is assigned to a node $j \in N$ for each object $k \in K$, incurring a specific cost according to a *cost function* $f(\cdot)$. For example, such a function may reflect the average latency for clients accessing objects in the system's nodes. An extensive sample of cost functions is shown in Table 2.2.

This cost function is augmented with a number of *constraints*. The binary variable y_{ijk} indicates whether client i sends its requests for object k to node j; x_{jk} indicates whether node j stores object k. The following four constraints are present in most problem definitions (the numbers refer to the equations below): (2.2) states that each client can only send requests for an object to exactly one node; (2.3) states that only nodes that store the object can respond to requests for it; (2.4) and (2.5) imply that objects and requests cannot be split. Optional additional constraints are described later in this section. The basic problem is thus to find a solution of either minimum or maximum cost that satisfies constraints (2.2) – (2.5).

$$minimize/maximize \ \ f(\cdot) \qquad\qquad (2.1)$$

subject to

$$\sum_{j \in N} y_{ijk} = 1 \quad \forall i, k \qquad\qquad (2.2)$$

$$y_{ijk} \le x_{jk} \quad \forall i, j, k \qquad\qquad (2.3)$$

$$x_{jk} \in \{0, 1\} \quad \forall j, k \qquad\qquad (2.4)$$

$$y_{ijk} \in \{0, 1\} \quad \forall i, j, k \qquad\qquad (2.5)$$

A number of extra constraints can then be added.

Storage Capacity (SC): $\sum_{k \in K} size_k \cdot x_{jk} \le SC_j$, $\forall j$. An upper bound on the storage capacity of a node.

Number of Replicas (P): $\sum_{j \in N} x_{jk} \le P$, $\forall k$. A constraint limiting the number of replicas placed.

Load Capacity (LC): $\sum_{i \in C} \sum_{k \in K} (reads_{ik} + writes_{ik}) \cdot y_{ijk} \le LC_j$, $\forall j$. An upper bound on the load, characterized as the rate of requests a node can serve.

Node Bandwidth Capacity (BW):
$\sum_{i \in C} \sum_{k \in K} (reads_{ik} + writes_{ik}) \cdot size_k \cdot y_{ijk} \le BW_j$, $\forall j$. A constraint on the maximum rate of bytes a node can transmit.

Delay (D): $\sum_{j \in N} reads_{ik} \cdot dist_{ij} \cdot y_{ijk} \leq D, \forall i, k$. An upper bound on the request latency for clients accessing an object.

The cost functions of a representative sample of existing RPAs, as shown in Table 2.2, use the following parameters:

Reads $(reads_{ik})$: The rate of read accesses by a client i to an object k.

Writes $(writes_{ik})$: The rate of write accesses by a client i to an object k.

Distance $(dist_{ij})$: The distance between a client i and a node j, represented with a metric such as network latency, AS-level hops or link "cost". For update propagation costs, some algorithms use the minimum spanning tree distance between a node j and all the other nodes with a copy of object k, denoted mst_{jk}.

Fanout $(fanout_j)$: The fanout at node j measured in number of outgoing network links.

Storage Cost (sc_{jk}) : The cost of storing object k at node j. The storage cost might reflect the size of the object, the throughput of the node, or the fact that a copy of the object is residing at a specific node, also called *replication cost*.

Object Size $(size_k)$: The size of object k in bytes.

Access Time $(acctime_{jk})$: A time-stamp indicating the last time object k was accessed at node j.

Load Time $(loadtime_{jk})$: A time-stamp indicating when object k was replicated to node j.

In the literature, a number of additional constraint primitives have been added to constraints (2.2) – (2.5) of the problem definition:

Table 2.2 maps replica RPAs from many disparate fields into the proposed cost-function primitives and constraints. The list is not meant to be complete. Instead, we have chosen what we think is an interesting and disparate subset. The problem definitions have been broken down into five main groups. Group 1 only considers network metrics; Group 2 only looks at time metrics when a decision is made; Group 3 mainly accounts for read access metrics; Group 4 considers both read and network metrics, and finally Group 5 considers both read and write accesses, including update dissemination. These groups can be further divided into two subcategories according to whether a problem definition takes into account *single* or *multiple objects*. Single-object formulations cannot handle inter-object constraints, such as storage constraints, but they are easier to solve than multi-object formulations.

Table 2.2. Some cost function and constraints combinations used by popular RPAs. The various components of the cost function might be weighted. However, these are not shown in the table. For notational convenience $\sum_i = \sum_{i \in C}$, $\sum_j = \sum_{j \in N}$ and $\sum_k = \sum_{k \in K}$

#	COST FUNCTION	RPA(s)
	Group1: Network metrics only	
(1)	$\max_{i,j} dist_{ij} \cdot y_{ijk}$	Min K-center [Jamin et al., 2000]
(2)	$\sum_i \sum_j dist_{ij} \cdot y_{ijk}$	Min avg. distance [Jamin et al., 2001]
(3)	$\sum_j fanout_j \cdot x_{jk}$	Fanout [Radoslavov et al., 2002]
(4)	$\sum_j x_{jk}$	Set domination [Huang and Abdelzaher, 2004]
	Group 2: Time metrics only	
(5)	$\sum_j \sum_k acctime_{jk} \cdot x_{jk}$	LRU, Delayed LRU
(6)	$\sum_j \sum_k loadtime_{jk} \cdot x_{jk}$	FIFO
(7)	$\sum_i \sum_j \sum_k (acctime_{jk} + 1/size_k) \cdot y_{ijk}$	GDS [Cao and Irani, 1997]
	Group 3: Read access metrics mainly	
(8)	$\sum_j \sum_k reads_{ik} \cdot x_{jk}$	LFU, Popularity [Kangasharju et al., 2002]
(9)	$\sum_i \sum_j reads_{ik} \cdot y_{ijk}$	Greedy-local [Kangasharju et al., 2002]
(10)	$\sum_i \sum_j \sum_k (acctime_{jk} + reads_{ik}/size_k) \cdot y_{ijk}$	GDSF [O'Neil et al., 1993]
	Group 4: Read access and network metrics	
(11)	$\sum_i \sum_j reads_{ik} \cdot dist_{ij} \cdot y_{ijk}$	Greedy [Qiu et al., 2001]
(12)	$\sum_i \sum_j \sum_k reads_{ik} \cdot dist_{ij} \cdot y_{ijk}$	Greedy-global [Kangasharju et al., 2002]
(13)	$\sum_i \sum_j \sum_k reads_{ik} \cdot dist_{ij} \cdot size_k \cdot y_{ijk}$	[Baev and Rajaraman, 2001]
(14)	$\sum_i \sum_j (sc_{jk} \cdot x_{jk} + dist_{ij} \cdot reads_{ik} \cdot y_{ijk})$	[Korupolu et al., 2000]
	Group 5: Reads, writes and network metrics	
(15)	$\sum_i \sum_j reads_{ik} \cdot dist_{ij} \cdot y_{ijk} + writes_{ik} \cdot (dist_{ij} + mst_{jk}) \cdot y_{ijk}$	[Wolfson and Milo, 1991]
(16)	$\sum_i \sum_j (reads_{ik} \cdot dist_{ij} + writes_{ik} \cdot (dist_{ij} + \sum_{n \in N, n \neq j} dist_{jn} \cdot x_{nk})) \cdot y_{ijk}$	[Cook et al., 2002]
(17)	$\sum_i \sum_j reads_{ik} \cdot dist_{ij} \cdot y_{ijk} + writes_{ik} \cdot (dist_{ij} + mst_{jk}) \cdot y_{ijk} + \sum_j sc_{jk} \cdot x_{jk}$	[Kalpakis et al., 2001]
(18)	$\sum_i \sum_j \sum_k reads_{ik} \cdot dist_{ij} \cdot y_{ijk} + writes_{ik} \cdot (dist_{ij} + mst_{jk}) \cdot y_{ijk} + \sum_j \sum_k sc_{jk} \cdot x_{jk}$	[Awerbuch et al., 1993]

The drawback of the cost functions in Group 1 is that they place the P replicas of every object, in the same P nodes. Clearly, this is not practical, when many large objects are placed in the system. However, they are useful as a substitute of Group 3-5 problem definitions, if the objects are accessed uniformly by all the clients in the system and the utilization of all nodes in the system is not a requirement. In this case, Group 1 algorithms can be orders of magnitude faster than the ones for Group 3-5, because the placement is decided once and it applies to all objects. (1) is called Min K-center [Jamin et al., 2000, Jamin et al., 2001], (2) is a minimum average distance problem [Jamin et al., 2001], (3) places object at the P nodes with the greatest fanout [Jamin et al., 2001, Radoslavov et al., 2002], and (4) is together with a delay constraint (D) a set domination problem [Huang and Abdelzaher, 2004].

Group 2 uses only time metrics and the ones that are in Table 2.2 can be measured in a completely decentralized fashion. In fact, these cost functions are used together with a storage constraint in caching algorithms. (5) is used in LRU, (6) in FIFO and (7) in Greedy-Dual Size (GDS) [Cao and Irani, 1997]. To see that caching is nothing more or less than one of these cost functions plus a storage constraint that is greedily ranked at each access, consider the following conceptual example. Every time a request arrives at the node (cache) it will have to make a decision on what to store. What objects it cannot store, it will have to evict. Suppose we use (5). In this case, the access times of all the objects in the node plus the one object that was just accesses will be ranked. The algorithm will place all the objects it can in descending order of access time until it reaches the storage constraint, which is equal to the capacity of the cache. When the storage capacity is full, it will not store any more objects, and this will explicitly evict the objects not placed so far. Assuming a uniform object size, it will at this point contain the newly accessed object plus all the others that were in the node minus the one object that had the smallest access time. This is conceptually equivalent to LRU, however, nobody would implement it this way as it can be simplified to $O(1)$ in computational complexity. The important observation to take away is that caching is just an RPA with a storage constraint, an access history of one access and an evaluation interval of one access as seen in Table 2.1. If it has an evaluation interval greater than one access it is called delayed caching [Karlsson and Mahalingam, 2002] or it turns into an RPA that traditionally have other names (more about those below).

Almost all problem definitions proposed in the literature explicitly for use in CDNs fall under Groups 3 and 4. They are applicable to read-only and read-mostly workloads. Problem definitions (8), (9), (11), (12) and (13) have all been proposed in the context of CDNs. It has been shown that there are scalable algorithms for these problems that are close to optimal when they have a storage or replica constraint [Karlsson and Mahalingam, 2002, Qiu et al., 2001]. Group 3 contains cost functions that mainly considers read access metrics (plus object size in one case and access time in another). These have been frequently used both for caching heuristics (8) LFU [Abrams et al., 1996] and (10) GDSF (Greedy-Dual Size Frequency) [O'Neil et al., 1993], and for traditional CDN RPAs (8) popularity [Kangasharju et al., 2002], and (9) Greedy-local [Kangasharju et al., 2002]. The reason that they are popular for both types of heuristics, is that the cost functions can all be computed with local information.

Group 4 contains cost functions that use both read access measurements as well as network measurements in order to come up with a placement. Considering distances is generally a good idea if the variability between the distances is large. As this is the case in the Internet, this should in theory be a good idea. But on the other hand, these cost functions generally requires centralized computations or dissemination of the network measurements throughout all the nodes, and over a wide-area network the variance of the network measurements is large. (11) is the k-median problem [Hakimi, 1964] and Lili Qiu's greedy algorithm [Qiu et al., 2001], (12) is Greedy-global [Kangasharju et al., 2002], (13) can be found in [Baev and Rajaraman, 2001], and (14) is another facility location problem studied in [Korupolu et al., 2000, Balinski, 1965, Cidon et al., 2001, Kurose and Simha, 1989]. The cost function in (13) also captures the impact of allocating large objects and could preferably be used when the object size is highly variable.

The storage costs (sc_{jk}) in cost function (14) could be used in order to minimize the amount of changes to the previous placement. As far as we know, there have been scant evaluation in this field of the benefits of taking this into consideration. Another open question is whether storage, load, and nodal bandwidth constraints need to be considered. Another question is then; are there any scalable good heuristics for such problem definitions?

Considering the impact of writes, in addition to that of reads, is important, when users frequently modify the data. This is the main characteristic of Group 5, which contains problem definitions that probably will only be of interest to a CDN if the providers of the content or the clients are allowed to frequently update the data. These problem definitions represent the update dissemination protocol in many different ways. For most of them, the update dissemination cost is the number of writes times the distance between the client and the closest node that has the object, plus the cost of distributing these updates to the other replicas of the object. In (15) [Wolfson and Milo, 1991, Wolfson and Jajodia, 1992, Wolfson et al., 1997], (17) [Kalpakis et al., 2001, Krick et al., 2001, Lund et al., 1999] and (18) [Awerbuch et al., 1993, Awerbuch et al., 1998, Bartal et al., 1992], the updates are distributed in the system using a minimum spanning tree. In (16) [Cook et al., 2002] one update message is sent from the writer to each other copy. Note, that none of these problem definitions considers load or nodal bandwidth constraints and only few cost functions with writes in the literature consider storage constraints. As discussed before, it is unclear if these constraints will be important, thus there are open research issues in this space. In the next section, we will discuss the performance implications that these choices and the RPA characteristics in Section 1.1 have to the CDN as a system.

1.3   Performance Implications

The replica placement problem in a CDN is a dynamic problem. Clients arrive and depart, servers crash and are replaced, network partitions suddenly form, the latency of the Internet varies a lot, etc. It is commonplace to distinguish algorithms as static (having clairvoyant information) and dynamic (reacting to old information). However, we will here treat all RPAs as dynamic even though they might have been designed for the static case, as a real CDN is dynamic and we will always act on more or less old data.

The number one reason that a customer employs a CDN is for it to provide the its clients with a good request latency to the customer's site. It should provide this to almost all Internet locations, under heavy site load and under network partitions. Thus, we will start by examine what RPA characteristics that impacts the performance under these three scenarios.

The ability of an RPA to provide good client request latency under ideal conditions has been the most popular way of evaluating RPAs. The metric has usually been the average of all requests over the whole client population, or a percentile of the request latency over the same population. This has the tendency to provide better metric values to regions with many clients or for clients with many requests. It might be the case that this is the most effective way of satisfying clients within a limited infrastructure budget. But, is this the best way to maximize the number of satisfied clients? Studies [Huffaker et al., 2002] have shown that clients consider request latency of less than 300 ms to be fast, independently if they are 10 ms or 250 ms. A better metric might then be how many clients that get their requests served in less than 300 ms, as this will directly relate to the number of clients that are satisfied with the web-site's response, instead of the number of requests that are "satisfied". On one hand, an average measurement over all clients might look good on paper, but might really mean 50% of clients are satisfied clients and 50% are unsatisfied. More effort needs to go into defining a good metric that more accurately reflects the impact on the system level goal.

The ability of an RPA to cost effectively deal with flash crowds or hotspots is a metric that is rarely evaluated. There are two diametrically opposite ways for an RPA to deal with hotspots: react fast and replicate popular content to share the increased load and improve performance; or to statically over-provision. The former requires the RPA to have a low evaluation interval as otherwise it will not even be given the chance to redistribute the content. Caching is such an RPA as it has an evaluation interval of one access. But it also comes with an added networking cost due to all the mistakes that it makes and some added cost for extra storage space to compensate for this. Over provisioning, on the other hand, could work with potentially any RPA by increasing e.g., the storage capacity or the number of replicas. This has a more direct impact on cost than the former suggestion, but it is unclear what is the best strategy in battling flash crowds with RPAs. More research is needed in this space to get a clear picture of this.

The diurnal cycle and mobile clients have a similar effect on RPAs as hotspots. In this case the load is not increased, instead it is moved around. The same two strategies as before can be employed with similar trade-offs, and again there is no clear understanding of the trade-off between the two strategies.

Network partitions are formed when parts of the networking infrastructure fails or when it is misconfigured. This creates isolated islands of networks. When this happens, it is important that each partition contains the content that the clients in each of them access. Under this scenario, reacting fast by having a low evaluation interval will not help a single bit once the network partition has occurred. The best we can do is to preallocate replicas at strategic locations around the network in preparation of partitions. This can be done implicitly or explicitly. The former occurs if the RPA itself has no idea that this is a desired property. An example of this would be a centralized greedy algorithm [Qiu et al., 2001]. In the extreme case, if you put the number of replicas to be equal the number of nodes you would get 100% coverage of all possible network partitions. (This is if we exclude all partitions that could occur between a client and all servers in the CDN, in which case there is nothing we can do.) A number of replicas less than that, and a lower coverage would ensure. There is a non trivial mapping between the parameters of an RPA and the probabilistic assurance that it provides during network partitions. Thus, any RPA could be used to provide a probabilistic assurance in this way. How well or how bad, is an open question. The direct way has been tried [On et al., 2003, Dowdy and Foster, 1982], but it is unclear how it compares to the indirect way.

The information that an RPA receives in order to make a decision can be more or less accurate. The impact of information accuracy has been touched upon by some researchers [Qiu et al., 2001]. Metrics such as access time and load time are trivial to get 100% correct locally on a node. Others such as network distance measured in milliseconds, is notoriously hard and fickle [Savage et al., 1999]. This uncertainty of the measurements should be taken into account when evaluating an RPA. A fair number of RPAs have been proposed that take a large number of parameters into account, but it is unclear if any of them has a significant impact on the overall goal, as they many times are evaluated using perfect information. The evaluation interval also plays a role here. The longer the interval the more outdated and inaccurate aggregate measurements will be, and this might adversely affects performance. On the other hand, a short interval might mean that the RPA reacts to statistical outliers created by short disturbances.

The final performance measure we would like to mention is the computational complexity. If the time it takes to execute an algorithm is t, the evaluation interval need to be greater than t (unless you consider parallel computational resources). A complicated RPA that takes a long time to run, will thus have the same drawbacks discussed previously for an RPA with a high evaluation interval. E.g., it cannot react to hotspots unless it over-provisions. The computation complexity also decides what the abstraction of an object really can stand for. An algorithm with a high complexity regarding the number of objects is not well suited to place individual pages, but could scale well enough to deal with whole sites. A fast RPA, on the other hand, might be well equipped to deal with individual pages, but not with whole sites because it changes its placement so often that it would waste lots of bandwidth and provides bad performance moving large sites back and forth.

1.4 Some Important Problems

This section raises some more research problems that the author thinks are important and not sufficiently or at all addressed in the context of RPAs in CDNs. The main issues are: being able to satisfy probabilistic QoS goals in CDNs; dealing with updates; dealing with collusion attacks; and the impact of RPAs to the system cost and performance goal.

The service level agreements (SLA) that are signed between the CDN provider and the content providers are today at best fluffy. They can even be of the "better than before" type. It would be more desirable from a customers perspective if the SLAs of the CDNs could offer something more. E.g., "95% of the day the CDN will provide a first-byte request latency of 100 ms and a throughput of at least 1,000 requests.". There might be a number of these service-levels defined with an associated cost. The customer could then chose one that he believes has the best trade-off between the performance needed and the cost. One might even envision that the SLA itself is specified by the customer and that the CDN only sets a price on it as in a utility computing environment [Chase et al., 2001], or refuses to accept it if cannot or does not want to provide service to that customer.

There have been some first steps in order to move towards this vision. Huang *et al.* [Huang and Abdelzaher, 2004] proposed an RPA and a system architecture that can be used in order to provide latency goals to the customers with an unknown but high probability. Both a centralized and a distributed algorithm based on the set domination problem (4) was presented. Tang *et al.* [Tang and Xu, 2004] formulate an RPA that considers retrieval cost goals. The problem is a special case of the min-sucost problem, and the authors propose several greedy heuristics for solving the problem. On *et al.* [On et al., 2003] look into RPAs that are designed to provide availability goals. Several definitions of availability are defined and evaluated.

Many questions are still unanswered though. How can the above probability be taken into account? How can various performance, availability, reliability and maybe even security goals be taken into account, and the combination of these goals? When the system cannot satisfy all the SLAs, what shall it do? Can we use utility functions to be able to specify this, and how can these be taken into account when placing objects? Network partitions happen and these need to be taken into account in some way if we are going to provide QoS. These are some of the more pressing questions that we should understand and answer, to be able to proceed in this direction.

Another issue for CDNs with QoS goals is that customers can get better performance than they paid for through collusion. Let us consider the example of a CDN that uses a LRU caching policy at each single node, and with one of the customers only paying for the worst performance class. If the cache space on the node is shared among all customers, the colluder can now issue requests to all its content in all caches at repeated time intervals, in order to make sure that all or most of its pages are always in the cache. This provides it with the best possible latency without having paid for it. This can be alleviated by enforcing individual cache space bounds for the customers. But then this has other drawbacks, e.g., the overall cache space might not be used efficiently, and how do we determine those space bounds that satisfy the performance requirements and dynamically change the cache space bounds during run-time [Lu et al., 2002] to get good storage utilization. It is important to safe guard CDNs to these collusion attacks. Research in how to make RPAs less susceptible to this might be a fruitful avenue.

Writes, updates and consistency is of interest to a CDN if the providers of the content or the clients are allowed to frequently update the data. This could be useful in e.g., document sharing applications that large, global corporations use as they frequently are web-based. In this case, both the updates to these documents and the impact of the consistency requirements becomes something that the CDN should consider. E.g., a CDN infrastructure that states that your files will be "updated eventually within a day" might be of little use to the document sharing application. The customer would like something stronger, such as the documents will be consistent within one minute. It is actually unclear what consistency semantics that make sense to the applications that write on top of a CDN. Many have been proposed in this context [Sivasubramanian et al., 2005]. There is a trade-off between few replicas and less update traffic and possibly better, or at least less costly, consistency, and on the other hand, good read latency performance from having many replicas in the CDN. This trade-off could be studied in the context of CDNs.

This last issue which is unfortunately one of the least studied ones, is the impact to the overall system level goal all the RPA design choices have. What features of an RPA makes a difference for the system as a whole, and what features and parameters could be fixed or forgotten once and for all for use in

CDNs? The discussion in the previous section just highlighted some of the high-level performance implications of some of the choices, but clearly, in-depth studies are needed to answer this. The study of this question would help researchers in the field of RPAs for CDNs to focus on the important problems and identify new ones.

2. Request Routing

Request routing is the problem of deciding what node a client request should be directed to. Looking at this from a system-level point of view, requests should be directed to nodes in such a way that the overall system goal is met at the lowest possible cost. This usually means that some end-to-end latency goal should be satisfied as that is a good indicator of actual client experiences [Huffaker et al., 2002].

The request routing problem can be divided into two subtasks: a redirection algorithm and a redirection mechanism. A redirection algorithm decides what node to direct a request to in response to a given client request. Usually it is some algorithm taking network distances and server load into consideration in order to directly or indirectly minimize the client perceived latency. A redirection mechanism is a way of redirecting a client's request to the selected node. Redirection schemes are either implemented on the client (usually in the browser) or somewhere in the network between the client and the servers. This section will only focus on the redirection algorithms and not on the redirection mechanisms that enforce those choices. For a good survey of the latter, please consult [Sivasubramanian et al., 2005].

2.1 Existing Techniques

The simplest redirection algorithm imaginable is to statically assign each client to a server that is close in geographical distance. This works well as long as the server does not get overloaded or the network to that server does not get congested.

Another simple technique is to use round-robin request routing [Radware, 2002] over a number of servers. This would not work well if it was over the whole set of servers in the CDN, due to the high network distances in the Internet. But it is more successful over small subsets containing nodes that are close in network distance, such as ones selected using the previous scheme or some more advanced clustering scheme [Ng and Zhang, 2002]. An extension to round-robin is weighted round-robin that has been used in e.g., the Cicso DistributedDirector [Delgadillo, 1999]. With this policy, weights can be assigned to each server and the servers get a number of requests proportional to its weight. E.g., if one server has a weight of five and another one a weight of one, the former server will get five times as many requests as the latter. While this scheme can address heterogeneity in server and network infrastructure capacities that are static, it still cannot address server overload or network congestion which is dynamic in nature.

Cisco's DistributedDirector also supports various AS-level distance metrics. While these are easy to passively measure, it is unclear how well they reflect the real latencies on the network [Huffaker et al., 2002].

The CDN system RaDaR [Rabinovich and Aggarwal, 1999] implemented two request redirection policies that try to tackle the aforementioned problems. The first one [Rabinovich et al., 1999] ranks the servers according to how many requests each of them has served. It then redirects clients so that the requests are evenly distributed across the nodes and the network distance between client and server is low. The underlying assumption here is that load as a function of number of requests is the same function across all nodes. While this solves the problem of hotspots, it does ignore network congestion and it cannot deal with heterogeneous server resources. The second scheme proposed [Rabinovich et al., 1999], is a version of the first in which the load on each node is constantly monitored. Similar results are reported as for the other request routing algorithm.

There are some policies [Andrews et al., 2002, Delgadillo, 1999] that use client-server latency as the metric. They are interesting as this is the most directly observable metric of client perceived latency. They get these measurements either by client side access logs or by passive measurements. They both redirect the client to the server that has recently reported the lowest latency.

A rather different way of routing requests compared to all the previous policies described, is to use consistent hashing [Karger et al., 1999] and other routing schemes such as Plaxton's routing protocol [Plaxton et al., 1999]. This has been used by commercial companies such as Akamai [Akamai, 2005] and in P2P systems such as Chord [Stoica et al., 2001] and Pastry [Rowstron and Druschel, 2001]. On a high level, the techniques work as follows. A URL is hashed to a key through a cryptographic hash function. This key is then used to route the request to another server that is closer to the content but might not have the content. If it does not have the content, it forwards the request to another node that is even closer, and so on. There are even P2P routing scheme that consider load and network distances when routing. These routing schemes have been tremendously popular in the research community. A thorough survey of these algorithms can be found in [Androutsellis-Theotokis and Spinellis, 2004].

2.2   Discussion

The characteristics of request routing algorithms that mainly decide the performance of them are: the extent of knowledge of what nodes that hold some content, we call this *routing knowledge*; and the prediction of what request latency each node will provide. We will illustrate these performance implications with some examples. Consider the problem of request routing when the system only consists of local caches. In this case the routing knowledge is usually confined to one cache plus the origin node. If the content is not found in the cache, the request is sent to the origin node. On the other hand, with an RPA with an evaluation interval of e.g., 1 day, it would be possible to disseminate the information of what node stores what object to each single request routing device. These routing devices would then know of all nodes with a copy of a specific object. Thus, a more informed decision could be made using any measurements available that could be used to predict the request latency. The request routing device could then pick the one node in the whole system that it believes can return the requested object in the least amount of time.

When researchers have evaluated centralized or even decentralized RPAs they have generally assumed that the request in some way is always routed to the closest replica. As the performance of an RPA is a function of how well the request routing works, it would be interesting to see more evaluations of RPAs that take various request routing algorithms into account. More research that looks at these problems in a holistic way, such as RaDaR [Rabinovich and Aggarwal, 1999], is warranted.

To conclude, this chapter has surveyed the field of replica placement algorithms and request routing algorithms to be able to characterize them in a number of dimensions. This characterization was then used to get a high-level overview on the performance and cost of various algorithms during a number of situations that a CDN should be able to handle. These included, giving clients the performance they want, dealing with hotspots and tolerating network partitions. We then highlighted some important open questions, such as providing probabilistic performance guarantees in CDNs, dealing with writes and consistency requirements and factoring these in when placing content, and how to stifle collusion attacks in the CDN. Finally, one of the most important problem is to study RPAs and request routing algorithms and their impact on the overall system-level goal. That is, how does the cost and performance of the overall CDN system change as a function of the choice of request routing and replica placement algorithms? Answering this question has the potential to focus the field by pruning away algorithmic choices that we today have little intuition if they are useful or not in the context of content delivery networks.

References

Abrams, Marc, Standridge, Charles, Abdulla, Ghaleb, Fox, Edward, and Williams, Stephen (1996). Removal Policies in Network Caches for World-Wide Web Documents. In *ACM Conference of the Special Interest Group on Data Communication (SIGCOMM)*, pages 293–305, Stanford, CA.

Akamai (2005). *Akamai*. Cambridge, MA, USA. http://www.akamai.com.

Anderson, Eric, Kallahalla, Mahesh, Spence, Susan, Swaminathan, Ram, and Wang, Qian (2005). Ergastulum: quickly finding near-optimal storage system designs. *ACM Transactions on Computer Systems*.

Andrews, Matthew, Shepherd, Bruce, Srinivasan, Aravind, Winkler, Peter, and Zane, Francis (2002). Clustering and Server Selection using Passive Monitoring. In *IEEE Infocom*, New York, NY.

Androutsellis-Theotokis, Stephanos and Spinellis, Diomidis (2004). A survey of peer-to-peer content distribution technologies. *ACM Computer Surveys*, 36(4):335–371.

Awerbuch, Baruch, Bartal, Yair, and Fiat, Amos (1993). Competitive Distributed File Allocation. In *ACM Symposium on Theory of Computing (STOC)*, pages 164–173, San Diego, CA.

Awerbuch, Baruch, Bartal, Yair, and Fiat, Amos (1998). Distributed Paging for General Networks. *Journal of Algorithms*, 28(1):67–104.

Baev, Ivan and Rajaraman, Rajmohan (2001). Approximation Algorithms for Data Placement in Arbitrary Networks. In *ACM-SIAM Annual Symposium on Discrete Algorithms (SODA)*, pages 661–670, Washington, D.C.

Balinski, Michel (1965). Integer Programming: Methods, Uses, Computation. *Management Science*, 12:253–313.

Bartal, Yair, Fiat, Amos, and Rabani, Yuval (1992). Competitive Algorithms for Distributed Data Management (Extended Abstract). In *ACM Symposium on Theory of Computing (STOC)*, pages 39–50, Victoria, Canada.

Cao, Pei and Irani, Sandy (1997). Cost-Aware WWW Proxy Caching Algorithms. In *USENIX Symposium on Internet Technologies and Systems (USITS)*, pages 193–206, Monterey, CA.

Chase, Jeffrey, Anderson, Darrell, Thakar, Prachi, Vahdat, Amin, and Doyle, Ronald (2001). Managing Energy and Server Resources in Hosting Centres. In *ACM Symposium on Operating Systems Principles (SOSP)*, pages 103–116, Banff, Canada.

Cidon, Israel, Kutten, Shay, and Soffer, Ran (2001). Optimal Allocation of Electronic Content. In *IEEE Infocom*, pages 1773–1780, Anchorage, AK.

Cook, Stephen, Pachl, Jan, and Pressman, Irwin (2002). The optimal location of replicas in a network using a READ-ONE-WRITE-ALL policy. *Distributed Computing*, 15(1):57–66.

Delgadillo, Kevin (1999). *Cisco DistributedDirector*. Cisco Systems Inc.

Dowdy, Lawrence and Foster, Derrell (1982). Comparative Models of the File Assignment Problem. *ACM Computer Surveys*, 14(2):287–313.

Drezner, Zvi and Hamacher, Horst, editors (2001). *Facility Location Theory: Applications and Methods*. Springer-Verlag, Berlin. ISBN 3-540-21345-7.

Garey, Michael and Johnson, David (1979). *Computers and Intractability: A Guide to the Theory of NP-Completeness*. W.H. Freeman & Company. ISBN 0-7167-1045-5.

Hakimi, S. Louis (1964). Optimum Location of Switching Centers and the Absolute Centers and Medians of a Graph. *Operations Research*, 12:450–459.

Huang, Chengdu and Abdelzaher, Tarek (2004). Towards Content Distribution Networks with Latency Guarantees. In *International Workshop on Quality of Service (IWQoS)*, pages 181–192, Montreal, Canada.

Huffaker, Bradley, Fomenkov, Marina, Plummer, Daniel, Moore, David, and k. claffy (2002). Distance Metrics in the Internet. In *International Telecommunications Symposium (ITS)*, Natal, Brazil.

Jamin, Sugih, Jin, Cheng, Jin, Yixin, Raz, Danny, Shavitt, Yuval, and Zhang, Lixia (2000). On the Placement of Internet Instrumentation. In *IEEE Infocom*, pages 295–304, Tel-Aviv, Israel.

Jamin, Sugih, Jiu, Cheng, Kurc, Anthony, Raz, Danny, and Shavitt, Yuval (2001). Constrained Mirror Placement on the Internet. In *IEEE Infocom*, pages 31–40, Anchorage, AK.

Jiang, Yingyin, Wu, Min-You, and Shu, Wei (2002). Web Prefetching: Costs, Benefits and Performance. In *International Workshop on Web Content Caching and Distribution (WCW)*, pages 199–212, Boulder, CO.

Kalpakis, Konstantinos, Dasgupta, Koustuv, and Wolfson, Ouri (2001). Optimal Placement of Replicas in Trees with Read, Write, and Storage Costs. *IEEE Transactions on Parallel and Distributed Systems*, 12(6):628–637.

Kangasharju, Jussi, Roberts, James, and Ross, Keith (2002). Object Replication Strategies in Content Distribution Networks. *Computer Communications*, 25(4):367–383.

Karger, David, Sherman, Alex, Berkheimer, Andy, Bogstad, Bill, Dhanidina, Rizwan, Iwamoto, Ken, Kim, Brian, Matkins, Luke, and Yerushalmi, Yoav (1999). Web Caching with Consistent Hashing. In *International World Wide Web Conference (WWW)*, pages 1203–1213. Toronto, Canada.

Karlsson, Magnus and Karamanolis, Christos (2004). Choosing Replica Placement Heuristics for Wide-Area Systems. In *International Conference on Distributed Computing Systems (ICDCS)*, pages 350–359, Hachioji, Japan.

Karlsson, Magnus, Karamanolis, Christos, and Mahalingam, Mallik (2002). A Framework for Evaluating Replica Placement Algorithms. Technical Report HPL-2002-219, HP Laboratories. http://www.hpl.hp.com/personal/Magnus_Karlsson.

Karlsson, Magnus and Mahalingam, Mallik (2002). Do We Need Replica Placement Algorithms in Content Delivery Networks? In *International Workshop on Web Content Caching and Distribution (WCW)*, pages 117–128, Boulder, CO.

Korupolu, Madhukar, Plaxton, Greg, and Rajaraman, Rajmohan (2000). Analysis of a Local Search Heuristic for Facility Location Problems. *Journal of Algorithms*, 37(1):146–188.

Korupolu, Madhukar, Plaxton, Greg, and Rajaraman, Rajmohan (2001). Placement Algorithms for Hierarchical Cooperative Caching. *Journal of Algorithms*, 38(1):260–302.

Krick, C., Räcke, H., and Westermann, M. (2001). Approximation Algorithms for Data Management in Networks. In *ACM Symposium on Parallel Algorithms and Architectures (SPAA)*, pages 237–246, Heraklion, Greece.

Kurose, James and Simha, Rahul (1989). A Microeconomic Approach to Optimal Resource Allocation in Distributed Computer Systems. *IEEE Transactions on Computers*, 38(5):705–717.

Lu, Chenyang, Wang, Xiaorui, and Koutsoukos, Xenofon (2004). End-to-end utilization control in distributed real-time systems. In *International Conference on Distributed Computing Systems (ICDCS)*, Tokyo, Japan.

Lu, Ying, Abdelzaher, Tarek, Lu, Chenyang, and Tao, Gang (2002). An adaptive control framework for QoS guarantees and its application to differentiated caching services. In *International Workshop on Quality of Service (IWQoS)*, pages 23–32, Miami Beach, FL.

Lund, Carsten, Reingold, Nick, Westbrook, Jeffrey, and Yan, Dicky (1999). Competitive On-Line Algorithms for Distributed Data Management. *SIAM Journal of Computing*, 28(3):1086–1111.

Ng, Eugene and Zhang, Hui (2002). Predicting Internet Network Distance with Coordinates-Based Approaches. In *IEEE Infocom*, New York, NY.

On, Giwon, Schmitt, Jens, and Steinmetz, Ralf (2003). Quality of Availability: Replica Placement for Widely Distributed Systems. In *International Workshop on Quality of Service (IWQoS)*, pages 325–342, Monterey, CA.

O'Neil, Elizabeth, O'Neil, Patrick, and Weikum, Gerhard (1993). The LRU-K Page Replacement Algorithm For Database Disk Buffering. In *ACM SIGMOD International Conference on Management of Data (SIGMOD)*, pages 297–306, Washington, D.C.

Plaxton, Greg, Rajaraman, Rajmohan, and Richa, Andréa (1999). Accessing Nearby Copies of Replicated Objects in a Distributed Environment. *Theory of Computing Systems*, 32(3):241–280.

Qiu, Lili, Padmanabhan, Venkata, and Voelker, Geoffrey (2001). On the Placement of Web Server Replicas. In *IEEE Infocom*, pages 1587–1596, Anchorage, AK.

Rabinovich, Michael and Aggarwal, Amit (1999). RaDaR: A Scalable Architecture for a Global Web Hosting Service. In *International World Wide Web Conference (WWW)*, pages 1545–1561, Toronto, Canada.

Rabinovich, Michael, Rabinovich, Irina, Rajaraman, Rajmohan, and Aggarwal, Amit (1999). A Dynamic Object Replication and Migration Protocol for an Internet Hosting Service. In *International Conference on Distributed Computing Systems (ICDCS)*, pages 101–113, Austin, TX.

Radoslavov, Pavlin, Govindan, Ramesh, and Estrin, Deborah (2002). Topology-Informed Internet Replica Placement. *Computer Communications Review*, 25(4):384–392.

Radware (2002). *Web Server Director*. Radware Inc.

Rowstron, Anthony and Druschel, Peter (2001). Pastry: Scalable, distributed object location and routing for large-scale peer-to-peer systems. In *ACM/IFIP/USENIX International Middleware Conference (MIDDLEWARE)*, pages 329–350, Heidelberg, Germany.

Savage, Stefan, Collins, Andy, Hoffman, Eric, Snell, John, and Anderson, Thomas E. (1999). The End-to-End Effects of Internet Path Selection. In *ACM Conference of the Special Interest Group on Data Communication (SIGCOMM)*, pages 289–299, Cambridge, MA.

Sivasubramanian, Swaminathan, Szymaniak, Michał, Pierre, Guillaume, and van Steen, Maarten (2005). Replication for Web Hosting Systems. *ACM Computer Surveys*.

Stoica, Ion, Morris, Robert, Karger, David, Kaashoek, Frans, and Balakrishnan, Hari (2001). Chord: A Scalable Peer-to-peer Lookup Service for Internet Applications. In *ACM Conference of the Special Interest Group on Data Communication (SIGCOMM)*, pages 149–160. San Diego, CA.

Tang, Xueyan and Xu, Jianliang (2004). On Replica Placement for QoS-Aware Content Distribution. In *IEEE Infocom*. Hong Kong, China.

Vazirani, Vijay (2001). *Approximation Algorithms*. ISBN 3-540-65367-8. Springer-Verlag.

Wolfson, Ouri and Jajodia, Sushil (1992). Distributed algorithms for dynamic replication of data. In *ACM Symposium on Principles of Database Systems (PODS)*, pages 149–163, San Diego, CA.

Wolfson, Ouri, Jajodia, Sushil, and Huang, Yixui (1997). An Adaptive Data Replication Algorithm. *ACM Transactions on Database Systems*, 22(2):255–314.

Wolfson, Ouri and Milo, Amir (1991). The Multicast Policy and Its Relationship of Replicated Data Placement. *ACM Transactions on Database Systems*, 16(1):181–205.

Chapter 3

THE TIME-TO-LIVE BASED CONSISTENCY MECHANISM:

Understanding Performance Issues and Their Impact

Edith Cohen

AT&T Labs-Research
Florham Park, NJ, USA
edith@research.att.com

Haim Kaplan

Tel-Aviv University
Tel Aviv, Israel
haimk@post.tau.ac.il

Abstract   The Web is a large distributed database were copies of objects are replicated and used in multiple places. The dominant consistency mechanism deployed for HTTP (Hyper Text Transfer Protocol) and DNS (Domain Name Service) records is Time-to-Live (TTL) based weak consistency. Each object has a lifetime-duration assigned to it by its origin server. A copy of the object fetched from its origin server is received with maximum time-to-live (TTL) that equals its lifetime duration. Cached copies have shorter TTLs since the *age* (elapsed time since fetched from the origin) is deducted from the objects lifetime duration.

A request served by a cache constitutes a *hit* if the cache has a fresh copy of the object. Otherwise, the request is considered a *miss* and is propagated to another server. With HTTP, expired cached copies need to be validated, and if they turned out to be not modified, we refer to the request as a *freshness miss*.

We study how cache performance is affected by TTL-based consistency. Since cache misses induce user-perceived latency, a cache can reduce user perceived latency by refreshing its copies of popular objects proactively, before they are requested. For hierarchical caches, the number of cache misses depends in subtle ways on the age of the copies the cache receives. Thus, fresh copies obtained through another cache are less effective than fresh copies received from an authoritative server.

Keywords: TTL, Time To Live, Cache, Web caching, Domain Name System

1.   Introduction

Distributed databases such as the Web maintain a master version of each item and a possibly large number of cached copies. Caching offloads the server and expedites delivery of the item to end users but also requires some consistency mechanism, that makes sure that when the master copy is modified, this fact is propagated to the copies. Maintaining strong consistency, where all copies are updated promptly when the master is modified, can be very resource consuming. Time-to-Live (TTL)-based consistency is a simple and effective weak consistency mechanism where the lifetime of each copy is limited to some fixed duration. TTL-based consistency allows for the benefits of using cached copies without the need to maintain state on the location of all the copies. The cached copies can be stale, but are guaranteed to be almost (as determined by the TTL duration) up to date.

The Hyper-Text Transfer Protocol (HTTP) [Fielding et al., 1999] that governs the distribution of Web content, and the Domain Name (DNS) [Mockapetris, 1987a, Mockapetris, 1987b], that is responsible for translating between domain names and IP addresses, constitute examples of very large scale distribution systems that deploy TTL-based consistency. Objects are typically associated with one authority that originates and modifies them (their *origin* or *authoritative* server), but can be cached and further distributed from multiple *replicating* servers (caches). Caching and replication are widely deployed for reducing load on Web servers, network load, and user-perceived latency. Caches are located at different points in the network and include reverse proxies, proxy caches, and browser caches. By and large, servers rely on one widely supported and deployed mechanism for consistency of cached copies. Under this client-driven and expiration-based mechanism, the authoritative server provides an expiration time for each copy, beyond which it must be validated or discarded.

Each HTTP object has a URL which specifies its "location" and its authoritative server. The object is requested by sending an HTTP request and the content is sent back on the respective HTTP response. The response includes a header with important information on the object, including cache directives. The directives specify if the object can be cached, and may provide explicit expiration time or information that can be used to compute one. When an object is requested from the cache then if the cache has a *fresh* (non-expired) copy, the request is processed locally. If the cached copy is *stale* (expired), it must be validated by contacting an external server with a fresh copy. To this end, HTTP provides conditional GET requests. Similarly, if there is no cached copy, the cache must obtain a fresh copy from an external server.

An HTTP-compliant cache [Berners-Lee et al., 1996, Fielding et al., 1999, Squid, 2001] calculates from the header fields of an object a *freshness lifetime*, which is the time interval during which the copy remains fresh (non-expired) since it left its authoritative server. The freshness lifetime is typically fixed for each object. The cache also determines from the headers the *age* of the copy, which is the elapsed time since it left its authoritative server (and resided in caches). If the age is smaller than the freshness lifetime then by subtracting the age of the copy from its freshness lifetime the cache obtains a *time-to-live (TTL)* duration for the copy (during which it is considered fresh). If the age is larger than the freshness lifetime, the object is considered stale and its TTL is zero.

In the DNS database, each resource record (RR) has a freshness lifetime duration assigned to it by its authoritative administrator. These records are cached in multiple servers and the age is calculated in a similar way as with HTTP. DNS performance is critical to many applications. In particular, name translation is necessary and precedes HTTP transfers.

Among the different performance objectives of caches, improving end-user Web experience, in particular reducing using-percieved latency, is gradually becoming the most pronounced. Many organizations are deploying caching servers in front of their LANs, mainly as a way to speed up users Web access. Generally, available bandwidth between end-users and their Internet Service Providers (ISPs) is increasing and is complemented by short round trip times. Thus, the latency bottleneck is shifting from being between end-users and cache to being between cache and origin servers. From the viewpoint of Web sites and Content Distribution Networks (like Akamai [Akamai, 2001]), decreasing costs of server-machines and backbone connectivity bandwidth along with increasing use of the Web for commercial purposes imply that server and network load are gradually becoming a lesser issue relative to end-user quality of service. At the limit, these trends indicate that communication time between local caches and remote servers increasingly dominates cache service-times and user-perceived latency, and that technologies which provide tradeoffs between traffic-increase and latency-decrease would become increasingly worthwhile for both Web sites and ISPs. User-percieved latency is incurred on cache misses, when the cache has no cached copy or a stale cached copy and therefore must communicate with an external server before serving the request.

Web caches are placed close to clients, in Web browsers, and as proxy caches or as reverse proxies, close to web servers [Inktomi, 2001, Squid, 2001]. They are also sometimes configured in hierarchies [IRCache, 2001]. Thus, often there is more than one cache placed between the end user and the origin server. Different copies corresponding to the same URL and residing in different caches can have different ages and thus different TTLs. In particular, a copy obtained by a cache from another cache expires sooner than a copy obtained from an authoritative server. Therefore, a cache that forwards requests to another cache is likely to suffer more cache misses than a cache that forwards requests to an authoritative server. Furthermore, a cache is likely to obtain more client requests than an authoritative server since it serves older copies. So even if a cache maintains fresh copies, since the copies are aged, the cache is somewhat less effective than an authoritative server [Cohen and Kaplan, 2001a, Cohen and Kaplan, 2001b]. Age is a central performance factor where TTL-based consistency is used, as it affects frequently-requested objects, and it remains a performance issues even if storage is practically unlimited.

1.1   Overview

In Section 2 we start with a brief survey of other consistency mechanisms, before dwelling into exploration of TTL-based consistency. We also give an overview of the consistency mechanism used by HTTP.

In Section 3 we discuss validation latency: A considerable fraction of cache "hits" involve stale copies that turned out to be current (were not modified). These validations of current objects have small message sizes, but nonetheless, often induce latency comparable to full-fledged cache misses. Thus, the functionality of caches as a latency-reducing mechanism highly depends not only on content availability but also on its freshness.

Validation latency, and more generally, cache misses that occur on previously cached but already-expired objects can be confronted with *Refreshment policies*. Refreshment policies for Web caches were proposed and studied in [Cohen and Kaplan, 2002] and for the DNS system in [Cohen and Kaplan, 2001c]. We summarize work and results on these policies in Section 4.

TTL-based consistency affects the performance of cascaded caches, when there is more than a single cache on the path between the end user and the origin server and therefore caches can be served from caches. Sections 5 and 6 summarize results presented in [Cohen et al., 2001] and [Cohen and Kaplan, 2001b]. We will see how the miss rate of a client cache depends on the source from which it obtains its objects.

Section 5 presents and explores models for three different basic configurations. Under the first configuration, the client cache uses an authoritative server directly without a high-level cache. In the second configuration the client cache uses consistently for all its misses the same source cache. In the third configuration the client cache alternates between several source caches to resolve its misses. We will see that a cache which consistently uses the same source cache (for each object) would incur a lower miss rate than a cache that alternates between several caches. This suggests that when a set of caches handles the workload of a set of clients, it is better to partition the workload such that the same primary cache is used for each client-object pair. We then characterize how the miss rate degrades when using a source cache compared to using an authoritative server. For a single consistent source (a cache source that does not perform pre-term refreshes) we show that the miss rate is larger by at most a factor of 2. For alternating between sources, the miss rate could be somewhat worse, but not more than a factor of $e = 2.718\ldots$ larger than the miss rate through an authoritative server [Cohen et al., 2001].

Section 6 presents an extension of the basic configurations. The basic models assumed that only expired copies can be refreshed. HTTP caches, however, may refresh fresh items. Such *pre-term refreshes* occur when a client request contains a *no-cache* request header. When a cache received such a request it must forward it to the origin server even if it has a fresh copy. The cache uses the response to replace or refresh its older copy of the object. Conceivably, a cache can deploy configured periodic pre-term refreshes (*rejuvenations*) to reduce the age of cached copies and as a result, improve the miss-rate at its client caches and consequently, the number of requests it receives. Rejuvenation increases traffic between a cache and the authoritative server but can decrease traffic between the cache and its clients. As illustrated in Figure 3.1, a single cache can potentially serve a large number of (caching) clients, and thus rejuvenation can be very effective. As pre-term refreshes decrease the average age of cached copies, it may seem that they can only increase the effectiveness of a cache. We will see, however, that this is generally not the case. In particular, when pre-term refreshes occur in arbitrary points in time and "out of synch" with the expiration times of previous copies, performance can degrade by up to a factor of 2, which is tight under some robust conditions. We will also see, however, that when used "in synch" with previous expirations, pre-term refreshes can boost performance. The relative performance of rejuvenating sources is studied when inter-request times drawn from natural known distributions, namely, Poisson and Pareto arrivals and data from cache proxy logs.

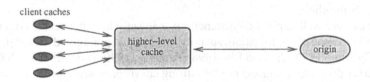

Figure 3.1. Client caches, higher-level cache, and origin server

1.2 Other work on TTL-based consistency

We summarize results that appeared in [Cohen and Kaplan, 2001c, Cohen and Kaplan, 2002, Cohen and Kaplan, 2001a, Cohen et al., 2001, Cohen and Kaplan, 2001b] but would like to mention some subsequent work on the subject.

Jung *et al* [Jung et al., 2001] explored the effect of the length of the freshness lifetime on the miss-rate. They concluded that relatively short freshness lifetime durations suffice to get most of the hits. Jung *et al* [Jung et al., 2003] supported their experimental work on DNS traces [Jung et al., 2001] with an analytical analysis. In this work they model requests as independent identically distributed random variable drawn from some fixed distribution. They develop formula for the miss rate generated by several particular distributions and analyze how freshness lifetime duration affects this miss-rate. For the distributions that fit best real traces they obtained results similar to the ones observed from the traces alone. That is, relatively short TTLs suffice to get low miss rate and the marginal affect of increasing the TTL further is small.

Hou *et al* [Hou et al., 2002, Hou et al., 2003] studied cache hierarchies with more than two levels. For requests generated by a Poisson distribution they calculate the miss-rate and average TTL at different levels of the hierarchy. Their analysis quantifies how the TTL shortens, and the miss rate increases, as we go to deeper caches in the hierarchy. They also analyze the effect of a rejuvenation mechanism on the TTL at various levels.

2.   Preliminaries

2.1   Consistency mechanisms

The appeal of TTL-based consistency is in its simplicity. In particular, it requires no end-to-end support (in particular server support). To place it in context, we provide a brief discussion of other proposed consistency mechanisms.

With server-driven mechanisms, clients are notified by the server when objects are modified (e.g. [Howard et al., 1988, Li and Cheriton, 1999]); With client-driven mechanisms, the cache validates with the server objects with a stale cached copy; with hybrid approaches, validations are initiated either at the server or the client.

Leases are well-studied consistency mechanism where the server commits to notify a cache of modification, but only for a limited pre-agreed period [Gray and Cheriton, 1989, Cao and Liu, 1998, Yin et al., 1999, Duvvuri et al., 2000].

Server-driven mechanisms provide strong consistency and can eliminate all freshness misses. Hybrid approaches can provide a good balance of validation overhead and reduced validation traffic. While obviously strong consistency can be critical for some applications, none of these mechanisms, however, is widely deployed or even standardized. Implementation requires protocol enhancements and software changes not only at the cache, but at all participating Web servers, and may also require Web servers to maintain per-client state. Except for some proprietary coherence mechanisms deployed for hosted or mirrored content [Akamai, 2001, InktomiCDS, 2001] (which require control of both endpoints), the only coherence mechanism currently widely deployed and supported by HTTP/1.1 is *client-driven* based on TTL (time-to-live).

2.2 HTTP freshness control

We provide a simplified overview of the freshness control mechanism specified by HTTP and supported by compliant caches. For further details see [Fielding et al., 1999, Berners-Lee et al., 1996, Squid, 2001, Nottingham, 1999, Mogul, 1999]. Caches compute for each object a *time-to-live (TTL)* value during which it is considered *fresh* and beyond which it becomes *stale*. When a request arrives for a stale object, the cache must validate it before serving it, by communication either with an entity with a fresh copy (such as another cache) or with the origin server. The cachability and TTL computation is performed using directives and values found in the object's HTTP response headers.

When the cache receives a client request for an object then it acts as follows:

- If the object is cached and fresh, the request constitutes *content and freshness hit* and the cached copy is immediately returned to the client.

- If the object is cached, but stale, the cache issues a conditional HTTP GET request to the origin server (or another appropriately-selected cache). The conditional GET uses the entity tag of the cached copy (with HTTP/1.1 and if an E-TAG value was provided with the response) or it issues an If-Modified-Since (IMS) request with the LAST-MODIFIED response header value (indicating last modification time of the object). If the source response is Not-Modified then the request constitutes a *content hit* but a *freshness miss*. If the object was modified, the request is a *content miss*.

- If the item is not found in the cache, then it is fetched from the origin server (or another cache) and the request constitutes a *content miss*.

- If the request arrives from the client with a no-cache header then the cache forwards it to the origin server. The cache must forward the request even if it has a fresh copy. The cache uses the response to replace or refresh its older copy of the object. We refer to such requests as *no-cache* requests.

The TTL calculation for a cachable object as specified by HTTP/1.1 compares the *age* of the object with its *freshness lifetime*. If the age is smaller than the freshness lifetime the object is considered fresh and otherwise it is considered stale. The TTL is the freshness lifetime minus the age (or zero if negative).

The age of an object is the difference between the current time (according to the cache's own clock) and the timestamp specified by the object's DATE response header (which is supposed to indicate when the response was generated at the origin). If an AGE header is present, the age is taken to be the maximum of the above and what is implied by the AGE header.

Freshness lifetime calculation then proceeds as follows. First, if a MAX-AGE directive is present, the value is taken to be the freshness lifetime. Otherwise, if EXPIRES header (indicating absolute expiration time) is present, the freshness lifetime is the difference between the time specified by the EXPIRES header and the time specified by the DATE header (zero if this difference is negative). Thus, the TTL is the difference between the value of the EXPIRES header and the current time (as specified by the cache's clock). Otherwise, no explicit freshness lifetime is provided by the origin server and a heuristic is used: The freshness lifetime is assigned to be a fraction (HTTP/1.1 mentions 10% as an example) of the time difference between the timestamp at the DATE header and the time specified by the LAST-MODIFIED header, subject to a maximum allowed value (usually 24 hours, since HTTP/1.1 requires that the cache must attach a warning if heuristic expiration is used and the object's age exceeds 24 hours).

3.   Validation latency

Servicing of a request by a cache involves remote communication if the requested object is not cached (in which case the request constitutes a *content miss*). Remote communication is also required if the cache contains a copy of the object, but the copy is *stale*, that is, its freshness lifetime had expired and it must be validated (by the origin server or a cache with a *fresh* copy) prior to being served. If the cached copy turns out to be modified, the request constitutes a content miss. Otherwise, the cached copy is *valid* and we refer to the request as a *freshness miss*. Validation requests that turn out as freshness misses typically have small-size responses but due to communication overhead with remote servers, often their contribution to user-perceived latency is comparable to that of full-fledged content misses.

Thus, cache service times can be improved by reducing both content and freshness misses. The content hit rate is measured per object or per byte and sometimes weighted by estimated object fetching cost. It is dictated by the available cache storage and the *replacement policy* used. Replacement policies for Web caches were extensively studied (e.g. [Williams et al., 1996, Cao and Irani, 1997, Bestavros et al., 1995, Cohen et al., 1998a, Cohen and Kaplan, 1999, Breslau et al., 1999, Feldmann et al., 1999, Young, 1998]).The freshness hit rate of a cache is not directly addressed by replacement policies or captured by the content hit rate metric.

The expiration time of each object is determined when it is brought into the cache, according to attached HTTP response headers provided by the origin server. Expired content must be validated before being served. Most current caching platforms validate their content *passively* i.e. only when a client request arrives and the cached copy of the object is stale. They perform validation via a conditional GET request (typically this is an If-Modified-Since (IMS) Get request). This means that validation requests are always performed "online," while the end-user is waiting. Here we promote proactive refreshment where the cache initiates unsolicited validation requests for selected content. Such "offline" validations extend freshness time of cached objects and more client requests can be served directly from the cache. Our motivation is that the most significant cost issue associated with freshness misses is their direct effect on user-perceived latency rather than their effect on server and network load, and thus it is worth performing more than one "offline" validation in order to avoid one performed "online."

A mechanism that reduces validation latency with TTL-based consistency is that the server piggy backs validations on responses to requests for related objects [Krishnamurthy and Wills, 1997, Cohen et al., 1998b, Cohen et al., 1999]. "Related" objects are those that are often requested after the current request; the cache then updates the freshness status of its content of these related objects and therefore eliminates validation latency on these requests. This scheme requires server support. Another line of work proposed to transfer stale cached data from the cache to the client's browser while the data validity is being verified [Dingle and Partl, 1996] or while the modified portion (the "delta") is being computed [Banga et al., 1997]. These schemes require browser support and are mostly effective when there is limited bandwidth between end-user and cache (such as with modem users).

Refreshment policies, which extend freshness periods of selected cached objects were proposed in [Cohen and Kaplan, 2002] (for Web caches) and in [Cohen and Kaplan, 2001c] for caches of Domain Name System (DNS) servers. With these policies, caches proactively validate selected objects as they become stale, and thus allow for more client requests to be processed locally. Refreshment policies operate within the existing protocols and exploit natural properties of request patterns such as frequency and recency. Although not yet supported by some widely deployed Web caching platforms (e.g., Squid [Squid, 2001]), proactive refreshment is offered by some cache vendors [Cacheman, 2001, IP-WorX, 2001]. Such products allow refreshment selections to be configured manually by the administrator or integrate policies based on object popularity.

For DNS caches, refreshing an object is equivalent to issuing a new request: there is no If-Modified-Since mechanism and also not much need for it as record sizes are typically small. Each DNS resource record (RR) has a TTL value initially set by its authoritative server. A cached RR becomes stale when its TTL expires. Client queries can be answered much faster when the information is available in the cache, and hence, refreshment policies which renew cached RRs offline increase the cache hit rate and decrease user-perceived latency.

4.   Refreshment policies

Refreshment policies are designed to balance the overhead cost of additional validation requests to origin servers against the increase in freshness hits. The decision of which objects to renew upon expiration varies between policies and is guided by natural properties of the request history of each object such as time-to-live (TTL) values, popularity, and recency of previous requests. Refreshment policies can also be viewed as prefetching of freshness. Their methodology and implementation, however, is closer to replacement policies than of prefetching algorithms. Refreshment policies resemble common cache replacement policies (such as LRU and LFU) in the way objects are prioritized. First, policies prefer renewing recently- or frequently-requested objects. Second, implementation is similar since object value is determined only by the request-history of the object rather than by considering request history of related objects. Another difference of refreshment and document prefetching is that validations typically have considerably smaller response-sizes than complete documents, but due to communication overhead, the latency gap is not nearly as pronounced. Hence, refreshment potentially provides considerably better tradeoffs of bandwidth vs. reduced latency compared to object prefetching.

The experimental study indicates that the best among the refreshment policies considered can eliminate about half of the freshness misses at a cost of 2 additional validation requests per eliminated freshness miss. Since freshness misses constitute a large fraction (30%-50%) of cache hits in a typical large scale Web cache, incorporating a refreshment policy can considerably improve latency.

4.1   Policies

Refreshment policies associate with every cached object a *renewal credit* (a nonnegative integer). When a cached copy is about to expire (according to its respective TTL interval), and it has nonzero renewal credit, a renewal request is sent to the respective authoritative server, and the renewal credit is decremented.

The association of renewal credits to objects is governed by the particular policy. The policies we consider may increment the renewal credit only upon a client request. Renewal scheduling can be implemented via a priority queue, grouping together objects with close-together expiration, or possibly by an event-triggered process.

- PASSIVE: passive validation, objects are validated only as a result of a freshness miss i.e. when a request arrives and there is a stale cached copy. This is the way most caches work today.

- OPT(i): An approximation to the optimal omniscient offline policy. This policy assumes knowledge of the time of the subsequent request for the object and whether the object copy would still be valid then. If the subsequent request is such that the current copy remains valid and it is issued within $c \leq i$ freshness-lifetime-durations after the expiration of the current copy, then the renewal credit is set to c. Otherwise, no renewals are performed. This policy viewed as analogous to Belady's cache replacement algorithm [Belady, 1966]. The approximation collapses to the optimal solution if renewals can be granted for fractional TTL values.

- RECENCY(k): The renewal credit is reset to k following any request for the object, including no-cache requests. RECENCY(k), similarly to the cache replacement policy LRU, exploits the *recency property* of request sequences, which states that future requests are more likely to be issued to recently-requested objects.

- FREQ(j, m): increment the renewal credit by j for any request that would have been a freshness miss under PASSIVE. In other words, we add j to the renewal credit upon any request which is issued more than freshness-lifetime-duration units of time after a previous request that caused the passive policy to contact the origin server. In addition, upon any request (except for no-cache requests) the renewal credit is set to m if it is less than m. With $m = 0$, this policy FREQ($j, 0$) purely exploits the *frequency property* that states that objects that were frequently requested in the past are more likely to be requested soon. (A cache replacement policy that exploits the frequency property is LFU.) For $m > 1$, the policy FREQ(j, m) is a hybrid of FREQ($j, 0$) and RECENCY(m).

- TH-FREQ(th, m) keep renewing objects until the ratio of would-have been PASSIVE freshness misses to number of freshness-lifetime-durations since beginning of log drops below a threshold. In other words, upon each request which would have been a freshness miss for PASSIVE we increment the renewal credit such that we would keep renewing until the ratio drops below a threshold. In addition, upon any request (except for no-cache requests) the renewal credit is increased to m if it was less than m. This policy exploits the frequency property, and normalizes it by freshness-lifetime-duration. It also naturally provides a more continuous range of tradeoffs, since th is not necessarily an integer. With $m = 0$ the policy is purely frequency-based whereas higher values of m correspond to hybrids with RECENCY(m) policy.

4.2   Simulation results

Simulations were performed using 6 days NLANR cache traces [IRCache, 2001] collected from the UC and SD caches from January 20th till January 25th, 2000. The NLANR caches run Squid [Squid, 2001] which logs and labels each request with several attributes such as the request time, service time, cache action taken, the response code returned to the client, and the response size.

Under the simulated baseline policy PASSIVE (where objects are refreshed only as a result of client requests), 48% of content hits constituted freshness misses on the UC trace, and 53% were freshness misses on the SD trace. The performance of the different refreshment policies is evaluated by the tradeoff of *overhead* vs. *coverage*. The coverage (reduction in freshness-misses) is calculated as the fraction of the number of freshness misses according to passive that are eliminated by the respective policy. More precisely, if x denotes the number of freshness misses of PASSIVE, and y the number of freshness misses of a policy P then the coverage of P is the fraction $(x - y)/x$.

The *overhead* of policy P is the difference between the number of validation requests issued by P and the number of validation requests issued by PASSIVE. Since the cache issues a validation request for each freshness miss, the request overhead is the total number of renewals performed minus the number of freshness misses eliminated (converted to freshness hits). The overhead is normalized by dividing it with the total number of freshness misses that were converted to freshness hits.

The coverage/overhead tradeoff for each type of policy is obtained by sweeping the value of its respective parameter. For example, the points on the curve of RECENCY correspond to runs with RECENCY(1), RECENCY(2), RECENCY(3), ... and the points for FREQ were obtained on runs with FREQ(1, 0), FREQ(2, 0), ... Note that OPT(0), RECENCY(0), FREQ(0, 0), and TH-FREQ(∞, 0) are in fact PASSIVE (these policies are able to achieve "continuous" tradeoffs by mixing two consecutive integral values of the respective parameter, for example, applying RECENCY(1) on some URLs and RECENCY(2) on others.) These tradeoffs are shown in Figure 3.2.

Under all types of policies, the coverage peaks at about 63%-67%. The remaining 33%-37% of freshness misses mostly occur on objects with freshness-lifetime-duration of 0, on which refreshment is not effective. The OPT policy eliminates all "addressable" freshness misses with overhead of about 1.3 requests per miss, and eliminates the bulk of these misses with an overhead of 0.5.

The simulation results for OPT and RECENCY show the locality effect, where most freshness misses that can be eliminated occur within a small number of freshness-lifetime-durations after a previous request. This goes well with the refreshment framework which keeps objects fresh continuously till the following "hit."

The left-most point on the curves of RECENCY and OPT, which correspond to RECENCY(1) and OPT(1), show that about 30% of freshness misses occur within one freshness-lifetime-duration after the expiration of the cached copy. The second points on the left correspond to RECENCY(2) and OPT(2) and in-

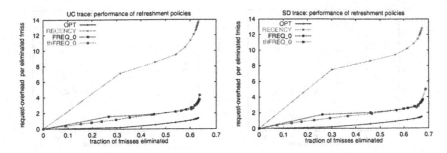

Figure 3.2. Performance of the different refreshment policies when simulated on the UC and SD traces

dicate that about additional 15% of freshness misses occur between one and two freshness-lifetime durations passed the expiration. We note that the observed fact that a very small number of freshness misses occur more than 10 freshness-lifetime-durations passed the expiration is not only due to locality but also reflects the interaction of the log duration of six days and the most common freshness-lifetime-duration of 24 hours [Cohen and Kaplan, 2001a].

The fact that coverage of RECENCY and the frequency-based policies peaks at about the same place indicates that a very small fraction of freshness misses are incurred on very infrequently requested objects (since the frequency-based policies do not perform any renewals on the first request and thus can not eliminate misses incurred on the second request.). The correspondence in peak coverage of OPT and other policy-types is due to a "threshold phenomenon" where most freshness misses occur on objects with a freshness-lifetime-duration of 0 or occur within a small number of freshness-lifetime-durations following a previous request.

The frequency-based policies FREQ$(j, 0)$ and TH-FREQ$(th, 0)$ significantly outperformed RECENCY(k). This reflects the fact that the vast majority of freshness misses which can be eliminated occur on the more popular URLs. The gap is caused by the very large number of cachable URLs that were requested only once. The RECENCY(k) policy performed up to k unproductive renewals on each such request. (It could be less than k since we did not perform renewals passed the termination time of the log.) The hybrid policies FREQ and TH-FREQ with $m > 0$ performed considerably worse than the pure frequency-based policies (that correspond to $m = 0$) and hence only results for $m = 0$ are shown. This behavior is not surprising given that RECENCY yielded much worse tradeoffs. Overall, the results indicate that frequency-based object prioritization is more effective than recency-based prioritization.

The domination of frequency-based policies is also consistent with studies of cache replacement policies for Web contents [Breslau et al., 1999, Cohen and

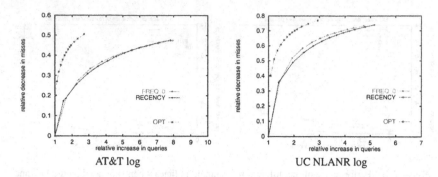

AT&T log   UC NLANR log

Figure 3.3. Performance of refreshment policies on DNS traces. The x-axis gives the increase in the number of DNS queries due to refreshments.)

Kaplan, 1999], since different URLs tend to have a wide range of characteristic popularities, a property that is captured better by frequency-based policies. It is interesting to contrast the performance of refreshment policies on DNS records (see Figure 3.3 and [Cohen and Kaplan, 2001c] for more details.) For DNS caches, the recency and frequency-based policies exhibited similar performance. We explain this by the observation that at the hostname level there is significantly smaller fraction of "objects" that are resolved only once.

The performance of FREQ and TH-FREQ is similar, although TH-FREQ, which normalizes the frequency by freshness-lifetime-duration, performed somewhat better. The similarity is mostly explained by the fact that the large majority of freshness-lifetime-durations are of the same length (one day) and also because for shorter durations, frequency of requests is correlated with the duration. The policy TH-FREQ provides a spectrum of tradeoffs and better performance, particularly in the low-overhead range. TH-FREQ, however, may require more book-keeping than FREQ. The particular tradeoffs obtained by the frequency-based policies shows that significant improvements can be obtained with fairly low overhead. About 10% of freshness misses can be eliminated with the overhead of half of a validation request per eliminated freshness miss; 25% of freshness misses can be eliminated with overhead of a single request per eliminated miss; 50% can be eliminated with overhead of two; and 65% of freshness misses can be eliminated with overhead of three.

For DNS caches, the data consisted from Web proxy logs, extrapolated DNS queries, and performed name resolutions to extract the corresponding TTL (freshness lifetime) durations (see [Cohen and Kaplan, 2001c] for more details). Figure 3.3 shows the performance of refreshment policies on two logs. For each policy we measure the tradeoff between the relative decrease in cache misses and the relative increase in DNS queries (issued by the name-server). As the natural baseline we use the passive policy, whose performance on the two logs is as follows. The UC NLANR log had 941K DNS misses (which were 8.7% from the total number of HTTP requests). Out of these misses, 9.7% were on the first logged request to an item. The AT&T log had 32K misses, that were 6.5% of the total number of logged HTTP requests. 33% of these DNS misses were on the first logged request to an item. The number of queries issued by the passive policy is equal to the number of DNS misses. Better tradeoffs were obtained for the larger (NLANR) log because the fraction of necessary misses that occur on the first request to an item decrease with log period and with the number of clients. On the UC NLANR log, RECENCY and FREQ eliminate about 60% of misses that occurred on previously-seen items with query overhead of 2 and eliminate 80% of these misses with query overhead of 5. The respective reductions for the AT&T log are 36% and 63%.

5.   Basic Source Types of Cascaded caches

We define three types of *sources* that capture different relationships between a client-cache and its data source(s). The different sources are illustrated in Figure 3.4. The TTL value obtained through each source as a function of time is illustrated in Figure 3.5.

1 AUTH: An authoritative source. AUTH always provides a copy with zero age (TTL that equals the freshness lifetime).

2 EXC: Let α be drawn uniformly at random from the interval $[0, T]$ (the distribution $U[0, T]$), where T is the lifetime of the object. We call α the *displacement*. At time t an EXC source provides a copy whose age is $(t - \alpha) \bmod T$ ("mod" is a generalized modulus operation to arbitrary nonnegative numbers $a \bmod b = a - b * \lfloor a/b \rfloor$. If $b = 0$ then we define $a \bmod b \equiv 0$.) TTL equals to $T - (t - \alpha) \bmod T$. Note that the choice of α is fixed for each "run" on the sequence, and the performance of EXC is the *expected* performance over all runs with different displacements.

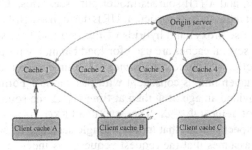

Figure 3.4.   Different types of sources: Cache A uses cache 1 as an EXC source. Cache B uses caches 1,2,... as an IND source. Cache C uses an AUTH source.

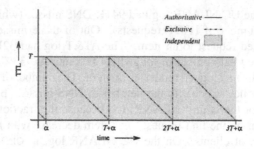

Figure 3.5. TTL obtained through different types of sources. AUTH source always provides zero age and TTL of T. EXC source (shown with displacement α) provides age that cycles from 0 to T and thus TTL which cycles from T to 0. IND source provides at each point in time age drawn independently from $U[0, T]$ and thus TTL drawn from $U[0, T]$.

This source models a scenario where the client-cache upon each miss fetches a copy from the *same* high-level-cache. This high-level-cache maintains a fresh copy by refreshing it through an AUTH source each time it expires. The averaging over different displacements captures independence of the request times at the client-cache and the particular "refresh period" of the high-level-cache.

3 IND: Upon each miss at the client-cache, the IND source provides a copy with age independently drawn from $U[0, T]$ (thus a TTL that is also drawn from $U[0, T]$).

This source models a scenario where upon each miss, the client-cache forwards the request to a different independent EXC-type high-level-cache. Independence means that the displacements of the different high-level-caches are not correlated.

The EXC, IND, and AUTH sources model pure scenarios. Currently, many web caches direct requests for a particular URL through a high-level-cache (e.g., a proxy or a reverse proxy) and hybrids of the IND and EXC sources capture scenarios where several caches are used for load balancing purposes.

We use the notion of source *consistency*. A source is *consistent* if the age provided at any given time is consistent with past values. Formally, if at time t, the source provided an age of Φ then at time $t + \Delta$ the source provides the object with age of at most $\Phi + \Delta$. The AUTH and EXC sources are consistent. In general, we expect sources that model a single server to be consistent.

Our analysis assumes that the request sequence is independent of the performance of the client-cache (that is, future requests do not depend on which previous requests constituted a hit or a miss).

5.1   Relationships Between the Basic Sources

We summarize results on basic relationships of the performances of a client cache through the different sources.

We first present proofs that on any request sequence

- The miss rate of a client-cache through an AUTH source is no greater than the miss rate of the client-cache through an EXC source, and

- The miss rate of a client-cache through an EXC source is no greater than the miss rate of the client-cache through an IND source.

The proof utilizes the following two basic lemmas that relate the miss rate at a client cache to the distribution of ages (and therefore TTLs) provided by the source. These lemmas will be also useful in later sections. (The proof of the second Lemma is omitted).

LEMMA 3.1 *Consider two consistent sources s_1 and s_2 such that at any given point in time, the TTL available from s_1 is at least as large as the TTL available from s_2. Then, for any sequence of requests, the number of misses through s_1 is at most the number of misses through s_2.*

Proof. The proof is by induction on the length of the request sequence. The lemma clearly holds for sequences of lengths 1 and 2. Consider a request sequence τ of length l. If the last request is either a miss or a hit through both s_1 and s_2, or a miss through s_2 but a hit through s_1, then the lemma follows by using the induction hypothesis on the prefix of length $l - 1$ of τ.

Consider the case where the last request is a miss through s_1 but a hit through s_2. Let the ith request be the last request on which the client working through s_2 had a miss. The client working through s_1 must have had a hit on the ith request and all the requests following it including the next to last request. (Otherwise our assumptions guarantee that it would have got a TTL that covers the last request.) Thus by applying the induction hypothesis on the prefix of τ of length $i - 1$ the lemma follows. ∎

LEMMA 3.2 *Consider two sources s_1 and s_2 that serve objects with TTLs that are independently drawn from distributions with CDFs (Cumulative Distribution Functions) F_1 and F_2, respectively. Suppose that for all $x \geq 0$, $F_1(x) \leq F_2(x)$, i.e. s_1 provides longer TTLs. Then for any sequence of requests, the expected number of misses through the source s_1 is no larger than the expected number of misses through the source s_2.*

As a consequence of Lemma 3.1 we obtain that AUTH has smaller miss rate than EXC. Furthermore, as a consequence of Lemma 3.2 we obtain that AUTH has smaller miss rate than IND. The following Lemma establishes that EXC always outperforms IND.

LEMMA 3.3 *For any sequence of requests, the miss rate through an* EXC *source is never higher than through an* IND *source.*

Proof. Consider the ith request. Its likelihood of being a miss with EXC is $\min\{1, (t_i - t_{i-1})/T\}$. Let $m[j]$ and $h[j]$ denote the events that the jth request is a miss or a hit respectively, with an IND source. The likelihood that the ith request constitutes a miss with IND is

$$
\begin{aligned}
p(m[i]) \quad = \quad & p(m[i-1]) \min\{1, \frac{t_i - t_{i-1}}{T}\} \\
& + p(h[i-1] \cap m[i-2]) \min\{1, \frac{t_i - t_{i-2}}{T}\} \\
& + p(h[i-1] \cap h[i-2] \cap m[i-3]) \min\{1, \frac{t_i - t_{i-3}}{T}\} + \dots \\
\geq \quad & \min\{1, \frac{t_i - t_{i-1}}{T}\} .
\end{aligned}
$$

Since the likelihood of every request to be a miss through an EXC source is smaller than through an IND source, we obtain that the miss rate through EXC is smaller than the miss rate through IND. ∎

Note that with respect to one fixed displacement value α, the EXC source could perform worse than IND. Consider the following sequence where requests are made at times $(2i - \epsilon)T$ and $(2i + \epsilon)T$ for integral $i > 0$. Suppose that the source refreshes at times iT. Then all requests would constitute misses with EXC, and only $1/2 + 2\epsilon$ would constitute misses with IND. Lemma 3.3 shows that on average over all displacements, EXC performs at least as well as IND.

6.   Rejuvenating Sources

We next consider replicating servers that refresh selected objects as soon as their TTL drops below some threshold (rather than wait for it to completely expire). We refer to such configured periodic pre-term refreshes as *rejuvenation*.

We extend the definitions of our basic sources to include rejuvenation. The source EXC$_v$ is an EXC source that refreshes its copy of the object when the age exceeds v fraction of the lifetime value. Formally, let α be drawn from $U[0, vT]$. At time t, an EXC$_v$ source return the object with age $(t - \alpha) \bmod (v * T)$ (so the TTL is $T - (t - \alpha) \bmod (v * T)$). As with an EXC source, α is fixed for a "run", and performance is the expected performance over runs with different displacements. We say that a client-cache uses an IND$_v$ source if upon each miss it forwards the request to a different independent EXC$_v$ source. Hence, IND$_v$ source returns copies with age drawn from $U[0, vT]$ and thus TTL drawn from $U[(1 - v)T, T]$. The TTL as a function of time for the different sources is illustrated in Figure 3.6. For both IND$_v$ and EXC$_v$ sources, a rejuvenation interval of $v = 1$ corresponds to the respective pure source: EXC$_1$ $\equiv$ EXC and

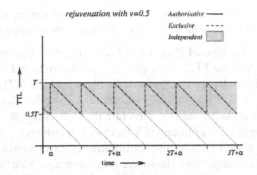

Figure 3.6. TTL as a function of time for rejuvenating sources with $v = 0.5$. $\text{EXC}_{0.5}$ has a period of $0.5T$ where the age cycles from $T/2$ to T and thus, the TTL cycles from T to $T/2$. For $\text{IND}_{0.5}$ the age at any point in time is independently drawn from $U[T/2, T]$ and thus the TTL is drawn from $U[T/2, T]$. The dotted lines correspond to expiration times of previously-served copies by $\text{EXC}_{0.5}$. The expiration times are at $iT/2 + \alpha$ for integral values of i.

$\text{IND}_1 \equiv \text{IND}$. A rejuvenation interval of $v = 0$ corresponds to a pure AUTH source. That is, $\text{EXC}_0 \equiv \text{AUTH}$ and $\text{IND}_0 \equiv \text{AUTH}$.

Intuitively, we might expect a monotonic improvement in miss rate as v decreases from $v = 1$ to $v = 0$. We show later on that this is the case with IND_v sources but not with EXC_v sources.

6.1 Does Rejuvenating Pay Off?

At first glance, it seems that rejuvenations can only reduce the miss rate of client caches. Somewhat surprising is the fact that this is not the case for EXC rejuvenating sources.

LEMMA 3.4 *Let $v < 1$, and let $u = \frac{1}{\lceil 1/v \rceil}$. Note that $v \leq u \leq 1$. Consider a request sequence $\{t_i\}$, such that the object is requested at least once every $(\lceil \frac{1}{v} \rceil v - 1)T$ time units. Let m_v denote the miss rate through EXC_v on $\{t_i\}$ and m_u the miss rate through EXC_u on $\{t_i\}$. Then, $m_v = \frac{u}{v} m_u$.*

Lemma 3.4 shows that the performance of a cache which receives frequent requests to the object can be strictly worse through EXC_v with $v < 1$ than through a non-rejuvenating EXC source. For example, for $v > 0.5$, and for sequences satisfying that the object is requested at least once every $(2v - 1)T$ time units, by Lemma 3.4 the miss rate is strictly worse through EXC_v than with a non-rejuvenating EXC source. In this case, rejuvenating does not pay off.

In contrast, the following lemma shows that IND sources do exhibit monotonic dependence of the miss rate on v.

LEMMA 3.5 *Let* IND_{v_1} *and* IND_{v_2} *be two sources such that* $v_1 \leq v_2$. *Then, the miss rate through* IND_{v_1} *is no larger than the miss rate through* IND_{v_2}.

Proof. By the definition of IND_v the TTL's through IND_{v_1} are drawn from $U[(1 - v_1)T, T]$ and the TTL's through IND_{v_2} are drawn from $U[(1 - v_2)T, T]$. Let F_1 be the CDF of $U[(1 - v_1)T, T]$ and let F_2 be the CDF of $U[(1 - v_2)T, T]$. Since for all $x \geq 0$, $F_1(x) \leq F_2(x)$ Lemma 3.2 implies that the miss rate through IND_{v_1} is no larger than the miss rate through IND_{v_2}. ∎

The following corollary of Lemma 3.1 shows that although generally rejuvenation does not always improve the performance, rejuvenation cannot degrade performance on any sequence if the source is *synchronized* with the client cache. (The source and client-cache are synchronized if after the client-cache contains a copy of the object which expires at some time t, requests directed to the source at times $t + \Delta$ (for any $\Delta > 0$) obtain a copy whose age is not more than Δ.)

COROLLARY 3.6 *Suppose a rejuvenating* EXC *source adheres to the original refresh schedule, refreshing the object at times* $\alpha + iT$ *for integral* i *in addition to possibly rejuvenating it at other points in time. Then on any sequence of requests, the number of misses is not higher than the number of misses through* EXC.

In particular it follows from Corollary 3.6 that the performance through EXC_v with integral $1/v$, (i.e., $v = 1/2, 1/3, \ldots$), is at least as good as through EXC. Moreover, even if we restrict ourselves to EXC_v, with integral $1/v$, the miss rate is not always monotonic as a function of v. The following example shows that EXC_v ($7/8 > v > 3/4$) can induce miss-rate even higher than through the basic IND source:

EXAMPLE 3.7 *Consider the source* EXC_v *with* $v = 3/4 + x$ *(for fixed* $0 < x < 1/4$*). Consider the sequence of requests to the client-level cache at regular intervals of* $1/2 + 2x$. *Since there is at least one request every* $(2v - 1)T$ *time, there is exactly one miss of the client-level cache every* vT *time. Consider now the performance of* IND. *With each miss we associate the time period till the next miss. We compute the expected length of that interval between misses. The interval length is* $(1/2 + 2x)$ *with probability* $(1/2 + 2x)$ *and is* $1 + 4x$ *otherwise. Thus, the expected length of the interval is* $3/4 + 2x - 8x^2$. *Note that* $2x - 8x^2 > x$ *for* $0 < x < 1/8$. *Hence,* IND *source would outperform* EXC_v *in this case.*

We saw that EXC_v sources are more effective when $1/v$ is integral (i.e., $v = 1/2, 1/3, \ldots$). Thus, since sporadic pre-term refreshes are better captured by non-integral $1/v$ values, they can degrade performance at client caches.

Poisson arrivals We now consider the performance of a client-cache that receives requests generated by a Poisson process with rate λ (we normalize the

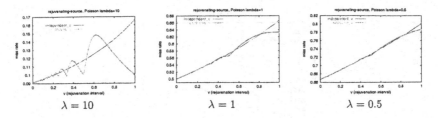

$$\lambda = 10 \qquad\qquad \lambda = 1 \qquad\qquad \lambda = 0.5$$

Figure 3.7. Miss rate dependence on rejuvenation interval for different Poisson arrivals rates.

rate by the freshness lifetime interval T, so the expected number of requests in time T is λ). The client cache contacts a rejuvenating source upon a miss. The miss rate as a function of v and λ is

- $\frac{1}{1+(2-v)\lambda/2}$, through an IND$_v$ source, and

- $\frac{1}{\lambda v(\lfloor 1/v\rfloor + \exp(\lambda v(1/v - \lfloor 1/v\rfloor))/(\exp(-v\lambda)-1))}$, through an EXC$_v$ source.

Figure 3.7 illustrates dependence of miss-rate on v, for 3 representative request rates, for a cache using EXC$_v$ and IND$_v$ sources.

Pareto arrivals The *Pareto* family of distributions is a widely-used model for inter-arrival times [Leland et al., 1993, Paxson and Floyd, 1995]. For a power $\alpha > 0$ and scale parameter $k > 0$, inter-request time durations have density function $f(x) = \alpha k^\alpha (x + k)^{-\alpha-1} (x \geq 0)$, and the respective CDF is $F(x) = 1 - (k/(x + k))^\alpha$. The parameter k is inversely proportional to the rate (average number of request per time unit), which is equal to $(\alpha - 1)/k$ for $\alpha > 1$. For $\alpha \leq 1$ the expectation of an inter-request duration is unbounded, and thus the rate is 0. We consider Pareto distributions with different values of α. For any given α, we vary "request-rates" by fixing $T = 1$ and sweeping k (it is symmetric to fix $k = 1$ and vary $1/T$). Simulations that we performed for Pareto arrivals when varying the scale parameter k (for a fixed power α) revealed patterns similar to those obtained for Poisson arrivals when varying $1/\lambda$. Figure 3.8 shows simulation results for some representative "request-rates" and values of the power α.

Trace-based simulations Figure 3.9 shows the miss rate as a function of the rejuvenation interval $v \in [0, 1]$ for the sources IND$_v$ and EXC$_v$. The results shown are for the UC NLANR trace mentioned in Section 4. The simulations show the presence of patterns obtained in our Poisson analysis.

Elementary derivations establish the following for Poisson arrivals, and simulations suggest that these patterns hold for Pareto arrivals and real traces as well.

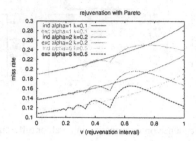

Figure 3.8.   Rejuvenation with Pareto arrivals

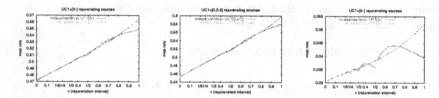

Figure 3.9. Miss rate dependence on rejuvenation interval for UC trace, UC[0.2–2], and UC[5–∞]. The notation UC[a–b] includes all requests made to objects with rate in [a, b).

- The miss rate of the client cache through IND_v and EXC_v converges to its miss rate through AUTH as v approaches 0, and to its miss rate through IND and EXC respectively as v approaches 1.

- The miss-rate through IND_v is monotone increasing with v and convex.

- The miss rate of EXC_v has local minima for v's such that $1/v$ is integral. For these values of v, EXC_v outperforms IND_v. EXC_v restricted to these points is a convex monotone increasing function of v. Between each pair of local minima EXC_v is a concave function of v, and has a local maxima around which it performs worse than IND_v. This is more pronounced for high rates ($\lambda \gg 1$). The ratio is less than 1 for integral values of $1/v$ and is improving with increasing $1/v$. For non-integral values and higher request rates the ratio is larger than 1. We note that even though we observed this for Pareto arrivals and in our traces, this is not universally true: There are sequences on which the miss-rate with $\text{EXC}_{1/2}$ is strictly lower than with $\text{EXC}_{1/3}$.

6.2   Worst-case analysis

We summarize some worst-case bounds on the performance of EXC and IND rejuvenating sources. For a source S and a request sequence $\{t_i\}$ let $\rho(\{t_i\}, S)$ be the ratio between the expected miss rate of $\{t_i\}$ through S and through an AUTH source. The maximum over all sequences $\{t_i\}$ of $\rho(\{t_i\}, S)$ is called the *competitive ratio* of S, and is denoted by $\rho(S)$. We use the term *rejuvenating policy* for any source that corresponds to a single high-level cache which maintains a fresh copy of the object by refreshing it (rejuvenating) from an authoritative server before or when it expires. In particular AUTH, EXC, and EXC_v, are rejuvenating policies. We start with a bound on the competitive ratio of any rejuvenating policy:

LEMMA 3.8 *The competitive ratio of any rejuvenating policy is at most 2.*

The following Theorem establishes a corresponding lower bound of 2 on the competitive ratio of any rejuvenating policy that cannot rejuvenate the object continuously but must have a small gap of ϵ between consecutive rejuvenations.

THEOREM 3.9 *Consider a rejuvenating policy P such that the time interval between any two rejuvenation points must exceed some $\epsilon > 0$. Then $\rho(P) = 2$.*

The Theorem implies that rejuvenating in fixed intervals, (an EXC_v source with $v > 0$), has a competitive ratio 2.

Another related problem is to compare the worst-case performance of an IND_v source with respect to an AUTH source:

THEOREM 3.10 *The competitive ratio of* IND_v *is* $\displaystyle\sum_{k=0}^{\lfloor \frac{1}{1-v} \rfloor} \frac{(1 - k(1 - v))^k}{k!v^k}.$

By Theorem 3.10, for $v < 1/2$, the competitive ratio of an IND_v source is 2, and as v approaches 1, the competitive ratio approaches $e \approx 2.718$. The higher competitive ratio of IND_v comparable to the competitive ratio of EXC_v fits well with the superiority of EXC on IND established earlier.

These worst-case bounds do not distinguish between the performance of sources with different rejuvenation rates, as all EXC_v sources ($0 < v \leq 1$) and all IND_v sources ($0 < v \leq 1/2$) have the same tight competitive ratio of 2.

6.3 Lessons

We learned that under a wide range of circumstances, sporadic pre-term refreshes (caused by requests with a no-cache request header) or rejuvenations that are not well-timed can result in inferior performance of a client-cache relative to its performance under a basic EXC source.

Synchronization between a client and its source cache would guarantee that the performance of the client is no worse than its performance through the basic EXC source. An EXC_v source is guaranteed to remain synchronized with all clients only if $1/v$ is integral. With sporadic pre-term refreshes, a source cache is only guaranteed to remain synchronized with the one client which invoked the most-recent pre-term refresh (delivered the no-cache request) and with clients with already-expired copies.

A source that serves sporadic no-cache requests can preserve synchronization with its other clients by performing one of the followings.

1) It can serve the no-cache request by contacting an origin server but refrain from updating the expiration time on its cached copy.

2) It can update the expiration time of its copy but perform another *follow-up* pre-term refresh of the object at its original expiration time.

Rejuvenation policies and follow-up refreshes increase traffic in the *upstream channel* between the high-level cache and origin servers while potentially reducing user-perceived latency and traffic in the *downstream channel* between the high-level cache and its clients (see Figure 3.1). This tradeoff should guide the selection of rejuvenation interval or the follow-up action on a sporadic pre-term refresh.

The objective of rejuvenation policies is to maximize the benefit, that is, minimize the total number of misses at client-caches given some bound on the cost, that is crudely measured by the number of unsolicited refresh requests issued by the high-level cache. Whereas the cost is independent of client activity and rather straightforward to estimate (for rejuvenation it is proportional to $1/v$), estimating the benefit, which is aggregated across all client caches, is a more involved task. A challenge left for future work is to efficiently estimate this benefit, possibly by keeping some summarized per-client history for a sample of the clients.

References

Akamai (2001). Akamai. http://www.akamai.com.

Banga, G., Douglis, F., and Rabinovich, M. (1997). Optimistic deltas for WWW latency reduction. In *Proceedings of the USENIX Annual Technical Conference*. USENIX Association.

Belady, L. A. (1966). A study of replacement algorithms for virtual storage computers. *IBM systems journal*, 5:78–101.

Berners-Lee, T., Fielding, R., and Frystyk, H. (1996). RFC 1945: Hypertext Transfer Protocol — HTTP/1.0.

Bestavros, A., Carter, R., Crovella, M., Cunha, C., Heddaya, A., and Mirdad, S. (1995). Application-level document caching in the internet. In *Proceedings of the Second Intl. Workshop on Services in Distributed and Networked Environments (SDNE '95)*. Available as http://cs-www.bu.edu/faculty/crovella/paper-archive/www-sdne95/paper.html.

Breslau, L., Cao, P., Fan, L., Phillips, G., and Shenker, S. (1999). Web caching and zipf-like distributions: Evidence and implications. In *Proceedings of the IEEE INFOCOM'99 Conference*.

Cacheman (2001). IBM WebSphere Cache Manager. http://www.software.ibm.com/webservers/cacheman.

Cao, P. and Irani, S. (1997). Cost-aware WWW proxy caching algorithms. In *Proceedings of the USENIX Symposium on Internet Technologies and Systems*, Monterey, California. http://www.usenix.org/events/usits97.

Cao, P. and Liu, C. (1998). Maintaining strong cache consistency in the world wide web. *IEEE Transactions on Computers*, 47(4):445–457.

Cohen, E., Halperin, E., and Kaplan, H. (2001). Performance aspects of distributed caches using TTL-based consistency. full version.

Cohen, E. and Kaplan, H. (1999). Exploiting regularities in Web traffic patterns for cache replacement. In *Proc. 31st Annual ACM Symposium on Theory of Computing*. ACM.

Cohen, E. and Kaplan, H. (2001a). The age penalty and its effect on cache performance. In *Proceedings of the 3rd USENIX Symposium on Internet Technologies and Systems*.

Cohen, E. and Kaplan, H. (2001b). Aging through cascaded caches: performance issues in the distribution of Web content. In *Proceedings of the ACM SIGCOMM Conference*. ACM.

Cohen, E. and Kaplan, H. (2001c). Proactive caching of DNS records: addressing a performance bottleneck. In *Proceedings of the Symposium on Applications and the Internet*. IEEE.

Cohen, E. and Kaplan, H. (2002). Refreshment policies for Web content caches. *Computer Networks*, 38:795–808.

Cohen, E., Krishnamurthy, B., and Rexford, J. (1998a). Evaluating server-assisted cache replacement in the Web. In *Proceedings of the 6th European Symposium on Algorithms*, pages 307–319. Springer-Verlag, Lecture Notes in Computer Science Vol. 1461.

Cohen, E., Krishnamurthy, B., and Rexford, J. (1998b). Improving end-to-end performance of the Web using server volumes and proxy filters. In *Proceedings of the ACM SIGCOMM'98 Conference*.

Cohen, E., Krishnamurthy, B., and Rexford, J. (1999). Efficient algorithms for predicting requests to web servers. In *Proceedings of IEEE Infocom '99 Conference*.

Dingle, A. and Partl, T. (1996). Web cache coherence. In *Proceedings of the Fifth International World Wide Web Conference*, pages 907–920. Computer Networks and ISDN Systems 28:7-11.

Duvvuri, V., Shenoy, P., and Tewari, R. (2000). Adaptive leases: a strong consistency mechanism for the World Wide Web. In *Proceedings of the 19th IEEE INFOCOM Conference*. http://www.ieee-infocom.org/2000/papers/.

Feldmann, A., Cáceres, R., Douglis, F., Glass, G., and Rabinovich, M. (1999). Performance of Web proxy caching in heterogeneous bandwidth environments. In *Proceedings of the IEEE INFOCOM'99 Conference*.

Fielding, R., Gettys, J., Mogul, J., Nielsen, H., Masinter, L., Leach, P., and Berners-Lee, T. (1999). RFC 2616: Hypertext Transfer Protocol — HTTP/1.1.

Gray, C. and Cheriton, D. (1989). Leases: an efficient fault tolerant mecahnism for distributed file cache consistency. In *Proceedings of the 12th ACM symposium on operating systems principles*, pages 202–210.

Hou, Y., Pan, J., Li, B., Tang, X., and Panwar, S. (2002). Modeling and analysis of an expiration-based hierarchical caching system. In *Proceedings of IEEE Globecom Internet Performance Symposium*. IEEE.

Hou, Y., Pan, J., Wang, C., and Li, B. (2003). On prefetching in hierarchical caching systems. In *Proceedings of IEEE ICC Global Services and Infrastructure for Next Generation Networking Symposium*. IEEE.

Howard, J., Kazar, M., Menees, S., Nichols, D., Satyanarayanan, M., Sidebotham, R., and West, M. (1988). Scale and performance in a distributed file system. *ACM Transactions on Computer Systems*, 6(1):51–81.

Inktomi (2001). Inktomi Traffic Server. http://www.inktomi.com.

InktomiCDS (2001). Inktomi Content Delivery Suite. http://www.inktomi.com.

IPWorX (2001). Lucent IPWorX. http://www.lucentipworx.com.

IRCache (2001). A Distributed Testbed for National Information Provisioning. http://www.ircache.net.

Jung, J., Berger, A., and Balakrishnan, H. (2003). Modeling TTL-based internet caches. In *Proceedings of the IEEE Infocom*.

Jung, J., Sit, E., Balakrishnan, H., and Morris, R. (2001). DNS performance and the effectiveness of caching. In *Proc. ACM SIGCOMM Internet Measurement Workshop*.

Krishnamurthy, Balachander and Wills, Craig E. (1997). Study of piggyback cache validation for proxy caches in the world wide web. In *Proceedings of the USENIX Symposium on Internet Technologies and Systems*, Monterey, California.

Leland, W. E., Taqq, M. S., Willinger, W., and Wilson, D. V. (1993). On the self-similar nature of Ethernet traffic. In *Proc. of ACM SIGCOMM '93*, pages 183–193.

Li, D. and Cheriton, D. R. (1999). Scalable web caching of frequently updated objects using reliable multicast. In *Proceedings of the USENIX Symposium on Internet Technologies and Systems*, pages 1–12.

Mockapetris, P. (1987a). Domain names – concepts and facilities. RFC 1034, ISI. http://www.dns.net/dnsrd/rfc/rfc1034/rfc1034.html.

Mockapetris, P. (1987b). Domain names – implementation and specification. RFC 1035, ISI. `http://www.dns.net/dnsrd/rfc/rfc1035/rfc1035.html`.

Mogul, J. C. (1999). Errors in timestamp-based HTTP header values. Technical Report 99/3, Compaq Western Research Lab. `http://www.research.digital.com/wrl/techreports/abstracts/99.3.html`.

Nottingham, M. (1999). Optimizing object freshness controls in Web caches. In *The 4th International Web Caching Workshop*. `http://www.ircache.nlanr.net/Cache/workshop99/Papers`.

Paxson, V. and Floyd, S. (1995). Wide area traffic: the failure of Poisson modeling. *IEEE/ACM Transactions on Networking*, 3(3):226–244.

Squid (2001). Squid internet object cache. `http://squid.nlanr.net/Squid`.

Williams, Stephen, Abrams, Marc, Standbridge, Charles R., Abdulla, Ghaleb, and Fox, Edward A. (1996). Removal policies in network caches for worldwide web documents. In *Proceedings of the ACM SIGCOMM Conference*, pages 293–305.

Yin, J., Alvisi, L., Dahlin, M., and Lin, C. (1999). Volume leases for consistency in large-scale systems. *IEEE transactions on knowledge and data engineering*.

Young, N. (1998). On line file caching. In *Proc. 9th ACM-SIAM Symposium on Discrete Algorithms*. ACM-SIAM.

Chapter 4

CONTENT LOCATION IN PEER-TO-PEER SYSTEMS: EXPLOITING LOCALITY

Kunwadee Sripanidkulchai and Hui Zhang
Carnegie Mellon University

Abstract   Efficient content location is a fundamental problem for decentralized peer-to-peer systems. Gnutella, a popular file-sharing application, relies on flooding queries to all peers. Although flooding is simple and robust, it is not scalable. In this chapter, we explore how to retain the simplicity of Gnutella while addressing its inherent weakness: scalability. We propose two complementary content location solutions that exploit locality to improve scalability. First, we look at *temporal locality* and find that the popularity of search strings follows a Zipf-like distribution. Caching query results to exploit temporal locality can significantly decrease the amount of traffic seen on the network by 3-times while using only a few megabytes of memory. As our second solution, we exploit a simple, yet powerful principle called *interest-based locality*, which posits that if a peer has a particular piece of content that one is interested in, it is very likely that it will have other items that one is interested in as well. We propose that peers loosely organize themselves into an interest-based structure on top of the existing Gnutella network. When using our algorithm, called *interest-based shortcuts*, a significant amount of flooding can be avoided, reducing the total load in the system by a factor of 3 to 7 and reducing the time to locate content to only one peer-to-peer hop. We demonstrate the existence of both types of locality and evaluate our solutions using traces of several different content distribution systems such as the Web and popular peer-to-peer file-sharing applications.

Keywords: Peer-to-peer, file-sharing, locality, search, content location

1.   Introduction

The invention of the World Wide Web over a decade ago revolutionized the process of publishing and disseminating information. Distributing bytes of information is much simpler than printing and transporting physical material. The Web is built on top of a client-server architecture. Content publishers provide the Web servers, network bandwidth, and content. The Internet carries the bytes of information from the server to the clients. While the success of the Web has been astronomical, with over 50 million Web sites reported in July 2004 [Netcraft, 2004], the publishing process often requires manual configuration and special domain knowledge. As a result, most of the Web sites on the Internet are built, operated, and maintained by professional content publishers. Individual end-users have not typically undertaken the role of publishing content.

In contrast, the recent birth of peer-to-peer file-sharing applications have enabled instant publishing for the masses. End-users only need to run the application and tell it which files are to be published. The application transparently makes the files available for other people to search and download. While peers are downloading content, they can also create and make available replicas to increase content availability. As the system grows, the supply of resources scales with demand. There are enough resources, even during flash crowds when many people access the same content simultaneously.

There are many challenges for peer-to-peer content distribution systems. In this chapter, we study one fundamental challenge: what is the appropriate strategy for locating content given that content may be replicated at many locations in the peer-to-peer system? If content cannot be located efficiently, there is little hope for using peer-to-peer systems.

There are two classes of solutions currently proposed for decentralized peer-to-peer content location. Unstructured content location, used by Gnutella, relies on flooding queries to all peers. Peers organize into an overlay. To find content, a peer sends a query to its neighbors on the overlay. In turn, the neighbors forward the query on to all of their neighbors until the query has traveled a certain radius. While this solution is simple and robust even when peers join and leave the system, it does not scale. Another class of protocols based on the Distributed Hash Table (DHT) abstraction [Ratnasamy et al., 2001, Rowstron and Druschel, 2001, Stoica et al., 2001, Zhao et al., 2000] and motivated by Plaxton et al. [Plaxton et al., 1997] have been proposed to address scalability. In these protocols, peers organize into a well-defined structure that is used for routing queries. Although DHTs are elegant and scalable, their performance under the dynamic conditions common for peer-to-peer systems is unknown [Ratnasamy et al., 2002].

Our design philosophy is to retain the simple, robust, and fully decentralized nature of Gnutella, while improving scalability, its major weakness. The key insight is to exploit locality in the query workload to the extent possible. We examine two types of locality: temporal locality and interest-based locality.

Query workloads exhibit *temporal locality* if queries that are issued recently by some peers are likely to be issued again by other peers. Peers may cache query results to improve the performance of content location. When a peer sees an incoming query for which it has a cached result, it can reply immediately without needing to forward that query to other peers. Caching query results can reduce the amount of query traffic in the system.

In addition, we identify a powerful principle: if a peer has a particular piece of content that one is interested in, then it is likely that it will have other pieces of content that one is also interested in. These peers exhibit *interest-based locality*. We propose a self-organizing protocol, *interest-based shortcuts*, that efficiently exploits interest-based locality for content location. Peers that share similar interests create shortcuts to one another and use shortcuts to locate content. When shortcuts fail, peers resort to using the underlying Gnutella overlay. Shortcuts provide a *loose* structure on top of Gnutella's unstructured overlay. Although we use Gnutella as the primary example in this chapter, shortcuts are also compatible with many other content location mechanisms, such as DHTs and supernode architectures such as Kazaa [Kazaa, 2005].

In Sections 2 and 3, we look at temporal locality and evaluate caching algorithms that exploit temporal locality. Next, we look at interest-based locality. We describe the design of interest-based shortcuts in Section 4. In Sections 5, 6, and 7, we present our metrics, simulation methodology, evaluation results, and the potential and limitations of shortcuts. We conclude with a discussion of the implications of our results in Section 8, and related work in Section 9.

2. Temporal Locality

In this section, we analyze the characteristics of Gnutella queries and its implications on scaling. We find that there is significant temporal locality in the query workload caused by the Zipf-like popularity of query strings. Taking advantage of temporal locality by caching a small number of query results can significantly decrease the amount of traffic seen on the network.

2.1 Trace Collection

To collect traces used in this study, we modified an open source Gnutella client (gtk-gnutella) [GTK-Gnutella, 2005] to passively monitor and log all queries and results that are routed through it. We run the modified client on monitoring hosts at Carnegie Mellon University (CMU). The details of our traces are listed in Table 4.1.

We also recorded packet traces of the activity from Gnutella on our local network during the measurement to obtain bandwidth usage information. On average, Gnutella was consuming a few Mbps for query and reply traffic. This amount of bandwidth exceeds the access bandwidth of many users, especially those with home broadband connections, making it difficult to participate in the system.

Table 4.1.   Statistics of the Gnutella traces. A – denotes that the particular statistic was not collected for that trace.

Traces	Duration	Number of queries	Number of results	Unique IP addresses	α
December 10-13, 2000	4 days	5,975,167	–	83,709	1.24
January 18, 2001	5 hours	570,361	5,282,668	–	1.13
January 19, 2001	3 hours	362,999	3,857,505	7,032	1.06
January 28, 2001	2.5 hours	352,396	2,083,615	7,288	0.78
January 29, 2001	5 hours	1,146,782	8,037,609	12,805	0.63

2.2   Popularity of Queries

In this section, we look at the characteristics of queries on Gnutella. About 17% of the queries contain non-ASCII strings perhaps caused by non-English queries and faulty clients. We removed such queries from the analysis. The most popular queries are for file extensions, artists and adult content. The top 20 queries for all traces are categorized and shown in Figure 4.1(a). In the December trace, the most popular queries were for file extensions. In the later traces, a larger portion of the queries were for artists and adult content.

Next, we look at the popularity of query strings. Note that temporal locality is directly related to popularity. A query stream has temporal locality if at the time a query for "foo" is observed, there is a high probability that another query for "foo" will arrive shortly. Very popular query strings will be issued more frequently, leading to temporal locality. The number of times a query is observed versus the ranking of the query for the December trace is shown in Figure 4.1(b) in log-log scale. Rank 1 is the most popular query. If each curve were to be a straight line, then the popularity of queries follows a Zipf-like distribution with the probability of seeing a query for the $i'th$ most popular query is proportional to $1/(i^{\alpha})$. The popularity follows a bimodal Zipf-like

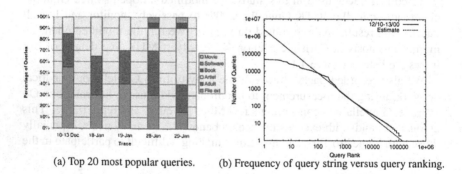

(a) Top 20 most popular queries.   (b) Frequency of query string versus query ranking.

Figure 4.1.   Popularity of query strings.

distribution with an inflection point at around query rank 100. The first portion of the curve for queries rank 1 to 100 is flatter. This implies that the most popular queries are roughly equally popular. The second portion of the curve, after query rank 100, fits a straight line reasonably well. We estimate the value of α, for the second portion of the curve. The values of α for all traces are between 0.63 and 1.24, and are listed in Table 4.1. We refer the reader to [Sripanidkulchai, 2001] for the popularity distribution curves for the other traces.

3. Exploiting Temporal Locality

In this section, we outline a protocol to implement caching of queries and results to exploit temporal locality for the popular queries.

3.1 Caching Query Results

A query initiated by the peer at the bottom is flooded to all peers in the system. Each query is tagged with a maximum Time-To-Live (TTL) to bound the number of hops it can travel. In addition, Gnutella employs a duplicate query detection mechanism so that peers do not forward queries that they have already previously forwarded. Despite such mechanisms, some amount of duplication is inherent to flooding algorithms and cannot be avoided. Peers reply to a query when the query string matches partially, or exactly, to files stored on their hard disks.

To implement caching, Gnutella nodes monitor and cache query strings and results that are routed through it. Cached results are valid only up to a timeout period, after which it is removed from cache. If a query result is cached at a node, the node directly answers the query and does not forward the query on as illustrated with the node on the bottom left of Figure 4.2(b). In the best case, a node may answer its own queries without needing to send any queries out on the network. If the cached result for a query is expired, the Gnutella node does not answer the query and forwards the query to its neighbors.

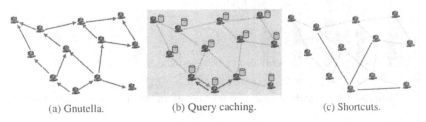

    (a) Gnutella.   (b) Query caching.   (c) Shortcuts.

Figure 4.2. Content location paths.

3.2   Caching Performance

Caching query results helps to reduce the time it takes for queries to be answered and also reduces the amount of traffic on the network. In this section, we evaluate the effectiveness of caching query results on both metrics using three caching policies based on timeouts: queries and results are cached for 1, 5, and 10 minutes.

In our simulations, query strings are directly associated with query results. For example, if a query for "foo.mpg" is received, we cache the query string "foo.mpg" and the associated replies. When a subsequent query for "foo.mpg" is received before timeout, it is a cache hit. Any subsequent queries for "foo", or "mpg" are considered misses even if received before the timeout. This gives a worst-case bound on the benefits of caching. A real implementation should allow for partial string matchings. We also assumed that it takes t_{max} after a query is received for a query result to be cached, where t_{max} is the maximum time it takes to receive a query result from any node. This gives a worst-case estimate on when a query result can be answered from cache. Our evaluation is for one Gnutella node, our monitoring node, implementing caching. As more nodes cache results, less traffic is seen overall, and most queries are answered within very few hops.

Figure 4.3(a) depicts the cache hit rate for each trace, where hit rates are defined as the number of queries that were answered from cache over the total number of queries. When results are cached for longer periods, it is more likely that a larger number of queries can be answered from cache, and the amount of query and reply traffic on the network is reduced. The hit rate ranges from 3% up to 73%, where the highest hit rate was observed when using a 10 minute caching interval with the December trace. Traffic is reduced by 3.7-times when the hit rate is 73%. The hit rate for the January 18 trace using a 1 minute caching interval was the lowest. This is because t_{max} for this trace is close to 1 minute.

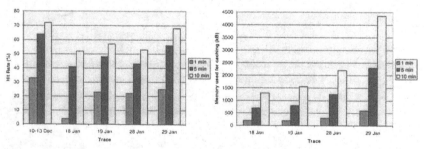

(a)Hit rates for each caching policy.   (b) Average amount of memory used for caching.

Figure 4.3.   Caching performance.

Although our findings suggest that having larger caching intervals results in a more significant reduction in traffic, there is a tradeoff. Cached results could become stale under dynamic conditions where peers can join and leave the network at any time and content on peers can change at any time. The longer a result is cached, the more stale it becomes. Finding a balance between high hit rates and staleness is key to achieving good performance.

Implementing caching requires additional memory at each node. Figure 4.3(b) depicts the average amount of memory used for caching. The longer the caching interval is, the more memory is needed. The amount of memory used ranges from 195 kB to 4.3 MB–which is acceptable for modern computers. However, if memory is scarce, a caching policy such as LRU may be used.

We have shown that the popularity of Gnutella queries has a bimodal Zipf-like distribution. Zipf-like distributions are common in content distribution workloads. For example, the frequency by which a Web document is accessed follows a Zipf-like distribution [Almeida et al., 1996, Breslau et al., 1999, Cunha et al., 1995, Kroeger et al., 1996]. Caching Gnutella query results, similar to caching web documents, is effective for locating popular content. In the next section, we look at a second type of locality called interest-based locality that has the potential to find both popular and unpopular content.

4. Interest-based Locality

In this section, we present a technique called interest-based shortcuts. We will show in Section 6 that this technique, while based on simple principles, can significantly improve the performance of Gnutella.

Figure 4.4 gives an example to illustrate interest-based locality. The peer in the middle is looking for files A, B, and C. The two peers in the right who have file A also each have at least one more matching file B or C. The peer on the upper right-hand corner has all three files. Therefore, it and the peer in the middle share the most interests, where interests represent a group of files, namely $\{A, B, C\}$. Our goal is to identify such peers, and use them for downloading files directly.

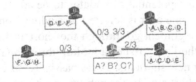

Figure 4.4. Peers that share interests.

4.1   Shortcuts Architecture and Design Goals

We propose a technique called shortcuts to create additional links on top of a peer-to-peer system's overlay, taking advantage of locality to improve performance. Shortcuts are implemented as a separate performance enhancement layer on top of existing content location mechanisms, such as flooding in Gnutella. The benefits of such an implementation are two-fold. First, shortcuts are modular in that they can work with any underlying content location scheme. Second, shortcuts only serve as performance-enhancement hints. If a document cannot be located via shortcuts, it can always be located via the underlying overlay. Therefore, having a shortcut layer does not affect the correctness of the underlying overlay. In general, shortcuts are a powerful primitive that can be used to improve overlay performance. For example, shortcuts based on network latency can reduce hop-by-hop delays in overlay networks. In this chapter, we explore the use of a specific kind of shortcut based on interests.

Figure 4.2(a) illustrates how content is located in Gnutella. A query initiated by the peer at the bottom is flooded to all peers in the system. Figure 4.2(c) depicts a Gnutella overlay with 3 shortcut links for the bottom-most peer. To avoid flooding, content is located first through shortcuts. A query is flooded to the entire system only when none of the shortcuts have the content.

Our design goals for interest-based shortcuts are simplicity and scalability. Peers should be able to detect locality in a fully-distributed manner, relying only on locally learned information. Algorithms should be lightweight. In addition, the dynamic nature of peer-to-peer environments requires that the algorithm be adaptive and self-improving. We incorporate the above considerations into our design, which has two components: shortcut discovery and shortcut selection.

4.2   Shortcut Discovery

We use the following heuristic to detect shared interests: peers that have content that we are looking for share similar interests. Shortcut discovery is piggy-backed on Gnutella. When a peer joins the system, it may not have any information about other peers' interests. Its first attempt to locate content is executed through flooding. The lookup returns a set of peers that store the content. These peers are potential candidates to be added to a "shortcut list." In our implementation, one peer is selected at random from the set and added. Subsequent queries for content go through the shortcut list. If a peer cannot find content through the list, it issues a lookup through Gnutella, and repeats the process for adding new shortcuts. Peers passively observe their own traffic to discover their own shortcuts. For scalability, each peer allocates a fixed-size amount of storage to implement shortcuts. Shortcuts are added and removed from the list based on their perceived utility, which is computed using the ranking algorithm described in Section 4.3. Shortcuts that have low utility are removed from the list when the list is full.

There are several design alternatives for shortcut discovery. New shortcuts may be discovered through exchanging shortcut lists between peers, or through establishing more sophisticated link structures for each content category similar to structures used by search engines. In addition, multiple shortcuts, as opposed to just one, may be added to the list at the same time. In Section 6, we study a basic approach in which one shortcut is added at a time, based on results returned from Gnutella's flooding. In Section 7, we explore the potential of two optimizations: adding k shortcuts at a time and learning about new shortcuts through one's current shortcuts.

4.3 Shortcut Selection

Given that there may be many shortcuts on the list, which one should be used? In our design, we rank shortcuts based on their perceived utility. If shortcuts are useful, they are ranked at the top of the list. A peer locates content by sequentially asking all of the shortcuts on its list, starting from the top, until content is found. Rankings can be based on many metrics, such as probability of providing content, latency of the path to the shortcut, available bandwidth of the path, amount of content at the shortcut, and load at the shortcut. A combination of metrics can be used based on each peer's preference.

Each peer keeps track of each shortcut's performance and updates its ranking when new information is learned. This allows for peers to adapt to dynamic changes and incrementally refine shortcut selection. In Section 6, we explore the use of probability of providing content (success rate) as a ranking metric. In this context, success rate is defined as the ratio between the number of times a shortcut was used to successfully locate content to the total number of times it was tried. The higher the ratio, the better the rank on the list.

5. Evaluation of Shortcuts

In this section, we discuss the design of experiments to expose interest-based locality and evaluate the effectiveness of our proposed shortcuts scheme.

5.1 Performance Indices

The metrics we use to express the benefits and overhead of shortcuts are:

Success rate: How often are queries resolved through shortcuts? High success rates indicate the potential of interest-based shortcuts to improve performance.

Load characteristics: How many query packets do peers process while participating in the system? Less load at individual peers is desirable for scalability.

Query scope: For each query, what fraction of peers in the system are involved in query processing? A smaller query scope increases system scalability.

Additional state: How much additional state do peers need to maintain in order to implement shortcuts? The amount of state measures the cost of shortcuts and should be kept to a minimum.

5.2   Methodology

We use trace-based simulations for our performance evaluation. First, we discuss our query workloads. Next, we describe how we construct the underlying Gnutella overlay that is used for flooding queries, and map peers from the query workload onto nodes in the Gnutella overlay. We then discuss our storage and replication models, and our simulation experiments.

Query workloads.   We use five diverse traces of download requests from real content distribution applications to generate query workloads. Our first three traces (labeled Boeing, Microsoft and CMU-Web in Table 4.2) capture Web request workloads, which we envision to be similar to requests in Web content file-sharing applications [Iyer et al., 2002, Padmanabhan and Sripanidkulchai, 2002, Bayardo et al., 2002, BitTorrent, 2005]. Our last two traces (labeled CMU-Kazaa and CMU-Gnutella in Table 4.2) capture requests from two popular file-sharing applications, Kazaa and Gnutella.

The Boeing trace [Meadows, 1999] is composed of one-day traces from five of Boeing's firewall proxies from March 1, 1999. The Microsoft trace is composed of one-day traces from Microsoft's corporate firewall proxies from October 22, 2001. The CMU-Web, CMU-Kazaa and CMU-Gnutella traces are collected by passively monitoring the traffic between Carnegie Mellon University and the Internet over a 24-hour period on October 22, 2002. Our monitoring host is connected to monitoring ports of the two campus border routers. Our monitoring software, based on tcpdump [Jacobson et al., 2005], installs a kernel filter to match packets containing an HTTP request or response header, regardless of port numbers. Although an HTTP header may be split across multiple packets, we find that it happens rarely (0.03% of packets). The packet filter was able to keep up with the traffic, dropping less than 0.026% of packets. We extend tcpdump to parse the packets online to extract source and destination IP addresses and ports, request URL, response code, content type, and cachability tags. We anonymize IP addresses and URLs, and log all extracted information to a log file on disk. Our trace consists of all Web transactions (primarily port 80), Kazaa downloads (port 1214), and Gnutella downloads (primarily port 6346) between CMU and the rest of the Internet.

Given the download requests in our traces, we generate query workloads in the following way: if peer P_1 downloads file A (or URL A) at time t_0, peer

Table 4.2. Trace characteristics.

Trace	Characteristics	1	2	3	4
Boeing	Requests	95,504	95,429	166,741	201,862
	Documents	42,800	44,153	75,833	79,306
	Clients	868	1,052	1,443	2,278
Microsoft	Requests	764,177	917,325	960,119	1,588,045
	Documents	102,548	164,505	198,559	285,711
	Clients	11,636	11,929	13,013	15,387
CMU-	Requests	125,138	104,781	132,405	155,847
Web	Documents	61,569	43,616	61,981	72,513
	Clients	6,322	6,426	7,054	7,602
CMU-	Distinct Requests	7,757	7,779	8,086	9,075
Kazaa	Documents	3,720	3,625	3,806	4,338
	Download Peers	6,482	6,514	6,732	7,468
	All Peers	6,985	6,968	7,217	8,064
CMU-	Distinct Requests	392	389	395	415
Gnutella	Documents	260	247	239	254
	Download Peers	256	270	271	296
	All Peers	464	383	373	405
Trace	Characteristics	5	6	7	8
Boeing	Requests	1,176,153	1,541,062	1,617,608	2,039,347
	Documents	305,092	391,229	434,766	513,264
	Clients	18,059	21,690	22,344	25,293
Microsoft	Requests	2,083,911	3,818,368	4,515,815	6,671,774
	Documents	416,784	662,986	718,444	956,617
	Clients	19,419	23,492	28,741	32,361
CMU-	Requests	338,656	358,778	432,843	495,119
Web	Documents	162,951	153,405	190,372	211,570
	Clients	11,176	12,274	13,892	15,408
CMU-	Distinct Requests	9,243	13,307	13,760	15,188
Kazaa	Documents	4,771	6,619	7,172	6,312
	Download Peers	7,601	10,977	11,362	12,558
	All Peers	8,542	11,983	12,660	13,590
CMU-	Distinct Requests	480	502	581	884
Gnutella	Documents	318	339	393	609
	Download Peers	320	341	383	542
	All Peers	543	477	590	735

P_1 issues a query for file A at time t_0. We model the query string as the full URL, A, and perform exact matching of the query string to filenames. We assume that P_1's intention is to search for file A, and all hosts with file A will respond to the query. Not modeling partial matches does not affect our results for the Web or CMU-Kazaa query workloads as a URL typically corresponds to a distinct piece of content. However, URLs in the CMU-Gnutella workload are based on filenames, which may not correspond to distinct pieces of content. For example, a file for my favorite song by my favorite artist could be named "my favorite song" or "my favorite song, my favorite artist." In our simulations, these two files would be considered different, although they are semantically the same. We use exact matches because it is difficult to partially match over anonymized names. As a result, it is likely that we underreport the number of peers who have a particular file, and overestimate the number of distinct files in the system.

We randomly selected eight one-hour segments from each query workload to use for our simulations. We limit our experiments to one hour, the median session duration reported for peer-to-peer systems [Saroiu et al., 2002]. The characteristics of all trace segments are listed in Table 4.2, sorted by number of clients.

Gnutella connectivity graphs.   Next, we discuss how we construct the underlying Gnutella overlay used for flooding queries, and how we map peers in the query workload described in the previous section to nodes in the Gnutella overlay.

To simulate the performance of Gnutella flooding, we use Gnutella connectivity graphs collected in early 2001 [Ripeanu et al., 2002]. All graphs have a bimodal power-law degree distribution with an average degree of 3.4. The characteristic diameter is small at 12 hops. In addition, over 95% of the nodes are at most 7 hops away from one another. The number of nodes in each graph vary from 8,000 to 40,000. For simulations, we selected Gnutella graphs that had the closest number of peers to the ones in each one-hour trace segment. Then, nodes were randomly removed from the graph until the number of nodes matched. The resulting graphs and the original graphs had similar degree distribution and pair-wise path length characteristics. Peers from each one-hour segment were randomly mapped to nodes in the Gnutella graphs. We used a maximum query TTL of 7, which is the application default for many Gnutella clients. Although it is possible that some content cannot be found because of the TTL limit, this was a problem for less than 1% of the queries.

Storage and replication model for Web query workloads.   Next, we describe how content is placed and stored in the system. For each trace segment, we assume that all Web clients participate in a Web content file-sharing system. To preserve locality, we place the first copy of content at the peer who makes the first request for it (i.e., this is a publish to the system, and a query lookup is not performed). Subsequent copies of content are placed based on accesses. That is, if peer P_1 downloaded file A at time t_0, P_1 creates a replica of file A and make it available for others to download after time t_0. Peers store all the content that they retrieve during that trace segment, and make that content available for other peers to download. Any request for content that a peer has previously downloaded (i.e., a repeated request) is satisfied locally from the peer's cache.

Only requests for static content in the Microsoft trace and the CMU-Web trace are used in our evaluation. Specifically, we removed requests for content that contained "cgi," ".asp," ".pl," "?," and query strings in the URL. In addition, for the CMU-Web trace we removed all requests for uncachable content as specified by the HTTP response headers, following the HTTP 1.1 protocol. The Microsoft trace did not have HTTP response header information. The Boeing trace did not contain sufficient information to distinguish between static and dynamic content. Therefore, all Boeing requests were used in our analysis.

Storage and replication model for CMU-Kazaa and CMU-Gnutella query workloads. We draw a distinction between two types of peers in the traces: peers that only serve files and peers that download files. Peers that only serve files do not issue requests for content in the trace, but provide a set of files for which other peers may download. It is likely that these are hosts outside of CMU who are providing files to hosts at CMU, or hosts at CMU that are not actively downloading any files. We assume that any peer that downloads files must make those files available for other peers. Table 4.2 lists the number of clients (peers that download files) and the total number of peers (both types) in each trace segment. Both types of peers are participants in the peer-to-peer system, but only peers who download content issue queries in the simulation.

Before running the simulation, we make one pass through each trace segment and build up a list of content available at each peer. Specifically, if a peer P_1 served a file A at some time t_0 in the trace segment, we assume that P_1 makes that file available for any other peer to download any time during that trace segment, even before t_0. This simulates a peer that has the file on disk before the beginning of the trace segment. However, if P_1 originally obtained file A by a download earlier in the trace, we make sure that A is available for other peers to download only after P_1 has downloaded it. We have only partial knowledge about content available at each peer because we are limited by the information present in the trace. For example, let's assume that peer P_1 has a copy of file B on disk. However, P_1 did not download the file during the trace segment. In addition, no other peer downloaded the file from him, either. Therefore, we have no information in the trace that P_1 has file B. When P_2 sends a query looking for file B in our simulations, P_1 would not reply although in reality P_1 has the file. As a result, we underestimate the number of peers who could potentially supply a file, and report pessimistic results for the CMU-Kazaa and CMU-Gnutella workloads.

Queries are performed only for distinct requests. For example, a Kazaa peer usually downloads multiple fragments of a file from multiple peers in parallel and may issue multiple HTTP requests for that one file. In our simulations, that peer issues only one query to find that file.

We assume that all peers in the trace segment participate in the file-sharing session, including peers outside of CMU downloading files from peers at CMU. We also ran a set of experiments where we looked only at peers at CMU downloading content and found that the results were similar to using all peers in the trace. We present results when using all peers in the trace in the following sections.

Simulation experiments.   We compare the performance of Gnutella, and Gnutella with shortcuts for each query workload. For each portion of the trace, we assume that peers that send any queries join the system at the beginning of the segment and stay until the end. Unless otherwise stated, peers maintain a fixed-size list of 10 shortcuts. Shortcuts are ranked based on success rates.

6.   Performance of Interest-Based Shortcuts

In this section, we present evaluation results comparing the performance of Gnutella against Gnutella with shortcuts.

6.1   Success Rate

Success rate is defined as the number of lookups that were successfully resolved through interest-based shortcuts over the total number of lookups. If the success rate is high, then shortcuts are useful for locating content. Note that peers who have just joined the system do not have any shortcuts on their lists, and have no choice but to flood to locate the first piece of content. We start counting the success rate after the first flood (i.e., when peers have one shortcut on their list).

Figure 4.5(a) depicts the average success rate for shortcuts for each query workload. The vertical axis is the success rate, and the horizontal axis is the time after the start of the simulation when the observation was made. The average success rate at the end of 1 hour is as high as 82%-90% for the Web workloads, and 53%-58% for the CMU-Gnutella and CMU-Kazaa workloads. For comparison, we also conducted experiments to select random peers from *all participating peers* to add as shortcuts (not depicted). Note that this is different from interest-based shortcuts where shortcuts are added based on replies from flooding through Gnutella. We find that the success rate for random shortcuts varied from 2-9% across all trace segments. The individual success rate (not depicted) observed at each peer increases with longer simulation times as peers learn more about other peers and have more time to refine their shortcut list. Although success rates for all workloads are reasonably high, success rates for Web workloads are distinctly higher than those for the CMU-Kazaa or CMU-

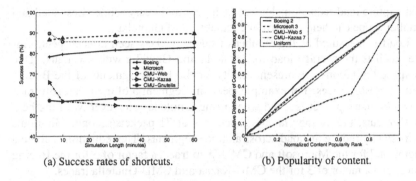

(a) Success rates of shortcuts. (b) Popularity of content.

Figure 4.5. The performance of interest-based shortcuts.

Gnutella workloads. We believe that this is because we only have a partial view of the content available at each peer for the CMU-Kazaa/Gnutella workloads and are likely to see conservative results, as discussed in the previous section.

Next, we ask what kind of content is located through shortcuts? Are shortcuts useful for finding only popular content? Figure 4.5(b) depicts the cumulative probability of finding content with the specified popularity ranking through shortcuts. We present results from one representative trace segment from each query workload. The x-axis is content rank normalized by the total number of documents in the trace segment. The normalized rank values range from 0 (most popular) to 1 (least popular). Each document is classified as found or not found. That is, if content with rank 0 was found at least once through shortcuts, it is labeled as found. Only content that is found is depicted in the figure. A reference line for the uniform distribution, when all documents have equal probability of being found, is also given. We find that the distributions for the Microsoft and CMU-Web traces closely match the uniform distribution, indicating that shortcuts are uniformly effective at finding popular and unpopular content. The distribution for the Boeing trace is also close to a uniform distribution, but has a slight tendency towards finding more popular content. On the other hand, shortcuts tend to find more unpopular content in the CMU-Kazaa trace. The distribution on the right of the sharp inflection point represents finding extremely unpopular content that is shared by only two people. We do not present the results for CMU-Gnutella because there were not enough file accesses to determine document popularity. The most popular file was accessed by a handful of people.

6.2   Load and Scope

We achieve load reduction by using shortcuts *before* flooding so that only a small number of peers are exposed to any one query. We look at two metrics that capture load reduction: load at each peer and query scope. Less load and smaller scope can help improve the scalability of Gnutella.

Load is measured as the number of query packets seen at each peer. Table 4.3 lists the average load for Gnutella and Gnutella with shortcuts. Due to space limitations, we present results for the last 4 segments of the Boeing and Microsoft traces. For example, peers in Segment 5 of the Microsoft trace saw 479 query packets/second when using Gnutella. However, with the help of shortcuts, the average load is much less at 71 packets/second. Shortcuts consistently reduce the load across all trace segments. The reduction is about a factor of 7 for the Microsoft and CMU-Web trace, a factor of 5 for the Boeing trace, and a factor of 3 for the CMU-Kazaa and CMU-Gnutella traces.

We also look at the peak-to-mean load ratio in order to identify hot spots in the system. The peak-to-mean ratio for flooding through Gnutella ranges from 5 to 12 across all traces, meaning that at some time during the experiment, the most loaded peer in the system saw 5 to 12 times more query packets than the average peer. For most trace segments, the peak-to-mean ratio for shortcuts is similar to Gnutella's, indicating that shortcuts do not drastically change the distribution of load in the system. However, for 3 segments in the Microsoft trace, the peak-to-mean ratio for shortcuts almost doubled compared to Gnutella. This is because shortcuts bias more load towards peers that have made a large number of requests. These peers have more content and are more likely to be selected as shortcuts compared to average peers. As a result, they tend to see more queries. We found that there were a number of peers that had significantly larger volumes of content in these 3 trace segments. Shortcuts have an interesting property that redistributes more load to peers that use the system more frequently. This seems to be fair as one would expect peers that make heavy use of the system to contribute more resources.

Scope for a query is defined as the fraction of peers in the system that see that particular query. Flooding has a scope of approximately 100% because all peers (except those beyond the TTL limit) see the query. Shortcuts, when successful, have a much smaller scope. Usually, only one shortcut will see a query, resulting in a query scope of less than 0.3%. When shortcuts are unsuccessful, then the scope is 100%, the same as flooding. The average scope when using shortcuts

Table 4.3. Load (queries/sec) and scope.

Trace	Protocol	5	6	7	8
Boeing	Gnutella Flooding Load	355	463	494	671
	Gnut. w/ Shortcuts Load	66	87	99	132
	Gnut. w/ Shortcuts Scope	19%	19%	20%	20%
Microsoft	Gnutella Flooding Load	479	832	1,164	1,650
	Gnut. w/ Shortcuts Load	71	116	162	230
	Gnut. w/ Shortcuts Scope	16%	15%	14%	14%

for the last four segments of the Boeing and Microsoft traces listed in Table 4.3 vary between 14%-20%. Shortcuts are often successful at locating content and only a small number of peers are bothered for most queries.

6.3   Path Length

Path length is the number of overlay hops a request traverses until the first copy of content is found. For example, if a peer finds content after asking 2 shortcuts, (i.e., the first shortcut was unsuccessful), the path length for the lookup is 2 hops. Note that a peer locates content by sequentially asking shortcuts on its list. For Gnutella, path length is the minimum number of hops a query travels before it reaches a peer that has the content. Peers can directly observe an improvement in performance if content can be found in fewer hops. Table 4.4 lists the average path length in number of overlay hops for all workloads. On average, content is 4 hops away on Gnutella. Shortcuts, when successful, reduce the path length by more than half to less than 1.6 hops. To further reduce the path length, all the shortcuts on the list could be asked in parallel as opposed to sequentially.

Table 4.4.   Shortest path to content.

Trace	Gnutella	Gnutella w/ Shortcuts
Boeing	4.0	1.3
Microsoft	4.0	1.6
CMU-Web	3.9	1.2
CMU-Kazaa	3.8	1.1
CMU-Gnutella	3.5	1.3

6.4   Additional State

Next, we look at the amount of additional state required to implement shortcuts. On average, peers maintain 1-5 shortcuts. Shortcut lists tend to grow larger in traces that have higher volumes of requests. We placed an arbitrary limit on the shortcut list size to at most ten entries. Although we could have allowed the list to grow larger, it does not appear to be a limiting factor on performance.

We also look at opportunities for downloading content in parallel through multiple shortcuts and find that for all trace segments, 25%-50% of requests could have been downloaded in parallel through at least 2 shortcuts.

We summarize the results from our evaluation below:

- Shortcuts are effective at finding both popular and unpopular content. When using shortcuts, 45%-90% of content can be found quickly and efficiently.

- Shortcuts have good load distribution properties. The overall load is reduced, and more load is redistributed towards peers that make heavy use of the system. In addition, shortcuts help to limit the scope of queries.

- Shortcuts are scalable, and incur very little overhead.

Although all five workloads have diverse request volumes and were collected three years apart, they exhibit similar trends in interest-based locality.

7.   Potential and Limitations of Shortcuts

In the previous section, we showed that simple algorithms for identifying and using interest-based shortcuts can provide significant performance gains over Gnutella's flooding mechanism. In this section, we explore the limits of interest-based locality by conducting experiments to provide insight on the following questions:

- What is the best possible performance when peers learn about shortcuts through past queries?

- Are there practical changes to the basic algorithm presented in the previous section that would improve shortcut performance to bring it closer to the best possible?

- Can we improve shortcut performance if we discover shortcuts through our existing shortcuts, in addition to learning from past queries?

In order to explore the best possible performance, we remove the practical limits imposed on the shortcuts algorithm evaluated in the previous section. First, peers add *all* peers returned from Gnutella's flooding as shortcuts. To contrast with the basic algorithm in the previous section, only *one* randomly selected peer was added at a time. Second, we removed the 10-entry limit on the shortcut list size and allowed the list to grow without bound.

Figure 4.6(a) depicts the best possible success rate averaged across all trace segments for all workloads. Also, note that the success rate is pessimistic for the CMU-Kazaa and CMU-Gnutella workloads as discussed previously. The average success rate at the end of 1 hour is as high as 97% and 65% for the Microsoft and CMU-Kazaa workloads. Although the upper-bound is promising, it is impractical for peers in the Boeing and Microsoft workloads because they need to maintain on average 300 shortcuts. Furthermore, the path length to the first copy of content is as long as tens of hops.

Rather than removing all practical constraints, we look at the performance when we relax some constraints to answer the second question posed at the beginning of this section. First, we observe that success rates for the basic shortcuts algorithm depicted in Figure 4.5(a) is only 7-12% less than the best

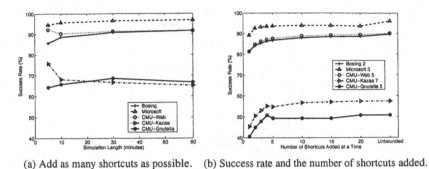

(a) Add as many shortcuts as possible.   (b) Success rate and the number of shortcuts added.

Figure 4.6. The potential of interest-based shortcuts.

possible. The basic algorithm, which is simple and practical, is already per-forming reasonably well. Now, we relax the constraints for adding shortcuts by adding k random shortcuts from the list of peers returned by Gnutella. Specif-ically, we looked at adding 2, 3, 4, 5, 10, 15, and 20 shortcuts at a time. We also changed the limit on the number of shortcuts each peer can maintain to at most 100.

Figure 4.6(b) depicts the success rates observed using this extended shortcuts algorithm. We report results for the segment with the lowest success rate when using the basic algorithm from each workload. The horizontal axis is k, the number of shortcuts added at a time, varying from 1 for the basic algorithm to "unbounded", where "unbounded" refers to adding as many shortcuts as possible for the best possible performance. The vertical axis is the success rate at the end of the 1-hour period. We find that the success rate increases when more shortcuts are added at a time. For instance, for segment 2 of the Boeing trace, when we add 5 shortcuts at a time, the success rate increases to 87% compared to 81% when adding 1 shortcut. Adding 5 shortcuts at a time produces success rates that are close to the best possible. Furthermore, we see diminishing returns when adding more than 5 shortcuts at a time. We find that the load, scope, and path length characteristics when adding 5 shortcuts at a time is comparable to adding 1 shortcut at a time. The key difference is the shortcut list size, which expands to about 15 entries. This is a reasonable trade-off for improving performance.

Next, we answer the third question. An additional improvement to the short-cut algorithm is to locate content through the shortcut structure in the following way: peers first ask their shortcuts for content. If none of their shortcuts have the content, they ask their shortcuts' shortcuts. This can be viewed as sending queries with a TTL of 2 hops along the shortcut structure. In our implementa-tion, peers send queries to each peer in the shortcut structure sequentially until

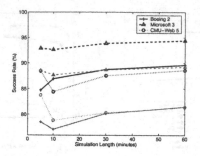

Figure 4.7.   Success rate for asking shortcuts' shortcuts.

content is found. If content is found at a peer who is not currently a shortcut, it gets added to the list as a new shortcut. Peers resort to Gnutella only when content cannot be found through the shortcut structure. We believe this could be an efficient way to learn about new shortcuts without needing to excessively flood through Gnutella.

Figure 4.7 depicts the success rates when using this algorithm for locating content. The vertical axis is success rate and the horizontal axis is the time the observation was made during the simulation. The gray lines, given as reference points, represent the success rates when using the basic algorithm. Again, we limit the shortcut list size to 10 entries. The success rates for discovering new shortcuts through existing shortcuts is higher than the basic algorithm. For segment 2 of the Boeing trace, the success rate increased from 81% to 90% at the end of the hour. And similarly, the success rate increased from 89% to 95%, and 81% to 89% for segment 3 of the Microsoft trace and segment 5 of the CMU-Web trace, respectively. In addition, the load is reduced by half. However, the shortest path length to content increases slightly to 2 hops. The results for the CMU-Kazaa and CMU-Gnutella traces have similar trends.

Our results show that the basic algorithm evaluated in the previous section performs reasonably well. In addition, a few practical refinements to the basic algorithm can yield further performance gains.

8. Conclusion and Discussion

In this chapter, we propose complementary techniques to exploit locality in peer-to-peer query workloads. First, we look at temporal locality and the the popularity of queries on Gnutella. We find that query popularity is Zipf-like and caching query results significantly reduces the amount of traffic seen on Gnutella. However, query caching is only effective for locating popular content.

To locate both popular and unpopular content, we exploit a second type of locality called interest-based locality which is a powerful principle for content distribution applications. We show that interest-based locality is present in Web content sharing and two popular peer-to-peer file-sharing applications. While we propose shortcuts as a technique to exploit interest-based locality, shortcuts are a generic approach to introduce performance enhancements to overlay construction algorithms and may optimize for other types of locality such as latency or bandwidth. Because shortcuts are designed to exploit locality, they can significantly improve performance. Furthermore, in our architecture, shortcuts are modular building blocks that may constructed on top of any large-scale overlay. Layering enables higher performance without degrading the scalability or the correctness of the underlying overlay construction algorithm.

In [Sripanidkulchai et al., 2003] , we conduct in-depth analysis to obtain a better understanding of the factors that contribute to the degree of interest-based locality observed in our workloads. We found that shortcuts are effective at exploiting interest-based locality at many levels of granularity ranging from locality in accessing objects on the same Web page, accessing Web pages from the same publisher, and accessing Web pages that span across publishers. In addition, interest-based structures are different from the HTML link structures in Web documents.

In our study, we find that interacting with a small group of peers, often smaller than ten, is sufficient for achieving high hit rates. Our results differ from previous Web caching studies [Wolman et al., 1999] that report that hit rates only start to saturate with population sizes of over thousands of clients. The difference is that in our approach, peers are grouped based on interests, whereas in Web caching, all clients are grouped together. Cooperation with small groups of peers who share interests provides the same benefits as cooperation with a large group of clients with random interests.

In addition to improving content location performance, interest-based shortcuts can be used as a primitive for a rich class of higher-level services. For instance, keyword or string matching searches for content and performance-based content retrieval are two examples of such services. Distributed hash tables [Ratnasamy et al., 2001, Rowstron and Druschel, 2001, Stoica et al., 2001, Zhao et al., 2000] do not support keyword searches. Interest-based short-cuts can be used to implement searches on top of those schemes in the following way. Peers forward searches along shortcuts. Then, each peer that receives a search performs a keyword match with the content it stores locally. There is a likely chance that content will be found through shortcuts because of interest-based locality.

Performance-based content retrieval can also be implemented using interest-based shortcuts. The advantage of such a service is that content can be retrieved from the peer with the best performance. Most peer-to-peer systems assume short-lived interaction on the order of single requests. However, shortcuts provide an opportunity for a longer-term relationship between peers. Given this relationship, peers can afford to carefully test out shortcuts and select the best ones to use based on content retrieval performance. In addition, the amount of state peers need to allocate for interest-based shortcuts is small and bounded. Therefore, peers can store performance history for all of their shortcuts. Peers can even actively probe shortcuts for available bandwidth if needed.

One potential concern about interest-based locality is whether exploiting such relationships infringes on privacy any more so than underlying content location mechanisms. We argue that it does not. Peers do not gain any more information than they have already obtained from using the underlying content location mechanism. Interest-based shortcuts only allow such information to be used intelligently to improve performance.

9.   Related Work

In this section, we review related work on peer-to-peer content location. Deployed peer-to-peer systems leverage "supernode" or server-based architectures. In a recent version of Kazaa and Gnutella (0.6) [Klingberg and Manfredi, 2002], certain well-connected peers are selected as supernodes to index content located on other peers. When locating content, peers contact their supernode who, in turn, may contact other supernodes. The BitTorrent [BitTorrent, 2005] system uses a server-based architecture where a dedicated "tracker" server maintains a list of all peers that have a copy of a particular piece of content. To locate content, peers contact the tracker. Shortcuts can be used in such environments to reduce load at trackers and supernodes, and to improve the efficiency of query routing between supernodes.

Improvements to Gnutella's flooding mechanism have been studied along several dimensions. Instead of flooding, different search algorithms such as expanding ring searches and random walks can limit the scope of queries [Lv et al., 2002]. Such approaches are effective at finding popular content. Query routing based on content indices can also replace flooding. Content is indexed based on keywords [Kumar et al., 2005, Zhang and Hu, 2005] or topics [Crespo and Garcia-Molina, 2002] and searches are forwarded towards nodes that have the desired content. Interest-based locality can be exploited to increase the effectiveness of routing by turning nodes that share similar interests into routing neighbors. Another dimension to improve search throughput and scalability is to exploit bandwidth heterogeneity such that nodes with higher capacity are visited more frequently [Chawathe et al., 2003]. This approach is complementary to exploiting locality.

Structured overlays such as DHTs [Ratnasamy et al., 2001, Rowstron and Druschel, 2001, Stoica et al., 2001, Zhao et al., 2000] are a scalable and elegant alternatives to Gnutella's unstructured overlays. However, DHTs only expose a simple exact match lookup interface. More recently, several schemes have been proposed to provide key-word search as an enhancement. For example, multi-keyword search can be implemented using Bloom filters [Reynolds and Vahdat, 2003]. Semantic search over text-based content can be implemented by encoding data and queries as semantic vectors and routing queries by matching the vectors to node IDs in the DHT [Tang et al., 2003]. PIER [Harren et al., 2002] implements traditional database search operators such as select and join on top of DHTs. Mechanisms to exploit locality such as query caching and interest-based shortcuts can be used to improve search performance for structured overlays.

Acknowledgments

This research was sponsored by DARPA under contract number F30602-99-1-0518, and by NSF under grant numbers Career Award NCR-9624979 ANI-9730105, ITR Award ANI-0085920, and ANI-9814929. Additional support was provided by Intel. Views and conclusions contained in this document are those of the authors and should not be interpreted as representing the official policies, either expressed or implied, of DARPA, NSF, Intel, or the U.S. government. We thank Venkat Padmanabhan for the Microsoft Corporate proxy traces, Matei Ripeanu for the Gnutella connectivity graphs, and Frank Kietzke and CMU Computing Services for running our trace collection software.

References

Almeida, V., Bestavros, A., Crovella, M., and de Oliveira, A. (1996). Characterizing Reference Locality in the WWW. In *Proceedings of 1996 International Conference on Parallel and Distributed Information Systems (PDIS '96)*.

Bayardo, Jr., R., Somani, A., Gruhl, D., and Agrawal, R. (2002). YouServ: A Web Hosting and Content Sharing Tool for the Masses. In *Proceedings of International WWW Conference*.

BitTorrent (2005). Available at http://bitconjurer.org/BitTorrent.

Breslau, L., Cao, P., Fan, L., Phillips, G., and Shenker, S. (1999). Web Caching and Zipf-like Distributions: Evidence and Implications. In *Proceedings of the IEEE INFOCOMM '99*.

Chawathe, Y., Ratnasamy, S., Breslau, L., Lanham, N., and Shenker, S. (2003). Making Gnutella-like P2P Systems Scalable. In *Proceedings of ACM Sigcomm*.

Crespo, A. and Garcia-Molina, H. (2002). Routing Indices for Peer-to-Peer Systems. In *Proceedings of the IEEE ICDCS*.

Cunha, C., Bestavros, A., and Covella, M. (1995). Characteristics of WWW Client Based Traces. Technical Report BU-CS-95-010, Computer Science Department, Boston University.

GTK-Gnutella (2005). http://gtk-gnutella.sourceforge.net.

Harren, M., Hellerstein, J., Huebsch, R., Loo, B., Shenker, S., and Stoica, I. (2002). Complex Queries in DHT-based Peer-to-Peer Networks. In *Proceedings of IPTPS*.

Iyer, S., Rowstron, A., and Druschel, P. (2002). Squirrel: A Decentralized Peer-to-Peer Web Cache. In *ACM Symposium on Principles of Distributed Computing, PODC*.

Jacobson, V., Leres, C., and McCanne, S. (2005). Tcpdump. Available at http://www.tcpdump.org/.

Kazaa (2005). http://www.kazaa.com.

Klingberg, T. and Manfredi, R. (2002). Gnutella 0.6. http://rfc-gnutella.sourceforge.net/src/rfc-0_6-draft.html.

Kroeger, T. M., Mogul, J. C., and Maltzahn, C. (1996). Digital's web proxy traces. Available at ftp://ftp.digital.com/pub/DEC/traces/proxy/webtraces.html.

Kumar, A., Xu, J., and Zegura, E. (2005). Efficient and Scalable Query Routing for Unstructured Peer-to-Peer Networks. In *Proceedings of IEEE Infocom*.

Lv, Q., Cao, P., Li, K., and Shenker, S. (2002). Replication Strategies in Unstructured Peer-to-Peer Networks. In *Proceedings of ACM International Conference on Supercomputing(ICS)*.

Meadows, J. (1999). Boeing proxy logs. Available at ftp://researchsmp2.cc.vt.edu/pub/boeing/.

Netcraft (2004). Web server survey. http://news.netcraft.com/archives/web_server_survey.html.

Padmanabhan, V.N. and Sripanidkulchai, K. (2002). The Case for Cooperative Networking. In *Proceedings of International Workshop on Peer-To-Peer Systems*.

Plaxton, C., Rajaraman, R., and Richa, A. W. (1997). Accessing Nearby Copies of Replicated Objects in a Distributed Environment. In *Proceedings of the 9th Annual ACM Symposium on Parallel Algorithms and Architectures*.

Ratnasamy, S., Francis, P., Handley, M., Karp, R., and Shenker, S. (2001). A Scalable Content-Addressable Network. In *Proceedings of ACM SIGCOMM*.

Ratnasamy, S., Shenker, S., and Stoica, I. (2002). Routing Algorithms for DHTs: Some Open Questions. In *Proceedings of International Peer-To-Peer Workshop*.

Reynolds, Patrick and Vahdat, Amin (2003). Efficient Peer-to-Peer Keyword Searching. In *Proceedings of the ACM/IFIP/USENIX Middleware Conference*.

Ripeanu, M., Foster, I., and Iamnitchi, A. (2002). Mapping the Gnutella Network: Properties of Large-Scale Peer-to-Peer Systems and Implications for System Design. *IEEE Internet Computing Journal*, 6(1).

Rowstron, A. and Druschel, P. (2001). Pastry: Scalable, Distributed Object Location and Routing for Large-Scale Peer-to-Peer Systems. In *IFIP/ACM International Conference on Distributed Systems Platforms (Middleware)*.

Saroiu, S., Gummadi, K. P., and Gribble, S. D. (2002). A Measurement Study of Peer-to-Peer File Sharing Systems. In *Proceedings of Multimedia Computing and Networking (MMCN)*.

Sripanidkulchai, K. (2001). The Popularity of Gnutella Queries and Its Implications on Scalability. http://www.cs.cmu.edu/~kunwadee/research/p2p/gnutella.html.

Sripanidkulchai, K., Maggs, B., and Zhang, H. (2003). Efficient Content Location Using Interest-Based Locality in Peer-to-Peer Systems. In *Proceedings of IEEE Infocom*.

Stoica, I., Morris, R., Karger, D., Kaashoek, M. F., and Balakrishnan, H. (2001). Chord: A Scalable Peer-to-Peer Lookup Service for Internet Applications. In *Proceedings of ACM SIGCOMM*.

Tang, C., Xu, Z., and Dwarkadas, S. (2003). Peer-to-Peer Information Retrieval Using Self-Organizing Semantic Overlay Networks. In *Proceedings of ACM Sigcomm*.

Wolman, A., Voelker, G., Sharma, N., Cardwell, N., Karlin, A., and Levy, H. (1999). On the Scale and Performance of Cooperative Web Proxy Caching. In *Proceedings of ACM SOSP*.

Zhang, R. and Hu, Y. (2005). Assisted Peer-to-Peer Search with Partial Indexing. In *Proceedings of IEEE Infocom*.

Zhao, B., Kubiatowicz, J., and Joseph, A. (2000). Tapestry: An Infrastructure for Wide-area Fault-tolerant Location and Routing. *U. C. Berkeley Technical Report UCB//CSD-01-1141*.

II

DYNAMIC WEB CONTENT

Chapter 5

TECHNIQUES FOR EFFICIENTLY SERVING AND CACHING DYNAMIC WEB CONTENT

Arun Iyengar

IBM T.J. Watson Research Center
P.O. Box 704
Yorktown Heights, NY 10598
aruni@us.ibm.com

Lakshmish Ramaswamy

College of Computing
Georgia Institute of Technology
Atlanta, GA 30332
laks@cc.gatech.edu

Bianca Schroeder

School of Computer Science
Carnegie Mellon University
Pittsburgh, PA 15213
bianca@cs.cmu.edu

Abstract   This chapter presents an overview of techniques for efficiently serving and caching dynamic web data. We describe techniques for invoking server programs and architectures for serving dynamic web content. Caching is crucially important for improving the performance of Web sites generating significant dynamic data. We discuss techniques for caching dynamic Web data consistently. Fragment-based web publication can significantly improve performance and increase the cacheability of dynamic web data. These techniques assume the existence of mechanisms for creating fragments. We discuss techniques for automatically detecting fragments in web pages.

It is often desirable to provide content with quality-of-service (QoS) guarantees. We examine techniques for providing QoS under overload conditions. We also look at techniques for providing differentiated QoS.

Keywords: Caching, dynamic Web data, fragment detection, quality of service

1.   Introduction

Dynamic data refers to content which changes frequently. Dynamic web content is created by programs which execute at the time a request is made. By contrast, static data is usually comprised of already existing files. Dynamic data requires more overhead to serve than static data; a request for a dynamic Web page might require orders of magnitude more CPU cycles to satisfy than a request for a static page. For web sites which generate significant amounts of dynamic data, the overhead for serving dynamic requests is often the performance bottleneck.

Another key problem presented by dynamic data is maintaining updated content. If a dynamic web page is changing frequently, then copies of the web page must be updated frequently to prevent stale data from being served. This chapter will discuss a number of techniques for maintaining consistent replicas of dynamic content. The dual problems of serving content efficiently and maintaining updated consistent data are what make dynamic data so challenging.

One method for improving performance which allows at least parts of dynamic web content to be cached is to generate web pages from fragments. A fragment is a portion of a web page which might recursively embed smaller fragments. Using the fragment-based approach, personalized, secure, or rapidly changing data can be encapsulated within fragments, allowing other parts of the web page to be stored in caches which have the ability to assemble web pages from fragments. This chapter discusses fragment-based web publication as well as techniques for automatically detecting fragments in web pages.

It is often in the economic interest of Web sites to offer some guarantee on the quality of service they deliver. Moreover, in many situations, it is desirable to provide different levels of quality of service, since requests vary in their importance and their tolerance to delays. We discuss techniques for both achieving system-wide performance guarantees and class-based service differentiation.

2.   Architectures for Serving Dynamic Content

The most common method of generating dynamic content used to be by invoking server programs through the Common Gateway Interface (CGI). This method is inefficient because a new process needs to be invoked for each dynamic request. More sophisticated methods for creating dynamic content are now commonplace. Web servers generally provide interfaces for invoking server programs which incur significantly less overhead than CGI. One approach to implementing faster interfaces is for a server program to execute as part of a web server's process. This can be done by dynamically loading the server program the first time that it is invoked. Alternatively, a server program can be statically linked as part of the web server's executable image.

There are drawbacks to running a server program as part of a web server process, however. Using this approach, a server program could crash a web server or leak resources such as memory. In addition, the server program should be thread-safe so that another thread within the server process cannot affect the state of the server program in unpredictable ways; this can make writing server programs more difficult. Another approach which alleviates these problems to a large degree at the cost of slight overhead is for server programs to run as long-running processes independent from a web server's process. The server communicates with these long-running processes to invoke server programs.

One commonly used method for creating dynamic web content is via JavaServer Pages (JSP) technology. JSP pages consist of special tags in addition to standard HTML or XML tags. A JSP engine interprets the special tags and generates the content required. Subsequently, the results are sent back to the browser in the form of an HTML or XML page.

JSP pages may be compiled into Java platform servlet classes (A servlet is a program that runs on the server, compared with an applet which runs on a client browser. Servlets are handled by special threads within a web server process and run as part of the web server process.). A JSP page needs to be compiled the first time the page is accessed. The resulting Java servlet class can remain in memory so that subsequent requests for the page do not incur compilation overhead. A JSP page typically has the extension .jsp or .jspx to indicate to the web server that the JSP engine should be invoked to handle the page.

Microsoft has a similar approach for handling dynamic web content known as Active Server Pages (ASP). However, ASP technology is restricted to Microsoft platforms. JSP technology was developed using the Java Community Process and is available on a much wider variety of platforms than ASP technology.

Figure 5.1 shows an end-to-end flow of how a web request might proceed from a client to a server. After the request is made by a browser, it may go through a proxy server which is shared by several clients. Web content may be cached at several places within the network as shown in the figure. Caching can significantly reduce the latency for accessing remote data.

A proxy cache will store static data on behalf of several clients which share the use of the proxy. By contrast a content distribution network will cache data on behalf of content providers; content providers pay a content distribution network such as Akamai to cache content in geographically distributed locations so that a client can obtain a copy from a cache which is not too far away.

A key problem with caching web data is maintaining consistency among multiple copies. Later in the chapter, we will discuss different cache consistency methods which can be used for caching dynamic data. Proxy caches and CDN's typically only cache static data.

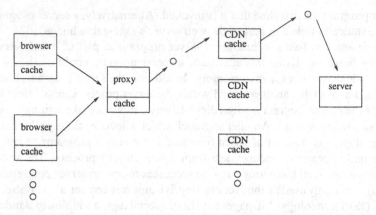

Figure 5.1. Path of a request from a client browser to a server. *CDN* stands for content distribution network.

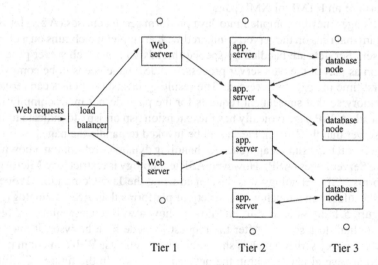

Figure 5.2. A three-tiered system for serving dynamic web content. The boxes labeled "app. server" represent application servers.

A web site which serves dynamic content to a large number of clients will need several servers. Figure 5.2 depicts a three-tiered system for serving dynamic data at a web site. Requests come into a load balancer which sends requests to Tier 1 consisting of web servers. Static requests are handled by the web servers in Tier 1. Dynamic requests are handled by the application servers in Tier 2. Application servers may incur significant overhead in satisfying dynamic requests. Therefore, there should be enough application servers to prevent Tier 2 from becoming a bottleneck during periods of high request rates for dynamic data. Balancing resources among the tiers is important for preventing one of the tiers from becoming a bottleneck while not wasting money on excessive resources in a tier which are under-utilized.

High availability is a critically important requirement for commercial web sites which should be robust in the presence of failures. Multiple servers improve availability as well as performance. If one server fails, requests can be directed to another server.

3.   Consistently Caching Dynamic Web Data

Caching may take place at any of the tiers in Figure 5.2. For example, many databases employ some form of caching. A web site might also have one or more reverse proxy caches [Song et al., 2002]. We now discuss techniques for achieving consistency among multiple cached copies.

Web objects which are cached may have expiration times associated with them. A cache continues to serve an object before its expiration time has elapsed. If a request is received for an object which has expired, the cache sends a get-if-modified-since request to the server; the server then either returns an updated copy of the object or indicates to the cache that the previous version is still valid. In either case, a new expiration time should be assigned to the object.

Expiration times require relatively low overhead for consistency maintenance. They only provide weak consistency, however. An application needs to know in advance when an object will expire, and this is not always possible. If the application overestimates the lifetime of an object, caches may serve obsolete copies. If the application underestimates the lifetime of an object, the cache will send extraneous authentication messages to the server which add overhead and increase latency for satisfying client requests.

There are a number of approaches for achieving stronger forms of cache consistency. In strong cache consistency, any cached copy of an object must be current; even a slight degree of inconsistency is not acceptable. A key problem with strong consistency is that updates require considerable overhead. Before performing an update, all cached copies of the object need to be invalidated first. Considerable delays can occur in making sure that all cached copies have been invalidated.

Strong consistency is often not feasible for web data because of the high overhead it entails. For much of the data on the web, slight degrees of inconsistency are tolerable. Therefore, true strong consistency is overkill for most web data. Other forms of consistency exist which offer stronger degrees of consistency than expiration times but don't have the overhead of strong consistency. These schemes generally make use of server-driven consistency or client polling.

In server-driven consistency, servers must notify caches when an object has changed. The notification message may either be a message to simply invalidate the object or it could contain a copy of the new object (prefetch). Prefetching is advantageous for hot objects which are highly likely to be accessed before they are updated again. For objects which are not accessed all that frequently relative to the update rate, prefetching is not a good idea because of the added bandwidth consumed by the prefetch; if the object is not accessed before the next update, then the prefetch will not have achieved anything useful.

Server-driven consistency has overhead when an update to a cached object is made. All caches storing the object need to be notified, and the number of update messages grows linearly with the number of caches which need to be notified. The server also needs to maintain information about which caches are storing which objects; this adds storage overhead.

In client polling, caches are responsible for contacting the server in order to determine if a cached object is still valid or not. Cache consistency managed via expiration times is a form of client polling in which the expiration time reduces the frequency of polling. If expiration times are very short, more frequent polling is required. In the worst case, polling is required on each request to a cache. The overhead for these polling message can be quite significant.

One method which can reduce the overhead for maintaining cache consistency is *leases*. In the lease-based approach, a server grants a lease to a cache for a duration. During the lease duration, the server must continue to send update messages to the cache. After the lease duration has expired, the server is no longer required to send update messages to the cache. If the cache wants to continue to receive update messages for an object, it must renew the lease. Leases combine elements of server-driven consistency and client polling. Note that if the lease duration is zero, the cache consistency scheme degenerates into pure client polling. If, on the other hand, the lease duration is infinite, the cache consistency scheme degenerates into pure server-driven consistency. Leases were used for distributed file cache consistency before they were applied to the web [Gray and Cheriton, 1989].

Leases provide a number of advantages. They bound the length of time that a server needs to provide updates to a cache. This is important because a cache might become unresponsive to a server or be taken off the network. The server might not know which caches are responsive and which ones are not. Leases provide an upper bound on how stale a validly cached object can be. In the worst case, a cached object is updated multiple times but a cache fails to receive any invalidation messages for the object due to an event such as a network failure. In this worst case scenario, the cache will still not serve a copy of the object obsolete by more than the lease duration.

There are a number of variations on leases which have been proposed. A *volume lease* is a single lease which is granted to a collection of several objects [Yin et al., 1999]. *Cooperative leases* have been proposed for CDN's and involve cooperation between multiple caches to reduce the overhead of consistency maintenance [Ninan et al., 2002].

3.1   Determining how Changes to Underlying Data Affect Cached Objects

A key problem with generating and caching dynamic web data is determining which cached pages have changed when changes occur. Web pages are often constructed from underlying data in a non-obvious fashion. When the underlying data changes, several web pages may be affected. Determining the precise ones which change can be nontrivial. For example, a news web site might have information about the latest news stories, stock quotes, sporting events, and other similar items. Suppose the web pages are constructed from databases which store the latest information received. When new information is received, the database tables are updated. The problem then becomes how to determine which web pages need to be updated as a result of the new information.

Data update propagation (DUP) provides an effective solution to this problem. In data update propagation, correspondences between web pages and underlying data are maintained in an object dependence graph. When underlying data changes, graph traversal algorithms are applied to determine which web pages are affected by the change [Challenger et al., 1999].

Figure 5.3 depicts a simple object dependence graph in which none of the nodes have both an incoming and outgoing edge. If underlying data $u1$ changes, then web pages $W1$, $W3$, and $W4$ also change. If $u2$ changes, then $W2$ also changes, while if $u3$ changes, then $W4$ is affected.

Figure 5.4 depicts a more general object dependence graph in which paths of length longer than one exist. If either $u1$ or $u3$ change, then both web pages $W1$ and $W2$ are affected.

The relationships between web pages and underlying data can change quite frequently. Object dependence graphs can thus be quite dynamic.

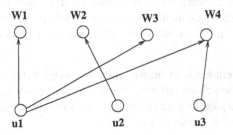

Figure 5.3.   A simple object dependence graph representing data dependencies between web pages and underlying data.

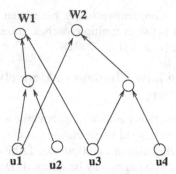

Figure 5.4. A more general object dependence graph representing data dependencies between web pages and underlying data.

4. Fragment-based Web Caching

The primary motivation for fragment-based web caching comes from some of the recent trends in web publishing. A considerable fraction of dynamic web pages exhibit the following distinct properties.

- Web pages rarely have a single theme or functionality. Most web pages have several document segments which differ in the information they provide or the functionality they encapsulate. For example, a web page from a news provider web site, in addition to containing an article about a news event, may also have links and synopses of other headlines of the day. Recent stock market data might also be listed on the web page. Further, the web page might also have a welcome bar containing personalized greetings to each registered user. These segments provide very different information, but are still present in the web page whose predominant theme is the news item with which it is associated.

- Most dynamic web pages contain a considerable amount of static content. The dynamic contents are often embedded in static web page segments. Similarly web pages are usually not completely personalized; Web pages generated for different users often share significant amounts of information.

- These different kinds of information may exhibit different lifetime and personalization characteristics. For example the stock market information in a web page might expire every few minutes whereas the synopses of headlines might change every few hours.

- Web pages hosted by the same web site tend to have similar structure and may exhibit considerable overlap in terms of HTML segments.

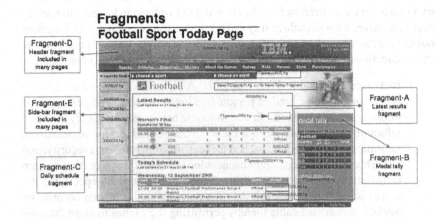

Figure 5.5. Fragments in a Web Page

Fragment-based publishing, delivery and caching of web pages are designed with the aim of utilizing these characteristics to improve the cacheable content on the web and to reduce data invalidations at caches. In fragment-based dynamic web pages, various information segments are clearly identified and demarcated from one another.

Conceptually, a fragment is a portion of a web page which has a distinct theme or functionality associated with it and is distinguishable from the other parts of the page. In the fragment-based model, each fragment is an independent information entity. The web pages have references to these fragments, which are served independently from the server and stored as such in the caches.

Figure 5.5 provides an example of a fragment-based web page. This was one of the web pages on a web site hosted by IBM for a major sporting event. The figure shows several fragments in the web page. Fragment-A lists some of the recent results of the event. Fragment-B indicates the current medal tally. Fragment-C shows the day's schedule of events. Fragment-D is a header fragment. Fragment-E is a navigation side-bar aiding the users to navigate the web site. Note that the fragments shown in the figure have distinct themes, whereas the web page itself is a collage of various information pertaining to the sporting event.

As the fragments differ from one another in terms of the information and the functionality they provide, the properties associated with them are also likely to vary from one another. Important properties associated with a fragment include the time for which the information remains fresh, personalization characteristics such as whether the generated information is client-specific (based on cookies), and information sharing behavior exhibited by them. Fragment-based caching schemes recognize the variability of these fragment-specific properties. They try to improve cache performance by allowing the web page designer to specify cache directives such as cacheability and lifetime at the granularity of a fragment rather than requiring them to be specified at the web-page level. Specifying the cache directives at fragment-level provides a number of distinct advantages:

1 **Increases Cacheable Web Content:** A significant percentage of web pages contain some kind of personalized information. The personalized information may be as simple as a welcome bar, or may be highly sensitive information like credit card or bank account details. This personalized information should not be cached for reasons of privacy and security, and hence has to be marked as non-cacheable. However, the pages that contain them usually also have non-personalized information. By specifying the properties at fragment level, only the personalized information need be marked as non-cacheable thereby permitting the caches to store the non-personalized content; this increases the cacheable content.

2 **Decreases Data Invalidations:** Fragments in the same web page might exhibit very different lifetime characteristics. In our example, Fragment-A and Fragment-B are likely to change more frequently than Fragment-C which in turn changes less frequently than Fragments D or E. When lifetimes are specified at the page level, the entire page gets invalidated when any of its fragments change. Therefore, the lifetime of a web page is dictated by the most frequently changing fragment contained in it. With fragment-based caching, the lifetime information can be specified at fragment-level. This allows the caches to invalidate only the fragment that has expired, and to fetch only the invalidated fragment from the origin server. The rest of the web page remains in the cache and need not be re-fetched from the server.

3 **Aids Efficient Disk Space Utilization:** Web pages from the same web site often share content. It might be in the form of same information being replicated on multiple web pages or it might be structural content such as navigation bars, headers and footers. In fragment-based publication, content which is shared across multiple web pages would typically be generated as fragments. These fragments are stored only once rather being replicated with each web page, thus reducing redundancy of information at the caches.

Researchers have proposed several flavors of fragment-based publishing, delivery and caching of web data. A fragment-based publishing system for dynamic web data is presented in [Challenger et al., 2000]. This was one of the first works on the fragment-based web document model. Their system not only improves the performance of web-page construction, but also simplifies designing of web sites. The system allows embedding smaller and simpler fragments into larger and more complex fragments. This permits reuse of generated fragments, thereby avoiding unnecessary regeneration of the same information multiple times. Fragment-based publishing also facilitates designing of multiple web pages having a common look and feel, thereby simplifying the task of constructing large web sites. Further, if the information corresponding to a fragment changes, only that particular fragment needs to be updated rather than updating every single web page containing that fragment. This significantly reduces the overhead of maintaining complex web sites.

Datta et al. [Datta et al., 2002] argue that the dynamic nature of a web page is exhibited along two mutually orthogonal dimensions, namely, the layout of the web page and its content. They propose a fragment-based web caching scheme wherein the dynamic content is cached at proxy caches, whereas the layout of the web page is fetched from the server on each access to the web page.

When a request for a web page reaches a proxy cache, it is routed to the origin server. The origin server executes a script associated with the request, which generates the entire web page. A background process called back-end monitor (BEM) constantly monitors the script generating the web page. This process creates a layout for the page being generated. The background process creates the layout by removing those contents that are available at the proxy cache from the web page being generated by the application script. A reference containing an identifier of the removed fragment replaces the removed content. This document, which contains the layout information along with the fragments not available in the proxy cache, is sent to the proxy cache. The proxy cache, on receiving this document, parses it and introduces any missing fragments to generate the complete web page, which is then communicated to the user. While parsing the document received from the server, the proxy also stores fragments that are not available locally. This approach reduces the amount of data communicated from the server to the cache by transferring only the layout and the fragments that are not present in the cache.

Mohapatra and Chen [Mohapatra and Chen, 2001] apply the concept of fragments for providing efficient QoS support and security mechanisms for web documents. They propose a system called WebGraph, which is a graphical representation of the containment relationship among weblets, which are analogous to fragments. The nodes of the graph correspond to weblets (fragments), and the edges represent the containment relationships. In the proposed system the QoS and security attributes can be specified at the granularity of a weblet. For example fragments may carry attributes such as delay sensitive, throughput sensitive, loss sensitive, etc. The edges of the WebGraph can also carry attributes indicating whether the edge can be dropped under certain circumstances like server overload or inability to support the QoS requirements of the associated fragments. If an edge is dropped, the corresponding fragment is not included in the web page.

4.1   Edge Side Includes: A Standard for Fragment-based Caching

Although researchers have shown the benefits of fragment-based caching, adopting it in commercial systems presents additional challenges. One of the major challenges is to evolve a common standard for fragment-based caching so that various proxies and servers implemented by different vendors become interoperable. Recognizing the need for standardizing fragment-based publishing, caching and delivery of web data, the Internet and Web communities have evolved a standard called the **Edge Side Includes (ESI)** [ESI, 2005]. ESI is an XML-based markup language that can be used by content providers to publish web pages through fragments. The content providers can specify the fragments to be included in a web page. A cache supporting ESI understands that the specified fragment has to be included in the web page. It constructs the web page by inserting those fragments either from the cache, or by fetching them from the server.

ESI has been endorsed by companies like IBM, Akamai, Oracle and Digital Island. One of the goals of its design was to make it mark-up language and programming-model independent. The key functionalities provided by ESI are:

1 **Inclusion** The primary functionality of ESI is to provide support for specifying fragments to be inserted in a web page. The include element in the markup language is provided for this purpose. The content providers use the include element to instruct the caches to insert the indicated fragment in the web page. The caches which encounter an include statement check to see whether it is available locally. In case the fragment is not available at the cache, the fragment is fetched from the server. In addition to identifying the fragment, the include element also provides variable support. It can be used to specify the parameters to the script generating the web page.

2 **Conditional Inclusion/Exclusion:** Web page designers may want to include certain fragments when one or more conditions are satisfied, and may want to exclude them, or provide alternate fragments otherwise. The *choose, when* and *otherwise* clauses in the ESI specification provide support for such conditional inclusions and exclusion of fragments.

3 **Handling Exceptions:** At certain times, a particular fragment may become unavailable due to failure of the server or the network. ESI includes mechanisms to counter such exceptions through the *try, attempt* and *except* clauses. Web page designers can use these clauses to specify

alternate resources, or default fragments to be used by the caches when such exceptions occur.

4 **Fragment Invalidation Support:** An important issue with caching dynamic web data is maintaining consistency of the cached copies. Since such documents may become stale when the data on the back-end databases change, caching such documents needs stronger consistency mechanisms than the commonly used Time-to-Live schemes. ESI supports stronger consistency through explicit invalidation of cached fragments. ESI's fragment invalidation includes 2 messages: (1) Invalidation request, and (2) Invalidation response. A server instructs the caches to invalidate one or more fragments through the invalidation response. A cache receiving an invalidation request sends the invalidation response to the server informing it of the result of the invalidation.

While fragment assembly in proxy or CDN caches has been shown to be effective in reducing the loads on the backbone networks and origin servers, it does not reduce the load of the network link connecting the end clients to the cache. However, for clients which are connected through dial-ups, the dial-up links from the clients to the reverse proxy caches located at the ISPs (or the so called last-mile) often become bottlenecks, and the latency involved in transferring documents over the dial-up links forms a significant fraction of the total latency experienced by dial-up clients. Therefore, it is important to reduce the load on the last-mile links, especially for dial-up clients. Rabinovich et al. [Rabinovich et al., 2003] address this problem by taking fragment assembly one step further. They propose the *Client Side Includes* scheme, wherein the composition of web pages from fragments is done at the client itself, rather than within a network cache. The CSI mechanism enables the browsers to assemble the web pages from the individual fragments.

The paper also describes a JavaScript-based implementation of the CSI mechanism. In their implementation, the origin server returns a wrapper on receiving a request for a web page from a CSI-enabled client. This wrapper invokes a JavaScript-based page assembler at the client's browser. This assembler fetches individual fragments from the origin server and composes the web page, which is then displayed to the user. The clients can cache the wrapper-code of a web page in order to avoid the overhead of fetching it from the server on each access to the web page.

Another important question that needs to be addressed is how dynamic web pages can be fragmented so that servers and caches provide optimal performance. One obvious solution for this problem is to require that the web pages be fragmented by either the web page designer or the web site administrator. Manual fragmentation of dynamic web pages in this fashion is both labor intensive and error prone. Further, manual markup of fragments in web pages does not scale, and it becomes unmanageable for edge caches serving web data from multiple content providers. Ramaswamy et al. [Ramaswamy et al., 2004] present a scheme to automatically detect fragments in web pages. This scheme automatically detects and flags fragments at a given web site which exhibit potential benefits as potential cache units. Their approach depends upon a careful analysis of the dynamic web pages with respect to their information sharing behavior, personalization characteristics and change patterns.

4.2   Automatic Fragmentation of Dynamic Web Pages

Automatically fragmenting dynamic web pages presents a unique challenge. The conceptual definition of a fragment says that it is a part of a web page having distinct theme or functionality. While a human with prior knowledge of the web page's domain can easily and unambiguously identify fragments with different themes, it is not straightforward to build a system that can do the same. Not only should these systems be able to identify the themes associated with the fragments, but also they should efficiently detect fragments in web sites with thousands of web pages.

The proposed scheme detects fragments that form cost-effective cache units [Ramaswamy et al., 2004]. These fragments are referred to as *candidate fragments*. A candidate fragment is recursively defined as follows:

- Each Web page of a web site is a candidate fragment.
- A part of a candidate fragment is itself a candidate fragment if any one of the two conditions is satisfied:
  - The part is shared among "M" already existing candidate fragments, where $M > 1$.
  - The part has different personalization and lifetime characteristics than those of its encompassing (parent or ancestor) candidate fragment.

We distinguish between two types of fragments. The fragments that satisfy the first condition are called the *shared fragments* and those satisfying the second condition are referred to as the *Lifetime-Personalization based fragments* or the L-P fragments. The two kinds of fragments benefit the caching application in two different ways. Incorporating shared fragments into web pages avoids unnecessary duplication of information at the caches, thereby reducing disk space usage at caches. The L-P fragments, on the other hand, improve cacheable content and reduce the amount of data that gets invalidated.

The scheme has two algorithms: one to detect shared fragments and another to detect L-P fragments. The shared fragment detection algorithm works on a collection of different dynamic pages generated from the same web site and detects fragments that are approximately shared among multiple web pages. In contrast the L-P fragment detection algorithm detects fragments by comparing different versions of the same web page.

As both fragment detection algorithms compare several web pages, they need a data structure that permits efficient comparison of web pages. The automatic fragmentation scheme uses a web page model for this purpose which is called the *Augmented Fragment Tree* model, or the AF tree model. An AF tree model is a hierarchical model for web documents similar to the document object model (DOM) [DOM, 2005], with three distinct characteristics: First, it is a compact DOM tree with all the text-formatting tags (e.g., <Big>, <Bold>, <I>) removed. Second, the content of each node is fingerprinted with Shingles encoding [Broder, 1997]. Third, each node is augmented with additional information for efficient comparison of different documents and different fragments of documents.

Shingles are fingerprints of strings or text documents with the property that when the string changes by a small amount its shingles also change by a small amount. The similarity between two text documents can be estimated by computing the overlap between their shingles. Shared and L-P fragment detection algorithms use shingles to estimate similarity of web pages.

Shared Fragment Detection Algorithm.   The shared fragment detection algorithm compares different web pages from the same web site and detects maximal fragments that are approximately shared among at least $ShareFactor$ distinct web pages, where $ShareFactor$ is a configurable parameter.

Let us consider the two web page parts shown in Figure 5.6a. The first web page part appeared in the Americas page of BBC's web site, while the second one is taken from the World News web page from the same web site. These two web page parts essentially contain the same information, which makes them prime candidates for shared fragment detection. However, detecting these fragments automatically presents several challenges. First, although the two web page parts are similar, they are not exactly the same. For example, the order of the bullet points is different, and the text appearing in one of the bullet points is slightly different. The shared fragment detection algorithm should be able to detect the entire web page part as a single fragment, or detect individual items (like the heading, the text, the bullet points) as fragments depending on the web site's preference. Second, similar html segments in two web pages might appear in completely different positions (note that the bullet points have changed their relative positions in the two web page parts). Third, if two or more web page parts are deemed to be similar, and hence detected as a shared fragment, a large fraction of their sub-parts (like the heading, the text and the bullet points in the example) would also be similar to one another. However, these sub-parts are *trivial* fragments, and hence the algorithm should avoid detecting them as fragments.

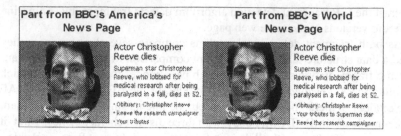

Figure 5.6a.   Example of Shared Fragments

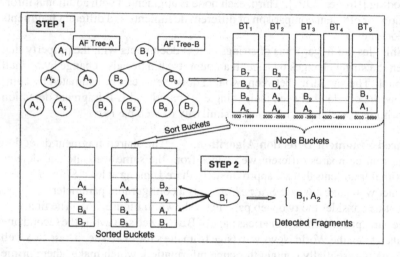

Figure 5.6b.   Illustration of Shared Fragment Detection Algorithm

The shared fragment detection algorithm addresses these challenges. It works in two steps as shown in Figure 5.6b. In the first step, the algorithm sorts the nodes of AF trees of the different web pages based on their sizes. In the second step the algorithm detects maximally shared fragments by grouping nodes that are similar to one another based on the overlap of their shingles.

The algorithm has three tunable parameters which can be used to control the quality of the detected fragments. The first parameter, $ShareFactor$, specifies the minimum number of web pages (or more generally other fragments) that should share a web-page part in order for it to be detected as a fragment. The web site administrator can use this parameter to avoid detecting fragments that are shared across a very minute fraction of the web pages. The second parameter, $MinMatchFactor$, which can vary between 0.0, and 1.0, is used to specify the similarity threshold among the AF tree nodes that form a shared fragment.

When this parameter is set to higher values, the algorithm looks for more perfect matches, thereby detecting larger numbers of small-sized fragments. For example, in the Figure 5.6a, if $MinMatchFactor$ is set to 0.6, the entire web page part is detected as a single fragment. If $MinMatchFactor$ is set to 0.9, the algorithm detects four fragments (a heading fragment, a fragment corresponding to the text, and two fragments corresponding to two bullet points). $MinFragSize$ is the third parameter, which specifies the minimum size of the detected fragments. One can use this parameter to avoid very small fragments being detected. If a fragment is very small, the advantages in incorporating it are limited, whereas the overheads of composing the web page from these very tiny fragments would be considerably high. A web site administrator can choose an appropriate value for these parameters based on the capability of the infrastructure, the user request patterns, and the invalidation rates.

L-P Fragment Detection. The L-P fragment detection algorithm can be used to detect fragments that have different lifetime or personalization characteristics than their encompassing fragments. The input to this algorithm is a set of different versions of the same web page. The different versions might either be time-spaced, or be obtained by sending in different cookies.

The L-P fragment detection algorithm compares different versions of the same web page and detects portions of the web page that have changed over different versions. A web page might undergo several different types of changes: contents might be added, deleted or they might change their relative position in the web page. Figure 5.7a shows two versions of a web page part appearing in two versions of the same web page from Slashdot's web site. This figure demonstrates the various kinds of changes web pages might undergo. Therefore, the algorithm should be sensitive to all these kinds of web page changes. Further, the algorithm should also detect fragments that are most beneficial to the caching application.

The L-P fragment detection algorithm discussed in the paper installs the AF tree of the first version available (in chronological order) as the base version. The AF tree of each subsequent version is compared against this base version. For each AF tree node of a subsequent version, the algorithm checks whether the node has changed its value or position when compared with an equivalent node from the base version and marks the node's status accordingly. In the second phase the algorithm traverses the AF trees and detects the L-P fragments based on its and its children's status, such that the detected fragments are most beneficial to caching. Figure 5.7b depicts the execution of the algorithm. The detected fragments and the object dependency graph are also shown in the figure.

Similar to the shared fragment detection algorithm, the L-P fragment detection algorithm also provides parameters which can be used by the web admin-

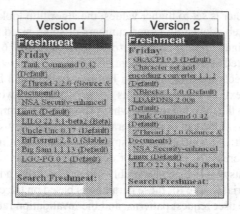

Figure 5.7a. Examples of L-P Fragments

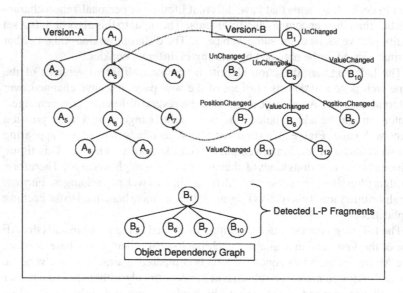

Figure 5.7b. Illustration of L-P Fragment Detection Algorithm

istrators to tune the performance of the algorithm. The first parameter called the $MinFragSize$ specifies the minimum size of the detected fragments. As in shared fragment detection, this parameter can be used to preclude very small fragments. By doing so one can detect only those fragments that are cost effective cache units. $ChildChangeThreshold$ is the second tunable parameter of the algorithm. This parameter in some sense quantifies the amount of change an html-segment has to undergo before being detected as a fragment. When *ChildChangeThreshold* is set to high values, fragments are detected at a finer granularity leading to larger numbers of small fragments. While finer granularities of fragmentation reduce the amount of data invalidations at caches, it also increases the page assembly costs at the caches. The web site administrator can decide the appropriate value for this parameter depending upon the available infrastructure and the web-site specific requirements.

The fragment detection scheme which includes these two algorithms outputs a set of fragments. These fragments are served as recommendations to the web site administrator.

5.   Providing quality of service for dynamic web content

Providing good quality of service (QoS) is crucial in serving dynamic content for several reasons. First, one of the main applications of dynamic content is in e-business web sites. For an e-business web site, the competitor is only one click away making it very easy for dissatisfied customers to take their business to a competitor. Second, poor quality of service affects the image of the company as a whole. Studies have shown that users equate slow web download times with poor product quality or even fear that the security of their purchases might be compromised.

In addition, it is often important for a site to offer different levels of service, since requests vary in how important they are and users vary in how tolerant they are to delays. For example, it is in the economic interest of an e-commerce retailer to differentiate between high-volume customer and low-volume customers. Moreover, some customers may have paid for service-level agreements (SLAs) which guarantee certain levels of service. Finally, studies [Bouch et al., 2000, Bhatti et al., 2000] indicate that customers' patience levels decline in proportion to the time spent at the site. Patience levels are also tied to the type of request users submit. Customers tend to be more tolerant of long search times and less tolerant of long purchase times.

How users perceive the quality of service they experience when accessing web content depends on several factors:

- The latency experienced by users
  When users rate the quality of service received at a web site as poor, the most common reason is high latency. Latency, or response time, is defined as the period of time between the moment a user makes a request and the time the user receives the response in its entirety. In order for a response to be perceived as immediate, the latency needs to be on the order of 0.1 seconds. For a user to be satisfied, delays should not exceed 5 seconds. Delays that are longer than 10 seconds are considered intolerable and lead users to assume that errors have occurred in processing their requests.

- The predictability of system performance
  Frequent customers at a site are used to a certain level of service. If the quality of service is not delivered as expected, users will not be happy. Unpredictable service compromises customers' opinions of the company.

- The overall system availability
  The worst quality of service is no service. Even short service outages can cost an e-business huge amounts in lost revenues. One common source of service outages is transient overload at the web site due to an unexpected surge of requests. Examples of this phenomenon include the overload of the Firestone web site after a tire recall, the outage of several large e-tailers during the holiday shopping season in 2000, and overload of the official Florida election site, which became overwhelmed after the presidential election of 2000.

- The freshness of data returned to the user
  Freshness of data is a quality of service aspect that is particular to dynamic content. It arises when web sites, in an attempt to serve a dynamic request more efficiently, rely on cached data from an earlier execution of the dynamic request. This approach is for example commonly used when serving dynamic requests that require access to a database back-end. While using cached data reduces work for the server, users might receive outdated data. Consider, for example, an e-commerce site that reports product availability based on cached values of stock levels. The site might realize only after accepting an order that the item is not actually in stock.

The network community has long studied the efficacy of providing quality of service guarantees and providing class-based service differentiation. However, much of this work relies on the assumption that the network is the typical bottleneck in web transfers. Serving dynamic content can require orders of magnitude more processing power at a web site compared with serving purely static data [Challenger et al., 2004]. For web sites that are dominated by dynamic content the bottleneck tends to shift from the network to the server, making it necessary to provide QoS mechanisms at the server.

In the remainder of this section, we will survey recent research on providing quality of service at a web server. We first discuss approaches for achieving system-wide QoS goals, i.e. achieving the same set of QoS goals across all requests served by a site. We then examine solutions for providing class-based QoS, where different classes of requests have different QoS goals.

5.1   Achieving system-wide QoS goals

The system load a site experiences is the main factor affecting the quality of service. The resources at a web site are limited, so providing a certain level of quality of service requires keeping the system load below some threshold. The main approach for guaranteeing a certain level of QoS is therefore load control in order to avoid *overload* conditions. Overload in this context refers not only to load that exceeds the system's capacity, but also to load that is too high to ensure the system's QoS specifications.

Load control typically consists of two steps; detecting when a system reaches overload and reacting by taking measures to reduce the load. The approaches suggested for load control vary depending on where they are implemented. Load control can be integrated into the operating system of the web server, it can be implemented at the application level, or it can be moved to the database back-end. Below we first describe different approaches for detecting overload and then discuss possible solutions to the problem.

Detecting Overload.   Approaches for overload detection at the *operating system level* fall into two categories. Approaches in the first category focus on the network stack and typically monitor the occupancy of the SYN queue or the TCP listen queue [Voigt et al., 2001]. While the occupancy of these queues provides only a very limited view of the overall state of the server, the back-pressure caused by over-utilization of resources in one of the higher system layers will eventually lead to a backlog in those kernel queues.

Another approach for overload detection at the operating system level is based on measuring the utilization of server resources. One of the motivations for considering server resource utilization is that some QoS algorithms can be theoretically proven to guarantee a certain level of service, assuming that the server utilization is below some threshold [Abdelzaher et al., 2002].

When using information on the utilization level of the system in load control decisions, it is important to distinguish between high utilization caused by a short, transient burst of new traffic, versus high utilization resulting from a persistent increase in traffic that calls for load control. Cherkasova et al. [Cherkasova and Phaal, 2000] therefore propose to use a predictive admission control strategy that is based on the weighted moving average of the utilization level observed in previous measurement periods, rather than the instantaneous utilization level.

Methods for detecting overload at the *application level* are either based on monitoring the occupancy of application internal queues, or on developing an estimate of the work involved in processing the currently active request.

The prior approach is taken by [Ramanathan and Singhal, 2000] and [Bhatti and Friedrich, 1999]. Both employ mechanisms for rapidly draining the TCP listen queue and managing the outstanding requests in an internal system of queues. The lengths of the internal queues can then indicate when to apply load control. Moving load control from the kernel queues to an application level queue helps to avoid TCP timeouts experienced by requests dropped in the kernel queues. Moving the load control to the application level also allows for the use of application-level information in the load control process.

Chen et al. [Chen et al., 2001] and Elnikety et al. [Elnikety et al., 2004] follow the latter approach, i.e. they approximate the current system load based on estimates of the work imposed by each request in progress. Chen et al. experiment with the CGI scripts included in the WebStone benchmark. They measure the CPU usage for each CGI script and use it as an estimate for the work associated with serving the corresponding dynamic request. Elnikety et al. consider Java servlets that communicate with a database back-end and find that estimates of per-servlet service time converge relatively quickly. Hence the per-servlet estimates can indicate the load a given dynamic request introduces to the system. Both studies then approximate the system load at any given time by summing up the per-request service time estimates for the requests in progress. Load control is triggered if the estimated load in the system is close to the system capacity, which is determined in off-line experiments.

Research on integrating load control into the *database server* has mostly focused on the avoidance of lock thrashing caused by data contention. A database-integrated approach offers the possibility of utilizing more detailed information on the transactions in progress. Rather than simply basing decisions on the number of transactions in progress, the load control can utilize knowledge of the state of the individual transactions (running vs blocked waiting for a lock) and the progress the transactions have made.

Choosing the right approach for implementing overload control involves several trade-offs. Integration into the operating system allows overload control by immediately dropping new requests before occupying any system resources. On the other hand, the advantage of application-level load control is that application-level information, e.g. the expected work to process a given request, can be taken into account. For complex applications like database systems, the application level and the operating system have only limited information of the state of the system, potentially allowing only for coarse-grained load detection and control. However, the more fine-grained approach of integrating QoS mechanisms into the database system comes at the price of modifying a complex piece of software.

Reacting to Overload.   After detecting an overload situation, measures must be taken to reduce the server load. One common approach is to reduce the number of requests at the server by employing admission control, i.e. selectively rejecting incoming requests. An alternative approach is to reduce the work required for each request, rather than reducing the number of requests, by serving lower quality content that requires less resources. The premise for using content adaptation rather than admission control is that clients prefer receiving lower quality content over being denied service completely.

- **Dealing with overload through content adaptation**
  Content adaptation to control overload has first been suggested by Bhatti et al [Abdelzaher and Bhatti, 1999]. Some of the proposed mechanisms apply mostly to static content, e.g. the suggestion to replace large, high resolution images by small, low resolution images to reduce the required bandwidth. Their approaches can also help reduce high load that is due to dynamic content. For example, the authors propose reducing the number of local links in each page, e.g. by limiting the web site's content tree to a specific depth. A smaller number of links in a page affects user behavior in a way that tends to decrease the load on the server.

  The work in [Chen and Iyengar, 2003] shows how to apply the concept of service degradation to dynamic content that is generated by accessing a back-end information systems, such as a database server. They propose to generate a less resource intensive, lower quality version of this type of content, by compromising the freshness of the served data by using cached or replicated versions of the original content.

  Chen et al. implement this notion of service degradation by complementing the high-end database back-end server at a web site with a set of low-end servers that maintain replicated versions of the original data with varying update rates. If the load at the high-end server gets too high, traffic can be off-loaded to the low-end servers at the price of serving more outdated data.

  Li et al. [Li et al., 2003] propose a similar approach for database content that is replicated in data centers across a wide area network. They characterize the dependency between request response times and the frequency of invalidating cached content (and hence the freshness of the cached content) and exploit this relationship by dynamically adjusting the caching policy based on the observed response times.

  A famous example for the application of service degradation in practice includes the way CNN handled the traffic surge at its site on Sept 11, 2001 [LeFebvre, 2002]. CNN's homepage, which usually features a complex page design and extensive use of dynamic content, was reduced to static content with one page containing 1247 bytes of text, the logo, and one image.

- **Dealing with overload through admission control**
  The simplest form of admission control would be to reject all incoming

requests, either in the network stack of the operating system or at the application level, until the load drops below some threshold. There are at least two problems caused by the indiscriminate dropping of requests in this naive approach.

1 The decision to drop a request does not take into account whether the request is from a new user or part of a session that has been lasting for a while. As a result, long sessions are much more likely to experience rejected requests at some point during their lifetime than short sessions. However, it is often the long sessions at an e-commerce server that finally lead to a purchase.

2 The decision to drop a request does not take the resource requirements of the request into account. To effectively shed load through admission control, one ideally wants to drop incoming requests with high resource requirements. On the other hand, despite high load, the server might want to accept a request if this request has very small resource requirements or requires only little service at the bottleneck resource.

The work of Cherkasova et al. [Cherkasova and Phaal, 2002] and Chen et al. [Chen and Mohapatra, 2003] address the first problem by taking session characteristics into account when making admission control decisions. Simply put, if the load at the server exceeds a specified threshold, only requests that are part of an active session are accepted, while requests starting new sessions are rejected. In practice, this approach can be implemented by using cookies to distinguish whether an incoming request starts a new session or is part of a session in progress.

[Elnikety et al., 2004] and [Chen et al., 2001] base admission control decisions on estimates of the service requirements of incoming requests and estimates of the server capacity (determined as described above). The system load at any given time is computed as the sum of the service requirements of all requests in progress. Elnikety et al. admit a new request to the system only if adding its service requirement to the current load does not increase the load beyond the server capacity. Requests that would increase the server load beyond its capacity are stored in a backup queue. Requests are only dropped after the backup queue fills up.

Orthogonal to the above approaches, Welsh et al. [Welsh and Culler, 2003] propose a whole new design paradigm for architecting internet services with better load control that they call SEDA (Staged-event-driven-architecture). In SEDA, Internet services are decomposed into a set of event-driven stages connected with request queues. Each stage can control the rate at which to admit requests from its incoming request queue and decide which requests to drop in the case of excessive load. This approach allows fine-grained admission control. Moreover, combating overload can be focused on those requests that actually lead to a bottleneck (since requests that never enter an overloaded stage are not affected by the admission control).

As mentioned earlier, work for load control in the database community is mostly concerned with avoiding thrashing due to data contention. Database internal methods reduce data contention not only by employing admission control, but also by canceling transactions that are already in progress. The conditions for triggering admission control and the canceling of transactions depends on the state of the transactions in progress. One option is to trigger admission control and transaction cancellation once the ratio of the number of locks held by all transactions to the number of locks held by active transactions exceeds a critical threshold [Moenkeberg and Weikum, 1992]. Another possibility is to apply admission control and cancel an existing transaction if more than half of all transactions are blocked waiting for a lock after already having acquired a large fraction of the locks they require for their execution [Carey et al., 1990]. In both cases, the transaction to be canceled is one that is blocked waiting for a lock and at the same time is blocking other transactions.

5.2 Differentiated quality of service

There are two different types of differentiated quality of service.

- Best effort performance differentiation
  Different classes with different priorities, where higher priority classes should receive better service than lower priority classes.

- Absolute guarantees
  Each class has a concrete QoS goal that it needs to meet, e.g. a latency target specified in number of seconds.

Best effort performance differentiation. Methods for providing best effort performance differentiation typically follow one of the following three approaches:

1. providing different quality of content depending on the priority of a request.

2. changing the order in which requests are processed based on request priorities.

3. adapting the rate at which a request is served according to the request priority.

We first discuss how to implement these approaches for non-database driven requests, and we then turn to the question of how to achieve performance differentiation at a database back-end server.

For non-database driven requests the first two approaches can be implemented as extensions of methods discussed previously for achieving system-wide QoS goals. The first approach can be implemented by applying the methods for content degradation described above, where the degree of content degradation is chosen according to request priorities. The second approach can be implemented as a straightforward extension of any of the mechanisms presented earlier that involve queues. More precisely, the processing order of requests can be changed based on request priorities, by either prioritizing the kernel SYN and listen queue [Voigt et al., 2001], or by prioritizing application internal queues such as those used in the work by [Bhatti and Friedrich, 1999] and by [Ramanathan and Singhal, 2000]. The former approach is limited to the case where class priorities can be determined based on the client IP address, since at this point no application level information is available.

Mechanisms for changing the rate at which requests are processed (approach 3 in the above list) include limiting the number of server processes available to low priority requests and adjusting the operating system priorities of server processes [Eggert and Heidemann, 1999]. The applicability of both of these mechanisms is limited in that they assume a process-based server architecture.

When it comes to database-driven requests, most commercial databases ship with tools that allow the database administrator to assign priorities to transactions in order to affect the rate at which transactions are processed. The implementation of those tools usually relies on CPU scheduling [Rhee et al., 2001, IBM DB2, 2005] and is therefore most effective when applied to CPU-bound workloads.

For database-driven workloads whose performance is limited by data contention, effective service differentiation requires prioritization applied at the lock queues. McWherter et al. [McWherter et al., 2004, McWherter et al., 2005] evaluate different lock scheduling strategies and find that simple reordering of lock queues according to priorities provides a relatively good level of service differentiation. However, to allow for optimal performance of high priority transactions, preemptive lock scheduling policies are necessary, i.e. scheduling policies that allow high priority transactions to abort and restart low priority transactions in case of a lock conflict. McWherter et al. show that naive preemptive policies impose harsh performance penalties onto the low priority transactions due to the large amounts of wasted work introduced by transaction aborts and restarts. They go on to propose a new preemptive lock scheduling policy that is able to balance the cost (in terms of wasted work due to rollbacks) and the benefit of preemptive lock scheduling.

Achieving absolute guarantees.   One approach for achieving absolute delay guarantees is by adapting the approaches for best-effort differentiation (described above) through feedback control. For example, admission control could be used in combination with one of the approaches that maintains internal request queues to adjust the drop rate of low priority requests if the response times of high priority requests are higher or lower than their target. This approach has been shown to work sufficiently well in the presence of only two priority classes, where one is best-effort and one has a delay bound [Ramanathan and Singhal, 2000]. However, multi-class latency targets call for more complex methods.

[Chen et al., 2001] propose the use of priority scheduling in combination with admission control guided by queuing theory to ensure multi-class latency targets. More precisely, requests are scheduled from an application internal queue in strict priority order. The priority of a request is determined by the latency target of its class: requests from classes with low latency targets always have priority over requests from classes with higher latency targets. This scheduling policy implies that the share of the system capacity received by a class equals the total system capacity minus the capacity used up by higher priority classes. The per-class share of the system capacity can be determined based on estimates for request service requirements, the per-class arrival rate, and the overall system capacity. Chen et al. then use known queuing formulas to compute the maximum arrival rate a class can sustain while staying in its delay target and apply admission control to ensure that a class stays within this maximum rate.

The above work focuses only on requests that are not database driven. There is relatively little work in the area of database systems for supporting per class QoS targets. Most work that is concerned with providing performance guarantees is in the large domain of real-time database systems (RTDBMS). The goal in RTDBMS is not improvement of mean execution times for high priority classes of transactions, but rather meeting (usually hard) deadlines associated with each transaction. In achieving this goal RTDBMS often rely on their specialized architecture with features such as optimistic concurrency control mechanisms, which are not available in the general purpose database systems used as web server back-ends.

The existing work in the area of general purpose databases systems for providing multi-class response time goals relies on buffer management strategies [Brown et al., 1993, Brown et al., 1996, Sinnwell and Koenig, 1997]. However, as of now these, there has been little work evaluating these approaches for web-driven database workloads.

References

Abdelzaher, Tarek F. and Bhatti, Nina (1999). Web content adaptation to improve server overload behavior. *Computer Networks: The International Journal of Computer and Telecommunications Networking*, 31(11–16):1563–1577.

Abdelzaher, Tarek F., Shin, Kang G., and Bhatti, Nina (2002). Performance guarantees for Web server end-systems: A control-theoretical approach. *IEEE Transactions on Parallel and Distributed Systems*, 13(1):80–96.

Bhatti, Nina, Bouch, Anna, and Kuchinsky, Allan (2000). Integrating user-perceived quality into web server design. In *Proceedings of the 9th International World Wide Web Conference*.

Bhatti, Nina and Friedrich, Rich (1999). Web server support for tiered services. *IEEE Network*, 13(5):64–71.

Bouch, Anna, Kuchinski, Allan, and Bhatti, Nina (2000). Quality is in the eye of the beholder: meeting users requirements for internet quality of service. In *Proceedings of the SIGCHI conference on Human factors in computing systems*.

Broder, Andrei (1997). On resemblance and Containment of Documents. In *Proceedings of SEQUENCES-97*.

Brown, Kurt P., Carey, Michael J., and Livny, Miron (1993). Managing memory to meet multiclass workload response time goals. In *Proceedings of the Very Large Database Conference*, pages 328–341.

Brown, Kurt P., Carey, Michael J., and Livny, Miron (1996). Goal-oriented buffer management revisited. In *Proceedings of the 1994 ACM SIGMOD Conference on Management of Data*, pages 353–346.

Carey, Michael J., Krishnamurthy, Sanjey, and Livny, Miron (1990). Load control for locking: The 'half-and-half' approach. In *Proceedings of the ACM Symposium on Principles of Database Systems*.

Challenger, Jim, Dantzig, Paul, Iyengar, Arun, Squillante, Mark, and Zhang, Li (2004). Efficiently serving dynamic data at highly accessed web sites. *IEEE/ACM Transactions on Networking*, 12(2).

Challenger, Jim, Iyengar, Arun, and Dantzig, Paul (1999). A Scalable System for Consistently Caching Dynamic Web Data. In *Proceedings of IEEE INFOCOM'99*.

Challenger, Jim, Iyengar, Arun, Witting, Karen, Ferstat, Cameron, and Reed, Paul (2000). A publishing system for efficiently creating dynamic Web content. In *Proceedings of IEEE INFOCOM*.

Chen, Huamin and Iyengar, Arun (2003). A tiered system for serving differentiated content. *World Wide Web*, 6(4).

Chen, Huamin and Mohapatra, Prasant (2003). Overload control in qos-aware web servers. *Computer Networks: The International Journal of Computer and Telecommunications Networking*, 42(1):119–133.

Chen, Xiangping, Mohapatra, Prasant, and Chen, Huamin (2001). An admission control scheme for predictable server response time for web accesses. In *Proceedings of the International World Wide Web Conference (WWW)*, pages 545–554.

Cherkasova, Ludmila and Phaal, Peter (2000). Predictive admission control strategy for overloaded commercial web server. In *Proceedings of the 8th International Symposium on Modeling, Analysis and Simulation of Computer and Telecommunication Systems*, page 500.

Cherkasova, Ludmila and Phaal, Peter (2002). Session-based admission control: A mechanism for peak load management of commercial web sites. *IEEE Transactions on Computers*, 51(6):669–685.

Datta, A., Dutta, K., Thomas, H., VanderMeer, D., Suresha, and Ramamritham, K. (2002). Proxy-Based Accelaration of Dynamically Generated Content on the World Wide Web: An Approach and Implementation. In *Proceedings of SIGMOD-2002*.

Document Object Model - W3C Recommendation (2005). http://www.w3.org/DOM.

Eggert, Lars and Heidemann, John S. (1999). Application-level differentiated services for web servers. *World Wide Web*, 2(3):133–142.

Elnikety, Sameh, Nahum, Erich, Tracey, John, and Zwaenepoel, Willy (2004). A method for transparent admission control and request scheduling in e-commerce web sites. In *Proceedings of the 13th International Conference on World Wide Web*, pages 276–286.

Edge Side Includes - Standard Specification (2005). http://www.esi.org.

Gray, Cary G. and Cheriton, David R. (1989). Leases: An efficient fault-tolerant mechanism for distributed file cache consistency. In *Proceedings of the Twelfth ACM Symposium on Operating Systems Principles*.

IBM DB2 (2005). Technical support knowledge base; Chapter 28: Using the governor. http://www-3.ibm.com/cgi-bin/db2www/data/db2/udb/winos2unix/support/document.d2w/report?fn=db2v7d0frm3toc.htm.

LeFebvre, William. CNN.com: Facing a world crisis. Invited talk at the USENIX Technical Conference, June 2002.

Li, Wen-Syan, Po, Oliver, Hsiung, Wang-Pin, Candan, K. Selcuk, and Agrawal, Divyakant (2003). Engineering and hosting adaptive freshness-sensitive web applications on data centers. In *Proceedings of the twelfth international conference on World Wide Web*, pages 587–598. ACM Press.

McWherter, David T., Schroeder, Bianca, Ailamaki, Anastassia, and Harchol-Balter, Mor (2005). Improving preemptive prioritization via statistical characterization of OLTP locking. In *Proceedings of the 21th IEEE Conference on Data Engineering (ICDE'2005)*.

McWherter, David T., Schroeder, Bianca, Ailamaki, Annastassia, and Harchol-Balter, Mor (2004). Priority mechanisms for OLTP and transactional web applications. In *Proceedings of the 20th IEEE Conference on Data Engineering (ICDE'2004)*.

Moenkeberg, Axel and Weikum, Gerhard (1992). Performance evaluation of an adaptive and robust load control method for the avoidance of data-contention thrashing. In *Proceedings of the Very Large Database Conference*, pages 432–443.

Mohapatra, Prasant and Chen, Huamin (2001). A Framework for Managing QoS and Improving Performance of Dynamic Web Content. In *Proceedings of GLOBECOM-2001*.

Ninan, Anoop, Kulkarni, Purushottam, Shenoy, Prashant, Ramamritham, Krithi, and Tewari, Renu (2002). Cooperative leases: Scalable consistency maintenance in content distribution networks. In *Proceedings of the Eleventh International World Wide Web Conference (WWW2002)*.

Rabinovich, Michael, Xiao, Zhen, Douglis, Fred, and Kalman, Charles R. (2003). Moving Edge-Side Includes to the Real Edge - the Clients. In *Proceedings of Usenix Symposium on Internet Technologies and Systems*.

Ramanathan, P. Bhoj S and Singhal, S. (2000). Web2K: Bringing qos to web servers. Technical Report HPL-2000-61, HP Laboratories.

Ramaswamy, Lakshmish, Iyengar, Arun, Liu, Ling, and Douglis, Fred (2004). Automatic Detection of Fragments in Dynamically Generated Web Pages. In *Proceedings of the 13th World Wide Web Conference*.

Rhee, Ann, Chatterjee, Sumanta, and Lahiri, Tirthankar (2001). The Oracle Database Resource Manager: Scheduling CPU resources at the application level.

Sinnwell, Markus and Koenig, Arnd C. (1997). Managing distributed memory to meet multiclass workload response time goals. In *Proceedings of the 15th IEEE Conference on Data Engineering (ICDE'99)*.

Song, Junehwa, Iyengar, Arun, Levy, Eric, and Dias, Daniel (2002). Architecture of a Web server accelerator. *Computer Networks*, 38(1).

Voigt, Thiemo, Tewari, Renu, Freimuth, Douglas, and Mehra, A. (2001). Kernel mechanisms for service differentiation in overloaded web servers. In *Proceedings of the USENIX Annual Technical Conference*, Boston, MA.

Welsh, Matt and Culler, David (2003). Adaptive overload control for busy internet servers. In *Proceedings of the 2003 USENIX Symposium on Internet Technologies and Systems*.

Yin, Jian, Alvisi, Lorenzo, Dahlin, Mike, and Lin, Calvin (1999). Volume leases for consistency in large-scale systems. *IEEE Transactions on Knowledge and Data Engineering*, 11(4):563–576.

Chapter 6

UTILITY COMPUTING
FOR INTERNET APPLICATIONS

Claudia Canali

University of Parma
Parco Area delle Scienze 181A, 43100 Parma, Italy
claudia@samba.ing.unimo.it

Michael Rabinovich

AT&T Labs - Research
180 Park Avenue, Florham Park, NJ 07932
misha@research.att.com

Zhen Xiao

AT&T Labs - Research
180 Park Avenue, Florham Park, NJ 07932
xiao@research.att.com

Abstract   With the growing demand for computing resources and network capacity, providing scalable and reliable computing service on the Internet becomes a challenging problem. Recently, much attention has been paid to the "utility computing" concept that aims to provide computing as a utility service similar to water and electricity. While the concept is very challenging in general, we focus our attention in this chapter to a restrictive environment - Web applications. Given the ubiquitous use of Web applications on the Internet, this environment is rich and important enough to warrant careful research. This chapter describes the approaches and challenges related to the architecture and algorithm design in building such a computing platform.

Keywords: Utility computing, Web applications, application servers, resource provisioning

1.   Introduction

The past decade saw an exponential growth in the amount of computing power, storage capacity, and network bandwidth. Various applications have been developed that utilize the available computing resources to better serve our society. For business big or small, the IT spending usually constitutes a substantial part of the overall budget. For ordinary people, our daily lives have become more and more computerized: we use computers to communicate with friends, read news, manage finance, etc.

As the demand for computing is increasingly becoming an integral part of our daily lives, a challenge that arises is how to provide reliable, highly available, and affordable computing service to everyone. The computing model as it exists today is far from satisfying these needs. With the rapid decrease of hardware expense, the labor costs have become a major expense in IT spending: the typical monthly salary of a system administrator is higher than the price of a group of high-end PCs. Moreover, as computer systems grow more and more complex, the expertise required to maintain such systems increases rapidly. It can be expensive for many businesses to retain the necessary computer staff. For ordinary home users, dedicated system support is seldom available. If a machine crashes, hangs, or is infected by viruses, significant effort is needed to remedy the situation.

Ideally, we want computing service to be provided like a utility service similar to water and electricity. Clearly, we understand the convenience of existing utility services: if we want to get water, we only need to turn on the tap. Imagine that the electric wires or water pipes in your home had to be "patched" or "rebooted" every so often! A similar approach to computing, where maintenance complexity is outsourced and maintenance costs are shared across a number of customers, would be very desirable.

While realizing the utility computing concept is a very challenging problem in general, we restrict our scope in this chapter to Web applications. Given the ubiquitous use of Web applications on the Internet, we believe that focusing on these applications is an important step towards providing a more generic utility computing service.

We can envision the Web-based utility computing model as a specialized distributed system with "transparency" being a major design objective. Under this model, a business can adjust the resource provisioning for its Internet applications dynamically based on user demand. For example, if an application suddenly becomes popular and receives a large number of user requests, the application service provider will allocate more servers for this application automatically to accommodate the surge in demand. Later, when the popularity of the application decreases, these servers can be re-purposed for other applications. Such a computing model can achieve a much higher degree of efficiency in resource utilization than a traditional model where each application has its dedicated infrastructure. Moreover, the locations of the computing resources are transparent to the end users. In other words, a service provider can optimize its resource provisioning based on any criteria it considers important (e.g. load, proximity, pricing, fault-tolerance, etc.) as long as the end users are provided with a single image of reliable, uninterrupted service.

There are several issues that need to be addressed in developing a utility computing system for Web applications:

- **Application distribution**: How does the system distribute instances of the application across its network? Also, how does the system maintain the consistency of different replicas of an application?

- **Resource isolation**: Given that the platform runs multiple applications on a shared platform, how can the applications be isolated from affecting each other? For example, if one application becomes a victim to a denial of service attack, this should not affect other applications.

- **Application placement**: How much resources should be allocated to an application and where (i.e., in which nodes within the platform) should the application instances be placed? A variety of metrics can be considered here, including: user proximity, server load, billing, security, relocation cost, customer preferences, DNS caching effect[1], etc..

- **Request distribution**: When a user sends a request, where should the system direct the request? A naive approach is to always distribute requests to the closest application servers. However, as we will see later, consideration of other factors is necessary for the stability of the system.

The rest of the chapter is organized as follows. We first give an overview of related work in Section 2. Then we describe a typical architecture for Web applications in Section 3 and explore some alternative architectures for utility computing in Section 4. Section 5 details our framework that allows sharing of servers at the application level. Server clusters and the maintenance of session state are discussed in Section 6 and 7, respectively. Section 8 discusses algorithmic challenges and, in particular, the danger of vicious cycles. Section 9 concludes.

2. Related Work

Related research has been conducted in Web caching, content delivery, and other distributed system areas. The literature is vast on caching and replication of Web objects, consistency maintenance of different replicas, and efficient generation of dynamic responses, with too many sources to cite here. Of special interest is work on "Edge Computing", where the computation is pushed to the edge of the network for better efficiency and performance. For example, several proposals assemble a Web response dynamically at the edge from static and dynamic components [Douglis et al., 1997, ESI, 2005]. Further, the authors and others have developed the *Client-Side Includes* mechanism that pushes the dynamic assembly of the Web response all the way to the browser [Rabinovich et al., 2003b]. As another example, Globule is an object-oriented system that encapsulates content into special Globule objects for replication [Pierre and van Steen, 2001]. Each object can specify its own policy on distribution and consistency maintenance.

Research in grid computing focuses on how to utilize networked computing resources in an efficient manner [Foster et al., 2001]. It shares many common objectives with utility computing. In fact, an approach for implementing scalable Web services using grid technology is described in [Ueda et al., 2005]. Both grid and utility computing represent important directions for further research. Grid technology stresses support for sharing computing resources contributed by different organizations. Utility computing has a special emphasis on transparency and convenience, characteristics necessary for common utility services. An important goal in utility computing is to offload the management of computing resources from individual businesses to a separate organization. Similar to a public utility company that generates electric power and delivers it though the wires, a utility computing company manages the computing resources (e.g. CPU, memory, storage, etc.) in a number of nodes (often referred to as "data centers" in industry) and delivers the computing power through a high speed network. Because implementing the general utility computing concept is difficult, existing approaches concentrate on providing specialized utility services for particular resources, such as storage or database.

In our work, we are exploring a utility computing service that targets a particular class of applications, namely, the Internet applications. The specifics of these applications simplify the problem, yet they are so widely used that a solution targeting just these applications is worthwhile and interesting in its own right. The following are the characteristics of Internet applications that we exploit:

- Client-server computing. Internet applications are inherently client-server. Invocations of an application never result in long-running tasks. These invocation define natural boundaries in computation, and we can limit resource reassignment to these boundaries. Thus, when reassigning resources between applications, we do not need to migrate running tasks, but rather install new instances of an application and uninstall old instances of applications.

- Single carrier. Unlike general grid, we assume that the entire utility computing platform is operated by a single organization which is trusted by the application provider. This simplifies the issues of security and privacy that are challenging in general grid computing [Foster et al., 2001]. This also simplifies the accounting of resource usage and billing.

- Tiered architecture. Internet applications typically use a tiered architecture that relies on centralized core database servers (see Section 3). This simplifies data consistency issues.

3.   A Tiered Architecture of Web Applications

Web applications are usually implemented in a tiered fashion. Typically, three tiers are distinguished as illustrated in Figure 6.1: the first tier includes Web gateways that accepts HTTP requests from users, the second tier contains application servers which execute the application code, and the third tier is database servers containing company data accessed or recorded by the application. Often, the first tier servers act as both Web gateways and applications servers and thus assume some functionality of the second tier. Therefore, the system can be often viewed as consisting of just two tiers: the utility computing tier and the back-end servers tier. This architecture is depicted on Figure 6.2. The utility computing tier includes servers that are operated by the utility computing platform, with the common resources shared appropriately between different services. The utility computing tier includes first and some of the second tier servers. The back-end tier includes servers that are outside the scope of the utility computing platform, with statically allocated resources. These typically include back-end database servers (which are often located on customer sites) and can also include some application servers.

Note that back-end database servers themselves could use some sort of dynamic resource sharing. However, this sharing is done using different mecha-

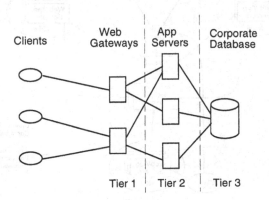

Figure 6.1. A three tier architecture for Internet applications

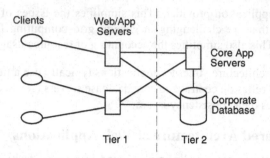

Figure 6.2.   A two-tier architecture for Internet applications

nisms and is outside the scope of this paper. An approach to improve scalability
of back-end databases is described in [Sivasubramanian et al., 2005].

4.   Architectural Alternatives for Utility Computing

The general architecture at a high level is similar to a traditional content
delivery network (CDN) and is shown in Figure 6.3. It includes a request
distribution component which routes client requests to a particular application
server, the utility computing tier of servers, and back-end servers. We assume
that DNS-based request distribution, the prevalent mechanism in traditional

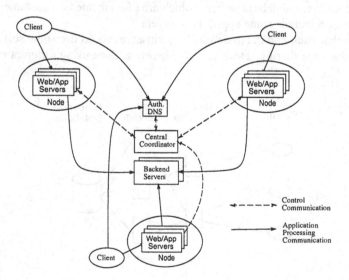

Figure 6.3.   A utility computing platform for Internet applications: high-level view

CDNs, is used here as well. (There are multiple mechanisms for request distribution. See [Cardellini et al., 1999] for a survey.) Consequently, a Web application is identified by the host name of its URLs, with specific requests and parameters forming the remaining parts of the URLs. For example, we may have an on-line stock broker application www.SellStocks.com and a specific request https://www.SellStocks.com/buy?ticker=T.

Before invoking the application, a client needs to resolve the host name, www.SellStocks.com in our example, to an Internet address. Thus, the client sends a DNS query to the platform's authoritative DNS server, which chooses an appropriate server for this query and responds with the corresponding IP address. The client will then contact the chosen application server. Note that due to DNS response caching, several subsequent HTTP requests to this service from the same client, as well as from other clients using the same client DNS server, will also go to the same server. The server processes the request, contacting backend servers using secure communication such as IPsec [IPSec, 2005]. In parallel, each server monitors the demand and performance of its applications. The particular architecture shown contains the central coordinator that collects these measurements and makes periodic policy decisions on replica placement and request distribution. According to these decisions, the coordinator sends instructions to application servers to install or uninstall applications, and request distribution rules to the authoritative DNS server. The coordinator may have other functions such as maintaining consistency of application replicas by propagating updates from the primary server. The specific functionality of the coordinator can vary because some functionality can be implemented in a distributed fashion by application servers directly [Rabinovich et al., 2003a].

Within this general framework, there are several alternatives for architecting the system, depending on the granularity of resource sharing and on the mechanism for request routing between application replicas within one platform node.

In terms of requests routing mechanisms within a node, one possibility is to allow the DNS server select individual application servers when responding to client DNS queries, and send client requests to these servers directly. This is the alternative shown in Figure 6.3. Another possibility is to connect the application servers at each node to a *load-balancing switch* [Rabinovich and Spatscheck, 2001]. The authoritative DNS server in this case selects only a node and sends clients to the corresponding switch. The switch then load-balances received requests among servers that have the requested application.

Turning to resource sharing, one can achieve fine-grained resource sharing when the same application server (such as Tomcat [Tomcat, 2005]) is shared by multiple applications. In this case, applications are installed by simply placing them into appropriate directories on the application server. On the other extreme, resource sharing may occur at the granularity of the whole servers, so each server may belong to only one application at a time. Many application servers offer clustering capabilities which simplify implementation of this approach. Finally, one can use server-grained allocation and clustering technologies as above, but employ virtual machine monitors to run multiple virtual application servers on the same physical machine. We consider these alternatives in more detail next.

5.   Application Server Sharing

An application server can be configured to host multiple applications. In this approach, creating an application replica requires simply putting the application in an appropriate directory on the application server. We implemented a prototype of this approach in our ACDN system [Karbhari et al., 2002, Rabinovich et al., 2003a]. In particular, our implementation showed that the entire system can be implemented on top of the standard HTTP protocol and off-the-shelf application servers. (We used Apache [Apache, 2005] in our prototype, with Fast CGI [FastCGI, 2005] as the implementation mechanism for applications.) Not only does this simplify the adoption of the system, but it also allows easy traversal of firewalls and network address translation devices, and hence permits the deployment of the system over public Internet.

The architecture of the system is shown in Figure 6.4. The system operates in cooperation between the central coordinator and local agents deployed on individual servers. The local agents implement functionalities related to application distribution. They contain sets of CGI scripts, and so are a pure add-on to any standard Web server. Before starting to use a server, the central coordinator invokes its *start-up script*. This script forks a *decision process* that periodically examines every application on the server and decides if any of them must be replicated or deleted. This is due to the fact that replica placement decisions in ACDN are distributed among individual servers: each server makes decisions about the applications that it currently deploys based on its own local usage.

The global central coordinator keeps track of application replicas in the system, collects periodic load reports from servers (by periodically invoking the *load reporter script* on each server), recomputes request distribution policy, communicates this policy to the load-balancing DNS server, and maintains application replicas on all servers consistent with the primary copy (by periodically invoking the *updater script* on each server). The coordinator also gives permission to servers to delete underused application replicas, which ensures that at least one replica of each application remains in the system even in the face of simultaneous decisions to delete the application by all servers. Finally, the central coordinator also answers queries from servers for the least-loaded server in the system. The servers use this information in some of their replica placement decisions.

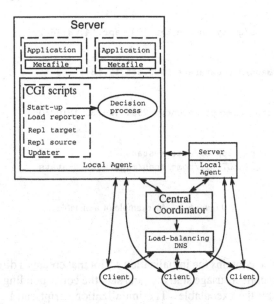

Figure 6.4. ACDN architecture

Although the central coordinator is theoretically a bottleneck, this is not a concern in practice since the amount of processing it does is minimal; it can in fact be physically co-located with the DNS server. The central coordinator is also a single point of failure. However, it is not involved in processing user requests. Thus, its failure only leads to a stop in application migrations or replications and does not affect the processing of requests by the existing replicas. Furthermore, the central coordinator's state can be reconstructed upon its recovery without a halt to processing of user requests.

5.1 Application Distribution Framework

We are not aware of any off-the-shelf support for the application distribution framework with application server sharing. Thus, the system must implement the entire framework itself. The ACDN implementation is based on the concept of a metafile, inspired by ideas from the area of software distribution such as the technology by Marimba Corp. [Hoff et al., 1999].

Conceptually, the metafile consists of two parts: the list of all files comprising the application along with their last-modified dates; and the *initialization script* that the recipient server must run before accepting any requests. Figure 6.5 provides an example of a metafile that represents a map-drawing application consisting of three files: an executable file that is invoked on access to this application and two data files used by this executable to generate responses.

```
<FILE>
  /home/apps/maps/query-engine.cgi 1999.apr.14.08:46:12
</FILE>
<FILE>
  /home/apps/maps/map-database 2000.oct.15.13:15:59
</FILE>
<FILE>
  /home/apps/maps/user-preferences 2001.jan.30.18:00:05
</FILE>
<SCRIPT>
  mkdir /home/apps/mapping/access-stats
  setenv ACCESS_DIRECTORY /home/apps/maps/access-stats
</SCRIPT>
```

Figure 6.5. An example of a metafile

The metafile also contains the initialization script that creates a directory where the application collects usage statistics and sets the corresponding environment variable used by the executable. The initialization script can be an arbitrary shell script. When the initialization script is large, the metafile can include just a URL of the file containing the script. The metafile is treated as any other static Web page and has its own URL.

Using the metafile, all the tasks of the application distribution framework can be implemented over standard HTTP. The process of replica creation is initiated by the decision process on an ACDN server with an existing replica. It involves the *replication target script* on the target server and the *replication source script* at the source server. Once the replication is complete, the replica target script informs the central coordinator about the new application replica. The central coordinator recomputes its request distribution policy based on the new replica set and sends the new policy to the DNS server.

Replica deletion is initiated by the decision process on a server with the application replica. This server first must notify the central coordinator of its intention to delete its replica. The coordinator in turn needs to notify the DNS server to exclude this replica from its request distribution policy. After that, the coordinator can grant the ACDN server the permission to delete the replica. The actual deletion, however, happens after a delay corresponding to the DNS time-to-live (TTL) value associated with the domain name of the application. This is to accommodate residual requests that might arrive due to earlier DNS responses still cached by the clients.

Application migration can be implemented as replication followed by deletion. We will describe consistency maintenance in the following subsection. More details on these tasks in application distribution can be found in [Rabinovich et al., 2003a].

5.2 Consistency Maintenance

Maintaining consistency of application replicas is important for the correct functioning of our system. There are three problems related to replica consistency:

- **Replica coherency:** An application typically contains multiple components whose versions must be mutually consistent for the application to function properly. A replica for an application can become incoherent if it acquired updates to some of its files but not others so that there is a version mismatch among individual files.

- **Replica staleness:** A replica for an application can become stale if it missed some updates to the application.

- **Replica divergence:** Replica divergence occurs when multiple replicas for an application receive conflicting updates at the same time.

The metafile described earlier provides an effective solution to the replica staleness and coherency problems. With the metafile, whenever some objects in the application change, the application's primary server updates the metafile accordingly. Other servers can update their copies of the application by downloading the new metafile as well as all modified objects described in the metafile. This ensures that they always get the coherent new version of the application. Thus, the metafile reduces the application staleness and coherency problems to the cache consistency of an individual static page – the metafile.

In our system, application updates are performed asynchronously with requests arrivals: a server keeps using the current version of an application to serve user requests until the new version is ready. This is to avoid a prohibitive delay to the user perceived latency that will otherwise occur. If an application has stringent consistency requirements, it may use application level redirection to redirect user requests to the server with the most recent version of the application.

The final problem related to replica consistency is replica divergence. It happens when an application is updated simultaneously at multiple replicas. In general, there are two types of updates:

- **Developer updates:** These are updates introduced by the application authors or maintainers. It can involve changes to the application code (e.g. software upgrades or patches) or to the underlying data (e.g. updates of product pricing).

- **User updates:** These are updates that occur as a result of user accesses (e.g. updates during e-commerce transactions). It involves changes to the data only.

Our system avoids replica divergence by restricting developer updates to only one application replica at any given time. This replica is called the *primary* replica for the application. It ensures that all the updates to the application can be properly serialized. The coordinator keeps track of the location of the primary replica for each application. The idea is similar to classic token-based schemes where a token circulates among a group of servers and only the server that holds the token can perform updates. For updates that occur as a result of user accesses, we either assume they can be merged periodically off-line (which is the case for commutative updates such as access logs) or that these updates are done on a shared back-end database and hence they do not violate replica consistency.

5.3   Discussion

One advantage of application server sharing is that replication of an application is often very quick. Indeed, unless the deployment of a new application instance requires server restart (which may happen when the application requires server reconfiguration, such as changing a log file), it involves little more than just copying and unpacking a tar file with the application components. In our prototype, this takes in the order of single seconds. Another advantage is the efficient utilization of server resources. When one application does not utilize the server, spare capacity can be used by another application.

Unfortunately, application server sharing also has a very serious drawback, namely, poor resource isolation. Different applications sharing the same server can affect each other in a variety of undesirable ways. If one application falls a victim to a denial of service attack, other applications on the same server will be affected. If one application fails and manages to hang the computer, other applications will be affected (this is referred to as fault isolation). No matter how well an application is hardened against hacker break-ins, its resiliency may be affected by a less secure application that shares the same server. Finally, billing and resource usage accounting is more complicated with server sharing. Although much work has been done on addressing these issues, they continue to impede this approach.

6.   Server Clusters

To avoid the poor resource isolation of application server sharing, the platform can always run each application instance on its own dedicated application server. The dedicated server approach further allows two main alternatives, depending on whether or not each application server runs on a dedicated physical machine. We consider these alternatives next.

6.1   Physical Server Clusters

In this approach, the system runs each application replica on a dedicated application server, and each application server on a dedicated physical machine. In other words, the system performs resource allocation at physical server granularity. This scheme allows almost absolute resource isolation. Furthermore, this approach is well-supported by existing server cluster technologies including WebLogic [BEA, 2005], WebSphere [IBM WebSphere, 2005], and Oracle's Application Server 10g [Oracle, 2005]. In particular, server clusters implement consistency management for the application, and quick fail-over capabilities with session state replication discussed later in Section 7. For example, WebLogic allows all replicas of an application that run within the same node to form a cluster, and all clusters of this application to form a single *domain*. Then WebLogic can ensure the consistency of all the application replicas in the domain, while performing fast fail-overs only among servers within each cluster.

On the other hand, this scheme is characterized by slow resource allocation. Indeed, moving a physical machine from one application cluster to another involves restarting the application server on this machine in the new cluster, which may take around a minute in our experience on a popular commercial application server. Another disadvantage of this scheme is that it may result in poor resource utilization. An application replica ties up an entire physical machine. So if this application does not fully utilizes the machine, the spare capacity is wasted.

6.2   Virtual Server Clusters

One can try to combine the advantages of the application server sharing and physical server sharing by utilizing the virtual machine technology. This technology allows several *virtual machines* to share the same physical machine. Each virtual machine provides an illusion of a dedicated machine to the operating system and any application running on it. In fact, different virtual machines sharing the same physical machine can run different operating systems. The operating systems running on the virtual machines are called *guest* operating systems, and the operating system that runs directly on the physical machine and enables the virtual machine sharing is called the *host* operating system.

With the virtual machine technology, one can still run each application replica on a dedicated application server, and use existing clustering technologies to facilitate replication and fail-over. However, each application server can now run on a virtual rather than a physical machine. Virtual machines allow very good resource and fault isolation, and at the same time permit good resource utilization, because the physical resources are shared among virtual machines (and hence applications).

Yet this approach is not without its own limitations. A technical issue is the overhead of running a guest operating system on top of the host operating system. A study using an open source implementation of a virtual machine monitor found that system calls on a Linux guest OS running on top of a Linux host OS experienced up to a factor of 30 slowdown [Jiang and Xu, 2003]. The same study found that sample applications ran 30-50% slower in this environment. Commercial virtual machine implementations such as VMWare apparently are more efficient, with performance penalties within single percentage points on standard benchmarks [Devara, 2005]. However, these products are expensive – the price of a VMWare license can be higher than that of a typical physical machine. Thus, the economy from better resource utilization can only be realized if a significant number of virtual machines can be multiplexed on the same physical server.

7.   Session State Maintenance

Many Internet applications require prolonged sessions between the client and the server, which span multiple HTTP interactions. Figure 6.6 shows an example of a user browsing an on-line travel site. A session in this case may

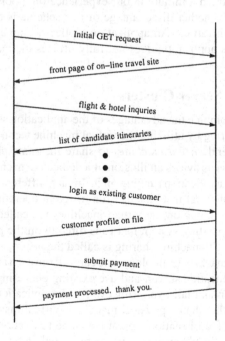

Figure 6.6.   An example session of an on-line travel Web site.

involve a sequence of interactions including flight and hotel inquiry, filling out the itinerary and customer profile, and finally completing the payment. Each inquiry depends on the context of the session, and the server must maintain session state from one interaction to the next. In the simplest case, this state can be maintained on the client using cookies. However, in most cases, the session state is too large or too valuable to hand off to the client, and servers maintain it themselves.

The need to maintain session state poses two challenges to the utility computing platform. First, for the duration of the session, requests from the same client must go to the same server that holds the session state. We refer to this behavior as *client stickiness*. Second, fulfilling the promise of high reliability requires the recovery of the session state from a failed server. Being able to move from a failed to an operational server in the middle of a session is referred to as *session fail-over*.

The basic idea to address both problems is the same: it involves encoding the identity of the server that has the session state into the response to the client and making the client include this information in subsequent requests. The easiest way to accomplish this is through the use of cookies as illustrated in Figure 6.7 (top diagram): when a server receives the first request of the session, it chooses a secondary server with the application and replicates the session state to the secondary server. In response to the client, the original (also called the primary) server sets a cookie, which records the identity of both the primary and secondary servers for this session.

Because clients cache DNS responses and load-balancing switches (if used) try to select the same server for the same client, client stickiness will be upheld most of the time. However, should a different server receive a subsequent request in the session, the request's cookie will have all the information to resolve the situation. If the original server is up, the new server can use an HTTP redirect to send the client to the original server and thus enforce client stickiness.[2] If the original server is down, the new server can implement session fail-over by obtaining the session state from the secondary server and taking over processing of this and all subsequent requests for this session. This is illustrated in the bottom diagram of Figure 6.7. (The cookie is modified accordingly to record the identity of the new server in place of the original server.) Because session fail-over requires tight communication between the original and the secondary servers for continuous state updates, it is typically only used between servers in the same site.

8.   Algorithmic Challenges

As already mentioned, a utility computing platform for Internet applications involves two main algorithms: the algorithm for application replica placement

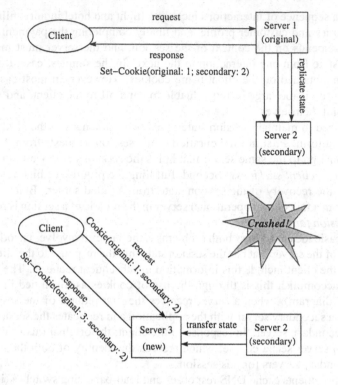

Figure 6.7.   Support for client stickiness and session fail-over.

and the algorithm for distributing requests among those replicas. Designing these algorithms involves several alternatives. The first choice has to do with the extent of central coordination in the algorithm. The architecture of Figure 6.3 assumes a central point for request distribution (DNS) and so it is natural to assume that the request distribution algorithm be centralized. However, the choice is less clear for the replica placement algorithm. While a centralized algorithm has a view of the entire system and can result in highly optimized placement, a distributed algorithm can be more scalable.

Within the centralized approach to replica placement, another fundamental choice is between a greedy incremental approach and a global optimization approach. The greedy approach utilizes feedback from monitoring the application to make incremental adjustments in replica placement. The global optimization approach uses monitoring results to periodically solve a mathematical optimization formulation from scratch, independent of the current configuration [Jain and Vazirani, 2001]. In our work, we explored a distributed approach to replica placement, where each server examines its own access log and decides whether any of its applications should be migrated or replicated to another server [Rabinovich et al., 2003a].

In this chapter, rather than describing a specific algorithm, we concentrate on an interesting issue faced by any such algorithm, namely, the possibility of vicious cycles. Because the issues we discuss are independent of the number of servers in each node of the platform, we assume for simplicity that each node contains only one server.

8.1   Vicious Cycles in Request Distribution

As an example of vicious cycles in request distribution, consider a natural request distribution algorithm as follows:

> The authoritative DNS server resolves a query to the closest non-overloaded server, where overload is determined by a load threshold, e.g., 80% server utilization.

Assume that the system periodically reconsiders the request distribution policy based on performance observed prior to the decision. This simple and intuitive algorithm can easily lead to oscillations due to a herd effect [Dahlin, 2000]. Consider, for example, two servers with an application replica and assume that all demand comes from the vicinity of server 1 (see Figure 6.8, top diagram). At decision time $t1$, the system realizes that server 1's utilization is over 80% and stops using it for future requests. Consequently, utilization of server 1 declines and by the next decision time $t2$ drops below 80%. At time $t2$ the system finds that server 1 is no longer overloaded and starts using it again for all future requests. Its load increases and by the next decision time exceeds 80%, and the cycle repeats. As a result, the request distribution is never optimal: either too many requests are sent to an overloaded server 1, or too many requests are sent to a distant server 2.

8.2   Vicious Cycles in Replica Placement

Replica placement algorithms also face a danger of vicious cycles, even with resource allocation at the whole server granularity. Assume for example that content providers are billed based on resource usage and, in particular, on server usage, a natural billing model for the utility computing paradigm. Then, customers will want to keep the number of application replicas at the minimum, and it is natural for them to specify how much demand for a given application replica warrants the extra costs of having the replica. We will refer to this demand as the *demand threshold*. At the same time, customers do not want the servers running their application to be overloaded, and hence it is natural for them to specify (or rely on the platform's default values of) a load of existing servers that should trigger the deployment of additional replicas. We will refer

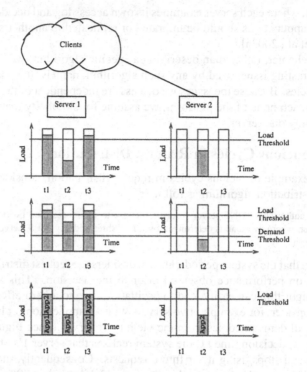

Figure 6.8. Vicious cycle examples in request distribution (top diagram), replication (middle diagram), and migration (bottom diagram).

to this load as the *load threshold*. The demand threshold is expressed in such units as request rate or traffic volume, and the load threshold in CPU or memory utilization. Normally, the load threshold governs overload-induced replication and demand threshold affects the proximity-induced replication.

However, if the two thresholds are not carefully coordinated, the scenario illustrated on Figure 6.8 (middle diagram) may occur. As in the previous example, assume that all demand comes from the proximity of server 1, and the demand overloads this server. Then, the algorithm may trigger replication. If no spare server is available in server 1's platform node, the new replica may be created elsewhere. However, because the new replica is more distant to the demand, the request distribution favors the old replica and sends only excessive load to server 2. Then, depending on the computational requirements of the application, the excessive load may translate to the request rate that is below the demand threshold. If this happens, the replica placement algorithm can later drop the new replica, reverting to the initial configuration.

The bottom diagram in Figure 6.8 illustrates another vicious cycle that may occur in a platform with shared servers. Again, consider a platform with two servers, server 1 and 2, where server 1 is shared between two applications. Assume all demand for both applications comes from server 1's own region, and its overall load is above the load threshold. Further, consider the case where the demand on each application separately does not exceed the demand threshold, and so replication is not possible. To offload the server, the system may resort to migration, for example, moving application 1 to server 2. Once this is done, neither server is overloaded. Then, the next time the application placement is considered, the system may migrate application 1 back to server 1 because this would improve client proximity.

To prevent such cycles, the replica placement algorithm must predict how dropping a replica would affect the load on remaining servers in the second example above, or how migrating a replica would affect the load on the recipient server in the last example. Because the load on individual servers depends on request distribution algorithm, direct load prediction introduces an interdependency between the request distribution and replica placement algorithms. Such prediction is especially difficult for fine-grained server sharing. Indeed, the load imposed by an application replica on its server depends on the load distribution among all application replicas, and the load distribution depends on the aggregate server load. Thus, the prediction of load due to one application may depend on other applications sharing the same servers.

9.   Conclusion

This chapter focuses on the issues and challenges in building a utility computing service for Web applications. We described a typical architecture for Web applications and discussed some alternatives in designing a utility computing platform for running these applications. In particular, we discussed tradeoffs in various approaches to resources sharing in this environment, and the issue of session state maintenance, the issue that is very important in practice but often overlooked in research in the Web performance arena. We also presented some fundamental algorithm issues in building such a platform, namely, how to avoid vicious cycles during request distribution and application replication.

Notes

1. As we will see later in the chapter, residual requests due to DNS caching may hinder the removal of the last replica for an application in a data center.

2. The only subtlety is that the new server must specify the (virtual) IP address of the original server in the redirect response. Indeed, if the new server used the host name for the redirection, the client would have to resolve this name again, and the cycle would repeat.

References

The Apache HTTP Server Project (2005). http://httpd.apache.org.

BEA Web Logic (2005). http://www.bea.com.

Cardellini, Valeria, Colajanni, Michele, and Yu, Philip S. (1999). Dynamic load balancing on web-server systems. *IEEE Internet Computing*, 3(3):28–39.

Dahlin, M. (2000). Interpreting stale load information. *IEEE Transactions on Parallel and Distributed Systems*, 11(10):1033–1047.

Murthy Devaraconda (2005). Personal Communication.

Douglis, Fred, Haro, Antonio, and Rabinovich, Michael (1997). HPP: HTML macro-preprocessing to support dynamic document caching. In *Proceedings of the USENIX Symposium on Internet Technologies and Systems*, pages 83–94.

ESI–Accelerating E-business Applications (2005). http://www.esi.org/.

FastCGI (2005). http://www.fastcgi.com/.

Foster, I., Kesselman, C., and Tuecke, S. (2001). The anatomy of the grid: Enabling scalable virtual organizations. *International J. Supercomputer Applications*, 15(3).

Hoff, A. Van, Payne, J., and Shaio, S. (1999). Method for the distribution of code and data updates. U.S. Patent Number 5,919,247.

IBM WebSphere Software Platform (2005).
http://www-306.ibm.com/software/info1/websphere.

IPsec (2005).
http://www.ietf.org/html.charters/ipsec-charter.html.

Jain, Kamal and Vazirani, Vijay V. (2001). Approximation algorithms for metric facility location and k-median problems using the primal-dual schema and lagrangian relaxation. *Journal of the ACM*.

Jiang, Xuxian and Xu, Dongyan (2003). SODA: A service-on-demand architecture for application service hosting utility platforms. In *Proceedings of the 12th IEEE International Symposium on High Performance Distributed Computing*.

Karbhari, Pradnya, Rabinovich, Michael, Xiao, Zhen, and Douglis, Fred (2002). ACDN: a content delivery network for applications. In *Proceedings of ACM SIGMOD (project demo)*, pages 619–619.

Oracle Application Server (2005). http://www.oracle.com/appserver.

Pierre, Guillaume and van Steen, Maarten (2001). Globule: a platform for self-replicating Web documents. In *Proceedings of the 6th International Conference on Protocols for Multimedia Systems*, pages 1–11.

Rabinovich, M. and Spatscheck, O. (2001). *Web Caching and Replication*. Addison-Wesley.

Rabinovich, Michael, Xiao, Zhen, and Aggarwal, Amit (2003a). Computing on the edge: A platform for replicating Internet applications. In *Proceedings of* the Eighth International Workshop on Web Content Caching and Distribution.

Rabinovich, Michael, Xiao, Zhen, Douglis, Fred, and Kalmanek, Chuck (2003b). Moving edge-side includes to the real edge—the clients. In *Proceedings of the 4th USENIX Symposium on Internet Technologies and Systems.*

Sivasubramanian, Swaminathan, Alonso, Gustavo, Pierre, Guillaume, and van Steen, Maarten (2005). GlobeDB: Autonomic data replication for web applications. In *Proceedings of the 14th International World Wide Web Conference.*

Tomcat, The Apache Jakarta Project (2005). http://jakarta.apache.org/tomcat.

Ueda, Ryoichi, Hiltunen, Matti, and Schlichting, Richard (2005). Applying grid technology to Web application systems. In *Proceedings of the IEEE Conference on Cluster Computing and Grid.*

Chapter 7

PROXY CACHING
FOR DATABASE-BACKED WEB SITES

Qiong Luo

Department of Computer Science
The Hong Kong University of Science and Technology
Clear Water Bay, Kowloon, Hong Kong
luo@cs.ust.hk

Abstract   Database-backed web sites face great challenges in performance and scalability, due to the large and growing amount of online activity at these sites. To address this performance and scalability problem, we study research issues in improving common proxy caching techniques for database-backed web sites. The key insight of the work in this area is to add some query processing capability to web proxies so that they can share the workload of the backend database server. We discuss alternatives and considerations on adding a query processing capability to a web proxy using our work as examples. We find that it is feasible and useful to have web proxies perform advanced caching beyond exact URL matching for database-backed web sites.

Keywords: Active query caching, database-backed web sites, proxy caching

1.   INTRODUCTION

Database-backed web sites have emerged as an important class of database applications. With the maturity of commercial database engines and rapid developments of the Internet and Web, these web-based applications have drawn more and more attention in the database community [Bernstein et al., 1998, Mohan, 2001]. Due to the large and growing Internet population, a major problem that these web sites face is performance and scalability.

One approach that the networking community created for improving the web scalability and performance is web-caching proxies. These proxies can bring the content closer to the users and share the web server workload. While caching proxies are widely deployed on the Internet and improve the performance significantly for some web sites, they are generally ineffective for database-backed web sites. This ineffectiveness is because common proxies only cache static web objects, while user requests to database-backed web sites often contain queries and the resulting pages are generated dynamically from the backend databases.

Considering the scalability problem of database-backed web sites and the advantages of common caching proxies to static web objects, we survey the state of the art on enhanced proxy caching techniques that can work for database-backed web sites efficiently. We find that the main technique used to improve proxy caching for database-backed web sites is to add some query processing capability to the proxies. This technique is used in the early work of our own [Luo et al., 2000, Luo and Naughton, 2001, Luo et al., 2002] as well as in the later work by others [Altinel et al., 2003, Amiri et al., 2003].

In this section, we first describe web caching proxy servers and database-backed web sites in more detail, and then motivate the research on adding a query processing capability to web proxies.

1.1   Database-Backed Web Sites

Many web sites managing significant amounts of data use a database system for storage. For example, Amazon.com and eBay. The dotted box in Figure 7.1 illustrates a basic configuration of such a site. Because a database-backed web site acts as a whole, we also call it a *database web server*. When users access such a web site, clicking on a URL or filling in a form in the HTML page they are viewing causes an application at the web site to generate database queries. After the database server executes these queries, the application at the web site takes the result of the queries, embeds it in an HTML page, and returns the page to the user. Under heavy loads, the database system can become the bottleneck in this process.

Compared with traditional database applications such as OLTP (On-Line Transaction Processing), database-backed web sites have a few interesting fea-

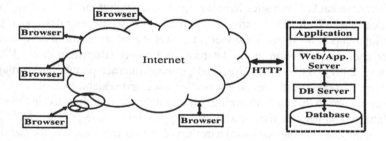

Figure 7.1.   A Database-Backed Web Site

tures. First, users on the Internet seem to have a high degree of tolerance to out-of-date data or inconsistent data. Second, the read-to-write ratio (total number of read requests over total number of write requests) is high. Even at large e-commerce sites, a read-to-write ratio of 60 is not surprising [Conner et al., 2000]. Third, the workload at the sites seems to vary significantly over time, and peaks and surges are common. All of these characteristics create opportunities for proxy caching for database-backed web sites.

1.2   Web Caching Proxy Servers

Web caching proxy servers are everywhere on the Internet (illustrated in Figure 7.2). Depending on the context, they are called accelerators, edge caches, firewalls, mirror servers, reverse proxies, web caches, and so on. They are deployed by the Internet content providers, Internet service providers, Content Delivery Network services, and network administrators. These proxies are used for increasing availability, sharing server workload, and improving response time. The major advantages of the caching proxies include easy deployment, flexibility, and cost effectiveness. However, even the state-of-the-art dynamic content caching in proxies has been mostly limited to exact match of specified URLs or simple result equivalence checking.

There are two kinds of deployment for these proxies. One is a traditional deployment (or *forward proxy caching*), in which the proxies serve the content from the Internet to a group of users. In this case, the web sites being proxied may not even know of the existence of the proxies. An example is a campus proxy for speeding up the Internet access of local users. The other is *reverse proxy caching*, in which the proxies serve a specified set of servers to general Internet users. In this case, the web sites and the proxies can collaborate. For example, web sites often set up their own reverse proxies or contract with the Content Delivery Network services to use theirs.

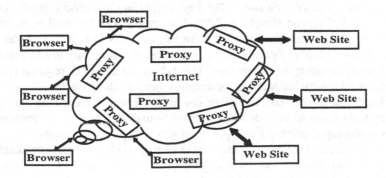

Figure 7.2.   Web Caching Proxy Servers

In either deployment scheme, the function of these proxies is simple - if a proxy has seen a URL before, and has cached the page corresponding to that URL, it can return the cached page without accessing the web site that is the "home" for that page. This simple logic apparently is insufficient for caching web pages generated from database-backed web sites. One reason is that users may submit a large number of different queries such that proxies have to cache those many pages if the exact-match style of caching is used.

Finally, application servers are also closely related to web proxy servers. A web proxy server is a special web server, in that it either serves files from its local cache, or forwards the requests to the original web servers and then serves the files from the servers to the users. In comparison, an application server is another kind of special web server, in that it does not serve files but executes programs such as servlets and EJBs (Enterprise Java Beans). If we enhance a web proxy to let it execute programs, it then has the function of an application server. On the other hand, if we distribute application servers to the edge of the Internet, they become enhanced edge servers. Because database-backed web sites usually use application servers and these application servers already have the underlying framework for executing programs, advanced caching in application servers is also attractive for database-backed web sites. In the remainder of this chapter, we will include application servers into the category of web proxies unless otherwise specified.

1.3   Adding Query Processing Capabilities to Proxy Servers

Having described database-backed web sites and web caching proxies, we motivate the work on adding query processing capabilities to proxy servers.

Since database-backed web sites need workload sharing, and traditional web proxies can share the workload of serving static web pages, we explore how to enhance web caching proxies so that they can efficiently provide caching for database-backed web sites. The key insight in our previous work [Luo et al., 2000, Luo and Naughton, 2001, Luo et al., 2002] as well as in later work by others [Altinel et al., 2003, Amiri et al., 2003] is that, in order to share the workload of database-backed web sites, it is necessary to add a query processing capability to web proxies. This is because the HTTP requests going to the database-backed web sites eventually become database requests to the backend database servers. Therefore, one effective way to reduce the requests going to the backend database servers would be to distribute at least some query processing capability to the web proxy servers or application servers.

Adding a query processing capability to web proxies has several advantages. The major advantage is that, by distributing the database capability to the large number of edge servers on the Internet, we can potentially scale up a database-backed web site to handle arbitrarily heavy workloads. Another advantage is that because of the geographically distributed nature of these proxies, it is easier to add customizations such as quality of service for the web sites. Finally, it is more cost-effective and more flexible to deploy and maintain these web proxies since they are simpler software than the backend database servers are.

Along with its advantages, adding a query processing capability to proxies also poses several research questions. First, how can we add this capability to the proxies or application servers? We need to address the collaboration issues between the proxies and the original web sites. Second, what query processing capability do we add? It can range from the traditional function of answering queries that exactly match the cached queries, to more sophisticated query caching techniques or data caching solutions. Moreover, how can we take advantage of the characteristics of queries submitted to database-backed web sites? Third, how do these enhanced caching proxies perform? On one hand, adding a query processing capability makes the proxies more powerful; on the other hand, it brings certain performance overhead. In addition, consistency maintenance is always an issue for caching.

This chapter attempts to answer the above questions through a survey of the work in the area. As we are more familiar with our own work, we will mostly use it as examples. More specifically, there are three parts of our research, each of which touch upon all the three questions while focusing on different aspects of the general problem of adding a query processing capability to web proxies. The three parts of our research include (1) active query caching in an existing enhanced web proxy [Luo et al., 2000], (2) form-based proxy caching [Luo and Naughton, 2001], and (3) middle-tier database caching for e-Business [Luo et al., 2002].

In the first part of our research [Luo et al., 2000], we demonstrate that a simple query processing capability can be added dynamically to an existing enhanced web proxy server in the form of a piece of Java code sent from the web server. The focus is to utilize the existing proxy framework to address the collaboration issue with the original web servers, and to add as little as possible overhead to the proxy. Consequently, we have developed query containment-based active query caching for simple selection queries within this framework. It improves the proxy cache hit ratio on a search engine trace, but there is a performance overhead associated with code mobility.

In the second part of our research [Luo and Naughton, 2001], we present a new form-based proxy framework, and use this framework to explore the performance tradeoffs among exact match style of caching, query containment based caching, and full semantic caching. The focus is to study what query processing capability should be added to the proxy for database-backed web sites. Our key observation is that HTML form-based interfaces, which are commonly provided by database-backed web sites, enable a useful variety of query caching techniques that would be impractical or impossible for arbitrary SQL queries. As a result, our query caching techniques take advantage of the common structure that an HTML form enforces on the queries that it generates. We have identified a common class of web queries, which we term Top-N Conjunctive Keyword Queries, and studied form-based caching techniques for them.

In the last part of our work [Luo et al., 2002], we investigate middle-tier database caching for e-Commerce applications, in which a full-fledged database server is deployed at the application server as a database cache. The focus is performance. This is mainly because of the requirements of e-Commerce applications, and the concerns about the long code path of an industrial-strength database engine. Using an e-Commerce benchmark on real systems, we show that the performance overhead of adding this cache is negligible when a web site is under heavy workload, and that using this cache the scalability and performance of the web site can be improved significantly.

In summary, our research indicates that proxy caching techniques beyond exact-match URL matching are feasible and useful for web-based database applications. In this chapter, we describe mainly the first part of our work, active query caching, as a simple example to discuss the research questions in this area.

1.4   Chapter Outline

The remainder of this chapter is organized as follows. In Section 2, we use our work as examples to illustrate the considerations in adding query processing capabilities to proxies. In Section 3, we discuss some other work related to this topic. In Section 4, we draw our conclusions and outline future research directions.

2.   Adding Query Processing to Proxies

In this section, we present issues and alternatives of adding a query processing capability to web proxies in order to offload the database server and to improve the performance of the database-backed web sites. We use our own work as examples and reference other work as necessary.

2.1   How to add a query processing capability

The first question about adding a query processing capability to proxies is how. A straightforward way is to install a database server at each proxy so that the proxy can use the local database server to perform some query processing over its cached data. Indeed, this approach is suitable for certain network environments, e.g., a corporate network, where the proxy and the database-backed web site are in close collaboration. The effectiveness of this approach has been demonstrated in the existing work such as the DBCache [Luo et al., 2002, Altinel et al., 2003], the DBProxy [Amiri et al., 2003] and the MTCache [Larson et al., 2004].

However, there are times that a proxy and a database-backed web site have little collaboration, as in forward proxy caching. In such a non-collaborative environment, adding a query processing capability, or in general, adding any server-desired functionality to the proxy, is a real problem. In our previous work on active query caching [Luo et al., 2000], we utilized an experimental, enhanced web proxy server called an *active proxy* [Cao et al., 1998] to facilitate the collaboration.

The active proxy follows the Active Cache scheme, in which a server is allowed to provide a piece of custom Java code (called a *cache applet*) to be associated with a document. These cache applets get their name because of their similarity to Java applets, which are lightweight, originate from a server, and can communicate with the server. An active proxy can cache these cache applets from web servers, along with their documents. For efficiency or security reasons, the active proxy has the freedom of not invoking a cache applet but directly forwarding a request to the server. However, if the proxy regards a request as a hit in its cache, it will invoke the corresponding cache applet to do the specified processing rather than just sending back the cached document to the user.

Through the cache applets, web servers gain more control over how proxies should behave upon the user requests addressed to the servers. For example, servers can ask the proxy to send them log information about user accesses, which are considered precious to servers. In addition, servers can execute other important policies such as consistency maintenance through cache applets while the proxy keeps its hands off. The other benefit to servers, in which we are more interested, is that servers can migrate some tasks to active proxies when needed and these tasks may even involve generating dynamic content at proxies.

In our approach, the database-backed web site collaborates with the active proxy by passing simple query processing ability to the proxy when needed, through a *query applet*. Figure 7.3 shows the system architecture along with the handling process of the prototype system we developed. The shaded parts represent the components that we implemented.

In this system, we used a modified version of the active proxy [Cao et al., 1998], which was originally developed on the CERN httpd code base from W3C (http:///www.w3c.org/). The modifications included allowing CGI requests with query strings in GET or POST methods to be cached, and loosening certain security inspections and resource limits on cache applets. We also used a CERN httpd as the web server. The database server was the IBM DB2 Universal Database Server V5.2 with a JDBC driver.

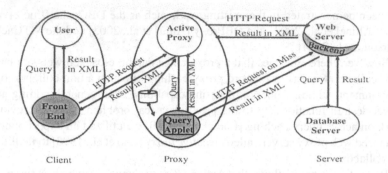

Figure 7.3. System Architecture

As illustrated in Figure 7.3, the three components we have implemented are the query front-end, query applet, and query back-end. They reside on the client side, the proxy (after the proxy gets the applet from the server), and the web server correspondingly. When a user submits a query to the query front-end, the front-end program will convert the user query into an HTTP request and send it to the proxy. The proxy then examines the URL to see if it is a cache hit at the proxy. If it is a cache hit and the server URL has a corresponding query applet in the proxy, the proxy will invoke the query applet. Otherwise, the proxy will forward the request to the web server.

On the web server, the query back-end program transforms an HTTP request into a SQL query and sends it through JDBC to the back-end database. It then retrieves result tuples from the database server, wraps them into an XML file with an XML representation of relational data, and sends the XML file to the proxy. If the server decides to send a query applet to the proxy, the query back-end program will send a query applet header along with the query result.

If a query applet header is sent to the proxy along with the document, the proxy will obtain the applet from the server and associate it with the server form URL. The next time the proxy receives a request to the server form URL with a query, it will invoke the corresponding query applet. The query applet maintains a mapping between the cached queries and their corresponding results. When the query applet is invoked upon a request, it extracts the query from the request parameters and examines its own cache. If a new query is the same as a cached query, the cached result will be returned; if the new query is more restrictive than a cached query, it is then evaluated on the result of the cached query, and new query results are generated and sent back to the user. Otherwise, the query applet forwards the request to the web server and caches the query and result from the server before passing the result to the client.

In practice, one HTTP request may be transformed into several SQL queries or involve more complex operations at the server side. However, the proxy does not need to know about it because all it sees is single table views expressed by forms. In addition, in our implementation, we only dealt with XML files not HTML files. If HTML pages are needed, servers can modify the query applet code to generate the HTML.

In our implementation, each query applet corresponds to a form URL at a web server and so it answers all the queries submitted to that form. When multiple query applets are present at the proxy, each of them manages its own query cache.

In summary, dynamically adding simple query processing ability to proxies is feasible and flexible. Nevertheless, we will see that this dynamicity and flexibility comes at a price of runtime overhead in our initial implementation with the Active Proxy. Compared with this dynamic approach, the static approaches of adding query processing capabilities to proxies require more setup effort, e.g., describing query statement templates [Luo and Naughton, 2001] or creating tables to be cached [Luo et al., 2002, Altinel et al., 2003, Amiri et al., 2003, Larson et al., 2004]. The amount of the setup effort depends on how much query processing ability to add as well as the requirements on performance and data consistency.

2.2 What query processing capability to add

Related to how to add a query processing capability, the next question is what query processing capability to add in order to improve proxy caching for database-backed web sites. Again, a straightforward approach is to put a full-fledged database server at the proxy so that a full SQL (Structured Query Language) processing capability is added to the proxy. The additional advantage of this approach is that the proxy gets the full features of a database server such as transaction management and concurrency control [Luo et al., 2002, Altinel et al., 2003, Larson et al., 2004]. However, the downside is that these features have performance implications and that sometimes it is unnecessary to have a full SQL query processor at the proxy.

Let us take our previous work [Luo et al., 2000] as an example again to illustrate our considerations on what query processing capability to add in the context of the Active Proxy. Our goal was to answer as many queries as possible at the proxy while keeping the overhead of the query applet low. A straightforward function of the query applet would be to cache the query results at the proxy and return the results to users when they ask queries that are identical to a cached query. We call this *passive query caching*. To further reduce the workload on the server, we have added two more functions to the query applet - query containment checking and simple selection query evaluation. Having these two functions, the query applet can perform *active query caching*, where the proxy not only answers queries that are identical to a cached query, but also answers queries that are more restrictive than a cached query.

Query Caching Scheme.   We chose caching at the query level rather than at the table level or semantic region level for a number of reasons. The most prominent reason is its low overhead, which is crucial to the proxy. The queries that database web servers allow users to submit are usually form-based. At the proxy, these form-based queries are treated as selection queries with simple predicates over a single table view whose columns are the form attributes. This simplifies query containment checking and query evaluation at the proxy because the actual queries on the back-end database schema at the server may be much more complex. For instance, queries submitted through a search form of an online bookstore may be viewed as selections with some title, author, and price range predicates on a virtual table books.

Moreover, the query level granularity fits well in the Web context. Firstly, each query corresponds to an individual user request so that later refinement queries from a user can be answered easily based on earlier queries. Secondly, if there are some hot queries during a period, many queries can be answered from the results of these hot queries. Finally, caching individual queries is convenient for possibly maintaining user specific information and generating tailored results for individual users.

In contrast, table level caching does not seem to apply naturally for the active proxy. It requires the proxy to get the base data, store all of it, translate simple form queries into complex SQL queries on base data, and evaluate them at the proxy. These requirements makes table level caching unsuitable for the active proxy, with the resource consumption and proxy autonomy considered. However, table level caching becomes appropriate when a full-fledged DBMS is deployed as a database cache for an application server [Luo et al., 2002, Larson et al., 2004].

Another alternative would be semantic caching ([Dar et al., 1996]), which has a finer granularity than query level caching and has the nice feature of non-redundancy. However, this advantage does not come for free. The expense of checking overlap among regions, coalescing regions, splitting queries among regions, and merging regions into the final query result is a lot more expensive than simple query containment checking and selection query evaluation. More importantly, it requires closer collaboration with the original server to get the remaining base data when answering a cache-intersecting query at the proxy. The small size of web query results causes region fragmentation and constantly triggers coalesce. Finally, it is complex to determine how current a coalesced region is in cache replacement. Nevertheless, when queries are not arbitrary but have the same structure due to their submission from HTML forms, the complexity of semantic caching is greatly reduced [Luo and Naughton, 2001].

Query Containment Checking. Query containment testing for general conjunctive queries is NP-complete [Chandra and Merlin, 1977]. However, there are polynomial time algorithms for special cases [Ullman, 1989]. For simple selection queries, which are a very special case, we identify a sufficient condition to recognize subsumed queries efficiently. The worst-case time complexity of our query containment recognition algorithm is polynomial in terms of the number of simple predicates in the Conjunctive Normal Form (CNF) query condition. The following illustrates our checking criteria.

Query1	Query2
SELECT List1	SELECT List2
From Table1	From Table2
WHERE WhereCondition1	WHERE WhereCondition2

Given the above two queries, Query1 and Query2, whose where-conditions have been transformed into the CNF by our query processor, we recognize that Query1 is subsumed by Query2 (we call Query2 a *super-query* of Query1, and Query1 a *subsumed query* of Query2) if all of the following conditions are satisfied:

- Table1 and Table2 are the same table (view).

- Fields in List1 are a subset of the fields in List2.

- WhereCondition1 is more restrictive than WhereCondition2.

- If WhereCondition1 and WhereCondition2 are not equivalent, all fields that appear in WhereCondition1 also appear in List2.

In general, the last condition is not a necessary condition. We specify it because eventually we need to evaluate the subsumed query on the query result of the super-query. Thus, we must guarantee that the result of the super-query contains all fields that are evaluated in the where-condition of the subsumed query. Therefore, we use the current sufficient condition for simplicity and efficiency.

At this point, our query containment checking reduces to the problem of recognizing if one CNF condition is more restrictive than another CNF condition. The following two propositions further reduce the problem to testing if a simple predicate is more restrictive than the other simple predicate.

Proposition 1. Given $WhereCondition1 = P1$ AND $P2$ AND $\ldots Pm$, $WhereCondition2 = Q1$ AND $Q2$ AND $\ldots Qn$, $WhereCondition1$ is more restrictive than $WhereCondition2$ if $\forall i, 1 \leq i \leq n, \exists k, 1 \leq k \leq m, Pk$ is more restrictive than Qi.

Proposition 2. Given $Pk = R1$ OR $R2$ OR $\ldots Rx$, $Qi = S1$ OR $S2$ OR $\ldots Sy$, Pk is more restrictive than Qi if $\forall v, 1 \leq v \leq x, \exists u, 1 \leq u \leq y, Rv$ is more restrictive than Su.

Finally, given two simple predicates $F1$ $op1$ $c1$, $F2$ $op2$ $c2$, where $F1$ and $F2$ are field names, $c1$ and $c2$ are constants, and $op1$ and $op2$ are numeric comparison operators or string LIKE operator, it is straightforward to test whether the former is more restrictive than the latter. Intuitively, $F1$ and $F2$ should be the same field, and the relationship among the two operators $op1$, $op2$, and the two constants $c1$, $c2$, should make the first predicate more restrictive than the second one. For example, $price \leq 10$ is more restrictive than $price \leq 20$.

Query Cache Management.   Since our cached query definitions use the CNF format, we transform user queries into CNF and store the AND-OR tree format at the proxy. The query cache consists of these query trees and their corresponding query results. A mapping table (called a *query directory*) is used to record the correspondence between queries and their results. Note that query definitions and their actual results are stored separately because query containment checking can be done by only comparing query trees and does not need the actual query results.

There is a choice whether we should cache the query result of a subsumed query. One argument for caching it is that we may answer new queries faster on it because its result size is smaller relative to its super-query's. The problem is the large redundancy between this query and its already cached super-query. Since web queries tend to return a small size of records per request, we chose not to cache any subsumed queries of a cached query. As a result, cache hit ratio is improved because of less data redundancy in the cache.

There are three cache replacement schemes available in our implementation: LFU (Least Frequently Used), LRU (Least Recently Used), and benefit-based. The first two are straightforward. The third one is a combination of the other two in that it uses reference frequency and recency as parameters of the benefit. We define the benefit of a cached query as a weighted sum of the reference frequency and the recency. The heuristic behind the benefit metric is intuitive. If a query was used as a super-query for many new queries, it is likely that it will serve later queries also. This is a reflection of spatial locality - that query covers a hot region of data. If a query was used as a super-query recently, we believe that it will probably be used as a super-query for subsequent queries soon if users are doing query refinement. This can be thought as temporal locality.

2.3   Performance

After answering questions about how to add a query processing capability and what query processing capability to add to a proxy for caching for database-backed web sites, we then examine the performance issues in such an enhanced proxy. In general, we see that adding a query processing capability induces certain performance overhead to the proxy. However, when there are locality patterns in the workload, active caching using the query processing capability reduces server workload and improves the performance and scalability of the web site. We still use results from our previous work on active query caching as examples to illustrate the performance issues.

On an Excite Query Trace.   Many web caching studies have used real traces [Douglis et al., 1997, Wills and Mikhailov, 1999] or synthetic web workloads [Barford and Crovella, 1998]. However, these real traces or generated workloads usually do not include CGI script requests or queries. What we really needed was a trace that recorded user queries to a specific database web server. Fortunately, we obtained a real query trace of around 900K queries over one day from a popular search engine, Excite (http://www.excite.com/).

Search engines have their special features that may differ from other database web servers. The main differences include: their search forms conceptually have only one column (keywords), their query results are URLs, and these results are sent page by page upon user requests. Despite these differences, we feel that it is useful to investigate the effect of active query caching on search engine queries, because these queries represent the patterns of web user queries to a popular class of web information sources.

A recent study [Markatos, 2000] has shown that 20-30% of the 900K queries in the Excite query trace can be answered from cache if the query results are cached. This caching is equivalent to the exact-match passive query caching. We set out our experiments to examine how much more opportunity exists for active query caching. We transformed the search engine trace into a SQL query stream on two columns - keywords and page number - and ran it through our query caching module. All experiments started from a cold query cache. The cache replacement policy was LRU.

We compared hit ratios of active query caching and passive query caching at various cache sizes. The legend 20KQ passive in Figure 7.4 means passive query caching using a cache of 20K queries. Other legends have similar meanings. If we use the assumption of 4KB query result page [Markatos, 2000], the query cache sizes of 20KQ, 50KQ, and 100KQ can be roughly translated into 80MB, 200MB, and 400MB correspondingly, which is smaller than previously used cache sizes between 500MB to 2GB [Markatos, 2000].

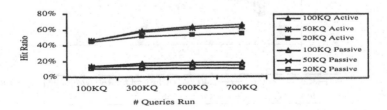

Figure 7.4.   Query Cache Hit Ratios on Excite Query Trace

From Figure 7.4 we can clearly see that there is much more opportunity for active query caching than passive query caching. The whole trace of 900K queries has 29% non-unique queries, which is the upper limit of the cache hit ratio of passive query caching with a sufficiently large cache. In contrast, we can achieve 45%-65% hit ratios in active query caching with a small to medium size cache. Notice that active query caching with a query cache size of 20K queries outperforms passive query caching with a cache size of 100K queries by a factor of three.

On Synthetic Data and Queries.   No matter how high the cache hit ratios are, they are just part of the story. To identify the performance implications of our prototype system, we generated synthetic relational data and query streams for our experiments and measured actual query response times.

In the following experiments, we ran the CERN httpd server and the active proxy on two Sun Ultra10 300Mhz machines with the SunOS 5.6 Operating System. The DB2 server was running on a Pentium Pro 200MHz PC with Windows NT Operating System. All machines were in our department local area network and query caches started cold.

First, we measured the response times of a query stream when the workload of the database server was varied. We used a stream of 100 queries to measure the response time when the database server was idle, when it had 6 other clients, and when it had 12 other clients. The measurements were made with R20, R40 and R60 query streams (RX reads that X% queries are subsumed queries). In this experiment, a cache size of 10 queries was sufficient to achieve the performance gain, since we generated subsumed queries immediately after their super-queries. In practice, the cache size should be sufficiently large to ensure that the super-queries are in the cache when their subsumed queries arrive.

The response time variation in Figure 7.5 shows the impact of subsumed query distribution on response times with active query caching. Unlike the case

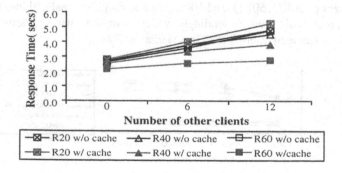

Figure 7.5.   Response Time as Server Workload Varies

without caching, the query response times with active query caching decrease when the percentage of subsumed queries increases. For the R40 and R60 query streams, the response time for the proxy with the cache is better than the case without the cache, which means these hit ratios offset the query applet overhead at the proxy. Although for the R20 query stream the response time with caching is slightly more than the response time without a cache, the proxy with caching can still share 20% of the workload with the server.

We then measured the breakdown of the time spent by a query at the various stages in a query applet. We considered the three cases - the new query could be identical to a query in the cache, be a subsumed query to a cached query, or need to be evaluated at the server. Load + Save refers to the time that the query applet takes to load the query directory from disk when it is invoked by the proxy plus the time taken for saving the query directory to disk before it finishes. Check + Evaluate includes the time that the query applet spends checking the query cache to see if the new query is subsumed by any cached query, and the time that the query applet spends evaluating the query from the cache. Finally, Fetch from Server is the time spent sending the query to the server and waiting for the result back, if the query cannot be answered from the cache. The results are shown in Figure 7.6.

The breakdown of the time spent at the various stages in the query applet shows that even in an intra-departmental network, the time taken to contact the server and get the result back is a major portion of the total time. We observed that roughly 40% of the Fetch from Server time was spent at the database server and the remaining 60% was spent on the network. The time taken to evaluate the subsumed query from the result of the cached query is considerable. This time was also seen to be proportional to the size of the result file of the cached query as the file I/O of reading this file and writing the result back was seen to dominate this time. Within Check + Evaluate the portion of the time taken to check and find a super-query is quite small. Finally, we see that the time

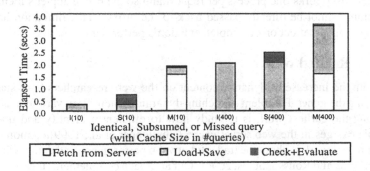

Figure 7.6.   Breakdown of Time Spent in the Query Applet

taken to load and save the cache directory is considerable. This time increases almost linearly with increase in cache size, and becomes comparable to the time taken to contact the server when the cache size is 400 queries. This cost can be avoided if the query directory could be kept in memory in the active proxy. However, this is not feasible in the existing implementation of the active proxy.

2.4   Summary

In this section, we have studied the three questions about adding a query processing capability to proxies in order to improve proxy caching for database-backed web sites. We used our active query caching work as an example to discuss these questions. We have shown the opportunities that active query caching brings through a trace-driven simulation on real query traces and a prototype implementation. We have also identified the performance bottlenecks in the existing implementation of the active proxy framework.

The focus of our previous work has been to utilize the existing active proxy framework to achieve the collaboration with a database web server. Therefore, we make as little as possible modifications to the framework, and encapsulate query containment checking and simple query processing logic into a query applet. Because the original server sends this code dynamically, it maintains close control over the requests at the proxy, and the proxy maintains its own simplicity despite of the possible complexity in the mobile code.

The active proxy made it possible for us to study active query caching at proxies for database web servers. Nevertheless, since the active proxy was in its prototype stage and active query caching was a brand-new application of the active proxy, we learned a few lessons from our experience. One major issue is that the active proxy does not provide any memory-resident structure for cache applets. This is not a limitation of the Active Cache protocol but is related to the CERN proxy design and implementation. Two factors are involved. One is that the CERN proxy does not have memory-resident cache. The other is that CERN proxy forks one process per request and so the cache applet's memory structure cannot be directly passed back to the proxy. This limitation had a strong negative effect on our implementation's performance.

3.   Related work

With the increase of dynamic content on the web, researchers have started studying the general problem of caching dynamic content from various aspects. Among the earliest work is to study how to efficiently identify and update obsolete pages in the web server cache [Challenger et al., 1999]. Among the most recent work is about the tradeoff between performance and data freshness [Labrinidis and Roussopoulos, 2004]. Our approach complements these server-side techniques because it addresses the problem in the context of web proxies and aims at sharing database web server workload and reducing network traffic. In this sense, DBProxy [Amiri et al., 2003] is most related to our work except it intercepts SQL statements from the JDBC driver and thus has full knowledge about the base data schema and the SQL queries.

Caching dynamic content at proxies has also been studied in [Smith et al., 1999]. Their approach allows web content providers to specify result equivalence in generated documents so that the proxy can utilize the equivalence to return a cached result to a new request. Most recently, several groups have also worked on caching and replication for data-intensive web sites [Candan et al., 2001, Datta et al., 2002, Li et al., 2003, Tang and Chanson, 2003, Gao et al., 2005]. However, they do not consider database query containment or evaluate subsumed query at the proxy.

Unlike other proxy caching schemes, which only cache non-executable web objects, the Active Cache scheme [Cao et al., 1998] allows servers to provide a piece of Java code (called a cache applet) associated with a document. Compared with the declarative nature and limited scope of the Dynamic Content Caching Protocol [Smith et al., 1999], the Active Cache scheme provides a simple and flexible interface to web servers at the price of a possible overhead associated with the mobile code.

Most recently, several companies have proposed an open standard ESI (Edge Side Includes). Edge Side Includes (ESI) is a simple mark-up language used to define Web page components for dynamic assembly and delivery of Web applications at the edge of the Internet. It is more advanced than the Active Cache Protocol in the sense that it includes specifications for the mark-up language, cache-control headers in the HTTP messages, as well as a library for usage of ESI tags with JSP applications. Recent work [Rabinovich et al., 2003] has been done on pushing ESI to web clients.

Finally, our active query caching can be viewed as a special case of answering queries using views [Levy et al., 1995] in the database field, if we consider cached queries as materialized views. However, these views come and go dynamically because of the nature of caching. Moreover, as a first step of query caching at web proxies, we only consider answering a query using one view instead of multiple views and thus reduce the problem to simple query containment checking. Both IBM's DBCache [Altinel et al., 2003] and Microsoft's MT-Cache [Larson et al., 2004] focused more on answering complex SQL queries at the middle-tier database cache.

4. CONCLUSIONS

Dynamic content caching has received an increasing amount of attention from both academia and industry. Database-backed web sites will continue to be one of the major sources of dynamically generated web content. In this chapter, we have explored several important aspects of advanced proxy caching specifically for database-backed web sites.

4.1 Put It All Together

As an example, we have used our early work on active query caching [Luo et al., 2000] to illustrate the issues in adding query processing capabilities to web proxies for caching for database-backed web sites. To give the reader a wider view of the issues in this area, we compare it with two other pieces of our work, Form-Based Proxy [Luo and Naughton, 2001], and DBCache [Luo et al., 2002]. The central point of each of these three pieces is adding a query processing capability to a proxy. Nevertheless, they differ significantly in various aspects such as research focus, targeted workloads, framework, and caching schemes. The comparison is shown in Table 7.1.

It would be ideal if there were such a proxy caching scheme with the best attributes of all schemes: handling all sorts of workloads, maintaining cache consistency, having a short code path, requiring little server collaboration, fitting with various framework, and possibly migrating from one place to another dynamically! Unfortunately, most of the attributes in the table are related to one another. For example, targeted workloads, queries handled, and caching schemes; caching schemes, length of code path, updates/consistency, and required server collaboration; length of code path and code mobility.

Table 7.1. Comparison of the Three Pieces of Our Research Work

Attributes	Active Query Caching	Form-Based Proxy	DBCache
Research Focus	Collaboration with the server	Caching schemes	Performance study
Targeted Work-loads	Web searches, browsing	Form-based Web searches, browsing	E-Commerce
Queries Handled	Simple selections	Top-N Conjunctive Keyword queries	Full SQL
Caching Scheme	Query-containment based active caching	Form-based variety of active caching	Full table caching
Proxy Framework/ Application Server	Existing research prototype	Open source + home-grown code	Commercial Product
Code Mobility	Yes	Maybe	No
Length of Code Path	Moderate	Short	Long
Updates/ Consistency	Maybe	Maybe	Yes
Required Server Collaboration	Moderate (Providing query applets)	Depends (Providing query templates + maybe remainder)	High (Providing data + SQL processing)

More specifically, if the length of code path of the added query processing capability is as long as that of a full-fledged DBMS (DBCache), it is natural that the cache can handle a full set of SQL as well as updates and consistency maintenance. Then it is hard to mobilize the code, as what was done with the query applets in the active proxy framework in Section 2. Moreover, with full SQL processing capability, table level caching is a natural choice, but table level caching in turn requires that the backend database server to provide the base data as well as to answer arbitrary queries on the uncached tables. This is probably only feasible for caches within the same organization. In addition, because of the long code path, a full-fledged DBMS serving as a cache will not improve the response time significantly unless the backend is heavily loaded and the cache is not.

In comparison, when the targeted applications are web searches with form-based interfaces, the caching scheme can take advantage of the query templates, in other words, the common structure that forms enforce on the queries. As a result, the proxy with form-based active caching needs the server collaboration up to the level of providing the query templates, and possibly remainder query processing if full semantic caching is desired. With the short code path, the caching code can answer a query much faster than the backend does, especially when the backend is heavily loaded. In addition, it is possible to move the code around dynamically and port to other platforms easily.

Similar to the form-based proxy, the target applications in the active proxy are web searches with little transactional semantics. However, different from the form-based proxy, the active proxy focus on enabling code mobility. Consequently, the query containment-based caching scheme and simple selection queries were chosen for low overhead and minimum server collaboration. The lightweight code can be sent dynamically from the server to the proxy, which is still attractive considering the autonomy and various changes of web sites. Nevertheless, the security and resource concerns at the proxy need to be addressed in order to reduce the performance overhead associated with the code mobility.

4.2 Possibilities for Future Work

There are several lines of future work. In the area of hosting mobile code at the active proxy, we suggest a shared memory structure between the proxy and the query applet to alleviate the performance overhead. Application servers have already adopted this kind of process model. Using more advanced interfaces than the Java Native Interface between the Java mobile code and the C-code base of the proxy might be beneficial to the performance as well.

In terms of the query cache management, utilizing indices on the query directory or other techniques would further reduce the time of query containment checking and query evaluation. Cache replacement policies and cache consistency always have more issues to study. We can also use our form-based framework to study caching for classes of queries other than the top-N conjunctive keyword queries.

Future work on extending the DBCache prototype includes handling special SQL data types, statements, and user-defined functions. We are also investigating alternatives for handling updates at the front end. Usability enhancements, such as cache performance monitoring, and dynamically identification of candidate tables and subsets of tables for caching are important directions for us to pursue.

At a thirty thousand feet level, I still believe that the mobile code approach is useful in some context of caching. One reason is that code has better encapsulation mechanism than declarative ways such as ESI, and web sites may appreciate this "privacy" more than having to write their policies into HTML pages or HTTP messages. Proxies can improve their performance for database query caching by adding a common query caching capability to their own framework, and leave the customization part of caching to mobile code from individual web sites.

With respect to what query processing capability to add at the proxies, I feel that while commercial DBMS products have been in advance in this area for application servers, we still need a more lightweight approach so that it can be really pushed widely throughout the Internet. Industrial-strength DBMS's have the advantage of large user bases, abundant development tools, and powerful functionalities. However, the usability and maintainability issues still need more attention. More importantly, it is not clear that web-based applications all require full-fledged DBMS's as a database cache. In contrast, lightweight approaches probably can take more advantage of locality patterns in the workloads, and improve end-to-end performance better for ordinary web applications.

In summary, the explorations in this chapter have set the stage for building a unified proxy caching framework for database-backed web sites. We can study various caching techniques for different workloads once the framework is ready, and gain more insights into challenging problems. It is our hope that the query processing capability will eventually be distributed to the millions of edge servers on the Internet, and advanced caching techniques will enable database-backed web sites to serve more and more Internet users faster and faster.

References

Altinel, Mehmet, Bornhövd, Christof, Krishnamurthy, Sailesh, Mohan, C., Pirahesh, Hamid, and Reinwald, Berthold (2003). Cache tables: Paving the way for an adaptive database cache. In *VLDB*, pages 718–729.

Amiri, Khalil, Park, Sanghyun, Tewari, Renu, and Pamanabhan, Sriram (2003). Dbproxy: A dynamic data cache for web applications. In *ICDE*, pages 821–831.

Barford, P. and Crovella, M. E. (1998). Generating representative web workloads for network and server performance evaluation. In *Proc. Performance '98/ACM SIGMETRICS '98*.

Bernstein, Philip A., Brodie, Michael, Ceri, Stefano, DeWitt, David J., Franklin, Michael J., Garcia-Molina, Hector, Gray, Jim, Held, Gerald, Hellerstein, Joseph M., Jagadish, H. V., Lesk, Michael, Maier, David, Naughton, Jeffrey F., Pirahesh, Hamid, Stonebraker, Michael, and Ullman, Jeff D. (1998). The asilomar report on database research. In *SIGMOD Record 27(4)*, pages 74–80.

Candan, K. Selcuk, Li, Wen-Syan, Luo, Qiong, Hsiung, Wang-Pin, and Agrawal, Divyakant (2001). Enabling dynamic content caching for database-driven web sites. In *SIGMOD Conference*.

Cao, Pei, Zhang, Jin, and Beach, Kevin (1998). Active cache: Caching dynamic contents on the web. In *Proc. IFIP International Conference on Distributed Systems Platforms and Open Distributed Processing (Middleware '98)*.

Challenger, Jim, Iyengar, Arun, and Dantzig, Paul (1999). A scalable system for consistently caching dynamic web data. In *Proc. IEEE INFOCOM*.

Chandra, Ashok K. and Merlin, Philip M. (1977). Optimal implementation of conjunctive queries in relational data bases. In *Conference Record of the Ninth Annual ACM Symposium on Theory of Computing*, pages 77–90.

Conner, Mike, Copeland, George, and Flurry, Greg (2000). Scaling up e-business applications with caching. In *DeveloperToolbox Technical Magazine*.

Dar, Shaul, Franklin, Michael J., Jonsson, Bjorn, Srivastava, Divesh, and Tan, Michael (1996). Semantic data caching and replacement. In *VLDB*.

Datta, Anindya, Dutta, Kaushik, Thomas, Helen, Vandermeer, Debra, Suresha, and Ramamritham, Krithi (2002). Proxy-based acceleration of dynamically generated content on the world wide web: An approach and implementation. In *SIGMOD*.

Douglis, Fred, Feldmann, Anja, Krishnamurthy, Balachander, and Mogul, Jeffrey (1997). Rate of change and other metrics: a live study of the world wide web. In *Symposium on Internet Technology and Systems*. USENIX Association.

Gao, Lei, Dahlin, Mike, Nayate, Amol, Zheng, Jiandan, and Iyengar, Arun (2005). Improving availability and performance with application-specific data replication. *IEEE Transactions on Knowledge and Data Engineering*, 17(1):106–120.

Labrinidis, Alexandros and Roussopoulos, Nick (2004). Exploring the tradeoff between performance and data freshness in database-driven web servers. *The VLDB Journal*, 13(3):240–255.

Larson, Per-Ake, Goldstein, Jonathan, and Zhou, Jingren (2004). Transparent mid-tier database caching in sql server. In *ICDE Conference*, pages 177–189.

Levy, Alon Y., Mendelzon, Alberto O., Sagiv, Yehoshua, and Srivastava, Divesh (1995). Answering queries using views. *PODS*.

Li, Wen-Syan, Po, Oliver, Hsiung, Wang-Pin, Candan, K. Selçuk, and Agrawal, Divyakant (2003). Freshness-driven adaptive caching for dynamic content web sites. *Data and Knowledge Engineering*, 47(2):269–296.

Luo, Qiong, Krishnamurthy, Sailesh, Mohan, C., Pirahesh, Hamid, Woo, Honguk, Lindsay, Bruce G., and Naughton, Jeffrey F. (2002). Middle-tier database caching for e-business. In *SIGMOD*, pages 600–611.

Luo, Qiong and Naughton, Jeffrey F. (2001). Form-based proxy caching for database-backed web sites. In *VLDB*, pages 191–200.

Luo, Qiong, Naughton, Jeffrey F., Krishnamurthy, Rajasekar, Cao, Pei, and Li, Yunrui (2000). Active query caching for database web servers. In *WebDB*, pages 92–104.

Markatos, Evangelos P. (2000). On caching search engine query results. In *Proceedings of the fifth International Web Caching and Content Delivery Workshop*.

Mohan, C. (2001). Caching technologies for web applications (tutorial). In *VLDB*.

Rabinovich, Michael, Xiao, Zhen, Douglis, Fred, and Kalmanek, Chuck (2003). Moving edge-side includes to the real edge—the clients. *USENIX Symposium on Internet Technologies and Systems*.

Smith, Ben, Acharya, Anurag, Yang, Tao, and Zhu, Huican (1999). Exploiting result equivalence in caching dynamic web content. In *Proc. of 1999 USENIX Symp. on Internet Technologies and Systems*.

Tang, Xueyan and Chanson, Samuel T. (2003). Coordinated management of cascaded caches for efficient content distribution. In *ICDE*, pages 37–48.

Ullman, Jeffrey D. (1989). Principles of database and knowledge-base systems, volume II. *Computer Science Press*, pages 877–907.

Wills, Craig E. and Mikhailov, Mikhail (1999). Examining the cacheability of user-requested web resources. In *Proc. of the 4th International Web Caching Workshop*.

III

STREAMING MEDIA DELIVERY

Chapter 8

GENERATING INTERNET STREAMING MEDIA OBJECTS AND WORKLOADS

Shudong Jin
Computer Science Department
Case Western Reserve University
jins@cwru.edu

Azer Bestavros
Computer Science Department
Boston University
best@cs.bu.edu

Abstract   Characterization and synthetic generation of streaming access workloads are fundamentally important to the evaluation of Internet streaming delivery systems. GISMO is a toolkit for the generation of synthetic streaming media objects and workloads that capture a number of characteristics empirically verified by recent measurement studies. These characteristics include object popularity, temporal correlation of request, seasonal access patterns, user session durations, user interactivity times, and variable bit-rate (VBR) self-similarity and marginal distributions. The embodiment of these characteristics in GISMO enables the generation of realistic and scalable request streams for use in benchmarking and comparative evaluation of Internet streaming media delivery techniques. To demonstrate the usefulness of GISMO, we present a case study that shows the importance of various workload characteristics in evaluating the bandwidth requirements of proxy caching and server patching techniques.

Keywords: Streaming media delivery, performance evaluation, Internet characterization

1.   Introduction

The use of the Internet as a channel for the delivery of streaming (audio/video) media is paramount. This makes the characterization and synthetic generation of streaming access workloads of fundamental importance in the evaluation of Internet streaming delivery systems. While many studies have considered the characterization and synthesis of HTTP workloads [Almeida et al., 1996, Arlitt and Williamson, 1996, Barford et al., 1999, Breslau et al., 1999, Crovella and Bestavros, 1996, Cunha et al., 1995, Gribble and Brewer, 1997, Jin and Bestavros, 2000, Padmanabhan and Qiu, 2000, Barford and Crovella, 1998, SPECweb96, 1996], just to name a few, very few studies focused on characterizing streaming media workloads [Acharya et al., 2000, Almeida et al., 2001, Chesire et al., 2001, Padhye and Kurose, 1998, Cherkasova and Gupta, 2002, Veloso et al., 2002, van der Merwe et al., 2002, Costa et al., 2004, Li et al., 2005], and just two [Jin and Bestavros, 2001, Tang et al., 2003] have tried to generate representative streaming media workloads. Because HTTP requests and streaming accesses are different, HTTP request generators are not suitable for generating streaming access workloads. These differences include the duration of the access, the size of the objects, the timeliness requirements, *etc.*

In the absence of synthetic workload generators, and in order to evaluate the performance of streaming access techniques, one has to seek alternatives, such as using real traces, or using analysis/simulation under simplifying and often incorrect assumptions (*e.g.*, using independent reference model, sequential access, *etc.*). Indeed, these alternatives have been used in prior work on caching and on patching [Hua et al., 1998, Gao and Towsley, 1999], for example. While the use of such alternatives allows analysis and performance evaluation, the resulting conclusions may not be accurate enough, and certainly could not be reliable enough to assess performance when conditions under which the traces were collected (or modeling assumptions made to simplify analysis) are violated. For example, when a limited trace is used in a trace-driven simulation, it may not be possible to generalize the conclusions of such a simulation when the system is subjected to scaled-up demand, or when the distribution of some elements of the trace (*e.g.*, size and popularity distributions of objects) are changed. Synthetic workload generators have the advantage of being able to produce traces with controllable parameters and distributions. The challenge is in ensuring that such synthetic workload generators reflect (in a parameterizable fashion) known characteristics of streaming media and their access patterns.

This chapter overviews GISMO—a tool for synthesizing streaming access workloads that exhibit various properties observed in access logs and in real traces. One of the salient features of our work is the independent modeling of both session arrival processes and individual session characteristics. For session arrival processes, we use a Zipf-like distribution [Breslau et al., 1999, Zipf, 1929] to model reference correlation due to streaming object popularity. For individual sessions, we use a model that exhibits rich properties, including session durations, user interactivity times, VBR self-similarity and heavy-tailed marginal distributions. These properties have been observed and validated by studies on streaming access workload characterization. Using GISMO, we are able to generate synthetic workloads with parameterizable characteristics. To demonstrate the usefulness of GISMO, we present results from a case study comparing the effectiveness of recently proposed proxy caching and server patching techniques. We show how workload characteristics affect the performance of these techniques.

2.   Related Work

HTTP Workload Characterization.   Workload characterization is fundamental to the synthesis of realistic workloads. Many studies [Almeida et al., 1996, Arlitt and Williamson, 1996, Barford et al., 1999, Breslau et al., 1999, Cunha et al., 1995, Gribble and Brewer, 1997, Jin and Bestavros, 2000] focused on the characterization of HTTP requests. Main findings include the characterization of Zipf-like document popularity distribution [Barford et al., 1999, Breslau et al., 1999, Cunha et al., 1995], the characterization of object and request size distributions [Barford et al., 1999, Cunha et al., 1995], and the characterization of reference locality properties [Almeida et al., 1996, Arlitt and Williamson, 1996, Jin and Bestavros, 2000].

Web traffic is self similar, exhibiting burstiness at different time scales [Crovella and Bestavros, 1996, Leland et al., 1994]. A representative self-similar Web traffic generator, SURGE [Barford and Crovella, 1998] models the overall request streams as the aggregation of many individual user request streams, which have heavy-tailed inter-arrival time distribution, and/or heavy-tailed request size distribution. Request streams generated in such a way have significantly different characteristics than the ones from the workloads generated by HTTP benchmark tools such as SpecWeb96 [SPECweb96, 1996].

Streaming Media Workload Characterization.   As we mentioned at the outset, there have been few studies that considered the characteristics of streamed media on the Web [Acharya and Smith, 1998] and the characteristics of access patterns for streamed media [Acharya et al., 2000]. These studies revealed several findings that are also known for non-streamed Web media, including: high variability in object sizes, skewed object popularity, and temporal locality of reference. In addition, these studies highlighted the preponderance of partial accesses to streamed media—namely, a large percentage of responses to user requests are stopped before the streamed object is fetched in its entirety. [Chesire et al., 2001] analyzed a client-based steaming-media workload. They found that most streaming objects are small, and that a small percentage of requests are responsible for almost half of the total transfers. They also found that the popularity of objects follows a Zipf-like distribution and that requests during periods of peak loads exhibit a high degree of temporal locality. [Almeida et al., 2001] analyzed workloads from two media servers for educational purposes. They studied the request arrival patterns, skewed object popularity, and user inter-activity times. Examples of characterization efforts targeted at non-web environments include the work of Padhye and Kurose [Padhye and Kurose, 1998], which studied the patterns of user interactions within a media server, and the work of [Harel et al., 1999], which characterized a workload of media-enhanced classrooms, and observed user inter-activity such as "jumping behavior". More recently, Cherkasova and Gupta [Cherkasova and Gupta, 2002] analyzed enterprise media server workloads, in particular locality of access and evolution of access patterns. They pointed out a number of differences from traditional Web server workloads. Based on this, they have also designed the MediSyn [Tang et al., 2003] workload generator. [Veloso et al., 2002] presented the first study on live streaming access workload characterization at different granularity level, namely users, sessions, and individual transfers. In another work, [van der Merwe et al., 2002] analyzed streaming access logs from commercial service. The assessed the potential benefit of using distribution infrastructures to replicate streaming media objects and to improve bandwidth efficiency. A recent study [Costa et al., 2004] provides a more thorough analysis of pre-stored streaming media workloads, focusing on the typical characteristics of client interactive behavior.

In Section 3, we incorporate many of these characteristics in the models we use for workload generation in GISMO. To the best of our knowledge, GISMOis the first streaming workload generator developed and made available to public. Another more recent effort, the MediSyn project by [Tang et al., 2003] adopted similar methodology and models.

Evaluation Methodologies.   In the absence of a unified model for workload characteristics, various proposals for streaming media protocols and architectures have used a variety of assumptions and models. We discuss these below, focusing only on caching and patching [Carter and Long, 1997, Hua et al., 1998, Gao and Towsley, 1999] protocols—protocols we will be contrasting in a case study using GISMO in Section 5.

In particular, the patching technique [Carter and Long, 1997, Hua et al., 1998, Gao and Towsley, 1999, Eager et al., 2001] leverages large client buffer to enable a client to join an ongoing multicast for prefetching purposes, while using unicast communication to fetch the missed prefix. A few patching protocol studies have considered the effect of Zipf-like popularity distributions on performance [Gao and Towsley, 1999, Hua et al., 1998]. In these studies, the arrival processes for requests were assumed to follow a Poisson distribution [Gao and Towsley, 1999, Hua et al., 1998]. None of the studies we are aware of considered other workload characteristics, such as stream length or user inter-activity.

3. Workload Characteristics in GISMO

Accurate workload characterization is essential to the robust evaluation of streaming access protocols. In fact, several studies on streaming access workload characterization [Acharya et al., 2000, Almeida et al., 2001, Chesire et al., 2001, Padhye and Kurose, 1998] considered the implications of observed characteristics on the performance of various protocols, including caching, prefetching, and stream merging techniques.

In order to generate realistic synthetic streaming access workloads, we need to adopt an access model. We define a *session* as the service initiated by a user's request for a transfer and terminated by a user's abortion of an on-going transfer (or the end of the transfer). The workload presented to a server is thus the product of the *session arrivals* and the *properties of individual sessions*. The first three distributions in Table 8.1 specify the characteristics of session arrivals, whereas the remaining distributions characterize properties of individual sessions.

Session arrivals could be described through the use of appropriate models for: (1) object popularity, (2) reference locality, and (3) seasonal access characteristics. In GISMO, and given the preponderance of findings concerning the first two of these models, we use a Zipf-like distribution to model object popularity, implying a tendency for requests to be concentrated on a few "popular" objects, and we use a heavy-tailed Pareto distribution to model reference locality (*i.e.*, temporal proximity of requests to the same objects). Given the application-specific nature of seasonal access characteristics, we allow the overall request arrival rate to vary with time according to an arbitrary user-supplied function.

An individual session could be described through the use of appropriate models for: (1) object size, (2) user inter-activity, and (3) object encoding characteristics. In GISMO, we model object size (which determines the total playout time of the streamed object) using a Lognormal distribution. We model user inter-activity times which reflect user interruptions (*e.g.*, VCR stop/fast-forward/rewind functionalities) using a Pareto distribution. Finally, we model object encoding characteristics by specifying the auto-correlation of the variable bit rate needed to transfer that object in real-time. Multimedia objects are known to possess self-similar characteristics. Thus, in GISMO, we model the VBR auto-correlation of a streaming object using a self-similar process. Also, we use a heavy-tailed marginal distribution to specify the level of burstiness of the bit-rate.

3.1 Modeling Session Arrivals

The first aspect of a workload characterization concerns the model used for session arrivals. We define the *session inter-arrival time* to be the time between two session arrivals. We consider both the inter-arrival time of *consecutive sessions* (*i.e.*, general inter-arrival time), and the inter-arrival time of *sessions*

Table 8.1.   Distributions used in the workload generator

Component	Model	PDF $f(x)$	Params
Popularity	Zipf-like	$\frac{1}{x^\alpha}, x = 1, 2, ..., N$	α, N
Temporal Correlation	Pareto	$\frac{\alpha k^\alpha}{1-k^\alpha} x^{-\alpha-1}, k < x < 1$	α, k
Seasonal Access Frequency	User-specified		
Object Size	Lognormal	$\frac{e^{-(\ln x-\mu)^2/2\sigma^2}}{x\sigma\sqrt{2\pi}}, x > 0$	μ, σ
User Inter-activities	Pareto	$\frac{\alpha k^\alpha}{1-k^\alpha} x^{-\alpha-1}, k < x < 1,$	α, k
VBR Auto-correlation	Self-similarity		H
VBR Marginal Dist.(body)	Lognormal	$\frac{e^{-(\ln x-\mu)^2/2\sigma^2}}{x\sigma\sqrt{2\pi}}, 0 < x < C$	μ, σ
VBR Marginal Dist.(tail)	Pareto	$\alpha k^\alpha x^{-\alpha-1}, x \geq C$	α, k

requesting the same objects, which is a measure of temporal locality of reference [Almeida et al., 1996, Arlitt and Williamson, 1996, Breslau et al., 1999].

General inter-arrival times can be generated by distributing the requests over the spanning time of the synthetic workload. If the requests are distributed uniformly, then general inter-arrival times roughly follows the exponential distribution. However, several studies have shown that streaming accesses exhibit diurnal patterns [Acharya et al., 2000, Almeida et al., 2001, Chesire et al., 2001, Harel et al., 1999, Luperello et al., 2001]. We call such phenomena *seasonal patterns*, *i.e.*, there are, hourly, daily, and weekly patterns. Users are more likely to request streaming objects during particular periods, making a uniform distribution of requests over the spanning time of the synthetic workload unrealistic.

For HTTP requests, the distribution of inter-arrival time of requests to the same object was found to be the result of two phenomena: the popularity distribution of objects and the temporal correlation of requests [Jin and Bestavros, 2000]. The skew in Web object popularity was found to be directly related to the skew in the inter-arrival time distribution [Breslau et al., 1999, Jin and Bestavros, 2000]. This skew was further increased by temporal correlations of requests. For streaming media accesses, we need to model both of these phenomena.

Popularity Distribution.   The skewed popularity of streaming media objects was documented in [Acharya et al., 2000, Aggarwal et al., 1996, Almeida et al., 2001, Chesire et al., 2001, Luperello et al., 2001]. In particular, several studies observed a Zipf-like distribution of streaming object popularity [Almeida et al., 2001, Chesire et al., 2001, Luperello et al., 2001]. Zipf-like distributions imply that the access frequency of an object is inversely proportional to its popularity (rank), *i.e.*, $P(r) \sim r^{-\alpha}, 1 < r \leq N$, where N is the number of objects, r is the rank, and P is the access frequency of the r-ranked object. A discrete form of the probability density function is $f(x) = \frac{1}{\Omega x^\alpha}$, $x = 1, 2, ..., N$, where $\Omega = \sum_{i=1}^{N} i^{-\alpha}$. The parameter α is called the *shape parameter* since it determines the level of skewness in the popularity profile. The parameter N is called the *scale parameter*.

Temporal Correlation. If requests to the same object are independent, then they are distributed randomly. This was shown not to be accurate enough for HTTP requests [Jin and Bestavros, 2000]. Similarly, in a number of recent studies, streaming media accesses were shown to exhibit temporal correlations [Acharya et al., 2000, Almeida et al., 2001, Chesire et al., 2001]. For example, it was observed that streaming accesses have much higher overlap during peak loads. To reflect this, we assume that a portion of all request arrivals are correlated, while the remaining request arrivals are independent.

To model correlated inter-arrival times, we use a Pareto distribution. The Pareto distribution has a density function $f(x) = \alpha k^\alpha x^{-\alpha-1}$, where $\alpha, k > 0$ and $x > k$. In [Jin and Bestavros, 2000], it was observed that temporal correlations were stronger when request inter-arrival times were shorter. The Pareto distribution models such a condition well. The Pareto distribution used to characterize temporal correlations has two parameters. The *shape parameter* (α) indicates the skewness of inter-arrival time distribution. The *scale parameter* (k) indicates the time scale of observations. Since we are only interested in a finite period but the random variable with a Pareto distribution can have arbitrarily large values, we need to cut off the Pareto distribution at unity (corresponding to the maximum possible inter-arrival time, or the spanning time of synthetic request stream). Introducing a cutoff for the Pareto distribution necessitates that we normalize it. We do so by defining a *truncated Pareto distribution* with a PDF $f(x) = \alpha \frac{k^\alpha}{1-k^\alpha} x^{-\alpha-1}$, where $\alpha, k > 0$ and $k < x < 1$. In implementation, we use inverse method to generate Pareto-distributed random values.[1] Figure 8.1 illustrates such a truncated PDF.

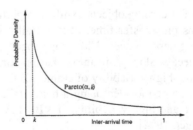

Figure 8.1. Truncated Pareto PDF for interarrival time of correlated requests. The cutoff point is unity, the maximum possible inter-arrival time.

Seasonal Access Frequency.   In GISMO, we do not make any assumptions related to the seasonal patterns of the overall access frequency. Such patterns are application-specific, and depend on various aspects of location and time. For example, several studies [Acharya et al., 2000, Almeida et al., 2001, Chesire et al., 2001, Harel et al., 1999, Luperello et al., 2001] observed such patterns over significantly different time scales (from hours to months). Hence, we assume that a histogram of access frequency (request arrival rate) at different times is provided by users of GISMO. Namely, given the histogram of the overall request arrival rate at different times, we can approximate the CDF $F(t)$, $t \in (0, 1)$. For each request generated in the last step, assume $t \in (0, 1)$ is the request time, then we transform t to another request time $F^{-1}(t)$.

3.2   Modeling Individual Sessions

The second aspect of a workload characterization concerns the model used for determining the specifics of each user session.

First, the distribution of object sizes is a main determinant of session duration—the larger the object, the longer the session. HTTP requests are usually shorter, while streaming accesses have much longer durations (typically a few KB for Web objects but up to hundreds of MB for streaming objects). Several studies have found that the session length has heavier tails than an exponential distribution [Almeida et al., 2001, Luperello et al., 2001, Padhye and Kurose, 1998, Chesire et al., 2001].

Second, user activities (including VCR-like stop/fast-forward/rewind/pause functionalities) affect session duration. User interventions are not unique to streaming access and were documented for HTTP requests (*e.g.*, "interrupted" transfers). Such effects are much more common for streaming accesses. For example, it has been observed that nearly a half of all video requests are not completed [Acharya et al., 2000]. In addition, jumps become popular in streaming media access workloads [Almeida et al., 2001, Harel et al., 1999, Padhye and Kurose, 1998].

Third, the bit-rate of streaming objects exhibits important properties which may have implications on transfer time. Specifically, streaming media bit rates exhibit long-range dependence. With long-range dependence, the auto-correlation function decays slowly, meaning that burstiness persists at large time scales. In addition, high variability of frame sizes (a property of the encoding scheme used) can be modeled using a heavy-tailed distribution. Both long range dependence and high variability of VBR have been characterized in [Garrett and Willinger, 1994].

Object Size Distribution.   In GISMO, we use the Lognormal distribution to model streaming object sizes. Several studies on workload characterization [Almeida et al., 2001, Luperello et al., 2001, Padhye and Kurose, 1998] found that the Lognormal distribution fits the distribution of object sizes well. The Lognormal distribution has two parameters, μ, the mean of $\ln(x)$, and σ, the standard deviation of $\ln(x)$. To generate a random variable that follows the Lognormal distribution, we first generate x from an approximation of the standard Normal distribution, and then return $e^{\mu+\sigma x}$ as the value of the Lognormally-distributed random variable representing the object size.

Notice that GISMO allows our choice of the Lognormal distribution to be changed. Specifically, several other distributions (*e.g.*, Pareto and Gamma) were found to provide a good fit for streaming object sizes measured empirically [Almeida et al., 2001, Padhye and Kurose, 1998]. This is one way in which GISMO is extensible: Users of GISMO can easily replace the module for generating object sizes for the synthetic workload with their own module.

User Inter-activity Times. In GISMO, two forms of user interventions (or activities) are modeled—namely, partial accesses due to "stop" activity and jumps due to "fast forward and rewind" activities.

For partial accesses (resulting from a "stop" activity), we need to model the duration of an aborted session. Unfortunately, there are very few empirical studies characterizing partial accesses. The work presented in [Acharya et al., 2000] implies that the stopping time (time until a session is stopped) is not uniformly or exponentially distributed. Instead, stopping is more likely to occur in the beginning of a stream playout. We model such a behavior with a Pareto distribution. We make this choice since stopping probability decreases as the session grows longer (indicating interest in the streamed content, and hence a lower probability of stoppage). A Pareto distribution models this behaviors very well.

For intra-session jumps (resulting from a "fast forward" or "rewind" activity), we need to model the distribution of *jump distances*. In previous work [Padhye and Kurose, 1998], it was found that jump distances tend to be small but that large jumps are not uncommon. In our current implementation of GISMO, we model jump distances using Pareto distributions. In addition to jump distances, we also need to model the duration of continuous play (*i.e.*, intra-jump times). In our current implementation of GISMO, we assume that the duration of continuous play follows an exponential distribution $e^{-\lambda t}$, where λ is the *frequency* of jumps.

Two previous studies [Almeida et al., 2001, Padhye and Kurose, 1998] have used active period (ON period) and silent period (OFF period) in modeling user interactivities. The duration of continuous play (ON period) tends to be heavier-tailed, but for small objects exponential distribution is the most observed [Almeida et al., 2001]. The duration of the silent period is best fit by a Pareto distribution.

VBR Self-Similarity.   We model the sequence of frame sizes for a streaming object as a self-similar process [Garrett and Willinger, 1994]. A time series X is said to be *exactly second-order self-similar* if the corresponding "aggregated" process $X^{(m)}$ has the same correlation function as X, for all $m \geq 1$, where the process $X^{(m)}$ is obtained by averaging the original X over successive non-overlapping blocks of size m. The variance of the aggregated process behaves for large m like $Var(X^{(m)}) \approx m^{-\beta}(\sigma^2)_X$, resulting in a single Hurst parameter $H = 1 - \beta/2$. A property of self-similar processes is that the auto-correlation function decays much slower when $H > 0.5$. This means that burstiness persists at large time scale, and implies the ineffectiveness of buffering to smooth out burstiness.

In GISMO, we generate fractional Gaussian noise by generating a fractional Brownion motion (FBM), and then obtaining FGN from the increments of FBM. We implemented a simple and fast approximation of FBM called "Random Midpoint Displacement" (RMD). The RMD method was proposed in [Lau et al., 1995]. RMD works in a top-down fashion. It progressively subdivides an interval over which to generate the sample path. At each division, a Gaussian displacement, with appropriate scaling (d^H, where d is the length of the interval and H is the target Hurst parameter), is used to determine the value of the midpoint. This recursive procedure stops when it gets the FBM process of the required length. The time complexity for RMD is only $O(n)$, where n is the length of the FBM process. Note that RMD generates a somewhat inaccurate self-similar process and that the resulting Hurst parameter may be slightly smaller than the target value. Other methods such as the fast Fourier Transform [Paxson, 1997] can be implemented.

VBR Marginal Distribution.   To model the high variability of streaming media bit rates, we use a heavy-tailed marginal distribution to characterize the bit rate. A heavy-tailed distribution is one whose upper tail declines like a power law, *i.e.*, $P[X > x] \sim x^{-\alpha}$, where $0 < \alpha < 2$. In [Garrett and Willinger, 1994], it was found that the tail of the VBR marginal distribution can be modeled using a Pareto distribution. The CDF of Pareto distribution is $F(x) = P[X \leq x] = 1 - (k/x)^{\alpha}$, where $k, \alpha > 0$ and $x \geq k$. Pareto distributions yield random variables with high variability. If $1 < \alpha < 2$, the random variable with Pareto distribution has finite mean and infinite variance; if $\alpha \leq 1$, it has infinite mean and variance.

In addition to modeling the "tail" of the distribution, we also need to model the "body" of the distribution. Garrett and Willinger [Garrett and Willinger, 1994] found that the Gamma distribution is a good fit for the body, so they used a hybrid Gamma/Pareto for the marginal distribution. We use a Lognormal distribution for the body along with a Pareto tail.

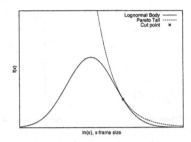

Figure 8.2. A hybrid distribution with Lognormal body/Pareto tail.

Finally, to complete our model of VBR marginal distribution, we use the following approach to "connect" the body to the tail. Given the Lognormal distribution for the body with parameters u and σ, and the cut point between the body and the tail, we can derive the scale and shape parameter of the Pareto tail by equalizing both the value and the slope of the two distributions at the cut point. The resulting hybrid distribution needs to be normalized. One can get different tail distributions by moving the cut point. Figure 8.2 illustrates the fit of a Lognormal distribution and a Pareto distribution.

We use a transformation to generate the required marginal distribution from the FGN Gaussian marginal distribution (CDF $G_{\mu,\sigma}$). The parameters μ and σ can be computed from FGN samples. Then we transform it to a hybrid Lognormal/Pareto distribution with CDF F_{hybrid}. To do this, for each sample value x in the FGN process, the new value is computed as $F_{hybrid}^{-1}(G_{\mu,\sigma}(x))$.

We test the Hurst parameter of the resulting VBR frame size series using *variance-time plot*. A variance-time plot should show that if the sample is aggregated by a factor of m, then the variance decreases by a factor of $m^{-\beta}$, where $\beta = 2 - 2H$. Since the RMD algorithm is an approximation, and the transformation of marginal distribution may not preserve the Hurst parameter very well, we repeat the last two steps if the resulting H value is not close enough to the target value.

For example, we generate a VBR series for 100000 frames with target Hurst parameter 0.8. The given parameters are $\mu = 6$, $\sigma = 0.4$, and cut point 560. We derive other parameters $\alpha = 2.05$ and $k = 335$ for the Pareto tail. The hybrid distribution needs to be normalized by a factor 0.876. Figure 8.3(a) shows the marginal distribution of the synthetic trace. It fits the target distribution well. We test the Hurst parameter using larger number of samples. Figure 8.3(b) shows the variance-time plot from a sequence of one million frame sizes. It shows that the resulting H value is smaller than the target value when the aggregation level is low. At intermediate and high aggregation level, the difference between the target Hurst value and the resulting is less than 0.01.

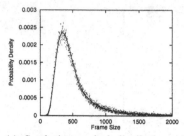

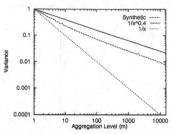

(a) Synthetic marginal distribution with Lognormal body and Pareto tail. The solid line is the target distribution and the dots show the histograms of the synthetic trace.

(b) Variance-time plot test of self-similarity yields Hurst parameter value close to the target value, especially at the intermediate aggregation level when $10 < m < 10000$.

Figure 8.3.   Comparisons of synthetic VBR sequence with target parameters.

4.   Adapting GISMO to Various Architectures

GISMO was designed as a "toolbox" that allows the evaluation of various streaming delivery architectures. A typical architecture would involve a set of *users* accessing a set of streaming *objects* stored on a set of streaming *servers* via a *network*. Figure 8.4 illustrates such an architecture. The media players are usually the *Plug-ins* of the Web browsers (we show them coupled). When a user is browsing an HTTP page with links to streaming objects, a media player is launched. The media player may be using different protocols to stream the data from the streaming server, *e.g.*, UDP, TCP, and RTSP. In addition to the entities shown in Figure 8.4, there could be other components that may play a role in the delivery of streaming media (*e.g.*, caching proxies inside the network or replicated servers for parallel downloads).

The workload generated by GISMO for the performance evaluation of a given architecture consists of two parts: (a) the set of phantom streaming objects[2] available at the server(s) for retrievals, and (b) a schedule of the request streams generated by various clients.[3] To use such a workload, the set of streaming objects are installed on the servers and schedules specifying client accesses are installed on the clients. Once installed, a GISMO workload can be played out simply by having clients sending requests to the server(s) according to the schedule of accesses at such a client.

By virtue of its design, GISMO allows the evaluation of any "entity" in the system (lying between request generating clients and content providing servers). To do so requires that such entities be "coded" as part of an end-to-end architecture to be evaluated. While a user of GISMO is expected to develop one or more modules for the entity to be evaluated (*e.g.*, a caching or patching algorithm), he/she is not expected to provide the many other entities necessary

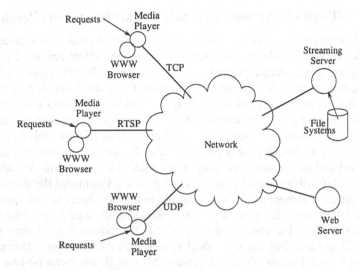

Figure 8.4. Synthetic workload components: (1) Access schedules generated by client requests, and (2) Streaming objects stored on servers.

to complete the end-to-end architecture. To that end, and in addition to the above two main components of a workload (the objects on the servers and the schedules at the clients), GISMO provides support for various other ingredients of a streaming media delivery system. Examples of these include modules to implement simple transport protocols (*e.g.*, UDP, TCP, RTP) and modules to interface clients and server to an emulated network (*e.g.*, NistNet).

The following are examples of "use cases" for GISMO: (1) To evaluate the capacity of a streaming server, a number of clients are used to generate requests to the server under test. This can be done on a LAN and clients do not have to be real media players. The interesting aspects of the server performance (that a GISMO user may want to evaluate using simulations) may include its scheduling, its memory and CPU behavior, and caching, etc. (2) Evaluating network protocols for streaming data transmission. For this purpose, the data is streamed using the protocol under investigation, but one may use simple implementation of media players and streaming servers. An example of using GISMO in such a study is our work on stream merging and periodic broadcasting protocols [Jin and Bestavros, 2002]. (3) Evaluating streaming data replication techniques. For this purpose, one can study how streaming objects are replicated via the Internet to provide better services to the users. The replication techniques include proxy caching, prefetching, work-ahead smoothing, and multicasting etc. An example of using GISMO in such a study is our work on partial caching [Jin et al., 2002] as well as the case study we present in the next section.

5.   GISMO in Action: Evaluating Caching versus Patching

To demonstrate its usefulness, we describe how GISMO was used to generate realistic workloads, which were used to compare the effectiveness of proxy caching and server patching techniques in reducing bandwidth requirements.

We conducted a base experiment to measure the server bandwidth requirements for a system using neither caching nor patching. GISMO was used to generate a total of 50000 requests to 500 streaming objects stored on the server. Requests were over a one-day period, with three hours of peak activities. We used $\alpha = 0.7$ to describe the popularity skew. Requests were not temporally correlated and the streams were played out without interruptions. We used a Lognormal distribution with $\mu = 10.5$ and $\sigma = 0.63$ to model the streaming object sizes (in number of frames), resulting in a mean object size of approximately 43K frames. To model the VBR frame sizes, we used Lognormal with $\mu = 5.8$, $\sigma = 0.4$ to model the body of the distribution and a Pareto with $\alpha = 1.82$ and $k = 248$ bytes to model its tail, with the cut point between the body and the tail set to 400 bytes. Under this model, the mean bit-rate was close to $100Kbps$ with 24 frames per second. The sequences of frame sizes were generated with a target Hurst parameter $H = 0.8$. Figure 8.5 shows the base bandwidth (bytes per second) needed by the server.

Next, we conducted a number of experiments to study the effectiveness of proxy caching and server patching techniques. To that end, we considered *bandwidth reduction ratio* as the metric of interest. This metric is computed by normalizing the mean bandwidth requirement for a system using caching or patching with respect to the base bandwidth requirement (similar to that shown in Figure 8.5). In our experiments, we varied various parameters of the workload and report the bandwidth reduction ratio (as a function of such parameters), focusing only on the 3-hour period of peak load.

To study the effectiveness of caching, we considered a system with 100 proxies, each with infinite cache size. A proxy can satisfy a request if it has a previously-fetched copy of the streaming object in its cache. To study the

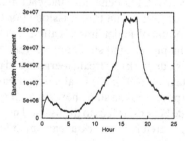

Figure 8.5.   Base server bandwidth requirements.

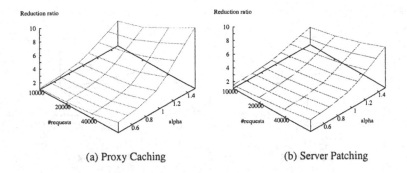

(a) Proxy Caching   (b) Server Patching

Figure 8.6. Server bandwidth reduction ratios of proxy caching and server patching schemes when popularity parameters change. Larger α is more important for caching.

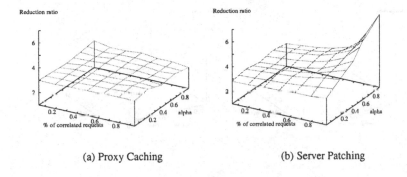

(a) Proxy Caching   (b) Server Patching

Figure 8.7. Server bandwidth reduction ratios of proxy caching and server patching schemes when correlation parameters change. Strong temporal correlation favorites server patching.

effectiveness of patching, we considered a system in which the server patches its response to requests it receives (to the same object) within a short period of time. This was done using the optimal threshold-based patching schemes proposed in [Gao and Towsley, 1999] (assuming that clients had enough buffer space).

Figure 8.6 shows the performance of proxy caching and server patching when the total number of requests and the skewness parameter α change. We observe that for proxy caching, a larger α results in higher bandwidth reduction ratio. This means that for proxy caching, the concentration of requests on a smaller number of "popular" objects is much more important than it is for server patching techniques. Recent studies [Acharya et al., 2000, Chesire et al., 2001, Almeida et al., 2001] of streaming access logs suggest that such popularity

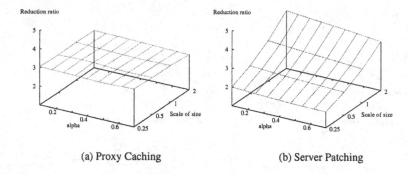

(a) Proxy Caching   (b) Server Patching

Figure 8.8.   Server bandwidth reduction ratios of proxy caching and server patching schemes when size distribution parameters change. Larger sizes favorites server patching.

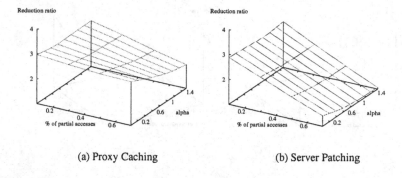

(a) Proxy Caching   (b) Server Patching

Figure 8.9.   Server bandwidth reduction ratios of proxy caching and server patching schemes when partial access parameters change. Early stops degrade server patching performance significantly, but only affect caching moderately.

skew for streaming media access is limited, *i.e.*, α is likely to have small values. This suggests that it is difficult to achieve high bandwidth reduction ratios using proxy caches. From Figure 8.6, we also observe that increasing the number of requests in the workload increases the efficiency of both techniques. Since we assume a fixed number (100) of proxies, increasing the number of requests in effect increases sharing among users.

Figure 8.7 shows the performance of proxy caching and server patching when the percentage of temporally correlated requests and the correlation skewness α are changed. For proxy caching, the correlation of requests is almost irrelevant.[4] For server patching, increasing the percentage of correlated requests or increasing the skewness of correlated inter-arrival times results in higher reduction ratios. Nevertheless, when correlation is not strong, the reduction ratio is only slightly higher than when no correlation exists. Thus, for evaluating server patching techniques, Poisson arrivals are adequate in workloads with weak correlations.

Figure 8.8 shows the performance of proxy caching and server patching when object sizes are scaled and the size skewness parameter α changes. Again, the effectiveness of proxy caching is not affected by size distribution. For server patching, the larger the objects, the higher the reduction ratio. This is expected since long streams offer more opportunities for patching. However, the skewness parameter has less of an effect, suggesting that it is adequate to use a mean-size streaming object to study the effectiveness of server patching. One implication from this experiment is that a good hybrid strategy would involve using caches for smaller objects and patching for longer streams.

Figure 8.9 shows the performance of proxy caching and server patching, when the probability of partial accesses and the partial access skewness parameter α are varied. Increasing the fraction of partially-accessed objects (*i.e.*, probability of early stops) hurts the performance of both proxy caching and server patching. While the impact on proxy caching performance is marginal, the impact on server patching is disastrous. This suggests that for streaming access allowing a high degree of user inter-activity, server patching is not a promising technique at all.

To summarize, our case study demonstrates the importance of a realistic and scalable streaming access workload generator by showing that the characteristics of a workload may have great impacts on the effectiveness of a streaming content delivery solution. Changing the workload characteristics does indeed change the relative performance of various techniques.

6.   Summary

GISMO generates streaming access workloads, which are parameterized so as to match properties of real workloads, including object popularity, temporal correlation of requests, seasonal access patterns, user session durations, user inter-activity, and VBR long-range dependence and marginal distribution. We demonstrated the value of GISMO by showing that the relative performance of proxy caching and server patching techniques is inherently dependent on properties of the workload used to evaluate them.

Notes

1. To generate a random variate following Pareto distribution $f(x)$, we first compute the inverse CDF $F^{-1}(x)$. A random variable $r \in (0, 1)$, *i.e.*, uniformly-distributed r is generated, and the inter-arrival time is $F^{-1}(r)$.

2. While the contents of "phantom" objects generated by GISMO are not comprehensible (not real audio or video), their characteristics conform to the specific parameters of desired distributions (*e.g.*, VBR auto-correlation, VBR marginal distributions, sizes, *etc.*)

3. A GISMO client is a software entity that mimics a configurable set of *real users*, each generating requests conforming to the various distributions of popularity, inter-activities, *etc.*

4. Request correlation (a.k.a. locality of reference) would be relevant for finite-size proxy caches because it impacts the effectiveness of cache replacement algorithms.

References

Acharya, Soam and Smith, Brian (1998). An experiment to characterize videos stored on the Web. In *Proceedings of MMCN*.

Acharya, Soam, Smith, Brian, and Parns, Peter (2000). Characterizing user access to videos on the World Wide Web. In *Proceedings of MMCN*.

Aggarwal, Charu C., Wolf, Joel L., and Yu, Philip S. (1996). On optimal batching policies for video-on-demand storage servers. In *Proceedings of ICMCS*.

Almeida, Jussara, Krueger, Jeffrey, Eager, Derek, and Vernon, Mary (2001). Analysis of educational media server workloads. In *Proceedings of NOSS-DAV*.

Almeida, Virgilio, Bestavros, Azer, Crovella, Mark, and de Oliveira, Adriana (1996). Characterizing reference locality in the WWW. In *Proceedings of PDIS*.

Arlitt, Martin and Williamson, Carey (1996). Web server workload characteristics: The search for invariants. In *Proceedings of SIGMETRICS*.

Barford, Paul, Bestavros, Azer, Bradley, Adam, and Crovella, Mark (1999). Changes in Web client access patterns: Characteristics and caching implications. *World Wide Web*, 2(1):15–28.

Barford, Paul and Crovella, Mark (1998). Generating representative Web workloads for network and server performance evaluation. In *Proceedings of SIGMETRICS*.

Breslau, Lee, Cao, Pei, Fan, Li, Phillips, Graham, and Shenker, Scott (1999). Web caching and Zipf-like distributions: Evidence and implications. In *Proceedings of INFOCOM*.

Carter, S. W. and Long, D. D. E. (1997). Improving video-on-demand server efficiency through stream tapping. In *Proceedings of ICCCN*.

Cherkasova, Ludmila and Gupta, Minaxi (2002). Characterizing locality, evolution, and life span of accesses in enterprise media server workloads. In *Proceedings of NOSSDAV*.

Chesire, Maureen, Wolman, Alec, Voelker, Geoff, and Levy, Henry (2001). Measurement and analysis of a streaming workload. In *Proceedings of USITS*.

Costa, Cristiano P., Cunha, Italo S., Borges, Alex, Ramos, Claudiney Vander, Rocha, Marcus M., Almeida, Jussara M., and Ribeiro-Neto, Berthier A. (2004). Analyzing client interactivity in streaming media. In *Proceedings of WWW Conference*.

Crovella, Mark and Bestavros, Azer (1996). Self-similarity in World Wide Web traffic: Evidence and possible causes. In *Proceedings of SIGMETRICS*.

Cunha, Carlos, Bestavros, Azer, and Crovella, Mark (1995). Characteristics of WWW client-based traces. Technical Report BU-CS-95-010, Computer Science Department, Boston University.

Eager, Derek, Vernon, Mary, and Zahorjan, John (2001). Minimizing bandwidth requirements for on-demand data delivery. *IEEE Transactions on Data and Knowledge Engineering*, 13.

Gao, Lixin and Towsley, Don (1999). Supplying instantaneous video-on-demand services using controlled multicast. In *Proceedings of ICMCS*.

Garrett, Mark W. and Willinger, Walter (1994). Analysis, modeling and generation of self-similar VBR video traffic. In *Proceedings of SIGCOMM*.

Gribble, Steven D. and Brewer, Eric A. (1997). System design issues for Internet middleware services: Deductions from a large client trace. In *Proceedings of USITS*.

Harel, Nissim, Vellanki, Vivekanand, Chervenak, Ann, Abowd, Gregory, and Ramachandran, Umakishore (1999). Workload of a media-enhanced classroom server. In *Proceedings of Workshop on Workload Characterization*.

Hua, Kien A., Cai, Ying, and Sheu, Simon (1998). Patching: A multicast technique for true video-on-demand services. In *Proceedings of ACM MULTIMEDIA*.

Jin, Shudong and Bestavros, Azer (2000). Temporal locality in Web request streams: Sources, characteristics, and caching implication (poster). In *Proceedings of SIGMETRICS*.

Jin, Shudong and Bestavros, Azer (2001). GISMO: Generator of Streaming Media Objects and Workloads. *Performance Evaluation Review*, 29(3).

Jin, Shudong and Bestavros, Azer (2002). Scalability of multicast delivery for non-sequential streaming access. In *Proceedings of ACM SIGMETRICS*.

Jin, Shudong, Bestavros, Azer, and Iyengar, Arun (2002). Accelerating Internet streaming media delivery using network-aware partial caching. In *Proceedings of IEEE ICDCS*.

Lau, W.-C., Erramilli, A., Wang, J. L., and Willinger, W. (1995). Self-similar traffic generation: The random midpoint displacement algorithm and its properties. In *Proceedings of ICC*.

Leland, Will E., Taqqu, Murad S., Willinger, Walter, and Wilson, Daniel V. (1994). On the self-similar nature of ethernet traffic (extended version). *IEEE/ACM Trans. on Networking*, 2(1).

Li, Mingzhe, Claypool, Mark, Kinicki, Robert, and Nichols, James (2005). Characteristics of streaming media stored on the web. To appear in *ACM Transactions on Internet Technology (TOIT)*.

Luperello, Dario, Mukherjee, Sarit, and Paul, Sanjoy (2001). Streaming media traffic: An empirical study. In *Proceedings of Web Caching Workshop*.

Padhye, J. and Kurose, J. (1998). An empirical study of client interactions with a continuous-media courseware server. In *Proceedings of NOSSDAV*.

Padmanabhan, Venkata N. and Qiu, Lili (2000). The content and access dynamics of a busy Web site: Findings and implications. In *Proceedings of SIGCOMM*.

Paxson, V. (1997). Fast, approximate synthesis of fractional gaussian noise for generat ing self-similar network traffic. *Computer Communication Review*, 27:5–18.

SPECweb96 Benchmark (1996). The Standard Performance Evaluation Corporation. Available at http://www.spec.org/osg/web96/.

Tang, Wenting, Fu, Yun, Cherkasova, Ludmila, and Vahdat, Amin (2003). Medisyn: A synthetic streaming media service workload generator. In *Proceedings of NOSSDAV*.

van der Merwe, Jacobus, Sen, Subhabrata, and Kalmanek, Charles (2002). Streaming video traffic: Characterization and network impact. In *Proceedings of Web Caching Workshop*.

Veloso, Eveline, Almeida, Virgilio, Meira, Wagner, Bestavros, Azer, and Jin, Shudong (2002). A hierarchical characterization of a live streaming media workload. In *Proceedings of SIGCOMM Internet Measurement Workshop*.

Zipf, George Kingsley (1929). *Relative Frequency as a Determinant of Phonetic Change*. Reprinted from Harvard Studies in Classical Philiology, XL.

Chapter 9

STREAMING MEDIA CACHING

Jiangchuan Liu
School of Computing Science
Simon Fraser University, British Columbia, Canada
jcliu@cs.sfu.ca

Abstract   Streaming media has contributed to a significant amount of today's Internet traffic.
Like conventional web objects (e.g., HTML pages and images), media objects
can benefit from proxy caching; yet their unique features such as huge size and
high bandwidth demand imply that conventional proxy caching strategies have to
be substantially revised. This chapter discusses the critical issues and challenges
of cache management for proxy-assisted media streaming. We survey, classify,
and compare the state-of-the-art solutions. We also investigate advanced issues
of combining multicast with caching, cooperating among proxies, and leveraging
caching in overlay/peer-to-peer networks.

Keywords: Streaming media, video, proxy, caching, overlay networks, multicast

1.   Introduction

With widespread penetration of the broadband Internet, multimedia service
is getting increasingly popular among users and has contributed to a significant
amount of today's Internet traffic. Media objects can be accessed similar to
conventional text and images using a download-and-play mode; but most users
prefer to quickly initiate and then continuously play back a media object while
it is being downloaded, i.e., to use a *real-time streaming* mode. We have
witnessed the initial and incremental deployment of streaming applications like
RealNetworks RealPlayer and Microsoft Windows Media Player in recent years.
The performance of such applications however is still far from satisfactory,
especially during the peak hours.

To reduce client-perceived access latencies as well as server/network loads,
an effective means is to cache frequently used data at proxies close to clients.
It also enhances the availability of objects and mitigates packet losses, as a

local transmission is generally more reliable than a remote transmission. Proxy caching thus has become one of the vital components in virtually all web systems. Streaming media, particularly those pre-stored, could also benefit significant performance improvement from proxy caching, given their static nature in content and highly localized access interests. However, existing proxies are generally optimized for delivering conventional web objects (e.g., HTML pages or GIF images), which may not meet the requirements of steaming applications. In the following, we list some important and unique features of streaming media and discuss their implications to proxy cache design.

Huge size: A conventional web object is typically on the order of 1K to 100K bytes. Hence, a binary decision works well for proxy caching: either caching an object in its entirety or not caching. In contrast, a media object has a high data rate and a long playback duration, which combined yield a huge data volume. For illustration, a one-hour standard MPEG-1 video has a volume of about 675 MB; caching it entirely at a web proxy is clearly impractical, as several such large streams would exhaust the capacity of the cache. One solution is to cache only portions of an object. In this case, a client's playback needs a joint delivery involving both the proxy and the origin server. To cache which portions of which objects thus has to be carefully managed, such that the benefit of caching outweighs the synchronization overhead of the joint delivery.

Intensive bandwidth use: Streaming nature of delivery requires a significant amount of disk and network I/O bandwidth, sustaining over a long period. Hence, minimizing bandwidth consumption becomes a primary consideration for proxy cache management, even taking precedence over reducing access latencies in many cases. Moreover, the bandwidth bottleneck limits the number of clients that a proxy can simultaneously support; employing multicast delivery and cooperation among proxies thus become particularly attractive for media streaming applications.

High interactivity: The long playback duration of a streaming object also enables various client-server interactions. As an example, recent studies found that nearly 90% media playbacks are terminated prematurely by clients [Chen et al., 2004b]. In addition, during a playback, a client often expects VCR-like operations, such as fast-forward and rewind. This implies the access rates might be different for different portions of a stream, which potentially complicates the cache management.

Given these unique features of media objects, novel caching algorithms have been developed in the literature. The objective of this chapter is to review the state-of-the-art caching techniques dedicated to streaming media caching. We begin with discussions on a generic proxy caching architecture and some protocol considerations. The caching strategies for streaming media are classified, examined, and compared in Section 3. Section 4 investigates some advanced issues. Finally, Section 5 concludes the chapter.

2. Architecture and Protocols for Streaming Caching

Streaming applications generally support diverse client-server interactions and have stringent demands on packet delay and jitter to ensure discontinuity-free playback. To meet these requirements, the Internet Engineering Task Force (IETF) has developed the RTP/RTCP/RTSP protocol suite. A generic system diagram of proxy-assisted media streaming using this suite is depicted in Fig. 9.1.

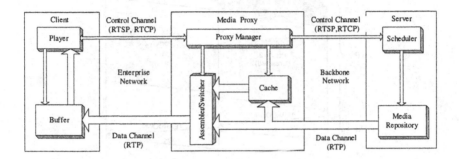

Figure 9.1. A generic system diagram of proxy-assisted media streaming using RTP/RTCP/RTSP.

In this system, the basic functionalities for data transferring are provided by the Real-Time Transport Protocol (RTP), including payload identification, sequence numbering for loss detection, and time stamping for playback control. Running on top of UDP, RTP itself does not guarantee Quality-of-Service (QoS), but relies on its companion, the Real-Time Control Protocol (RTCP), to monitor the network status and provide feedback for application-layer adaptation. The Real-Time Streaming Protocol (RTSP) coordinates the delivery of media objects and enables a rich set of controls for interactive playback. For the proxy-assisted streaming, the proxy has to relay these control messages between the client and the server. The problem is particularly involved if only part of a media object is cached at a proxy. In this case, the proxy must reply to the client PLAY request and initiate transmission of RTP and RTCP messages to the client for the cached portion, while request the uncached portion(s) from the server. Such fetching can be achieved through an RTSP Range request specifying the playback points, as illustrated in Fig. 9.2. The Range request also enables clients to retrieve different segments of a media object from multiple servers or proxies, if needed.

Beside this classical client/server paradigm, peer-to-peer streaming and other overlay streaming paradigms have also attracted much attention recently, which will be discussed in Section 4.C.

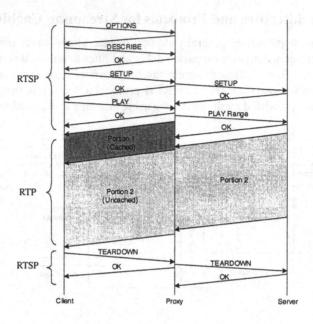

Figure 9.2. Operations for streaming with partial caching.

3. Caching Strategies: Homogeneous Clients and Heterogeneous Clients

Due to the aforementioned features of streaming media objects, media caching has many distinct focuses from conventional web caching. On one hand, since the content of a media object is rarely updated, management issues like cache consistency and coherence are less critical in media caching. On the other hand, given high resource requirements of media objects, effective management of proxy cache resources (i.e., space, disk I/O, and network I/O) becomes more challenging. In this section, we survey the state-of-the-art media caching strategies for both homogenous clients and heterogeneous clients, with an emphasis on how the strategies minimize resource demands.

3.1 Stream Caching for Homogeneous Clients

Most existing caching algorithms focus on homogeneous clients, which have identical or similar configurations and capabilities behind a proxy. As such, a single version of an object would match the bandwidth and format demands of all requests to the object. Nevertheless, what to cache (which portions of which objects) and how to manage cache (e.g., cache placement and replacement) at the proxy remain challenges. According to the selection of the portions to cache, we classify existing algorithms into four categories: *sliding-interval caching*, *prefix caching*, *segment caching*, and *rate-split caching*.

Sliding-Interval Caching [Tewari et al., 1998, Chen et al., 2004a]: This algorithm caches a sliding interval of a media object to exploit sequential access of streaming media. For illustration, given two consecutive requests for the same object, the first request may access the object from the server and incrementally store it into the proxy cache; the second request can then access the cached portion and release it after the access. If the two requests arrive close in time, only a small portion of the media object needs to be cached at any time instance, and yet the second request can be completely satisfied from the proxy (see Fig. 9.3). In general, if multiple requests for an object arrive in a short period, a set of adjacent intervals can be grouped to form a *run*, of which the cached portion will be released only after the last request has been satisfied.

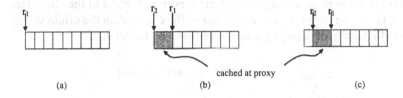

cached at proxy

(a)   (b)   (c)

Figure 9.3. An illustration of sliding-interval caching. The object consists of 9 frames, each requiring one unit time to deliver from the proxy to a client. Requests 1 and 2 arrive at times 0 and 2, respectively. To serve request 2, only two frames need to be cached at any time instance. (a) Time 0: request 1 arrives; (b) Time 1-2: frames 1 and 2 accessed by request 1 and cached; request 2 arrives; (c) Time 2-3: frame 3 accessed by request 1 and cached; frame 1 read by request 2 and released.

As the cached portion is dynamically updated with playback, the sliding-interval caching involves high disk bandwidth demands; in the worse case, it would double the disk I/O due to the concurrent read/write operations. To effectively utilize available cache resources, [Tewari et al., 1998] proposed a resource based caching (RBC) policy. The policy characterizes each object by its space and bandwidth requirements, and models the cache as a two-constraint knapsack. A heuristic algorithm was developed to dynamically select the caching granularity of an object with the objective of balancing its bandwidth and space usages. Depending on the object's characteristics and the available resources, the selected granularity could be a sliding interval, a sliding run, or the full object.

Sliding-interval caching can significantly reduce network bandwidth consumption and start-up delay for subsequent accesses. However, as the cached portion is dynamically updated with playback, the sliding-interval caching involves high disk bandwidth demands; in the worse case, it would double the disk I/O due to the concurrent read/write operations. [Chen et al., 2004a] proposed the Shared Running Buffer (SRB) approach, which argues that, with the falling price of memory, it is possible to allocate memory buffers to accommodate media data and thus avoiding the intensive disk read/write.

The effectiveness of sliding-interval caching diminishes with the increase of the access intervals. If the access interval of the same object is longer than the duration of the playback, the algorithm is degenerated to the unaffordable full-object caching. To address this issue, it is preferable to retain the cached content over a relatively long time period. Most of the caching algorithms to be discussed in the rest of this section fall into this category.

Prefix Caching [Sen et al., 1999]: This algorithm caches the initial portion of a media object, called *prefix*, at a proxy. Upon receiving a client request, the proxy immediately delivers the prefix to the client and, meanwhile, fetches the remaining portion, the *suffix*, from the server and relays to the client (see Fig. 9.4). As the proxy is generally closer to the clients than the origin server, the start-up delay for a playback can be remarkably reduced.

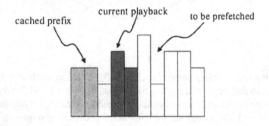

Figure 9.4. A snapshot of prefix caching with workahead smoothing.

To ensure discontinuity-free playback with a start-up delay of s, the proxy has to store a prefix of length $max(d_{max} - s, 0)$, where d_{max} is the maximum delay from the server to the proxy. If cache space is abundant, the proxy can also devote some space to assist in performing workahead smoothing for variable-bit-rate (VBR) media [Sen et al., 1999]. With this smoothing cache, the proxy can prefetch large frames in advance of each burst to absorb delay jitter and bandwidth fluctuations of the server-to-proxy path. The delay of prefetching can be hided by the prefix caching. Similar to sliding-interval caching, the content of the smoothing cache is dynamically updated with playback. However, the purposes are different: the former is to improve cache hit for subsequent requests, while the latter is to facilitate workahead smoothing.

Segment Caching [Chen et al., 2004b, Wu et al., 2001, Miao and Ortega, 2002, Fahmi et al., 2001]: Segment caching generalizes the prefix caching paradigm by partitioning a media object into a series of segments, differentiating their respective utilities, and making caching decision accordingly (see Fig. 9.5). Various segment caching algorithms have been proposed in the literature by employing different segmentations and utility calculations. [Wu et al., 2001] suggested grouping the frames of a media object into variable-sized segments, with the length increasing exponentially with the distance from the start of the media, i.e., the size of segment i is 2^{i-1}, which consists of frames $2^{i-1}, 2^{i-1} + 1, ..., 2^{i} - 1$. The motivation is that a proxy can quickly adapt to the changing access patterns of cached objects by discarding big chunks as needed. The utility of a segment is calculated as the ratio of the segment reference frequency over its distance from the beginning segment, which favors to cache the initial segments as well as those with higher access frequencies. [Chen et al., 2004b], however, argued that neither the use of a predefined segment length nor the favorable caching of the initial segments is the best strategy for reducing network traffic. They suggested postponing segmentation as late as possible (called *lazy segmentation*), thus allowing the proxy to collect a sufficient amount of access statistics to improve the effectiveness.

cached segments

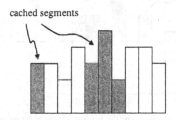

Figure 9.5. An illustration of segment caching.

A salient feature of segment-based caching is its support to VCR-like operations, such as random access, fast-forward, and rewind. As an example, [Fahmi et al., 2001] proposed to cache some key segments of a media object, called *hotspots*, which are identified by content providers. When a client requests the object, the proxy first delivers the hotspots to provide an overview of the stream; the client can then decide whether to play the entire stream or quickly jump to some specific portion introduced by a hotspot. Furthermore, in fast-forwarding and rewinding operations, only the corresponding hotspots are delivered and displayed, while other portions are skipped. As such, the load of the server and backbone network can be greatly reduced, but the client will not miss any important segments in the media object.

Rate-Split Caching [Zhang et al., 2000]: While all the aforementioned caching algorithms partition a media object along the time axis, the rate-split caching partitions a media along the rate axis: the upper part will be cached at the proxy, whereas the lower part will remain stored at the origin server (see Fig. 9.6). This type of partitioning is particularly attractive for VBR streaming, as only the lower part of a nearly constant rate has to be delivered through the backbone network. For a QoS network with resource reservation, the bandwidth reserved should be equal to the peak rate of a stream; caching the upper part at the proxy clearly reduces the rate variability and improves the backbone bandwidth utilization. A critical issue here is how to select the cut-off rate or, equivalently, the size of the upper part for caching. [Zhang et al., 2000] studied the impact of the cut-off rate for a single stream through empirical evaluation, and found that a significant bandwidth reduction can be achieved with a reasonably small cache space. They also formulated the multiple-stream case as a knapsack problem with two constraints: disk bandwidth and cache space, and developed several heuristics, e.g., caching popular objects only, or caching those with high bandwidth reduction.

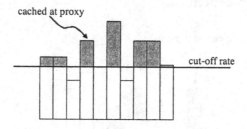

Figure 9.6.   An illustration of rate-split caching.

Summary and Comparison: Tab. 9.1 summarizes the caching algorithms reviewed for homogeneous clients. While these features and metrics provide a general guideline for algorithm selection, the choice for a specific streaming system also largely depends on a number of practical issues, in particular, the complexity of the implementation. In fact, only a few simple algorithms have been employed in commercial systems, though recently-built prototypes have practically demonstrated the viability and superiority of the intelligent algorithms, such as lazy segmentation [Chen et al., 2004b].

In addition, we emphasize that these algorithms are not necessarily exclusive with each other, and a combination of them may yield a better performance. For example, segment caching combined with prefix caching of each segment can reduce start-up latency for VCR-like random playback from any key-segment. Combination with conventional data caching algorithms has also been examined.

Table 9.1. Comparison of the caching algorithms for homogeneous clients

		Sliding-interval caching	Prefix caching	Segment caching	Rate-split caching
Cached portion		Sliding intervals	Prefix	Segments	Portion of higher rate
VCR-like support		No	No	Yes	No
Resource demand	Disk I/O	High	Moderate	Moderate	Moderate
	Disk space	Low	Moderate	High	High
	Sync overhead	Low	Moderate	High	High
Performance improvement	Bandwidth reduction	High*	Moderate	Moderate	Moderate
	Start-up latency reduction	High*	High	High**	Moderate

* There is no reduction for the first request in a run.
** Assume the initial segment is cached.

3.2   Stream Caching for Heterogeneous Clients

Owing to diverse network models and device configurations, clients behind the same proxy often have quite different requirements on the same media object, in terms of streaming rates or encoding formats. To accommodate such heterogeneity, a straightforward solution is to produce replicated streams of different rates or formats, each targeting on a subset of clients. Though being widely used in commercial streaming system, the storage and bandwidth demands of this approach can be prohibitively high [Liu et al., 2004]. An alternative is to transcode a media from one form to another of a lower rate or a different encoding format in an on-demand fashion [Tang et al., 2002]. The intensive computation overhead of transcoding however prevents a proxy from supporting a large, diverse client population.

Yet a more efficient approach to this problem is the use of layered encoding and transmission. A layered coder compresses a raw media object into several layers: the most significant layer, called *base layer*, contains the data representing the most important features of the object, while additional layers, called *enhancement layers*, contain the data that can progressively refine the quality. A client thus can subscribe to a subset of cumulative layers to reconstruct a stream commensurate with its capability. For layered caching, [Kangasharju et al., 2002] assumed that the cached portions are semi-static and only completed layers are cached. To maximize the total revenue, they developed effective heuristics based on an analytical stochastic knapsack model to determine the cache content. In their model, the client population and the distribution of their capacities are known *a priori*. For layered streaming under dynamic conditions, [Rajaie et al., 2000] studied segment-based cache replacement and prefecting policies to achieve efficient utilization of cache space and available bandwidth (see Fig. 9.7a). The main objective is to deal with the congestion problem for individual clients. To this end, the proxy keeps track of popularities of each object on a per layer basis. When the quality of the cached layers is lower than the maximum deliverable quality to an interested client, the proxy sends requests to the server for missing segments within a sliding prefetching window. On cache replacement, a victim layer is identified based on popularities, and its cached segments are flushed from the tail until sufficient space is obtained.

A critical drawback of the existing layered streaming systems is that the number of layers is pretty small, typically 2 or 3 only; hence, their adaptation granularity remains coarse. Fortunately, recent development in the coding area has demonstrated the possibility of fine-grained post-encoding rate control. An example is the MPEG-4 Fine-Grained Scalable (FGS) coder with bitplane coding, which generates embedded streams containing several bitplanes and each can be partitioned at any specific rate. As such, for narrowband clients, the proxy can reduce the streaming rate using a bitplane filter; for wideband clients, the proxy can fetch some uncached portion (i.e., higher-order bitplanes) from the server and assemble it with the cached portion to generate a high-rate stream. As illustrated in Fig. 9.7b, the available bandwidth of a client can be almost fully utilized, and, more importantly, both the filtering and the assembling operations in FGS can be done with fast response. Hence, we envision the FGS-based streaming and caching as a very promising solution to media steaming over the Internet comprising highly heterogeneous end-systems. Several caching algorithms have been proposed to minimize the bandwidth consumption and/or improve the client utility [Liu et al., 2004].

FGS video also facilitates QoS or quality-based cache replacement. As an example, [Yu et al., 2003] showed that differentiating the utilities of different

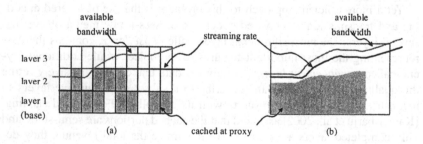

Figure 9.7.   Caching for layered streaming. (a) Coarse-grained layering; (b) Fine-grained layering.

video blocks in cache replacement can noticeably reduce the end-to-end quality distortion. The use of other advanced scalability tools, in particular, MPEG-4 object scalability, has been investigated in [Schojer et al., 2004, Schojer et al., 2003, Podlipnig and Boeszoermenyi, 2002] as well. They have implemented QBIX-G, a Quality Based Intelligent proXy Gateway, which performs both caching and filtering functionalities. It acts as a general broker accommodating heterogeneous user requirements and video variations. In addition, the MPEG-7 and MPEG-21 standards are employed to ensure inter-operability. The whole system enables a desired What You Need is What You Get (WYNIWYG) video services, which delivers videos to users exactly with the quality they expected.

4.   Enhancing Proxy Caching: Multicast Delivery and Proxy Cooperation

So far we consider a standalone proxy with only unicast delivery. While it can significantly reduce the access latencies and backbone bandwidth demands, the scalability and robustness of this simple architecture are still restricted. In this section, we discuss two effective enhancements: multicast and proxy cooperation.

4.1   Combining Proxy Caching with Multicasting

Like caching, multicasting also explores the temporal locality of client requests. Specifically, it allows a media server to accommodate concurrent client requests with shared channels through batching, patching, or periodic broadcast. However, multicast delivery suffers from two important deficiencies. First, to save more bandwidth, it is better to accommodate more requests in one multicast channel by using a large batching/patching window, which however leads to long start-up latencies. Second, while IP multicast is enabled in virtually all local-area networks, its deployment over the global Internet remains limited in scope and reach. Hence, it is unlikely that a multicast streaming protocol can be used for geographically dispersed servers and clients.

Interestingly, both deficiencies can be alleviated through the use of proxies. Specifically, a request can be instantaneously served by a cached prefix while waiting for the data from a multicast channel [Ramesh et al., 2001, Wang et al., 2002], and proxies can bridge unicast networks with multicast networks, i.e., employing unicast for server to proxy delivery while batching and/or patching local accesses. [Wang et al., 2002] have derived the optimal length of the prefix to be cached for most typical multicast protocols, and showed that a careful coupling of caching and multicasting can produce significant cost savings over using the unicast service, even if IP multicast is supported only at local networks.

4.2 Cooperative Proxy Caching

In general, proxies grouped together can achieve better performance than in-dependent standalone proxies. Specifically, the group of proxies can cooperate with each other to increase the aggregate cache space, balance loads, and improve system scalability [Acharya and Smith, 2000, Chae et al., 2002, Hofmann et al., 1999]. A typical cooperative media caching architecture is MiddleMan [Acharya and Smith, 2000], which operates a collection of proxies as a scalable cache cluster. Media objects are segmented into equal-sized segments and stored across multiple proxies, where they can be replaced at a granularity of a segment. There are also several local proxies responsible to answer client requests by locating and relaying the segments. Note that, in cooperative web caching, a critical issue is how to efficiently locate web pages with minimum communication costs among the proxies. This is, however, not a major concern for cooperative media caching, as the bandwidth consumption for streaming objects is of orders of magnitude higher than that for object indexing and discovering. Consequently, in MiddleMan, a centralized coordinator works well in keeping track of cache states. On the other hand, while segment-based caching across different proxies facilitates the distribution and balance of proxy loads, it incurs a significant amount overhead for switching among proxies to reconstruct a media object. To reduce such effects as well as to achieve better load balance and fault tolerance, [Chae et al., 2002] suggested a Silo data layout, which partitions a media object into segments of increasing sizes, stores more copies for popular segments, but still guarantees at least one copy stored for each segment.

5. Streaming Caching in Overlay/Peer-to-Peer Networks

In the above studies, we have focused on the client/server paradigm for media streaming, and proxies act as intermediaries between them. Generalizing the proxy functionalities into every end-host will shift the system to the recently popularized overlay communication paradigms, such as peer-to-peer communication or application-layer multicast. There have been many pioneering efforts on overlay streaming, which have demonstrated the superior scalability and deployability of these overlay systems [Xu et al., 2002, Jin and Bestavros, 2002, Padmanabhan et al., 2002, Cui et al., 2004]. The enormous buffer capacities distributed in end-hosts also enable efficient client-side caching and sharing to improve content availability as well as to support asynchronous streaming. An example that realizes such features is DONet (Data-driven Overlay Network) [Zhang et al., 2005].

DONet is a *data-centric* streaming overlay, where a node always caches and then forwards data to others that are expecting the data, with no prescribed roles like father/child, internal/external, and upstreaming/downstreaming, etc.

In other words, it is the availability of data that guides the flow directions, while not a specific structure (as in IP multicast) that restricts the flow directions. This data-centric design is quite suitable for overlay with highly dynamic nodes, particularly considering that a semi-static structure, no matter how efficient, is constantly rendered to suboptimal due to node dynamics. The core operations in DONet are very simple: every node periodically exchanges (cached) data availability information with a set of partners, and retrieves unavailable data from one or more partners, or supplies available data to partners. There are three salient features of this data-driven design: 1) *easy to implement*, as it does not have to construct and maintain a complex global structure; 2) *efficient*, as data forwarding is dynamically determined according to data availability while not restricted by specific directions; and 3) *robust and resilient*, as the partnerships as well as the periodically updated data availability information enable adaptive and quick switching among multi-suppliers.

To realize the data-driven design for live media streaming, a set of practical challenges have to be addressed, including how the partnerships are formed; how the data availability information are encoded and exchanged; and how the video data are supplied and retrieved among partners. DONet employs a scalable membership and partnership management algorithm together with an intelligent scheduling algorithm, which enable efficient and continuous streaming of medium- to high-bandwidth contents with low control overhead. They also evenly distribute the forwarding load among the participating nodes, and accommodate nodes with heterogeneous capabilities.

A prototype of DONet have been built and extensively evaluated over the PlanetLab testbed (http://www.planet-lab.org). The experiments, involving almost all the active PlanetLab nodes, demonstrated that DONet achieves high streaming quality in terms of rate and playback continuity. Meanwhile, its transmission delay and control overhead are both kept at low levels. A public Internet-based DONet implementation, called *CoolStreaming v.0.9*, was released on May 30, 2004, which has been used to lively broadcast sports programs offered freely by a video server. While initially attracted only 20 users, till July 2004, over 50000 distinct users (in terms of unique IP addresses) have tested this streaming system, and more than 6000 users have been simultaneously online at some peak times. The preliminary statistical results as well as the feedbacks from the users are quite encouraging, which reveal that the current Internet has enough available bandwidth to support TV-quality streaming ($\geq$ 450 Kbps).

Nevertheless, we are aware that, in contrast to the reliable and dedicated servers or proxies, the loosely-coupled autonomous end-hosts can easily crash, leave without notice, or even refuse to share its own data. Given that a media playback lasts a long time and consumes huge resources, we believe dedicated proxies will still play an important role in building high-quality media streaming systems; in particular, strategically placed proxies may effectively assist the

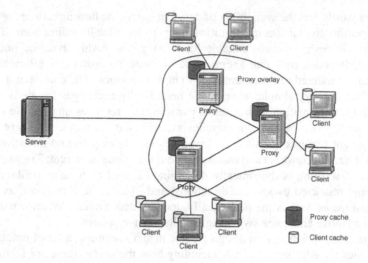

Figure 9.8.   An illustration of the cooperative proxy-client caching architecture.

construction and maintenance of large-scale overlays. On the other hand, we may also leverage the overlay paradigm in proxy design. As an example, [Guo et al., 2004] suggested a proxy and its clients be structured into a peer-to-peer system to collaboratively serve local streaming requests. Their work focused on local area collaboration. [Ip et al., 2004] extended it to a two-level streaming overlay, called Cooperative Proxy-Client Caching System, or COPACC.

Fig. 9.8 depicts a generic architecture of COPACC. A cluster of proxies are logically connected through direct or indirect peer links to form a proxy overlay, and each of them serves as the *home proxy* for a set of local clients. The proxies and their clients are closely located with relatively low communication costs, e.g., they could be in the same ISP domain or in the same metropolitan area. A server storing the repository of videos, however, is far away from them, and the remote communications incur much higher costs.

The video data are cached across both proxies and clients. Since the storage space of a proxy or a client is limited, the videos are partially cached only, and there is always a full copy at the server. Specifically, as shown in Fig. 9.9, a video stream is partitioned into a *prefix* and a *suffix*, and the beginning part of the later is also referred to as the *prefix-of-suffix*. The proxies are responsible to cache the prefix of video, whereas the clients cache the prefix-of-suffix of video. This setting not only reduces the initial playback latency but also facilitates the multicast delivery to local clients. When a client expects to play a video, it first initiates a playback request to its home proxy, which intercepts the request and computes a streaming schedule: when and where to fetch which portion of

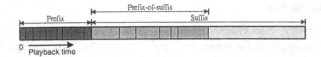

Figure 9.9. An illustration of the different portions of a video stream in COPACC. The prefix is to be cached by proxies, while the prefix-of-suffix by clients

the video. It then accordingly fetches the prefix, prefix-of-suffix, as well as the remaining part of suffix, and relays the incoming stream to the client. If needed, a proxy may also perform a verification operation, which detects forged video data through a simple signature mechanism.

There are two key issues to be addressed in the COPACC architecture:

- How to partition each video and allocate the prefixes and prefix-of-suffixes to different proxy and client caches? The objective is to minimize the total transmission cost of the COPACC system given the video access patterns, the heterogeneous transmission costs, and the storage constraints.

- How to manage, search, and retrieve the cached data in different proxies and clients? These operations should be highly efficient so as to deploy COPACC in large-scale networks with intensive requests.

In [Ip et al., 2004], a comprehensive suite of distributed protocols have been proposed to facilitate the interactions among different COPACC entities. Most operations in this protocol suite are executed by dedicated proxies. As such, it is not only suitable for clients with limited computation power, but also resilient to client failures. COPACC has also embedded an efficient indexing and searching algorithm for video contents cached across different proxies or clients, as well as a signature verification mechanism, which can effectively identify and block malicious clients.

Simulation results for COPACC demonstrated that it achieves remarkably lower transmission cost as compared to pure proxy-based caching with limited storage space. On the other hand, with the assistance from dedicated proxies, it is much more robust than a pure peer-to-peer system. Its transmission cost only slightly increases when a large portion of clients fail, even though the clients contribute a significant fraction in the total cache space. Moreover, It scales well to larger networks, and the cost generally reduces when more proxies and clients cooperate with each other.

6.   Summary

Proxy caching is an effective means to reduce access latencies as well as resource consumptions for networked applications. Due to the unique features of media objects like huge size and high bandwidth demand, a number of novel streaming caching solutions have been reported in the literature. This chapter serves as a pioneer survey to this field, though it by no means covers all aspects. Plenty of research issues have yet to be addressed, e.g., caching over the wireless mobile Internet, for large-scale dynamic overlays, and with advanced video coding/indexing schemes such as multiple description coding [Padmanabhan et al., 2002] and MPEG-7/21 standards, as well as security and privacy for cached media objects, to name but a few. We envision that streaming media caching remains a fertile area, and both theoretical and practical solutions to the listed problems are urged with rising demands on ubiquitous multimedia services throughout the world.

Acknowledgments

J. Liu's work is partially supported by a Canadian NSERC Discovery Grant and a SFU President's Research Grant.

References

Tewari, R., Vin, H. M., Dan, A., and Sitaram, D. (1998). Resource-based caching for Web servers. In *Proceedings of SPIE/ACM Conf. on Multimedia Computing and Networking (MMCN'98)*, San Jose, CA.

Chen, S., Shen, B., Yan, Y., Basu, S., and Zhang, X. (2004a). SRB: Shared running buffers in proxy to exploit memory locality of multiple streaming media sessions. In *Proceedings of the 24th IEEE International Conference on Distributed Computing Systems (ICDCS)*.

Sen, S., Rexford, J., and Towsley, D. (1999). Proxy prefix caching for multimedia streams. In *Proceedings of IEEE INFOCOM'99*, New York, NY.

Wu, K. L., Yu, P. S., and Wolf, J. L. (2001). Segment-based proxy caching of multimedia streams. In *Proceedings of World Wide Web Conference (WWW10)*, Hong Kong.

Miao, Z., and Ortega, A. (2002). Scalable proxy caching of video under storage constraints. *IEEE Journal on Selected Areas in Communications*, vol. 20, no. 7, pp. 1315-1327, Sep. 2002.

Fahmi, H., Latif, M., Sedigh-Ali, S., Ghafoor, A., Liu, P., and Hsu, L. (2001). Proxy servers for scalable interactive video support. *IEEE Computer*, 43(9): 54-60.

Zhang, Z.-L., Wang, Y., Du, D., and Su, D. (2000). Video staging: A proxy-server-based approach to end-to-end video delivery over wide-area networks. *IEEE/ACM Transactions on Networking*, 8(4): 429-442.

Liu, J., Chu, X., and Xu, J. (2004). Proxy Cache Management for Fine-Grained Scalable Video Streaming *Proceedings of IEEE INFOCOM'04*, Hong Kong.

Tang, X., Zhang, F., and Chanson, S. T. (2002). Streaming media caching algorithms for transcoding proxies. In *Proceedings of 31st International Conference on Parallel Processing (ICPP'02)*.

Kangasharju, J., Hartanto, F., Reisslein, M., and Ross, K. W. (2002). Distributing layered encoded video through caches. *IEEE Transactions on Computers*, 51(6), pp. 622-636.

Rejaie, R., Yu, H., Handley, M., and Estrin, D. (2000). Multimedia proxy caching mechanism for quality adaptive streaming applications in the Internet. In *Proceedings of IEEE INFOCOM'00*, Tel Aviv, Israel.

Ramesh, S., Rhee, I., and Guo, K. (2001). Multicast with cache (Mcache): An adaptive zero-delay video-on-demand service. In *Proceedings of IEEE INFOCOM'01*, Anchorage, AK.

Wang, B., Sen, S., Adler, M., and Towsley, D. (2002). Optimal proxy cache allocation for efficient streaming media distribution. In *Proceedings of IEEE INFOCOM'02*, New York, NY.

Acharya, S. and Smith, B. C. (2000). Middleman: A video caching proxy server. In *Proceedings of 10th International Workshop on Network and Operating Systems Support for Digital Audio and Video (NOSSDAV'00)*.

Chae, Y., Guo, K., Buddhikot, M. M., Suri, S., and Zegura, E. W. (2002). Silo, rainbow, and caching token: Schemes for scalable, fault tolerant stream caching. *IEEE Journal on Selected Areas in Communications*, 20(7), pp. 1328-1344.

Xu, D., Hefeeda, M., Hambrusch, S., and Bhargava, B. (2002). On peer-to-peer media streaming. In *Proceedings of IEEE International Conference on Distributed Computing Systems (ICDCS'02)*, Wien, Austria.

Jin, S. and Bestavros, A. (2002). Cache-and-relay streaming media delivery for asynchronous clients. In *Proceedings of the 4th International Workshop on Networked Group Communication (NGC)*, Boston, MA, USA.

Padmanabhan, V. N., Wang, H. J., Chou, P. A., and Sripanidkulchai, K. (2002). Distributing streaming media content using cooperative networking. In *Proceedings of 12th International Workshop on Network and Operating Systems Support for Digital Audio and Video (NOSSDAV'02)*, Miami, FL, USA.

Cui, Y., Li, B., and Nahrstedt, K. (2004). oStream: Asynchronous Streaming Multicast in Application-Layer Overlay Networks. *IEEE Journal on Selected Areas in Communications*, 22(1), pp. 91-106.

Guo, L., Chen, S., Ren, S., Chen, X., and Jiang, S. (2004). PROP: a scalable and reliable P2P assisted proxy streaming system. In *Proceedings of IEEE*

International Conference on Distributed Computing Systems (ICDCS'04), Tokyo, Japan.

Hofmann, M. , Ng, T. E., Guo, K., Paul, S., and Zhang, H. (1999) Caching Techniques for Streaming Multimedia over the Internet. *Technical Report, Bell Labs*.

Chen, S., Shen, B., Wee, S., and Zhang, X. (2004b). Designs of high quality streaming proxy systems. In *Proceedings of of IEEE INFOCOM'04*, Hong Kong.

Zhang, X., Liu, J., Li, B., and Yum, T.-S. P. (2005). CoolStreaming/DONet: A Data-driven overlay network for peer-to-peer live media streaming. In *Proceedings of IEEE INFOCOM'05*, Miami, FL, USA.

Ip, A. T.-S., Liu, J., and Lui, J. C.-S. (2004). COPACC: A cooperative proxy-client caching system for on-demand media streaming. *Technical Report, Chinese University of Hong Kong*.

Yu, F., Zhang, Q., Zhu, W., and Zhang, Y.-Q. (2003). QoS-adaptive proxy caching for multimedia streaming over the Internet. *IEEE Trans. on Circuit and System for Video Technology*.

Schojer, P., Böszörmenyi, L., and Hellwagner, H. (2004). QBIX-G: A Quality Based Intelligent proXy Gateway. em Technical Reports of the Institute of Information Technology, University Klagenfurt,TR/ITEC/04/2.16.

Schojer, P., Böszörmenyi, L., Hellwagner, H., Penz, B., and Podlipnig, S.(2003). Architecture of a quality based intelligent proxy (QBIX) for MPEG-4 videos. In *Proceedings of the 2003 ACM World Wide Web Conference (WWW'2003)*, Budapest,Hungary.

Podlipnig, S. and Böszörmenyi, L. (2002). Replacement strategies for quality based video caching. In *Proceedings of IEEE International Conference on Multimedia and Expo (ICME)*, Lausanne, Switzerland.

Chapter 10

POLICY-BASED RESOURCE SHARING
IN STREAMING OVERLAY NETWORKS

K. Selçuk Candan*, Yusuf Akca, and Wen-Syan Li[†]

NEC Laboratories America,
10080 North Wolfe Road, Suite SW3-350, Cupertino, CA 95014, USA
{candan,yakca,wen} @ sv.nec-labs.com

Abstract   In this chapter, we discuss peer-to-peer media streaming overlay network architectures and introduce a policy-based architecture for streaming live media
from media sources to end-users over independently owned and operated networks. This architecture (mSON) efficiently supports multiple simultaneous
media streams, with different sources and user populations, through *shared* overlay resources. The overlay network infrastructure takes into account the existence
of multiple content providers (media sources) and minimizes its footprint to use
available resources most effectively. In the meanwhile, it prevents resources
from being overutilized to prevent congestions, service rejections, and jitters in
the streams users receive. We report experimental results that show that the
policy-based mSON achieves these tasks efficiently and effectively.

Keywords: Overlay networks, multicasting, live media streaming, policy-based QoS, peer-
to-peer adaptation, multi-source, multi-sink

1.   Introduction

Wide-area data dissemination of streaming media poses significant challenges in the context of current Internet structure. Without appropriate multicasting mechanisms, network routes are quickly congested. IP multicasting
based solutions do not go far due to the incompatibility of the various independent network elements. Overlay based solutions address the incompatibility

---

*Current address: CSE Dept., Arizona State University, Tempe, AZ 85287, USA. This chapter describes
work performed during author's visit at NEC.

[†]Current address: IBM Almaden Research Labs, San Jose, CA 95120, USA. This chapter describes work
performed while the author was employed at NEC.

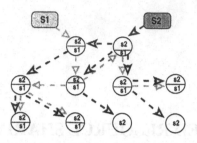

Figure 10.1. A multicasting overlay network supporting multiple content providers (media sources) s1 and s2 (proxies and network resources are shared)

and interoperability problems at the physical network layer by building virtual networks on top of the underlying physical network. By distributing the user load intelligently across alternative sources and by creating multicast hierarchies within the networks, the overlay networks reduce the overall load on each server and congestion on the network. Also, by regulating the number of proxies on the delivery path, they limit the jitter in the packets being delivered to end-users. Since they maintain service agreements with the ISPs and since they oversee the creation and maintenance of multicast hierarchies (with predictable lifetimes), they deploy policies and resource reservation protocols to prevent fluctuations in the service.

In this chapter, we present a policy-driven peer-to-peer media streaming overlay network (mSON) architecture for streaming live media over independently owned/operated networks (Figure 10.1). The physical network on which the overlay operates consists of multiple autonomous systems (ASs), each of which can host proxy servers that can act as Multicast Service Nodes or (MSNs) [Shi and Turner, 2002, Banerjee et al., 2003]. Each AS is an independent entity; therefore, the overlay has to compensate ASs for the resources consumed. The last mile (i.e., the final leg of the streams from the source to the end-users' systems), on the other hand, is charged to end-users by their ISPs (usually in terms of monthly cable modem or DSL subscription charges). Therefore, the goal of the overlay is to deploy its network-wide proxies to bring streamed media closer to the last-mile, while minimizing its own operational costs. The dynamic adjustment of proxy network is based on parameters including (1) concurrent media sources, (2) distribution of user requests, (3) network conditions, and (4) capacity of proxy servers.

mSON approach to peer-to-peer media streaming differs from most existing approaches in its optimization criteria. Most systems aim at creating multicast trees in a way that latency observed by the end-users of the corresponding media source is minimized. For instance, [Banerjee et al., 2003] formulates the overlay networking problem as a *degree constrained minimum average latency problem*

[Blum et al., 1994] and develops multicasting algorithms that addressed this problem. Most existing work, however, misses two critical constraints faced by media overlay networks:

- An overlay network has to support multiple simultaneous media streams, each with a different source and user population. The network infrastructure should take into account the existence of multiple media sources *sharing* the same resources (Figure 10.1).

- The overlay network should minimize its footprint on the network to minimize its operational costs and use its resources most effectively. However, resources should not be overutilized; otherwise, end-users will observe congestions, service rejections, and jitters.

The mSON architecture considers these two aspects of an effective media streaming architecture in addition to the average latency provided to the end-users. In other words, unlike most existing work, the overlay is explicitly optimized for resource (link and node) stress [Castro et al., 2003b] (or tension) along with the depth of the multicast trees. Unlike related work in resource allocation for overlay multicasts, such as [Cui et al., 2003] which presents optimal resource allocation schemes for single source network, mSON is specifically designed for shared, multi source, networks.

Another aspect that differentiates mSON style overlay networking from most recent peer-to-peer multicasting [Xu et al., 2002, Banerjee et al., 2003, Banerjee et al., 2002, Blum et al., 1994] work is that, instead of focusing on peers that independently arrive and leave the system, mSON is specifically designed to consider peer-to-peer negotiations between overlay's own proxies. Consequently, except during failures or at the edges where user arrival is not in overlay's control, the way proxies join and leave a multicast tree is controllable and is based on mutual agreements that will benefit the overlay in the long run. mSON leverages this to ensure that overlay's resources are used most efficiently.

1.1   End-Users and Network Resources

The Internet consists of autonomous systems (ASs). User requests are captured at (or redirected to) the proxies that are in the same AS as (or close to) the users. Overlay network resources (such as proxies) are placed in an AS after resource and QoS agreements signed. Consequently, the overlay service provider has to compensate each AS for the bandwidth streamed through it, while providing certain bandwidth and QoS guarantees as specified with the agreement. ASs are connected to each other through peering points (or borders) (Figure 10.2). Each peering point has a maximum bandwidth capacity as specified in the service agreements. Therefore, one of mSON's primary goals is to minimize the amount of traffic that flows across AS boundaries. On the

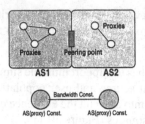

Figure 10.2. Two ASs connected with a peering point and the corresponding resource constraints

other hand, purchasing, deploying, and maintaining a proxy server in an AS is costly. Therefore, mSON also aims to minimize the total number of proxy servers that needs to be deployed to carry a given workload.

1.2   Policy Description

Most existing work on utility-based multicast routing, such as [Kelly et al., 1998] and [Kar et al., 2001], are focussed mainly on the use of pricing mechanisms to efficiently manage network resources. [Cui et al., 2003] provides a rate based overlay multicasting model based on the maximization of a utility function over all receivers in the overlay network. In overlay systems, however, resources of the proxies are as valuable as that of the underlying network [Amir et al., 2002]. In a streaming overlay network, the role of each overlay proxy server is to multiplex the stream it receives from another proxy and serve the resulting streams to other proxies or to end-users.

Without a loss of generality, let us model the proxies in a given AS as a single virtual proxy, analogous Multicast Service Nodes, as in [Banerjee et al., 2003]. Each AS has a multiplexing capacity, determined by the processing power of the available proxy servers in the AS and the local bandwidth availabilities. Given the amount of resources in a given AS, the overlay needs to maintain a level of resource utilization. Underutilization of the resources, such as bandwidth, is not desirable as in many cases the overlay service provider has to pay for resources allocated even if they are not utilized. Like underutilization, overutilization of the available resources is also not desirable as overutilization can lead to congestions, rejection of user requests, jitters, and vulnerability to sudden changes in the load. mSON models the effects of these two factors, underutilization and overutilization, in terms of an intuitive *policy* concept, which represents the underlying *costs* associated with deviating from the intended proxy resource utilization rate:

- resource tension is minimal (t_{pref}) when a resource is used at its intended load (l_{pref}).

- tension rises rapidly (to ∞) when the load on the resources reaches unacceptable high rates, l_{limit}.

- tension also increases as the utilization drops below the preferred rate as the overlay has to pay for these underutilized resources, and

- the resource tension is 0 when the resource is not utilized at all. If the workload can be maintained while keeping a particular resource at 0 utilization, then the resource can be removed from the system or can be re-allocated for other services the overlay provides.

Thus the concept of tension captures not-only real-time optimization needs (prevention of overutilization of resources), but it also favors releasing of resources altogether if possible, promoting mid- to long-term efficient allocation of resources. In general, an interaction between two resources, r_i and r_j is *desirable* if and only if

$$tension_i(l_{before,i}) + tension_j(l_{before,j}) > tension_i(l_{after,i}) + tension_j(l_{after,j}).$$

Although resource interactions are limited to those that reduce the overall tensions, user-resource interactions can increase the overall tension in the system. Although for an underutilized resource, addition of a new user will reduce its tension, for a resource being utilized at or above its preferred load, a new user will cause an increase in the tension. After a user interaction which increases the tension (such as a user leaving an already underutilized resource or a new user requesting an overutilized one) proxies can interact to reduce the overall tension in the system.

Given two alternative loads, l_1 and l_2, the policy graph describes which load is more desirable (i.e., $tension(l_1) < tension(l_2)$ or vice versa). Figure 10.3 presents two sample policy (tension) graphs, corresponding to different overlay service provider policies. These two policy graphs differ in that they represent different cost structures for underutilized and overutilized proxies. The graph in Figure 10.3(a) gets flatter as the utilization increases towards the preferred rate. If an overlay is using this policy graph, all *used* proxies are likely to fill up at the same rate. The slope in Figure 10.3(b) on the other hand gets steeper as the load increases towards the perfect utilization rate. Consequently, the second graph favors those proxies whose utilization is already close to perfect when choosing which proxy to use for new requests. The proxies that are almost empty are not loaded with additional loads. Thus, a few proxies would reach the perfect utilization quickly, and only after that other proxies would start being utilized. Both of these graphs provide high penalties to resources that are very lightly used; in other words, both graphs prefers a non-utilized proxy to a very lightly utilized one. In both cases, there is a cost associated with activating a new proxy in the proxy network and maintaining that proxy at a very light utilization rate.

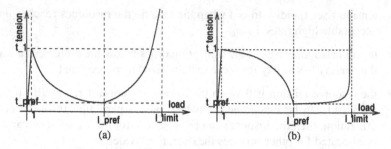

Figure 10.3. (a) An example resource policy graph favoring balanced utilization of available resources; (b) an alternative policy graph favoring the creation of a small *core* of resources carrying the current workload

The two graphs also differ in the way they treat overutilized proxies. While the penalty of overutilizing a proxy increases sharply for the resource presented in Figure 10.3(a), the policy modelled in Figure 10.3(b) allows proxies to be loaded very close to their limits.

1.3   Policy-based Resource Allocation on Shared Networks

Given the resource utilization policies described above, the overlay's task is to delivering multiple streams to end users, using as little resources as possible, while preventing congestions and reductions in QoS. Formally, at a given point in time, the state of the overlay network is described as follows:

- overlay owns and operates a set, $\mathcal{P}$, of proxies.

- overlay operates in an AS network, $G(\mathcal{V}, \mathcal{E})$, where $\mathcal{V}$ is the set of ASs the overlay has agreements with and $\mathcal{E}$ is the set of peering points (or borders) across these ASs. Each proxy $p_i \in \mathcal{P}$ is associated with a an as denoted as $loc(p_i)$. As stated earlier, without a loss of generalization, we assume that each network node contains at most one proxy).

- overlay's resource utilization policy that applies to a proxy $p_i \in \mathcal{P}$ is captured by a policy graph, $ptension_i$, as described earlier. Specifically, $pcap_i$ denotes the total multiplexing capacity (due to buffer, CPU, or local bandwidth limitations), of the proxy and $putil_i$ denotes its intended rate of utilization.

- each peering point $e_j \in \mathcal{E}$, has a maximum bandwidth capacity denoted as $bcap_j$ determined based on the service agreements. For each peering point, e_j, the overlay associates a policy $btension_j$ and an intended utilization $butil_j$.

- overlay simultaneously serves media from its media providers, S, where each provider has an associated source $s_i \in S$ hosted at an origin proxy $host(s_i) \in P$.

- end-users access streaming media by forwarding requests to the proxies of the overlay network. Therefore, at each proxy p_i, there is a $load(p_i, s_j)$ associated with the media served by source s_j.

The state of the network is subject to changes. The goal of the overlay is to adapt to these changes and deliver media streams using as little resource as possible, while providing low end-to-end delays. To achieve this task, mSON deploys proxy-based overlay multicasting structures. Given a set of proxies, an AS-level network structure, a set of media sources, and user access loads, mSON creates multicast trees such that

- resources are not overutilized,
- resources are not underutilized, and
- end-to-end delays are small.

Overlay proxies are shared resources, serving multiple streams simultaneously. Therefore, unlike other multicasting approaches, mSON does not focus on individual multicasts, but takes a holistic approach, where the shared resources are allocated in a way to support all streams the overlay serves at a given point in time. Therefore, mSON creates and maintains a set, T, of multicast trees for the overlay network over the shared resources. For each active media source s_i mSON maintains a (directed) multicast tree, $T_i(V_i, C_i) \in T$, where $V_i \subseteq V$ and each C_i is a path on $\mathcal{E}$. The root of the each tree T_i is a media source and the leaves of the tree are the proxies which serve end-users. A single proxy-to-proxy connection on the overlay network may pass through multiple ASs depending on the actual network structure. Therefore, each overlay connection $c_j \in C_i$ between two proxies has a corresponding set of edges (peering points), $path(c_j) \in 2^{\mathcal{E}}$, denoting the path it follows on the actual AS structure $\mathcal{G}$. The trees maintained by mSON respect the overlay's proxy and network resource utilization policies:

$$\forall p_i \in P \;\; pload_i = \sum_{T_j \in T} out_{j,loc(p_i)} \simeq putil_i,$$

and

$$\forall e_k \in \mathcal{E} \;\; bload_k = \sum_{T_j \in T} [c_l \in C_j][e_k \in path(c_l)] \simeq butil_k.$$

In other words, the overall resource tension in the system should be minimal:

$$\left(\sum_{e_j \in \mathcal{E}} btension_j \right) + \left(\sum_{v_j \in V} ptension_j \right).$$

Note that this formulation implicitly minimizes the latency of the resulting multicast trees; since each edge (even those edges that are used at their perfect utilization levels - see Figure 10.3) adds to the overall tension, the use of unnecessary edges is strongly discouraged. Thus, the latency of the resulting trees are implicitly minimized (subject to resource constraints and preferred utilization rates) as well.

1.4   Policy Cross-Talk

As described above, mSON identifies on two different types of resources: proxies and bandwidth. Although these are different, their policies need to be related. First of all, irrespective of its non-network resources (such as CPU and memory), a proxy can not multiplex more streams then the network bandwidth available at its outgoing peering points allow. Also, although an AS could tunnel streams to other ASs without having to use local multiplexing resources, the amount of available peering point resources bound the multiplexing power of the proxy; thus, since it consumes network bandwidth at the peering points, tunneling would impact (reduce) the multiplexing capacity of the proxy.

On the other hand, if network tunneling is cheap (i.e., network resources are not constrained), then overlay may not have an incentive to activate proxies closer to the edge and may choose to use such tunnels instead (Figure 10.4). As a result, the overlay may create shallow multicast trees with long proxy-to-proxy network connections, where most edge proxies are simply connected to the proxies closer to the root. Therefore, the cost of creating a new proxy, the network cost, and the multicast trees overlays create are interdependent.

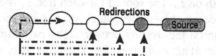

Figure 10.4.   Tunneling redirections instead of activating proxies close to the edge

In the next section, we provide an overview of the decentralized protocols mSON uses to achieve policy-driven resource allocation.

1.5   Protocols needed by Peer-to-Peer Media Streaming Overlay Network

Operation of a peer-to-peer media streaming overlay network requires three complementary protocols:

- a media streaming protocol,

- an information exchange protocol between peers to keep them aware of the status of the overlay network, and

- a multicast management protocol to create and manage the multicast trees for efficient utilization of resources.

In this section, we provide an overview of these three protocols. Since the underlying peer-to-peer decision making processes are embedded in the multicast management protocol, in the rest of the chapter, we focus on the third of these three protocols and discuss it in greater detail.

Media Streaming Protocol (MSP).   The media streaming protocol is specific to the media types delivered through the overlay and specifies how media is transmitted from the source to the end-users through a chain of proxies established by the overlay. These include control protocols, such as *Real-time Streaming Protocol* (RTSP) and *Realtime Control Protocol* (RTCP), and transport-level protocols, such as *Realtime Transport Protocol* (RTP). In this chapter, we do not assume any specific media streaming protocol.

Information Exchange Protocol (IEP).   In a decentralized overlay operating through negotiations between proxies in the network, there is a need for an information exchange protocol that will enable proxies to collect up-to-date information about the environment they operate in. Based on the formalism introduced earlier, in Table 10.1, we highlight the information that each proxy, $p_i \in \mathcal{P}$, collects from its neighbors and from the sources in a distributed fashion. Each proxy collects this information through regular communications with the other proxies it knows. This regular information exchange also helps proxies to identify when the connection between two proxies becomes broken. Note that, a link may be declared failed, when the QoS over the link becomes unacceptably low even though control-messages travel without any problem. This is taken care of network monitoring processes that run on each proxy. In addition to periodic information exchange, each proxy can also piggyback its current list of values to other messages it exchanges with its neighbors or can explicitly demand new information when it senses that the status may have been changed (due to a failure or insertion of new sources).

Although most of the information in Table 10.1 requires knowledge about only the immediate neighborhood. In other words, mSON needs to estimate current source to proxy distances that will be used by the multicast management protocol to guide multicast tree creation process. On the other hand, estimating the minimum cost, $minbcost_{i,j}$, of sending a stream from a source, s_j to a proxy, p_i, (the minimum cost of sending a stream from source s_j to p_i based on the current network and proxy utilizations) requires a distributed routing (or distance-vector) style algorithm running on the overlay proxies. To eliminate errors during the estimation of the source to proxy distances that will be used by the multicast management protocol to guide multicast tree creation process, mSON uses distance estimation protocols (such as DUAL [Garcia-

Table 10.1. Information collected and maintained by proxy p_i

Inform.	Meaning
$\mathcal{N}_i$	the list of proxies that are its *neighbors*. The concept of neighborhood is logical. Initially, the list contains its physical neighbors; however, as the load increases, the neighbor list may extend to include proxies that are not immediate neighbors.
$bload_k$ $btension_k$	the current load and the tension(respectively) of each path, e_k, to its neighbors,
$pload_j$ $ptension_j$	the current load and the tension (respectively) of each proxy $p_j \in \mathcal{N}_i$ in its neighborhood.
$minbcost_{i,j}$	the minimum cost of sending a stream from source s_j to p_i.

Lunes-Aceves, 1993], EIGRP [Albrightson et al., 1994], RIP-MTI [Schmid and Steigner, 2002], and LPA [Murthy and Garcia-Luna-Aceves, 1995]) which eliminate loops or minimize the undesirable effects of routing loops. Note that, even though the physical network may not be changing, the distance values (which measure the cost of streams) can vary during the operation of the over-lay based on the current load on the peering points. One way to eliminate the need for constant information exchange among proxies and to limit such exchange to only significant changes in the network structure, such as addition or removal of a proxy or network edge, is to calculates the shortest distance values based on the assumption that the network and the proxies are used at their preferred levels.

1.6   Multicast Management Protocol (MMP)

The multicast management protocol has two major tasks; creating the multicast trees that will be used for delivering streams from the sources to the end-users, and updating these multicast trees as the load and request characteristics in the overlay network changes. In the rest of this chapter, we provide an overview of how mSON achieves these tasks in a decentralized manner through communications and negotiations among neighboring proxies. mSON operates in a request-driven fashion. When a new source is inserted into the system, the only required *registration* or *initialization* process is to make the proxies aware of the new source. This can be achieved through a central lookup registry, by pushing the list of the sources to the proxies, or by letting proxies to discover sources in the system through the information exchange protocol discussed earlier. Otherwise, the operation of each proxy is driven by

- join requests from other proxies,

- stop requests from other proxies, and

- messages that initiate changes in the multicast tree structures.

In the sections, we discuss the various aspects of the Multicast Management Protocol (MMP) in detail.

2. Policy-Driven Peer Actions in a Shared Overlay Network

The mSON architecture uses decentralized proxy to proxy collaborations, including request redirections, load *redistributions*, and load *consolidations*, for optimizing resource utilization in the overlay network. Based on the available policy descriptions, a proxy which receives a request may redirect the request to a more suitable proxy in its neighborhood (Figure 10.5). An overloaded resource (Figure 10.6) may initiate a redistribution process which ships part of the load to a different proxy. Similarly, an underutilized resource may initiate consolidations (Figure 10.7) of overlay resources.

These policy-driven proxy actions ensure that the overlay network scales and adapts itself as media sources and end-users come and go and as multi-cast trees are created and torn apart. Consequently, unlike IP-multicasting [Eriksson, 1994], mSON understands and integrates AS-level service agreements. Furthermore, unlike most work in overlay multicasting (for example [Shi and Turner, 2002, Banerjee et al., 2003, Banerjee et al., 2002]), it is aware of the

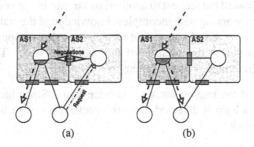

Figure 10.5. Request redirection: (a) before and (b) after

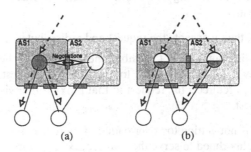

Figure 10.6. Load redistribution to prevent overutilization: (a) before and (b) after

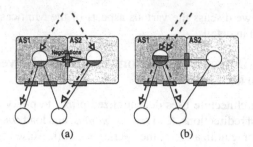

Figure 10.7. Load consolidation to prevent underutilization: (a) before and (b) after

shared nature of the overlay network and aims optimizing the utilization of the network and proxy resources along with the average delay *within an integrated framework*. Unlike static overlay-network based solutions [RealNetworks, 2005], mSON adapts to the varying data, network, and user conditions dynamically in a truly distributed, peer-to-peer manner.

2.1   Handling Join Requests

When a proxy p_i receives a request from a user or another proxy for access to the media stream multicasted at source s_j, it has to decide whether it should serve this request or forward the request to another, more suitable proxy (Figure 10.5). Since, proxies are working with incomplete knowledge of the status of the entire mSON, this step is especially important for ensuring that an appropriate search space is covered during the creation of the multicast trees. The decision to accept a new join request is based on the following criteria:

1 p_i checks if the request causes a service loop. Since loops are not desirable, if a loop is detected, then the request needs to be redirected to another proxy.

2 if p_i will get too overloaded when this request is admitted, p_i checks if redistributing its existing load to other servers can enable it to accept this new request.

   (a) if so, then it accepts the request and redistributes its load

   (b) if redistribution is not possible, then it checks if there is a suitable proxy in the neighborhood to serve the join request. If it finds one then p_i redirects the request to that proxy; otherwise, it denies the request.

3 even if p_i is not getting too overloaded, if there is a more suitable proxy in the neighborhood to serve the join request, p_i redirects the request to that proxy.

4 otherwise, if p_i is already serving the stream, then it admits the new request.

5 if p_i is not serving the stream yet,

   (a) if it has a more suitable neighbor, then it redirects the request to that neighbor,

   (b) otherwise, it admits the request and sends a join request to a *candidate* parent based on its neighbors' distances (costs) from the source and their current tensions.

Below, we discuss the underlying processes in greater detail.

Overload Detection and Elimination.   Before admitting a join request, p_i has to check whether it is becoming too overloaded. Obviously, if the proxy resource utilization reaches the absolute maximum, the proxy can not accept new requests. To promote overall system performance, instead of defining overload in absolute terms, we say that the proxy is too overloaded if shedding a fraction (Θ) of its load to some other server (say p_h) will be beneficial to the overall operation of mSON; in other words, p_i is overloaded when

$$t\_reduction\_at\_i > (1 + \gamma_d) \times t\_increase\_at\_h$$

or

$$plension_i(pload_i) - ptension_i((1 - \theta) \times pload_i) >$$
$$(1 + \gamma_d) \times ptension_h(\theta \times pload_i).$$

Here, $0.0 \leq \gamma_d$ is the threshold for initiating a load redistribution. If this condition is satisfied, then mSON uses redirection and redistribution negotiations (see below and Section 2.3) between proxies to identify and handle detected overloads.

Identification of a More Suitable Neighbor to Serve a Request and Redirection.   Before admitting a join request for a stream from source s_j, p_i checks if there is any proxy in its neighborhood better suited to admit this request than itself. p_i first calculates a self-cost of admitting the request (a negative cost denotes reduced tension; hence *benefit*). If p_i is already serving the stream, then the self-cost can be calculated as follows:

$$selfcost = ptension_i(new\_pl_i) - ptension_i(old\_pl_i)$$

If p_i is not yet serving the stream, on the other hand, the expected network cost (increase in the tension in the network resources) must be taken into account as well. Therefore, in that case, p_i estimates the cost of admitting this request as follows:

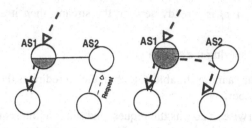

Figure 10.8.   Request redirection and tunneling: proxy resources of AS2 are not utilized

$$selfcost = ptension_i(new\_pl_i) - ptension_i(old\_pl_i) + minbcost_{i,j}$$

As discussed earlier , $minbcost_{i,j}$ is the cheapest distance based on the current tension values in the network between servers s_i and s_j. Clearly, this value is only an estimate of the actual network and costs: the request for a particular stream may be routed through a more costly route depending on actual resource loads or routing may cost much less if a multicast tree serving the stream is found nearby.

The costs of the request for the neighbors (say p_h) of p_i are also calculated in a similar manner:

$$cost_h = ptension_h(new\_pl_h) - ptension_h(old\_pl_h) + minbcost_{h,j} + \\ btension_{i,h}(new\_bl_{i,h}) - btension_{i,h}(old\_bl_{i,h})$$

The main difference from the calculation of the self-cost is that, while estimating the cost for a neighboring proxy, p_h, p_i also considers the cost associated with acting as a network tunnel for the request, in case the requesting proxy does not have a direct connection to p_h (Figure 10.8). Of course, if the proxy originating the request and p_h have a direct connection, then that connection may be used after redirection; however, at this point p_i does not have this information and has to account for the worst case scenario. Also, in order to speed up the process, the cost estimation for neighbors and networks are regularly pre-computed, refreshed, and kept in a local table in each proxy.

Once all these estimates are available, if p_i decides that it is not the best proxy to serve the request, then p_i sends the candidates and their costs (as it knows) to the requesting proxy along with a redirection message. With this additional information, the requesting proxy chooses the best proxy in the list and forwards its join request that proxy (Figure 10.9). Note that the redirection protocol does not allow backtracking; i.e., if proxy p_i chooses to redirect an incoming join request (say from proxy p_l) to proxy p_h based on its estimates, p_i is dropped from further considerations by p_l even though a join request accepted by p_h may eventually lead to a more costly path. Therefore, proper estimations of the costs of the future steps is the path creation is important.

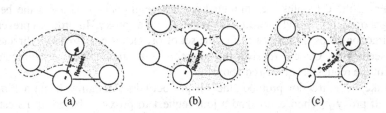

(a)   (b)   (c)

Figure 10.9. Expansion of the neighborhood through redirection: (a) A proxy sends a request to the best of its neighbors; (b) the neighbor chooses to redirect the request to one of its neighbors (it is either loaded or it knows that one of its neighbors can be better suited for this request; and (c) the original proxy now has a wider view of the neighborhood and can send a request to the best available proxy

Route Establishment. If p_i decides to serve the request and if the request is for a stream that is not already served by this proxy, then p_i has to find a way to join a multicast tree that serves the stream. For this purpose, it has to evaluate its neighbors and select the best one to send a join request. As shown in Figure 10.10, p_i considers all its neighbors when choosing the next proxy. For those neighbors (say p_l) that are already on the required multicast tree, p_i estimates the cost of connection simply as

$$cost_l = ptension_l(new\_pl_l) - ptension_l(old\_pl_l) + \\ btension_{i,l}(new\_bl_{i,l}) - btension_{i,l}(old\_bl_{i,l})$$

That is, it accounts for the increased tension at the new parent p_l as well as the increased tension on the network connection between itself and p_l. If p_l is not serving the stream, on the other hand, it also accounts for the fact that p_l will need to establish a route to the source:

$$cost_l = ptension_l(new\_pl_l) - ptension_l(old\_pl_l) + \\ btension_{i,l}(new\_bl_{i,l}) - btension_{i,l}(old\_bl_{i,l}) + \\ minbcost_{l,j}.$$

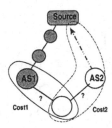

Figure 10.10. Cost estimation when selecting one of the alternative parents: one candidate parent is already delivering the stream whereas the other one has to account for the estimated distance to the source

After all the estimates are computed for the neighbors, p_i chooses the best neighboring proxy and forwards the request to that proxy. In order to prevent redirection loops, p_i keeps track of the set of proxies it has already redirected to (see below). Once p_l receives the join request, it can either deny, redirect, or admit the request as discussed above.

Like the redirection protocol, the join protocol does not allow backtracking; i.e., if proxy p_i chooses to send a join request to proxy p_l based on its estimates, unless p_l denies this request or explicitly redirects it to another proxy, all other neighbors of p_i are dropped from further considerations. Therefore, again, proper estimations of the costs of the future steps is the path creation is important.

Denies and Redirections.   A proxy p_i that has sent a join request can receive an *admit*, *deny*, or *redirection* message. Unless the request is admitted, the proxy has to find an alternative proxy to join to. As described above, redirection messages carry information about potential candidate proxies and their costs. p_i merges this information with the information it already has about its neighborhood and sends the request to the best candidate it now has. Note that unless a limit is established, a request may be redirected too many times. Therefore, mSON uses a limit, $redir_{limit}$, of the number of times each request can be redirected. Once the redirection limit is reached, p_i fails to join to the stream; if there is a downstream proxy waiting for the establishment of the route, p_i sends a deny message to it. The downstream proxy then initiates its own deny-message handling routines.

Loop Detection and Elimination.   A join request may originate from an edge proxy or from a proxy that is serving other proxies during the multicast tree establishment phase (Figure 10.11). In the latter case, it is essential to employ appropriate mechanisms to eliminate routing loops. As discussed earlier, there are various algorithms and protocols (such as DUAL [Garcia-Lunes-Aceves, 1993], EIGRP [Albrightson et al., 1994], RIP-MTI [Schmid

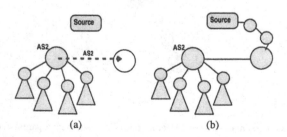

Figure 10.11.   Loop avoidance in join requests

and Steigner, 2002], and LPA [Murthy and Garcia-Luna-Aceves, 1995]) that aim at eliminating loops or minimizing the undesirable effects of routing loops.

In mSON, we opt to annotate each join request with the name of the AS where the request originates (Figure 10.11): If the receiving proxy has already a path to the source of the stream, it only has to verify that the list of its parents does not contain the AS where the join request originated. If there is not an already established path to the source, then the receiving proxy has to make sure that the path that it will create to the source does not contain the AS that it received request from. To achieve this, each join request is *also* annotated with the list of downstream proxies *waiting* for the establishment of the path to the route. Consequently, a proxy receiving a request can easily check whether admitting the request will cause a loop.

2.2 Stop Requests

When a proxy p_i receives a stop request from a user or another proxy for access to the media stream multicasted at source s_j, it simply drops the requesting proxy from the multicast tree and makes the corresponding resources available for future requests. In case there are no more child proxies consuming a stream served by p_i, then p_i also sends a stop request to the corresponding parent for that stream so that it can release all corresponding resources for other streams' use.

2.3 Redistribution

One of the scalability mechanisms used by the proxies in mSON is *redistribution*. When p_i detects any change in its neighborhood (as a result of the update messages it exchanges with its neighbors), such as nearby proxy becoming available or a configuration change, it checks if it is *overloaded* or *underloaded* relative to its neighbors. *Overload* is defined as having at least one server (p_h) in the neighborhood such that

$$t\_reduction\_at\_i > (1 + \gamma_d)t\_increase\_at\_h$$

as a result of the redistribution of one of the streams p_i is currently serving (see overload detection and elimination in Section 2.1). Here, γ_d is a threshold value to prevent very small gains to cause potentially expensive redistributions. Note that if proxy p_h is underutilized, redistribution can also decrease the tension at p_h benefiting both of the involved proxies. If p_i notices that this trigger condition is true for at least one of the streams, then it initiates a redistribution process aimed at re-balancing the overall tension.

During redistribution, p_i tries to find proxies in its neighborhood that can take a fraction (we used 50% in our implementation) of its load:

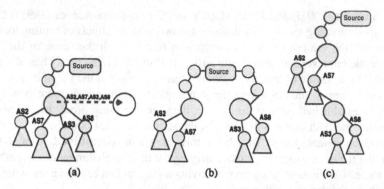

Figure 10.12. Loop avoidance in redistribution: (a) the requesting AS sends the list of the immediate children proxies to the chosen candidate; (b) if the candidate can establish a path that doesn't go through any children than the proxy can redirect any set of children; (c) if the path created by the proxy passes through a child, then a set that does not include this child is shipped to the candidate

1 It first chooses the stream, s_j, whose redistribution will bring the highest benefit to the system.

2 Then, for this stream, it chooses the best proxy, p_l, to take the fraction of the load it aims to redistribute. The process p_i uses to choose p_l is similar to the process it uses to choose the best proxy to redirect a request, except that during the redistribution more than one connection is redirected simultaneously. Hence, the loads that are used for calculating tension changes are based on the fraction of the load being shipped.

3 After it chooses the stream s_j and the proxy p_l to redistribute the load to, p_i contacts p_l and checks if it is indeed willing to take the required load. At this point p_l can either admit this load shipment request, deny it, or redirect it. Before admitting the request p_l makes sure that there is a loop free path to the source (Figure 10.12). As in the case of individual join request, if p_l chooses to redirect the shipment request, redirection messages are accompanied with the neighborhood list to help p_i choose the best one in its own and p_l's neighborhood based on its redirection past.

4 Once a proxy p_l accepts the shipment, p_i starts shipping the load. During this process it locks all resources (hence can not admit new requests). p_i chooses a fraction of its children consuming the streams s_j and redirects each one of them, individually, to p_l. p_l handles these join requests as a group and admits all of them.

5 Once the processing for s_j is over, p_i chooses another stream and continues this process until it ships the required load.

If a shipment to a proxy fails (for instance due to link failures), a timeout mechanism is used to prevent more time being wasted trying to connect to it in the future.

2.4 Consolidation

When p_i detects any change in its neighborhood (as a result of the update messages it exchanges with its neighbors), it checks if it becomes underloaded as a result of the change. If so, it tries *consolidating* its service with its neighbors. Consolidation is triggered when there is at least one server (p_h) in the neighborhood such that, if p_i ships one of its streams to p_h completely, the following would be true:

$$t\_reduction\_at\_i > (1 + \gamma_c)t\_increase\_at\_h$$

Consequently, the consolidation process is very similar to the redistribution process, except that the amount of load negotiated between the proxies and shipped from one proxy to the other is 100% of the load for each stream instead of being 50%. If the consolidation process is completed successfully for all streams, proxy p_i returns to zero utilization and can be taken out of the system.

Note that, despite their apparent similarities, there is a fundamental difference between consolidations and redistributions. In general, it is easier to sense when the system needs consolidations than it needs redistributions. This is because, consolidations aims solving a current challenge (resources are being underutilized), whereas redistributions also aim making enough resources available for future arrivals. Therefore, especially at times of rapid growth, rapid sensing of the need for redistributions is essential. To achieve this, join and redistribution requests can be augmented with expected load arrival rates based on short term statistics.

2.5 Parent Failure

When p_i detects one of its parents (p_i can have a different parent for each stream it is serving), it has to fix the broken connection. The process of fixing the broken connection is similar to redirection, in the sense that, p_i redirects itself to another proxy in its neighborhood based on the network and proxy tensions. A timeout mechanism is used to prevent the failed parent from being used in the considerations in the future. Also, during this process p_i locks all resources (hence can not admit new requests) for the failed streams.

3. Experimental Evaluation

In this section, we present experimental results of evaluating the effectiveness and usefulness of the mSON architecture and protocols for streaming media delivery. Each experiment has been repeated under the following five configurations and the results were compared:

Exp.	# Redirect.	Consol.	Redist.
0nCnR	0	Off	Off
3nCnR	3	Off	Off
3nCyR	3	Off	On
3yCnR	3	On	Off
3yCyR	3	On	On

All experiments presented here were conducted using software simulation in a network-emulated environment. In order to evaluate mSON and to observe the effects of various system parameters, we needed a large number of setups. Furthermore, we needed to change the parameters in a controlled fashion. Therefore, we systematically generated a large number of scenarios with various parameters and use these in our experimental evaluation. Next, we describe these scenarios.

In the experiments, we used two network models. The first network model is a three-layered network. In this network, the inner layer (L1) is densest and the outer layer (L3) is sparsest. This corresponds to the fact that a smaller number of backbone networks carry a large number of smaller networks. The number of nodes in each layer and the number of connections between and across each layer are controlled through a set of parameters (Table 10.2). Results are presented in Section 3.1. In addition to this network, we have also experimented with a network having transit-stub model widely used by other researchers [Banerjee et al., 2003, Castro et al., 2003b] to model Internet connectivity. We used GT-ITM topology generator [Zegura et al., 1996] to create transit-stub networks. As described in Section 3.2, the results on this alternative network model are similar. Figure 10.13 shows the proxy and network policy graphs used in our experiments. These graphs prefer almost full utilization of the proxy resources,

Table 10.2. The system parameters for the first set of experiments

Parameter	Value
Number of ASs(proxies)	100
Ratio of ASs(proxies) at L1 / L2 / L3	0.1/0.3/0.6
Intralayer density at (L1-L1) / (L2-L2)/ (L3-L3)	0.4/0.15/0.05
Interlayer density at (L1-L2) / (L2-L3)/ (L1-L3)	0.3/0.1/0.1
Number of proxies hit per source	80
Proxy hit ratio at L1 / L2/ L3	0.1/0.3/0.6
Number of sources	10
Source distribution at L1 / L2 / L3	0.1/0.3/0.6
Redirection limit	3
γ_d/γ_c	5%/10%

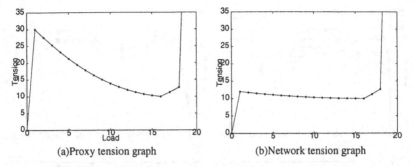

(a)Proxy tension graph (b)Network tension graph

Figure 10.13. (a) Proxy and (b) the network policy graphs used in the experiments

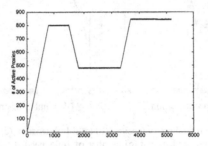

Figure 10.14. In the experiments, number of active sources in the system goes through extreme changes (50% additions/deletions)

whereas once a network connection is active, there is not much penalty unless it is highly overloaded.

We experimented with extreme variations in the source/client arrival patterns. In the setting presented in Figure 10.14, we start with 10 active sources. 50% of the sources (and their clients) dropped off at some point and later the same amount of (different) sources joined to the system.

3.1 Results on the Multi-layered Network Topology

In the first set of experiments, we aimed at observing the impact of proposed techniques on the overall performance of mSON.

As shown in Figure 10.15 (a) and (b), a combination of redirections, consolidations, and redistributions consistently achieve good proxy and link tensions. Note that, in Figure 10.15 (b), the lowest tension seem to be achieved when all adaptation mechanisms were turned off; but this is because a significant portion of the users were being declined by the system, which is highly undesirable. Figure 10.15 (c) shows that alternative $3yCyR$, where all adaptation mechanisms are on indeed achieves the best proxy utilization (where 1.0 de-

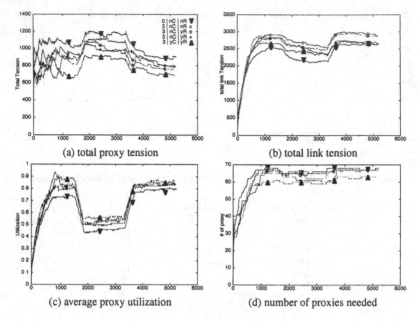

Figure 10.15. Results: (a) total proxy tension, (b) total link tension, (c) average proxy utilization, (d) number of proxies needed, and (e) number of links needed (*no-adaptation, 0nCnR,* **and** *all-adaptations, 3yCyR,* **cases have been highlighted more dominantly than the others**)

notes the preferred utilization rate). This increased utilization shows itself in the reduction in the number of proxies needed to serve the multicast trees (Figure 10.15(d)). Similarly, the number of network links needed is the lowest when all adaptation mechanisms are applied together (Figure 10.16(a)), except for option $0nCnR$ (without any adaptation) which results in too many denials to be a feasible option (we obviously do not want to cause client denials to reduce the number of network links used).

Figure 10.16(b) shows that consolidations and distributions also reduce the average depth (hence, the delay and possible QoS degradations) of the multicast trees. The figure also shows that, although consolidations enable a smaller depth, redistributions are essential to make sure that mSON is able to scale the depth of the tree in the case of sudden injections of a large number of sources.

Note that, in these experiments, each logical link between proxies was on the average 2 to 2.5 physical links; in general consolidations caused increases in this number as they led to sparser multicast trees with less number of proxies. However, overall, the total number of links used by the system was minimized by consolidations and redirections as shown earlier in Figure 10.16(a). Finally, Figures 10.16(c) and (d) show how mSON use redistributions and consolida-

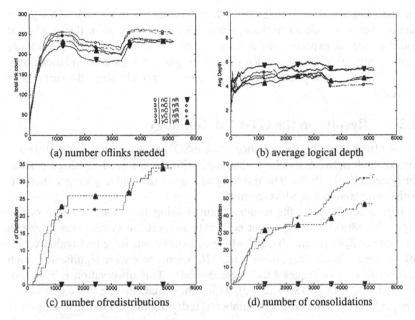

Figure 10.16. Results: (a) number of links needed, (b) average logical depth of the leaves, (c) number of redistributions, and (d) number of consolidations (*no-adaptation, 0nCnR,* and *all-adaptations, 3yCyR,* cases have been highlighted more dominantly than the others)

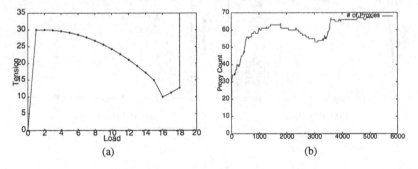

Figure 10.17. An experiment with (a) an alternative policy graph and (b) the corresponding proxy need

tions to tackle the sudden changes in the structure. Although not shown in this figure, redirections are also heavily used, especially by alternative $3yCyR$ which uses all adaptations.

We have also experimented with other policy graphs to verify that policy graph shapes have the expected impacts on the behavior of the system. Figure 10.17 shows an alternative policy graph and the resulting proxy utilization for the same experimental setup (with all adaptations allowed). This graph favors utilizations closer to the optimal. Consequently, when the number of sources drop, as expected, the number of proxies used by mSON drops more significantly. Furthermore, since this policy graph favors consolidations over redistributions, as expected it does not scale as quickly large fluctuations of sources.

3.2   Results on the GT-ITM Topology

We also studied the performance of the mSON architecture using a 100 node Transit-Stub network topology generated with the GT-ITM topology generator [Zegura et al., 1996]. The resulting network had relatively longer shortest-paths compared to three-layered model.

Figure 10.18 shows the results obtained using this model. As shown in Figure 10.18(a) the proxy count needed to support the system was lowest in alternatives $3yCnR$ and $3yCyR$ where consolidations were on (again excluding the case without adaptations, $0nCnR$, where there were significantly high number of service requests that were denied). This observation is also supported by Figures 10.18(b) and (c), which show that since in this case the system performs significantly less number of redistributions, a redistribution-only

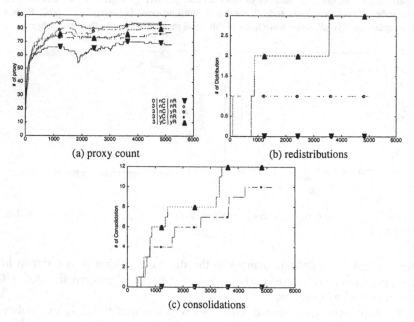

Figure 10.18.   Result on GT-ITM topology: (a) proxy count, (b) redistributions, and (c) consolidations

mechanism would not be enough to support adaptation to extremely high fluctuations (especially quick drops) of sources. Thus a redistribution+consolidation based scheme is the most desirable approach to adaptations to drastic network changes.

4. Related Work

Recently there has been considerable interest in using proxies and application level overlays for streaming data delivery [Shi and Turner, 2002, Banerjee et al., 2003, Banerjee et al., 2002, Castro et al., 2003b, Castro et al., 2002, Acharya and Smith, 2000, Rajaie et al., 2000, Jin et al., 2002, Wang et al., 1998, Sen et al., 1999, Miao and Ortega, 1999]. Su and Yemini [Su and Yemini, 2001] have proposed a virtual active network architecture over wide-area networks. The goal of this effort is to develop an API that will eventually be incorporated in vendor-supplied black-boxes which currently perform network layer functions such as routing. Other efforts in this direction include virtual local area networks (VLANs) [Passmore and Freeman, 1997] and virtual private networks (VPNs) [Scott et al., 1998].

The X-Bone [Touch, 2001] is a system for dynamic deployment and management of Internet overlay networks. Current overlay networks include commercial VPNs [Scott et al., 1998] and IP tunnelled networks M-Bone [Eriksson, 1994]. The X-Bone automatically discovers available components, configure, and monitors them. Due to its low-level implementation the X-Bone is limited in the level of functionality that is needed by advanced networking applications. Recently, [Lim et al., 2001] has proposed and implemented Virtual Network Service (VNS), a value added network service for deploying VPNs in a managed wide-are IP network. Their approach to provision customizable service leverages on a programmable router architecture that provides an open programmable interface [Takahashi et al., 1999]. The RON project [Andersen et al., 2001] at MIT has built a resilient overlay network that allows distributed Internet applications to detect and recover from path changes and period of degraded performance within several seconds.

Xu *et al.* introduced peer-to-peer streaming in [Xu et al., 2002]. Chawathe, McCanne and Brewer [Chawathe et al., 2002] have developed an architecture that provides application-level multicasting on top of existing IP networks with unicast capability. The architecture is referred to as *Scattercast* and is argued to be a more viable alternative to the efforts underway to integrate multicast at the IP level. The Scattercast architecture partitions a heterogeneous set of session participants into disjoint data groups. Each data group is serviced by a strategically located network agent. Agents organize themselves into an *overlay network*. Chu, Rao, and Zhang [Chu et al., 2000] have proposed end system multicast to support small-sized applications such as audio or video conferencing. This approach is not as scalable since it requires that every member maintain a complete list of every other member in the group.

Shi and Turner [Shi and Turner, 2002] have proposed a centralized greedy heuristic, called the Compact Tree algorithm to minimize the maximum latency from the source to a Multicast Service Node (equivalently, a proxy). Similarly, Banerjee et al. [Banerjee et al., 2003] have proposed a multicast overlay tree construction algorithm to minimize average-latency from the source to leaf level multimedia service nodes or proxies. Unlike mSON, these efforts are focused on the objective of optimization from the perspective of individual end-users. In contrast, our goal is to enable efficient distribution of streaming media by minimizing network and proxy resources needed.

SpreadIt [Deshpande et al., 2001] is an application level multicast architecture for delivering streaming live media over a network of clients, using the resources of the clients themselves. ZIGZAG [Tran et al., 2003] also takes a similar approach and create media stream hierarchies over clients themselves. Other cooperative peer-to-peer structures based on clients include, CoopNet [Padmanabhan et al., 2002]. In particular, the Bayeux builds on the P2P routing scheme based on Tapestry to create a highly redundant multicast tree over the peers in the network. The system also uses the Tapestry lookup mechanism to efficiently locate multimedia sessions. It relies on probabilistic approaches to minimize bandwidth usage. Kim, Lam, and Lee [M.S.Kim et al., 2003] presented a distributed algorithm that builds a multicast tree in which the average receiving rate, computed over all receivers in the tree, is maximized. Recently, Yang [Yang, 2003] considered a more elaborate model for streaming media approach where multiple delivery path(s) are established between source and destination(s) to improve service. SplitStream [Castro et al., 2003a] splits data is divided into disjoint sections, stripes, and delivers each stripe through a separate tree. In Chainsaw [Pai et al., 2005], instead of creating trees, the peer-to-peer system operates by an explicit notification-request mechanism between the peers. Nemo [Birrer and Bustamante, 2005] aims to add resilience to peer-to-peer multicasting systems, where peers are autonomous, unpredictable. FatNemo [Birrer et al., 2004], is one of the few overlay multicasting systems which recognizes the challenges associated with multi-source multicasting. It creates with larger clusters closer to the root, to eliminate bottlenecks closer to the root. Unlike mSON architecture presented here, oStream [Cui et al., 2004, Cui and Nahrstedt, 2003] focuses on the problem of asynchrony prevalent in systems which serve stored on-demand media.

In addition to these research activities, many CDN vendors provide various solutions for streaming media delivery on the Internet. In the solutions provided by Akamai[Akamai Technology, 2005], streaming media is distributed close to the users. It also reduces bandwidth requirement at the origin media server site because media is served from the edge cache servers. RealProxy by RealNetworks[RealNetworks, 2005] is software installed on a network or ISP gateway that aggregates and handles client requests for media streamed. In contrast mSON's dynamic adjustment of delivery network's structure to user population and distribution as well as network conditions, RealProxy requires manual specification and adjustment of multiplexing structure. [C-StarOne, 2005, Nguyen and Zakhor, 2002] propose streaming video from multiple sources to a single receiver to exploit path diversity and to reduce packet loss.

5. Conclusion

In this chapter, we presented a policy-driven peer-to-peer *media streaming overlay network* (mSON) for streaming live media from media sources to end-users. mSON is specifically designed to efficiently support multiple media streams with different sources and user populations at the same time. mSON minimizes its footprint on the overlay network to use its resources most effectively. For this purpose, mSON represents resource usage policies at the proxies (ASs - or Multicast Service Nodes, MSNs) as well as at the network peering points between them. The redirection, redistribution, and consolidation based negotiations between proxies prevent resources from being underutilized or overutilized, while maintaining small delays. This way, while maintaining a high resource utilization, they also prevent congestions, service rejections, and jitters in the streams users receive. We reported experimental results that show that mSON achieves these tasks effectively under a variety of conditions.

References

Acharya, S. and Smith, B. (2000). Middleman: A video caching proxy server. In *NOSSDAV*.

Akamai Technology (2005). http://www.akamai.com/.

Albrightson, R., Garcia-Luna-Aceves, J.J., and Boyle, J. (1994). Eigrp-a fast routing protocol based on distance vectors. In *Networld/Interop*.

Amir, Yair, Awerbuch, Baruch, Danilov, Claudiu, and Stanton, Jonathan (2002). Global flow control for wide area overlay networks: a cost-benefit approach. In *OPENARCH*, pages 155–166.

Andersen, David G., Balakrishnan, Hari, Kaashoek, M. Frans, and Morris, Robert (2001). Resilient overlay networks. In *Proc. SOSP 2001, Banff, Canada*.

Banerjee, S., Kommareddy, C., Kar, K., Bhattacharjee, B., and Khuller, S. (2003). Construction of an efficient overlay multicast infrastructure for real-time applications. In *IEEE INFOCOM*, pages 1521–1531.

Banerjee, Suman, Bhattacharjee, Bobby, and Kommareddy, Christopher (2002). Scalable application layer multicast. *SIGCOMM Comput. Commun. Rev.*, 32(4):205–217.

Birrer, S. and Bustamante, F.E. (2005). Nemo – resilient peer-to-peer multicast without the cost. In *MMCN*.

Birrer, S., Lu, D., Bustamante, F.E., Y.Qiao, and Dinda, P. (2004). Fatnemo: building a resilient multi-source multicast fat-tree. In *Ninth International Workshop on Web Content Caching and Distribution*.

Blum, Avrim, Chalasani, Prasad, Coppersmith, Don, Pulleyblank, Bill, Raghavan, Prabhakar, and Sudan, Madhu (1994). The minimum latency problem. In *STOC '94: Proceedings of the twenty-sixth annual ACM symposium on Theory of computing*, pages 163–171.

C-StarOne (2005). http://www.centerspan.com/.

Castro, M., Druschel, P., Kermarrec, A., and Rowstron, A. (2002). SCRIBE: A large-scale and decentralized application-level multicast infrastructure. *IEEE Journal on Selected Areas in communications (JSAC)*, 20(8).

Castro, M., Druschel, P., Kermarrec, A.-M., Nandi, A., Rowstron, A.I.T., and Singh, A. (2003a). Splitstream: high-bandwidth multicast in cooperative environments. In *SOSP*, pages 298–313.

Castro, M., Jones, M.B., Kermarrec, A.-M., Rowstron, A., Theimer, M., Wang, H., and Wolman, A. (2003b). An evaluation of scalable application-level multicast built using peer-to-peer overlay networks. In *IEEE INFOCOM*.

Chawathe, Y., McCane, S., and Brewer, E. (2002). An architecture for Internet content distribution as an infrastructure service. http://yatin.chawathe.com/~yatin/papers/scattercast.ps.

Chu, Y.-H., Rao, S.G., and Zhang, H. (2000). A case for end system multicast. In *Measurement and modeling of computer systems*, pages 1–12.

Cui, Y., Li, B., and Nahrstedt, K. (2004). ostream: asynchronous streaming multicast in application-layer overlay networks. *IEEE Journal on Selected Areas in Communications*, 22(1).

Cui, Y. and Nahrstedt, K. (2003). Layered peer-to-peer streaming. In *NOSS-DAV '03: Proceedings of the 13th international workshop on Network and operating systems support for digital audio and video*, pages 162–171.

Cui, Y., Xue, Y., and Nahrstedt, K. (2003). Optimal resource allocation in overlay multicast. In *ICNP*, pages 71–83.

Deshpande, H., Bawa, M., and Garcia-Molina, H. (2001). Streaming live media over a peer-to-peer network. Technical Report 2001-30, Stanford University.

Eriksson, H. (1994). MBone: the multicast backbone. *Communications of the ACM*, pages 54–60.

Garcia-Lunes-Aceves, J. J. (1993). Loop-free routing using diffusing computations. *IEEE/ACM Trans. Netw.*, 1(1):130–141.

Jin, S., Bestavros, A., and Iyengar, A. (2002). Accelerating Internet streaming media delivery using network-aware partial caching. In *International Conference on Distributed Computing Systems*.

Kar, K., Sarkar, S., and Tassiulas, L. (2001). Optimization based rate control for multirate multicast sessions. In *INFOCOM*, pages 123–132.

Kelly, F., Maulloo, A., and Tan, D. (1998). Rate control in communication networks: shadow prices, proportional fairness and stability. *Journal of the Operational Research Society*, 49(3):237–252.

Lim, L. K., Gao, J., Ng, T. S. E., Chandra, P. R., Steenkiste, P., and Zhang, H. (2001). Customizable virtual private network service with QoS. *Computer Networks*, pages 137–151.

Miao, Z. and Ortega, A. (1999). Proxy caching for efficient video services over the Internet. In *PVW*.

M.S.Kim, Lam, S.S., and Lee, D.-Y. (2003). Optimal distribution tree for Internet streaming media. In *ICDCS*, pages 116–125.

Murthy, S. and Garcia-Lunes-Aceves, J. J. (1995). Dynamics of a loop-free path-finding algorithm. In *IEEE Globecom*, pages 1347–1351.

Nguyen, T. and Zakhor, A. (2002). Distributed video streaming over the Internet. In *Multimedia Computing and Networking (MMCN)*.

Padmanabhan, V.N., Wang, H.J., Chou, P.A., and Sripanidkulchai, K. (2002). Distributing streaming media content using cooperative networking. In *NOSSDAV*, pages 177–186.

Pai, V., Kumar, K., Tamilmani, K., Sambamurthy, V., and Mohr, A. E. (2005). Chainsaw: eliminating trees from overlay multicast. In *4th International Workshop on Peer-to-Peer Systems*.

Passmore, D. and Freeman, J. (1997). The virtual LAN technology. Technical Report 200374-001, 3COM.

Rajaie, R., Yu, H., Handley, M., and Estrin, D. (2000). Multimedia proxy caching mechanism for quality adaptive streaming applications on the Internet. In *INFOCOM*.

RealNetworks (2005). http://www.real.com/.

Schmid, Andreas and Steigner, Christoph (2002). Avoiding counting to infinity in distance vector routing. *Telecommunication Systems*, 19(3-4):497–514.

Scott, C., Wolfe, P., and Erwin, M. (1998). *Virtual private networks*. OReilly, Sebastopol.

Sen, S., Rexford, J., and Towsley, D. (1999). Proxy prefix caching for multimedia servers. In *INFOCOM*.

Shi, S. and Turner, J. (2002). Routing in overlay multicast networks. In *IEEE INFOCOM*, pages 1200–1208.

Su, G. and Yemini, Y. (2001). Virtual Active Networks: Towards multi-edged network computing. *Computer Networks*, pages 153–168.

Takahashi, E., Steenkiste, P., Gao, J., and fischer, A. (1999). A programming interface for network resource management. In *Proceedings of the 1999 IEEE Open Architectures and Network Programming*, pages 34–44.

Touch, J. (2001). Dynamic Internet overlay deployment and management using the X-Bone. *Computer Networks*, pages 117–135.

Tran, D.A., Hua, K.A., and Do, T.T. (2003). Zigzag: an efficient peer-to-peer scheme for media streaming. In *INFOCOM*.

Wang, Y., Zhang, Z. L., Du, D. H., and Su, D. (1998). A network conscious approach to end-to-end delivery over wide-area networks using proxy servers. In *INFOCOM*.

Xu, D., Hefeeda, M., Hambrusch, S.E., and Bhargava, B.K. (2002). On peer-to-peer media streaming. In *ICDCS*, pages 363–371.

Yang, J. (2003). Deliver multimedia streams with flexible qos via a multicast DAG. In *ICDCS*, pages 126–137.

Zegura, Ellen W., Calvert, Kenneth L., and Bhattacharjee, Samrat (1996). How to model an internetwork. In *INFOCOM*, pages 594–602.

Chapter 11

CACHING AND DISTRIBUTION ISSUES FOR STREAMING CONTENT DISTRIBUTION NETWORKS

Michael Zink
Department of Computer Science
University of Massachusetts
Amherst, MA, USA
zink@cs.umass.edu

Prashant Shenoy
Department of Computer Science
University of Massachusetts
Amherst, MA, USA
shenoy@cs.umass.edu

Abstract   This chapter presents an overview of the state of the art in caching and distribution techniques for streaming media content. A content distribution network (CDN)—an overlay network of proxy servers—is typically employed for this purpopse. We present techniques for caching entire files as well as caching partial content at each proxy in a streaming CDN. We then present techniques for designing a cooperative cluster of streaming proxies as well as techniques for streaming using peer-to-peer networks.

Keywords: Content distribution networks, streaming, caching

1.   Introduction

1.1   Motivation

Content Distribution Networks (CDN) have become popular recently as a means to store web content closer to clients in a controlled manner. A content distribution network consists of an overlay network of proxy servers that are geographically distributed and cache popular content close to clients; user requests for content are serviced by forwarding the request to the nearest proxy. Unlike pure on-demand caching approaches that only store content requested by clients in the proxy's cache, in a CDN, owners of web servers can also actively distribute (i.e. replicate) content to proxies. Today, CDN services are offered by numerous commercial companies (e.g., Akamai) to both content providers and end users. Content providers subscribe to CDN services to provide their clients with faster access to their content.

While the first generation of CDNs were designed primarily for web content, modern CDNs can also store and serve streaming media content such as audio and video. However, streaming media objects have different characteristics when compared objects such as text and images—these objects are several orders of magnitude larger in size and have larger bandwidth requirements. Consequently, unlike web content, naive replication of popular objects on all proxy servers in a CDN may not be efficient, and new techniques for distributing and caching streaming media objects need to be devised.

A content distribution network for streaming media will need to exploit the following characteristics of video content [Acharya and Smith, 1998, Acharya et al., 2000, Chesire et al., 2001]:

- Unlike web content which may be modified after its creation, video content follows the write-once-read-many principle. Thus, streaming CDNs are simpler in that they do not need to consider cache consistency issues.

- Popularity of video files follow the Zipf distribution, and each file is typically accessed sequentially. Caching and distribution techniques employed by the CDN need to be tailored for these characteristics.

- Due to the significantly higher storage space and bandwidth requirements as well as the timeliness constraints imposed on video accesses, distribution and caching techniques for streaming content need to designed with these constraints in mind.

- Internet broadcast or multicast may be employed by an origin server to deliver live content to a large number of users [Sitaram and Dan, 2000, Hu, 2001, Hua and Sheu, 1997, Paris et al., 1999, Eager et al., 2001]. Broadcast or multicast techniques may also be used to deliver very popular files to a large user population. Proxy servers within a CDN will need to support such broadcast and multicast techniques as well.

Despite some of these differences, streaming CDNs retain some of the key advantages of traditional web CDNs. First, since proxy servers replicate content from origin servers, content can still be delivered to end-users if the origin server or some of the proxy servers suffer a transient failure. Second, by placing proxies close to the end-users and caching popular content at this proxies, a CDN can reduce the startup latency for accessing streaming content. Such caching also reduces the load on the origin servers and redistributes it across multiple proxies. Third, approximately 80% of the user requests access about 20% of the total available videos [Bianchi and Melen, 1997, Griwodz et al., 1997, Nussbaumer et al., 1995], indicating that, like in the web case, caching video content can be a very effective means for scalable delivery.

1.2   Outline

The remainder of this chapter is structured as follows. Section 2 describes the high level architecture of a streaming content distribution network. An overview on caching of complete objects is given in Section 3. Caching of partial streaming media objects is discussed in Section 4. Section 5 considers clusters of caches that are used to distribute the workload across several physical caches. Section 6 gives an overview of distribution networks based on peer-to-peer technology. Finally, Section 7 concludes this chapter.

2.   Architecture of a Content Distribution Network

A typical streaming content distribution network is assumed to contain three components: origin servers, proxy caches and end-clients (see Figure 11.1). We briefly discuss the role of each component.

Origin Servers Origin servers store the original versions of each streaming media file. These servers are generally controlled by content providers. The content providers are assumed to have complete control over the content stored at origin servers—they can add new files to the server and delete old files. Further, they can also place restrictions on whether a file may be cached within the CDN. For reasons of simplicity, in this chapter,

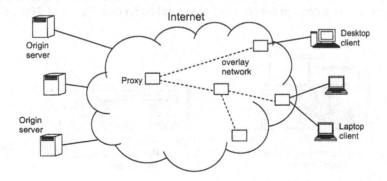

Figure 11.1.   Architecture of a Content Distribution Network

we assume that no restrictions are placed on files and that any file may be cached within the CDN if it is advantageous to do so. In general, a typical CDN will serve content from multiple origin servers.

Proxy Caches A typical CDN will consist of a large number of proxy caches that are geographically distributed. Each proxy has a disk cache that is used to store streaming content from the origin severs. Proxies are assumed to be deployed close to the end-clients of the origin servers. A request for a streaming media object is typically forwarded to the nearest proxy. If the requested object or portions of it are already cached at the local disk, then the proxy can stream these portions to the end-client. The mission portions are handled by forwarding a request for these portions to another proxy or the origin server. Typically, the disk cache at each proxy is finite, and it is not possible to store all content from all origin servers at each proxy. Hence, each proxy is assumed to employ a caching policy that decides what objects or subsets of objects should be cached locally.

Clients End-users are assumed to request content via a client. Clients are assumed to be heterogeneous and may range from set-top boxes to standard PCs and from PDAs to mobile phones. Clients can have heterogeneous network bandwidth, processing power and display capabilities, and the origin server needs to tailor the requested content to meet the needs of its clients. Each client is assumed to make requests to its nearest proxy; such a proxy may be statically configured at the client, or dynamically determined by the CDN based on the client's location.

In the simplest case, a video (audio) file at the origin server consists of a sequence of frames (samples). Since such a file can impose significant storage space and bandwidth requirement, it is possible to partition each file in time or space. In the former case, each file is split into segments, where each segment contains a contiguous chunk of video and audio (see Figure 11.2(a)). For

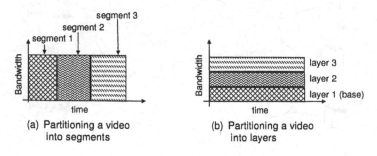

Figure 11.2.   Unscalable vs. scalable content

instance, a one hour movie may contain three segments, containing the first five minutes, the next ten minutes and the final forty-five minutes of the movie, respectively. Each segment is smaller in size, when compared to the complete object, and can be handled independently by the CDN. An alternate approach is to partition the video file in the bandwidth (spatial) dimension. In this approach, each file is partitioned into a base layer and multiple enhancement layers (see Figure 11.2(b)). The base layer contains a coarse resolution version of each frame or sample, and each enhancement layer contains additional information to successively refine the resolution of data contained in the previous layers. Thus, layered encoding provides a multi-resolution representation of streaming content—to reconstruct the information included in layer n, all of the information of the lower layers (0, ..., n-1) are needed. While the notion of temporal partitioning into segments is independent of the compression format used to encode content, specific support is needed in the compression format to support layered encoding. Many modern compression algorithms such as MPEG-2 [MPEG-1, 1993], H.263+ [H263, 1995], MPEG-4 [Pereira and Ebrahimi, 2002] support layered encoding. In a later section, we will discuss how a CDN can exploit both temporal and bandwidth partitioning to support more effective distribution of streaming content.

With the above background, we discuss caching and distribution issues in streaming CDNs.

3.   Complete Object Caching

In the simplest case, proxies within the CDN can cache entire audio or video files in their local disk cache. These files can be fetched from the origin servers on-demand as requests for these objects are received from clients, or by prefetching them *a priori*. In either case, since entire objects are cached at a proxy, due to their large sizes, only a limited number of files can be cached on disk. However, even this simple approach of caching entire objects can provide significant benefits, since caching very popular files locally can significantly reduce the burden on the origin servers.

Popularities of streaming media files tends to change over time as new files become popular and previously popular files see a reduced demand. Consequently, each proxy within the CDN needs to implement a caching policy that determines what files should be evicted and what new files to fetch into its cache. Typically, a *cache replacement policy* is employed to make such decisions. A common replacement policy that is widely used in web proxy caches is the *least recently used (LRU)* policy, where the least recently used object is evicted from the cache to make room for a new object. However, the LRU policy is not suitable for streaming media caches, due to the skewed popularities of these files. Studies have shown that the *least frequently used (LFU)* is more appropriate in such situations. The policy maintains the frequency of access (a measure of popularity) for each file and evicts the object with the least access frequency (i.e., the least popular) object from the cache. Thus, more popular objects are given preference over less popular objects in the cache.

Although LFU is a better choice than LRU for proxies caching streaming media content, it suffers from two drawbacks. First, a previously popular object continues to be associated with a high frequency count and is not evicted from the cache even though it is no longer popular. A simple modification that overcomes this drawbacks is to decrease the frequency count over time, so that the frequency count accurately reflects the current popularity of an object.

Second, depending on the encoded bit rate and the length of the clip, different audio and video files will have different sizes. Since LFU does not take the size of the file into account, two files with vastly different sizes and identical popularities see identical treatment. To overcome this drawback, the caching policy needs to normalize the popularity of an object by its size. The resulting policy is referred to as *bandwidth to space ratio (BSR)* based caching [Tewari et al., 1998]. In this policy, the proxy computes the ratio of the bandwidth and space requirement for each file. The bandwidth requirement is a measure of popularity, since it is the total bandwidth required to service all concurrent, asynchronous requests for a file. The space requirement is simply the storage space needed to stored the file in the cache. The BSR policy caches objects with the largest BSR ratio, thereby preferring objects with higher popularities and smaller sizes.

4. Partial Caching of Video Objects

Since the large size of streaming media objects limits the utility of complete object caching, several policies that cache portions of streaming media files have been proposed in the literature. These policies assumes that each streaming media file is partitioned in time (into segments) or in space (into layers), and subsets of these components are cached at proxies in the CDN. Caching partial objects allows greater flexibility and enables more judicious use of proxy resources in the CDN. When a client requests a file, the cached portions of the file are served from the local disk cache, while the remaining portions are fetched from another proxy or the origin server. The rest of this section discusses these techniques in detail.

4.1 Time-based Partial Caching

We discuss two techniques for caching portions of objects that are partitioned in time, namely prefix caching and caching of arbitrary segments.

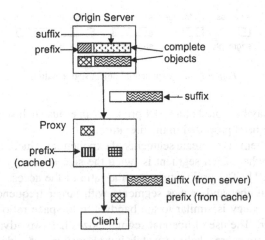

Figure 11.3. Prefix caching

Prefix Caching.   In prefix caching, each video file is partitioned into two segments—a prefix and a suffix. The prefix contains the the initial portion of the video while the suffix contains the remainder of the file. Proxies in the CDN only cache prefixes and the suffixes are stored at the origin servers (see Figure 11.3). When a request arrives, the proxy can immediately start streaming the requested object if its prefix is cached locally, while fetching the remainder of the file from the server. Doing so can significantly reduce the startup delay seen by the client. The prefix also servers as a "buffer" at the proxy and enables the proxy to mask jitter and loss on the server-proxy network path. Prefix caching is motivated by the observation that an initial portion of a video file is more likely be viewed than latter portions. This is because many users start viewing an audio or video file and then decide to no longer view the remainder of the file. In such a scenario, caching entire files at the proxy may be wasteful; instead it is more useful to store prefixes of popular files at proxy servers.

A key parameter in prefix caching is the size of the prefix cached at the proxy. The prefix length must be chosen carefully to balance the storage space at the proxy and factors such as the file popularity, jitter and loss on the server-proxy path. The problem of optimal prefix cache size selection has been studied in the literature [Wang et al., 2002].

Caching of Arbitrary Segments.   Prefix caching is the simplest time-based partial caching strategy, where each video file is partitioned into two segments, and proxies only cache the initial segment of a video file. The notion of caching partial file contents can be generalized to derive a variety of caching strategies, where a video file can be partitioned into multiple segments and different subsets

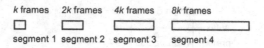

Figure 11.4. Exponential object segmentation

of segments may be stored at a CDN proxy. Numerous such segment caching strategies have been proposed in the literature.

One such scheme is to create segments of exponentially increasing sizes (see Figure 11.4), where each segment is twice the size of the previous segment [Wu et al., 2001]. The proxy computes the ratio of the access frequency and the segment number and caches segments with larger frequency to distance ratios. This strategy is similar to the bandwidth to space ratio (BSR) policy outlined earlier. The use of unequal segment sizes has two advantages. First, since viewers are more likely to watch initial portions of videos, the use of smaller segment sizes for the initial portions enables a proxy to favor these initial segments (over the subsequent larger segments) for caching. Second, unequal segment sizes enable a proxy to quickly free up a large amount of space by discarding a large segment that is no longer popular. In case of equal size segments, multiple evictions are necessary to free up the same amount of space. Consequently, it is easier for a proxy to adapt to changing segment popularities.

Another approach had advocated caching of the prefix as well as arbitrary segments of the video at the proxy, while storing the remainder of the file at the server. This approach is called selective caching [Miao and Ortega, 1999], and suggests storing intermediate segments or frames of the video at the proxy to permit efficient scan operations such as fast-forward, jump or rewind. Storing of the prefix allows the technique to provide similar benefits to prefix caching.

4.2   Bandwidth-based Partial Caching

In contrast to time-based partial cache, bandwidth-based partial caching requires that the video file be partitioned in the spatial dimension and involves storing portions of the file at proxies in the CDN and the remainder at the origin server. We discuss two techniques that are based on this idea.

Video Staging.   The video staging approach [Zhang et al., 2000] involves partitioning the file into two layers—a fixed rate lower layer and a variable rate upper layer. The lower layer is stored at the server, while the upper layer is stored at one or more proxies in the CDN (see Figure 11.5). When a client requests a file, the lower layer is streamed from the origin server and the upper layer from a proxy cache, thereby reducing the backbone bandwidth requirement. The main advantage of video staging is that it imposes a fixed overhead on the

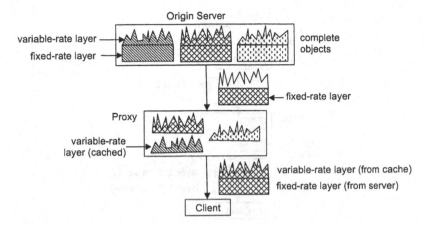

Figure 11.5. Video staging

server and the server-proxy network path due to the fixed rate of the lower layer. The variability in the video file is handled by the proxy. Observe that video staging is analogous to prefix caching, except for one important difference—in video staging, the lower layer is stored at the server, while in prefix caching, the prefix, which is the first segment, is stored at a proxy.

Caching of Layered Video. While bandwidth-based techniques for caching partial content have received little attention, some recent efforts have focused on caching of layered video files [Rejaie et al., 1999, Rejaie and Kangasharju, 2001a].

The Mocha proxy addresses this issue by assuming layered video files and caching different layers at a proxy, while fetching additional segments from the origin server in an on-demand basis [Rejaie et al., 2000, Rejaie and Kangasharju, 2001b]. User requests are serviced by streaming cached layers from the local disk, while fetching the missing layers from the origin servers (see Figure 11.6). A rate adaptive protocol is used to prefetch missing layers in the cache in a demand driven fashion in order to improve the quality of the cached video. Observe that, this technique is analogous to caching of arbitrary segments of the video at a CDN proxy. Other related efforts have also proposed caching of certain layers of a video file at CDN proxies and using user-perceived quality metrics to dynamically fetch additional layers from the origin server in order to improve video quality [Zink et al., 2004, Zink et al., 2003].

A disadvantage of partial time- or bandwidth-based caching techniques over caching complete objects is the reduced resilience to failures. Since only a subset of the file is stored in the CDN, the remaining content needs to be fetched from the server. Thus, a server failure will result in the content becoming

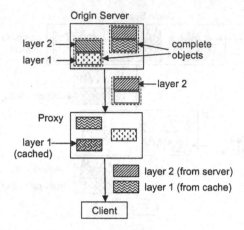

Figure 11.6.   Caching of layered video.

unavailable to the end-user. In contrast, caching complete objects enables the CDN to mask server failures from the end-user.

5.   Cluster-based Proxy Servers in a CDN

Our discussion thus far has focused on caching techniques at a single proxy in a CDN. However, in many scenarios, the CDN consists of multiple proxy clusters, where each cluster contains multiple proxy servers interconnected by a high-speed LAN (see Figure 11.7). In these environments proxies in the cluster can cooperate with one another to cache content; such cooperation often results in better service to the end-user. For instance, the cache at each proxy can be shared with other proxies in the cluster—in the event of a cache

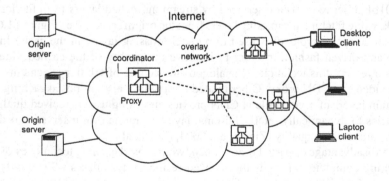

Figure 11.7.   Architecture of a clustered-based proxies in a CDN.

Table 11.1. Summary of Cluster-based Proxy Architectures.

Approach	Architecture	Content	Coordinator
Intelligent Agent	Centralized, LAN	Layered	Yes
Middleman	Centralized, LAN	Segments	Yes
Rcache/Silo	Distributed, LAN	Segments	No
Dynamic Reconfiguration	Distributed, LAN	Segments	No
SOCCER	Distributed, WAN	Segments	No

miss, a proxy can simply forward a user request to another proxy in the cluster, rather than fetching the missing content from the origin server. Similarly, proxy clusters can be employed for load balancing, where multiple proxies in a cluster can participate in servicing requests for very popular videos. In this section, we discuss several cluster-based proxy architectures that have been proposed recently. Table 11.1 summarizes these approaches.

Middleman Cluster Proxy: Early work on cluster-based proxies assumed a centralized coordinator for proxies in the cluster. The coordinator is assumed to have full knowledge about the files cached at each proxy as well as the requests currently served by each proxy in the cluster. The coordinator is responsible for implementing the caching policy on behalf of all proxies in the cluster as well as for determining which proxy should service an incoming request. The Middleman cluster proxy is an example of such an approach [Acharya and Smith, 2000]. Middleman employs a coordinator proxy to make decisions for all proxies in a cluster. Upon receiving a request, a proxy forwards the request to the coordinator, which determines the best proxy in the cluster to service the request. The requested file is then streamed from that proxy to the end-client. In the event of a cache miss or if all proxies are overloaded, the request is forwarded to the origin server. Middleman also implements an *LRU-k* cache replacement strategy.[1] Each video file is partitioned into equal size segments and the LRU-k policy is employed to determine which segments are cached locally by each proxy in the cluster.

While Middleman requires that a file be partitioned into segments and employs time-based partial caching within the proxy cluster, caching of layered video in a proxy cluster has also been studied in the intelligent agent cluster-based proxy [Paknikar et al., 2000]. Like in Middleman, a centralized coordinator is used to determine which layers of a video should be cached and at which proxy in the cluster.

Silo and RCache Cluster-based Proxy: Since a centralized coordinator can become a bottleneck and is a single point of failure, distributed architectures for proxy clusters have been studied recently. Such cluster-based proxy do not assume the presence of a coordinator and make all decisions in a distributed fashion.

The RCache approach employs a cluster of K cooperating proxies that randomize the placement of video segments onto proxies in the cluster [Chae et al., 2002]. RCache proxies assume equal size segments for a video and cache a segment with a fixed probability a/K, where a is a constant. A randomized strategy that maps video segments to proxies can avoid hot spots that occur when multiple popular segments are placed on a single proxy, resulting in overload. Note, however, that in the RCache approach, the probability of caching a segment is independent of its popularity.

The Silo approach overcomes this drawback by using unequal segment sizes and a randomized placement strategy that takes popularities into account [Chae et al., 2002]. The approach also assumes a cluster of proxies and employs exponentially increasing segment sizes and exponentially decreasing probabilities for caching later segments of a video. Specifically, the ith segment of a video has a size α^{i-1} and is cached with a probability $1/\beta^{i-1}$. Thus, initial segments are more likely to be cached (the first segment, also the smallest, is cached with a probability 1). Since different files can have different popularities, the probability of caching a segment can be biased by its current popularity. The approach also uses a cache replacement policy that takes both the local popularity of a segment (i.e., the popularity at a single proxy in the cluster) and the global popularity (the popularity across all proxies) when evicting segments.

Dynamically Reconfiguring Proxy Cluster: Since popularities of video files change dynamically over time, the set of segments cached at proxies in a cluster needs to be adapted to this changing popularity. Specifically, video segments that are increasing in popularity need to be fetched into the caches and segments that are no longer popular need to be replaced. A cluster-based proxy that can adaptively reconfigure the caches at proxies in the cluster was proposed in [Guo et al., 2003]. In this approach, a video file is partitioned into segments, that are ranked according to their *bandwidth to space ratio (BSR)*. The mapping of segments onto caches in the cluster is modeled as a two-dimensional knapsack problem, and a greedy first-fit heuristic is employed to place these segments onto proxies in the cluster. Depending on its popularity, each segment can be replicated at multiple caches, placed on a single proxy cache, or not cached at all. As the popularity of video file changes over time, the proxy cluster adapts this initial placement in an incremental fashion to match the new object popularities. This adaptation involves (i) determining an ideal mapping for the new popularities and (ii) use of a minimum weight perfect matching (MWPM) heuristic that transforms the current mapping to the new mapping such that the overhead of moving segments from one cache to another is minimized. Like in the Silo and the Middleman approaches, each user request is serviced by streaming available segments from the proxy cluster, while fetching the missing segments from the origin server.

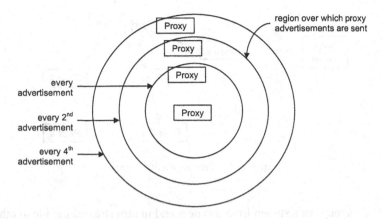

Figure 11.8. The expanding ring advertisement protocol.

Self-Organizing Cooperative Caching Architecture (SOCCER): While Middleman, Silo and the dynamically reconfiguring proxy architectures assume a cluster of proxies interconnected by a local area network, the SOCCER approach extends the notion of a proxy cluster to a wide area network [Hofmann et al., 1999]. In this approach, a collection of geographically distributed proxy servers cooperate with one another to service user requests. Cooperative caching requires a proxy to know the current status of other proxies in its cluster. While maintaining the state of all proxies is easy in a LAN setting, exchanging state updates is expensive in WAN environments. The SOCCER approach explicitly addresses this issue using an Expanding Ring Advertisement (ERA) protocol, where a proxy multicasts any updates to its cache with dynamic TTL values. Proxies that are further apart receive such advertisements less frequently, while nearby proxies have more up-to-date knowledge of each other's proxy cache contents (see Figure 11.8). The advertisements are also used to propagate load information to other proxies. The knowledge of a proxy load and its cache contents enables other proxies to determine whether to forward a user request to it.

6.   Peer-to-Peer Streaming Techniques

The previous sections have discussed streaming from a client-proxy-server perspective. In this section, we provide an overview of an alternative streaming approach, namely peer-to-peer streaming. Peer-to-peer streaming is motivated by a number of reasons. Origin servers as well as CDN proxies have limited capacity on the number of concurrent streams they can support. If an overloaded server or proxy is unable to service a client, then the client can request an object from another client (i.e., a peer) that is currently being served by the proxy. The

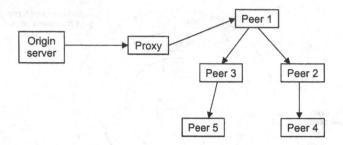

Figure 11.9. Peer-to-peer streaming

client then receives a stream from this peer and in turn streams the file to other interested clients. In other words, the proxy streams the file to a small number of client (or peers). Each peer in turn streams the file to other peers, until all interested clients receive a copy of the stream (see Figure 11.9). In effect, peer-to-peer streaming uses a form of multicast at the application level (referred to as application-level multicast). The network of peers form a multicast distribution tree rooted at the origin server or a CDN proxy. Observe that clients are inherently unreliable, since they can be disconnected or switched off by their owners at any time. Consequently, a peer-to-peer streaming technique must be able to adapt the distribution tree as peers dynamically join and leave the network. Further, the distribution tree needs to employ redundant streaming techniques to mask disruptions in the media playback caused by peers leaving the network. Consequently, much of the ongoing research in P2P streaming focuses on: (i) tree construction algorithms, (ii) handling dynamic joins and leaves, and (iii) redundant streaming techniques that mask packet losses due to peers leaving the network. This section discusses several peer-to-peer streaming approaches that have been proposed in the literature.

Zigzag streaming: The Zigzag P2P approach focuses on tree construction algorithms for streaming content to a large number of peers. The proposed tree construction causes the depth of the tree to grow logarithmically with the number of peers [Tran et al., 2003]. A distribution tree with a smaller depth reduces the number of intermediaries between the server and a leaf peer, which in turn reduces the end-to-end delay. The technique also bounds the number of children for each intermediate node in the tree, which in turn limits the network bandwidth requirement at each peer. Reducing the bandwidth requirements at each peer is especially important, since many peers tend to be connected over home broadband connections, which are asymmetric in nature with limited upload bandwidth. Departures of a peer are handled by reconnecting all peers in the subtree rooted at the departed peer with other live peers in the system.

CoopNet Resilient P2P streaming: The resilient P2P streaming approach [Padmanabhan et al., 2003] focuses on the use of redundant network paths (in the form of multiple distribution trees) and redundant data transmissions to minimize the disruptions due to peers leaving the network. A peer-to-peer streaming system called CoopNet ("cooperative networking") is proposed that employs multiple descriptive coding. Multiple description coding (MDC) is a method of encoding an audio and/or video stream into M separate streams, or descriptions, such that any subset of these descriptions can be received and decoded. The distortion with respect to the original signal is proportional with the number of descrip- tions received; i.e., the more descriptions received, the lower the distortion and the higher the quality of the reconstructed stream. This differs from layered coding in that in MDC every subset of descriptions must be decodable, whereas in layered coding only a nested sequence of subsets must be decodable. By using MDC to encode a video stream and by sending it on multiple paths to each peer, the CoopNet system ensures that a peer can decode the video so long as it receives some subset of the descriptions. The use of MDC also enables CoopNet to handle peer departures in a flexible manner—a departed peer results in a lower resolution video for all peers served by it until the tree is repaired.

SplitStream: The SplitStream system [Castro et al., 2003] combines a peer-to-peer overlay network with an application level multicast for the purpose of video distribution. In their approach a video is split into stripes which are distributed via separate multicast trees. The goal of SplitStream is to create a forest of separate multicast trees in such a way that a node is only an internal node for only one multicast tree and a leaf node in all other cases. This mechanism distributes the load equally over all nodes of the distribution system. This approach is well suited for the distribution of layer-encoded video, since each layer can be distributed via a separate multicast tree.

Layered Peer-to-Peer Streaming: The issue of streaming layered video in a peer-to-peer fashion has been explicitly studied in [Cui and Nahrstedt, 2003]. In this approach, each video is assumed to be encoded into a number of layers, and peers are assumed to be heterogeneous. An algorithm to determine what layers should be fetched by a peer from upstream peers and which of these layers to buffer and forward to downstream peers is proposed. The algorithm attempts to judiciously use the download and upload bandwidth available to each peer with the goal of maximizing overall viewing quality. For instance, a peer may fetch six layers from upstream peers, and depending on how many downstream peers it serves and when they join, only a subset of these six layers may be forwarded to others.

PROMISE P2P Streaming: The PROMISE peer-to-peer streaming system focuses on a set of services that are necessary to judiciously construct a P2P distribution tree [Xu et al., 2002, Hefeeda et al., 2003]. For instance, PROMISE supports a service to infer the underlying network topology between peers. The knowledge of the underlying topology can be employed to construct a tree where the number of hops between two connected peers is small. Another service supported by PROMISE involves monitoring the status of peers, so that peer departures can be detected with low latency. Detecting peer failures quickly is important for minimizing the disruptions in video delivery to downstream peers. A third service involves failure recovery, where the service dynamically switches peers to standby peers, when a parent peer fails. Together, these collection of services simplifies the building of peer-to-peer streaming services over a wide area network. This was demonstrated by designing a multi-path P2P streaming using these services [Xu et al., 2002].

7.   Conclusions

In this chapter, we presented a brief overview of the state of the art in caching and distribution techniques for streaming media content. Initial work in the area focused on full object caching. Given the large sizes of streaming media files, techniques for partial caching of objects have also been extensive studied. We classified partial caching techniques into two types: time-based partial caching and bandwidth-based partial caching. More recent research efforts have focused on caching techniques for a co-located cluster of proxy caches as well as techniques for streaming using peer-to-peer networks. The area continues to evolve as researchers shift their attention to distributing streaming content to small networked devices such as PDAs and next-generation mobile phones.

Notes

1. The *least recently used-K (LRU-K)* policy maintains a history of the K most recent access times and computes the K-distance of an object as the difference between the current time and the Kth access. The object with the greatest K distance is evicted from the cache. LRU-k is a generalization of the basic LRU policy, where LRU-1 is same as LRU.

References

Acharya, Soam and Smith, Brian (1998). Experiment to Characterize Videos Stored on the Web. In *Proceedings of SPIE/ACM Conference on Multimedia Computing and Networking (MMCN), San Jose, CA, USA*, pages 166–178.

Acharya, Soam and Smith, Brian (2000). MiddleMan: A Video Caching Proxy Server. In *Proceedings of NOSSDAV 2000, Chapel Hill, NC, USA*.

Acharya, Soam, Smith, Brian, and Parnes, Peter (2000). Characterizing User Access To Videos On the World Wide Web. In *Proceedings of SPIE/ACM Conference on Multimedia Computing and Networking (MMCN), San Jose, CA, USA*, pages 130–141. SPIE.

Bianchi, Giuseppe and Melen, Riccardo (1997). Non Stationary Request Distribution in Video-on-Demand Networks. In *Proceedings of the 16th Annual Joint Conference of the IEEE Computer and Communications Societies (INFOCOM'97), Kobe, Japan*, pages 711–717. IEEE Computer Society Press.

Castro, Miguel, Druschel, Peter, Hu, Y. Charlie, and Rowstron, Antony (2003). SplitStream: High-bandwidth Content Distribution in Cooperative Environments. In *Proceedings of the 2nd International Workshop on Peer-to-Peer Systems (IPTPS '03), Berkeley, CA, USA*, pages 103–107.

Chae, Youngsu, Guo, Katherine, Buddhikot, Milind M., Suri, Subhash, and Zegura, Ellen W. (2002). Silo, Rainbow, and Caching Token: Schemes for Scalable, Fault Tolerant Stream Caching. *IEEE Journal on Selected Areas in Communications*, 20, 7:1328–1344.

Chesire, Maureen, Wolman, Alec, Voelker, Geoffrey, and Levy, Henry (2001). Measurement and Analysis of a Streaming-Media Workload. In *Proceedings of USITS'02: The 3rd USENIX Symposium on Internet Technologies and Systems, San Francisco, CA, USA*.

Cui, Yi and Nahrstedt, Klara (2003). Layered peer-to-peer streaming. In *Proc. of International Workshop on Network and Operating Systems Support for Digital Audio and Video (NOSSDAV '03)*.

Eager, Derek, Vernon, Mary, and Zahorjan, John (2001). Minimizing Bandwidth Requirements for On-Demand Data Delivery. *IEEE Transactions on Knowledge and Data Engineering*, 13(5):742–757.

Griwodz, Carsten, Bär, Michael, and Wolf, Lars C. (1997). Long-term Movie Popularity in Video-on-Demand Systems. In *Proceedings of ACM Multimedia Conference 1997, Seattle, WA, USA*, pages 340–357.

Guo, Y., Ge, Z., Urgaonkar, B., Shenoy, P., and Towsley, D. (2003). Dynamic cache reconfiguration strategies for cluster-based streaming proxies. In *Proceedings of the Eighth International Workshop on Web Content Caching and Distribution (WCW 2003), Hawthorne, NY*.

H263 (1995). ITU-T: Video Coding for Low Bit Rate Communication. International Standard. ITU-T Recoomendation H.263.

Hefeeda, M., Habib, A., Botev, B., Xu, D., and Bhargava, B. (2003). Promise: Peer-to-peer media streaming using collectcast. In *Proceedings of ACM Multimedia 2003, Berkeley, CA*, pages 45–54. ISBN:1-58113-722-2.

Hofmann, Markus, Ng, T. S. Eugene, Guo, Katherine, Sanjoy, Paul, and Zhang, Hui (1999). Caching Techniques for Streaming Multimedia over the Internet. Technical report, Bell Labs, Holmdel, NJ, USA.

Hu, Ailan (2001). Video-on-Demand Broadcasting Protocols: a Comprehensive Study. In *Proceedings of the 20th Annual Joint Conference of the IEEE Computer and Communications Societies (INFOCOM'01), Anchorage, AK, USA*, pages 508–517. IEEE Computer Society Press.

Hua, Kien A. and Sheu, Simon (1997). Skyscraper Broadcasting: A new Broadcasting Scheme for Metropolitan Video-on-Demand Systems. In *Proceedings of the ACM SIGCOMM '97, Cannes, France*, pages 89–100.

Miao, Zhourong and Ortega, Antonio (1999). Proxy Caching for Efficient Video Services over the Internet. In *Proceedings of the 9th Packet Video Workshop, New York, NY, USA*, pages 36–44.

MPEG-1 (1993). International Organization for Standardisation (ISO). Information Technology – Coding of Moving Pictures and Associated Audio for Digital Storage Media at up to about 1,5 Mbit/s – Part 1: Systems. International Standard. ISO/IEC 11172-1:1993.

Nussbaumer, Jean-Paul, Patel, Baiju, Schaffa, Frank, and Sterbenz, James P. G. (1995). Networking Requirements for Interactive Video on Demand. *IEEE Journal on Selected Areas in Communications*, 13(5):779–787. ISSN 0733-8716.

Padmanabhan, V., Wang, H., and Chou, P. (2003). Resilient peer-to-peer streaming. In *Proceedings of IEEE Intl. Coference on Network Protocols (ICNP), Atlanta, GA*, pages 16–27. ISSN 1092-1648.

Paknikar, Shantanu, Kankanhalli, Mohan, Ramakrishnan, K.R., Srinivasan, S.H., and Ngoh, Lek Heng (2000). A Caching and Streaming Framework for Multimedia. In *Proceedings of the ACM Multimedia Conference 2000, Los Angeles, CA, USA*, pages 13–20.

Paris, Jehan-Francois, Long, Darell D. E., and Mantey, Patrick E. (1999). Zero-Delay Broadcasting Protocols for Video-on-Demand. In *Proceedings of the ACM Multimedia Conference 1999, Orlando, FL, USA*, pages 189–197.

Pereira, Fernando and Ebrahimi, Touradj (2002). *The MPEG-4 Book*. Prentice-Hall. ISBN 0-13-061621-4.

Rejaie, Reza, Handley, Mark, and Estrin, Deborah (1999). RAP: An End-to-End Rate-based Congestion Control Mechanism for Realtime Streams in the Internet. In *Proceedings of the Eighteenth Annual Joint Conference of the IEEE Computer and Communications Societies 1999 (INFOCOM'99), New York, NY, USA*, pages 395–399.

Rejaie, Reza and Kangasharju, Jussi (2001a). Mocha: A Quality Adaptive Multimedia Proxy Cache for Internet Streaming. In *Proceedings of the 11th International Workshop on Network and Operating System Support for Digital Audio and Video (NOSSDAV'01), Port Jefferson, NY, USA*, pages 3–10.

Rejaie, Reza and Kangasharju, Jussi (2001b). Mocha: A quality adaptive multimedia proxy cache for internet streaming. In *Proceedings of the International Workshop on Network and Operating Systems Support for Digital Audio and Video Port Jefferson, NY*.

Rejaie, Reza, Yu, Haobo, Handley, Mark, and Estrin, Debora (2000). Multimedia Proxy Caching for Quality Adaptive Streaming Applications in the Internet. In *Proceedings of the Nineteenth Annual Joint Conference of the*

IEEE Computer and Communications Societies 2000 (INFOCOM'00), Tel-Aviv, Israel, pages 980–989.

Sitaram, Dinkar and Dan, Asit (2000). *Multimedia Servers*. Morgan Kaufmann Publishers. ISBN 1-55860-430-8.

Tewari, Renu, Vin, Harrick, Dan, Asit, and Sitaram, Dinkar (1998). Resource-Based Caching For Web Servers. In *Proceedings of SPIE/ACM Conference on Multimedia Computing and Networking (MMCN), San Jose, CA, USA*, pages 191–204.

Tran, Duc T., Hua, Kien A., and Do, Tai (2003). ZIGZAG: An Efficient Peer-to-Peer Scheme for Media Streaming. In *Proceedings of the 22th Annual Joint Conference of the IEEE Computer and Communications Societies (INFOCOM'03), New York, NY, USA*, pages 1283–1292. ISSN 0743-166X.

Wang, B., Sen, S., Adler, M., and Towsley, D. (2002). Optimal Proxy Cache Allocation for Efficient Streaming Media Distribution. In *Proceedings of the 21th Annual Joint Conference of the IEEE Computer and Communications Societies (INFOCOM'02), New York, NY, USA*, pages 1726–1735.

Wu, Kun-Lung, Yu, Philip S., and Wolf, Joel L. (2001). Segment-Based Proxy Caching of Multimedia Streams. In *Proceedings of the Tenth International World Wide Web Conference, Hong Kong, China*, pages 36–44.

Xu, D., Hefeeda, M., Hambrusch, S., and Bhargava, B. (2002). On peer-to-peer media streaming. In *Proceedings of IEEE International Conference on Distributed Computing Systems (ICDCS 2002), Wien, Austria*, pages 363–371. ISSN 1063-6927.

Zhang, Zhi-Li, Wang, Yuewei, Du, David H.C., and Su, Dongli (2000). Prospects for Interactive Video-on-Demand. *IEEE/ACM Transactions on Networking*, 8(4):429–442.

Zink, Michael, Künzel, Oliver, Schmitt, Jens B., and Steinmetz, Ralf (2003). Subjective Impression of Variations in Layer Encoded Videos. In *Proceedings of the 11th IEEE/IFIP International Workshop on Quality of Service (IWQoS'03), Monterey, CA, USA*, pages 134–154. ISBN 3-540-40281-0.

Zink, Michael, Schmitt, Jens, and Griwodz, Carsten (2004). Layer-Encoded Video Streaming: A Proxy's Perspecive. *IEEE Communications*, 42(8):96–103.

Chapter 12

PEER-TO-PEER ASSISTED STREAMING PROXY

Lei Guo
Department of Computer Science
College of William and Mary
lguo@cs.wm.edu

Songqing Chen
Department of Computer Science
George Mason University
sqchen@cs.gmu.edu

Xiaodong Zhang
Department of Computer Science
College of William and Mary
zhang@cs.wm.edu

Abstract   The demand of delivering streaming media contents in the Internet has become increasingly high for scientific, educational, and commercial applications. This chapter first overviews three representative Internet technologies for delivering streaming media contents, and discusses the merits and limits of each. This chapter emphasizes on peer-to-peer streaming technology by presenting a design and its performance evaluation of a scalable and reliable media proxy system that effectively utilizes P2P sharing among media clients.

Keywords: Internet media streaming, peer-to-peer systems, proxy caching, distributed hash table

1.   Introduction

Delivering multimedia contents with high quality and low cost over the Internet is challenging due to the typical large sizes of media objects and the rigorous requirement of continuous streaming demand of clients. Three existing and representative solutions for media streaming are provided on the Internet, namely, proxy systems, content delivery/distribution networks (CDNs), and peer-to-peer systems. We will overview each of them with comments on their merits and limitations. To address these limitations, we focus on a novel technical approach of P2P assisted proxy streaming system in this chapter.

1.1   Streaming Media Proxy Systems

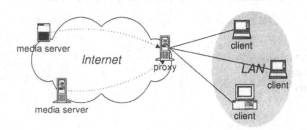

Figure 12.1.   The streaming media proxy system.

Proxy systems have been widely deployed at the edge of the Internet, and successfully used for delivering text- and image-based contents. Although small media clips can be cached in the same way as caching text-based Web objects, a full caching of high quality video objects will quickly exhaust the limited proxy cache storage. To handle the large sizes of media objects, researchers have developed a number of segment-based proxy caching strategies (e.g., [Wu et al., 2001] and [Chen et al., 2003]) to cache partial segments of media objects instead of their entirety.

Although the segment-based proxy caching technique has shown its effectiveness for media streaming, the quality of service it can provide is still not satisfactory to clients for the following reasons. First, the limited storage capacity of a proxy will restrict the amount of media data it can cache for clients. The work in [Chesire et al., 2001] shows that the reference locality of multimedia objects is much smaller than that of Web pages. Thus, the cache space problem is much more significant in streaming proxy systems than that in Web proxy systems. Second, the delivery of streaming media normally requires a dedicated reservation of continuous bandwidths for clients, thus, the highly demanded proxy bandwidths will limit the number of clients to be served simultaneously. Furthermore, a proxy easily becomes a system bottleneck, and also forms a single point of failure, being vulnerable to attacks. Due the above limitations, streaming proxies have not been widely used and there are no mentioned general-purpose commercial streaming proxies available so far. Most commercial streaming proxies are designed for specific streaming servers, such as Helix Universal Media Proxy [Realnetworks, 2005] and Windows Media Proxy Services [Cisco, 2005].

1.2 Content Delivery/Distribution Networks

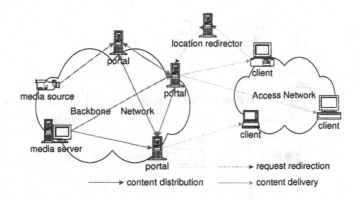

Figure 12.2. The architecture of Prism CDN.

Commercial content delivery/distribution networks (CDNs) have been built to replicate media servers across the Internet to move the contents close to the clients, such as Akamai [Akamai, 2005]. Prism (Portal Infrastructure for Streaming Media) [Cranor et al., 2001] is a CDN architecture for distributing and delivering high quality streaming media over the Internet. The Prism system consists of three kinds of elements: the media sources or content providers, portals, and clients. The main components of the system architecture are the *content distribution mechanism, data control mechanism,* and *content delivery mechanism.* The content distribution mechanism transfers media content from the video sources or content providers to one or more portals, or transfers content between two portals, in order to push the media content closer to end users in different networks and balance the workload among portals. The data control mechanism coordinates the media content storage among portals, locates content within the infrastructure, and redirects a user's requests to the portal satisfying the user best, which is normally a portal topologically close to the user. The content delivery mechanism streams media to clients via the selected portal. Today, CDNs have evolved from caching static Web contents such as text and image files to streaming media contents, dynamic contents, and even applications. Although the CDN approach is performance-effective, it is not cost-effective due to the expensive infrastructure. For example, Akamai uses more than 12,000 servers in over 1,000 networks to distribute contents at the edge of the Internet [Dilley et al., 2002]. Thus, for large commercial media providers, using server cluster or site mirrors may be more cost-effective than purchasing CDN services. Meanwhile, small media providers may not be able to afford the high cost of CDN services.

1.3   Client-based Peer-to-Peer Streaming Systems

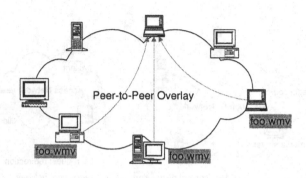

Figure 12.3.   Client-based peer-to-peer media streaming.

Although the capacity of a single proxy is limited, the resources of bandwidth, storage, and CPU cycles are richly available and under-utilized among the clients. Peer-to-peer (P2P) is a decentralized resource sharing model for client users, which is complementary to the client-server service models. In a peer-to-peer system, each peer acts both as a client who requests information and services, and as a server who produces and/or provides information and services. The P2P sharing model is very attractive for resource consuming services such as media streaming.

PROMISE [Hefeeda et al., 2003] is a client-based P2P streaming media system (see Figure 12.3). In this system, peers are self-organized into an overlay, where each peer contributes its media objects for sharing. Since the capacity of a single peer is limited, and peers may come and go frequently, multiple peers in PROMISE collaborate together to serve a streaming session. A CollectCast service is built in the system in order to find the best candidates for the streaming service.

A major limit of client-based P2P streaming systems, such as PROMISE, is that the availability and reliability of the streaming service are not guaranteed. First, since such a system is a streaming media sharing system, where each peer maintains its local media objects separately, the content distribution is not coordinated and the availability of the requested media cannot be ensured. Second, since client-based P2P systems are self-organized by end users, the demand of streaming service and the capacity of the systems is highly dynamic. As a result, it is not always possible to find enough peers for CollectCast to deliver the requested media. Third, the quality of service provided by multiple collaborative peers may not be sufficient for highly dynamic and bursty streaming media requests.

1.4   P2P Assisted Streaming Proxy Systems

In order to address the scalability problem of proxy-based techniques, and to deliver the high quality media content to clients, PROP, a scalable and reliable segment-based P2P media delivering system has been proposed [Guo et al., 2004a]. By organizing the proxy and its clients in the same intranet into a P2P system, the PROP system attempts to address both the scalability and the reliability issues for streaming media delivery in a cost-effective way. In such a system, the clients effectively coordinate and collaborate with the proxy to provide scalable media storage and to actively participate in streaming media delivery. Media objects are cached in segment units both in peers and in the proxy for the purpose of self-viewing and global sharing.

2.   Content Locating in P2P Systems

Decentralized peer-to-peer systems are self-organized by participating peers. The basic service of such systems is *content locating* or *lookup*. There are two kinds of P2P systems according to overlay organization: Unstructured P2P systems and structured P2P systems. In unstructured P2P systems, there is neither precise control nor global coordination over the overlay topology or object placement. Gnutella [Gnutella, 2005] is a representative unstructured P2P system for file sharing. In structured P2P systems, the overlay topology is precisely determined, so that the system can process queries efficiently. The system provides a hash table like interface for object placement and lookup service, called *distributed hash table*. The representative distributed hash table systems are CAN [Ratnasamy et al., 2001], Chord [Stoica et al., 2001], Pastry [Rowstron et al., 2001], and Tapestry [Zhao et al., 2001].

2.1   Content Locating in Unstructured P2P Systems

The basic approach to search in unstructured P2P systems is flooding. Flooding is the most effective way for content locating in such systems. However, it results in a great amount of redundant traffic on the underlying networks due to the redundancy of overlay connections. Many search optimization strategies have been proposed. For example, by organizing the P2P overlay into an approximated spanning tree and utilizing the power law distribution of node connectivity in P2P systems, LightFlood [Jiang et al., 2003] can reduce most of the redundant message traffic and retain the same performance as normal flooding. On the other hand, by exploiting the content locality and query patterns in P2P systems, CAC-SPIRP [Guo et al., 2004b] effectively reduces both query traffic and response time in P2P systems.

2.2 Content Locating in Structured P2P Systems

Content locating in structured P2P systems relies on a decentralized infrastructure – the distributed hash table (DHT). In such a system, each node maintains a routing table that is determined by the overlay structure of the distributed hash table. Each object is placed in a unique location in the system based on its key value, and can be reached by routing query between nodes according to the DHT routing rules. A one dimensional distributed hash table such as Chord, Pastry, and Tapestry uses skiplist-like routing or tree-like routing to pass the query to the destination node, and can provide $O(\log n)$ lookup with each node maintaining $O(\log n)$ routing table entries. Content addressable network (CAN) uses a multi-dimensional mapping mechanism that can provide $O(dN^{1/d})$ lookup with each peer maintaining $O(d)$ routing table entries, where d is the dimension of the system coordination space, and N is the number of nodes in the system.

Figure 12.4 shows how a message is routed from coordinate $(0.4, 0.1)$ to $(0.9, 0.7)$ in a two dimensional CAN structure. Each object is mapped into the two dimensional Cartesian space uniquely, and each node maintains a coordination zone and the objects associated with the zone. Each node also maintains a routing table, i.e., the coordination zones of its neighbors. Intuitively, routing in CAN overlay is performed by following the straight line path through the Cartesian space from the source to destination coordination in a decentralized way.

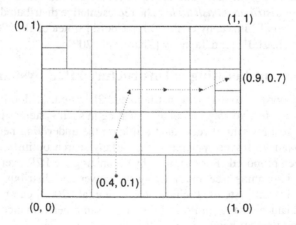

Figure 12.4. A two dimensional CAN structure.

3. PROP: A Scalable and Reliable P2P Assisted Streaming Proxy System

PROP is a scalable and reliable P2P assisted streaming proxy system for on-demand streaming media delivery, which is abbreviated from the technical theme of "collaborating and coordinating **PRO**xy and its **P**2P clients". The basic idea is to exploit resources available from end users to provide scalability for the streaming system and utilize a dedicated proxy to work as a backup service to provide the system reliability. The basic architecture of the PROP system is shown in Figure 12.5.

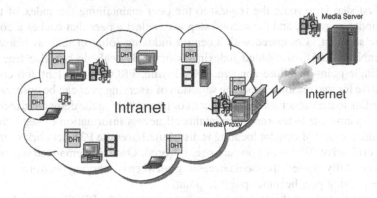

Figure 12.5. A sketch of the PROP system.

3.1 Infrastructure Overview

The two main components of the PROP system are (1) the proxy and (2) all the client peers receiving the media streaming service, which are connected via a P2P overlay network. The proxy is the bootstrap site of the P2P system and the interface between the P2P system and media servers. When an object is requested for the first time or when no peer in the system is able to serve a streaming request, the proxy is responsible for fetching the requested media object from the remote content server, caching it locally, and segmenting the object into small units evenly.

Each peer in the PROP system has three functionalities. First, a peer is a *client* that may request media data. Second, a peer is a *streaming server* that provides media streaming service to clients. Each peer caches the media data in segments while its content accessing is in progress, and shares the cached data with other peers in the system. Third, a peer is also an *index server* that maintains a subset of indices of media segments in the system for content locating. Peers in the PROP system are self-organized into a structured P2P overlay supporting a distributed hash table, which maps the identifier of each media segment to the index of the segment. The P2P operations in the PROP system can be overlay independent. Specifically, PROP uses content addressable network (CAN) as the overlay structure since it is more flexible for dynamic user environment due to the constant routing table size.

In the PROP system, the media segments and their corresponding indices are decoupled. In another words, they may be maintained by different peers. The index of a segment contains a location list of peers, each of which caches a copy of the media segment, and the access information of this segment, which is used for replacement operations. Segment locating is conducted in two steps: the first step is to route the request to the peer maintaining the index of the demanded segment, and the second step is to select a peer that caches a copy of the segment. Compared with a central indexing solution such as Napster [OpenNap, 2005], distributed indexing is not only scalable but also free of the single-point-of-failure concern. Meanwhile, PROP is efficient and cost-effective for two reasons. First, the selection of a serving peer can be optimized according to the capacities and workloads of peers caching the demanded media data, because the index server maintains all access information of segments. Second, the cost of content locating is distributed over the P2P network so that the workload of P2P routing on each peer is trivial. Once the demanded segment is successfully located, the media streaming between the serving peer/proxy and the requesting peer becomes point-to-point.

Figure 12.6 shows the data flow in an index server in the PROP system. Upon the arrival of a query, the index server first checks whether the query can be satisfied in its local distributed hash table. If yes, it performs a lookup on the

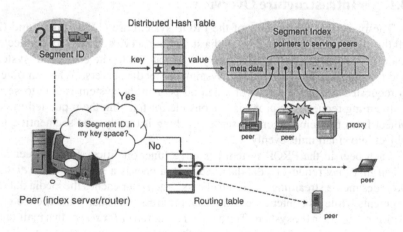

Figure 12.6. The data flow in a peer in PROP system.

table and returns a selected peer as the media server. Otherwise, it will route the query to other peers.

3.2   P2P Routing and Media Streaming

The distributed hash table supported by the P2P overlay stores the $(key, value)$ maps where each key is the identifier of a media segment and the corresponding $value$ is the index of the segment. The identifier of a media segment is a GUID (globally unique identifier) hashed from the URL of the media object and the offset of the segment in the object with SHA1 algorithm [RFC 3174, 2001]. In the PROP system, each peer is assigned a key space zone when joining the system, and maintains the segment indices mapped to this zone. Joining P2P routing entails getting the key space zone and taking over the corresponding indices from a neighbor, while leaving P2P routing entails handing over the segment indices and merging the key space zone to a neighbor [Ratnasamy et al., 2001].

The following operations on the distributed hash table are designed in the PROP system for content locating and data management: $publish, unpublish, request, update$ and $notify$.

Publishing and Unpublishing Media Segments.   The $publish(seg\_id, location)$ operation publishes a cached copy of media segment in the P2P system, in which seg_id is the segment identifier, and $location$ is the IP address and port number of the peer that caches the segment copy. Correspondingly, the $unpublish(seg\_id, location)$ operation unpublishes the copy of media segment stored in $location$. To publish or unpublish a segment, a peer routes its $location$ and the seg_id to the target peer that maintains the segment index. The target peer puts $location$ into or removes it from the location list in the segment index. Each segment index is created by the proxy upon object segmentation, and the index server is responsible for maintaining consistency between media segments and corresponding indices. A peer publishes a segment as soon as it caches the full segment and unpublishes a segment as soon as the segment is replaced. A peer publishes all segments it caches when joining the P2P system and unpublishes all segments it caches when leaving the P2P system.

Requesting and Serving Media Segments.   A peer requests a media object segment by segment, and searches in its local cache first. If the local search fails, it calls the $request(seg\_id, URL)$ operation, which requests a segment of the object designated by the URL. When a peer requests a media object that it does not cache, it routes the URL to the target peer that maintains the key space zone to which the identifier of the object's first segment is mapped. If the corresponding index does not exist, meaning the object is requested for the first time, the target peer sends a request to the proxy, which fetches the

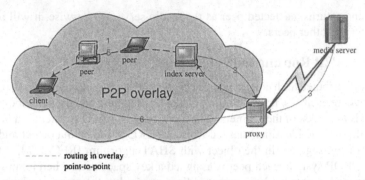

(a) The proxy fetches and serves the requested media data

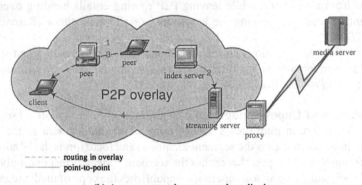

(b) A peer serves the requested media data

Figure 12.7.   The requesting and serving of media data.

requested object from the media server, and creates the index and publishes the object. Then the target peer routes the proxy's location back to the requesting peer, redirecting the peer to the proxy for the media data. If the target peer finds the segment index, but the location list is empty, the target peer sends a request to the proxy, which fetches the segment and publishes it. The first five steps are shown in Figure 12.7(a). If the location list is not empty, the target peer checks the validation of each location link, then returns the location of the peer with the maximal available bandwidth to the requesting peer. Figure 12.7(b) demonstrates the first three steps. Then the serving peer provides the requested data to the requesting peer, as the last step shown in Figure 12.7(a) and Figure 12.7(b). A client can buffer the next segment when the current segment is played back. If a serving peer wants to leave the P2P system before the current streaming terminates, it must push the rest of the segment to the requesting peer before exiting the P2P system.

Updating Segment Popularity and Utility Values. PROP uses the popularity and utility values of segments to manage cached data. These values depend on the access information and number of copies of corresponding media segments in the system. When the proxy or a peer finishes serving a segment streaming task, it calls $update(seg\_id, access\_info)$ operation, which routes the access information to the target peer maintaining the segment's index, and then the target peer updates the corresponding information items accordingly. When the segment popularity or utility values change, the index server notifies all peers that cache the segment with new values by the $notify(peerset, seg\_id, value)$ operation, where $peerset$ is the set of peers in the location list of the segment index, and $value$ is the popularity or utility value of the segment designated by seg_id.

Message Routing Overhead. In PROP, a $request$ and an $update$ message are generated for each segment a client requests. For each segment replica that is cached or evicted from the cache, a $publish$ or $unpublish$ message is generated. Although a $notify$ operation may generate multiple messages, it can be postponed if the popularity or utility value changes little. Furthermore, the replacement algorithm in PROP can keep the location list of the segment index being a moderate size. Thus, the routing overhead in PROP is trivial compared to the media data transfered. In PROP, the overhead is less than 1% of the streaming media data (including TCP/IP and Ethernet headers) for a segment size of 100 KB. To further reduce the routing overhead, the segment size can be increased, or variable-sized segmentation strategies, such as exponential segmentation [Wu et al., 2001] and adaptive and lazy segmentation [Chen et al., 2003], can also be adopted.

3.3 Global Replacement Policies

In the PROP system, the proxy serves as a persistent cache site, but storage size is limited. On the other hand, the total storage space contributed by peers is huge but the available contents change dynamically because peers come and go frequently. To fully utilize storage and to improve streaming service quality, PROP uses efficient replacement policies for both the proxy and peers based on the global information of segment accesses using the following parameters.

- T_0, the time when the segment is accessed for the first time;

- T_r, the most recent access time of the segment;

- S_{sum}, the cumulative bytes of the segment that have been accessed;

- S_0, the size of the segment in bytes;

- n, the number of requests to this segment;

- r, the number of replicas of the segment in the system.

Popularity-based Proxy Replacement Policy.   The proxy takes over the streaming service whenever the requested media segment cannot be served by any peer in the system. Thus, the proxy should store those popular media objects to minimize performance degradation due to peer failures. PROP uses a popularity-based replacement policy instead of the LRU policy, because LRU is not efficient for file scan operations, which are typical in media streaming services, and can only exploit the locality of reference to the proxy instead of the whole system. The *popularity* of a segment is defined as

$$p = \frac{\frac{S_{sum}}{S_0}}{T_r - T_0} \times \min(1, \frac{\frac{T_r - T_0}{n}}{t - T_r}), \tag{12.1}$$

where t is the current time instant, $\frac{\frac{S_{sum}}{S_0}}{T_r - T_0}$ represents the average access rate of the segment in the past, normalized by the segment size, and $\min(1, \frac{\frac{T_r - T_0}{n}}{t - T_r})$ represents the probability of future access: $\frac{T_r - T_0}{n}$ is the average time interval of accesses in the past. If $t - T_r > \frac{T_r - T_0}{n}$, the possibility that a new request arrives is small; otherwise, it is highly possible a request will come soon. The segment with the smallest popularity is chosen as the victim to be replaced when the proxy cache is full. Considering both the recent access and past access information, the proxy can cache the most useful media data for clients.

Study [Chen et al., 2003] uses a similar approach to estimate the popularity of objects in proxy caching systems. However, the system architecture and replacement policies of PROP are completely different from these systems. In order to quickly collect space for new media objects and to reduce the cache management overheads, the exponential segmentation approach [Wu et al., 2001] and the adaptive-lazy segmentation approach [Chen et al., 2003] have been proposed. In contrast, due to the distributed indexing and caching service provided by peers, the load on the proxy in the PROP system is much smaller than that in traditional proxy caching systems. PROP uses an evenly sized, fine grained segmentation with low overheads, and it is more efficient than coarser grained data management for cache utilization.

Utility-based Replacement Policy for Client Peers.   Independently exploiting reference locality on each client side is neither efficient from the system's perspective nor effective from the user's perspective. First, driven by typical client access patterns, popular objects get more accesses from peers and thus have more copies cached in the system, which are already cached at the proxy side. Keeping too many copies of popular objects degrades cache efficiency since the cache space could have been used to cache data of other

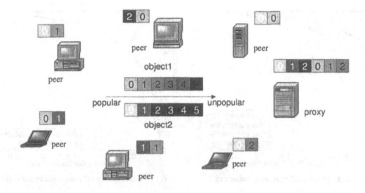

Figure 12.8. The distribution of media segments in PROP system.

objects. Second, the locality on each client side is limited and the cached data is prone to be flushed in a long streaming session. Third, the segments of a media object may be cached in a single peer, thus the data availability is very sensitive to the peer failure and leaving. On the other hand, the reference locality of all clients is much more significant than that of a single client and the difference between the access latency in an intranet and the local disk is not important for media streaming. Thus, in the PROP system, the collection of cached data of all clients is maintained collectively in a decentralized manner with replacement operations.

The purpose of the peer replacement policy is to use an adaptive mechanism to dynamically adjust the distribution of media data cached in the system. The peer replacement policy is designed to replace both those media segments with diminishing popularities because they rarely get accessed, and those popular media segments with too many copies being cached. As a result, peers accessing media objects completely will cache the latter segments and evict the beginning segments of the objects because they are more popular and have more replicas in the system than the latter segments. Peers that access only the beginning segments will cache the beginning segments. Thus, naturally a peer will cache only a few segments of each object it has accessed, while the segments of each object are distributed across many peers in the system according to their popularities, reducing the negative effects caused by peer failures. Figure 12.8 shows the distribution of media segments in the system using the replacement policies in PROP.

For the peer replacement policy, the *utility function* of a segment is defined as

$$u = \frac{(f(p) - f(p_{min})) \times (f(p_{max}) - f(p))}{r^{\alpha + \beta}}, \quad (12.2)$$

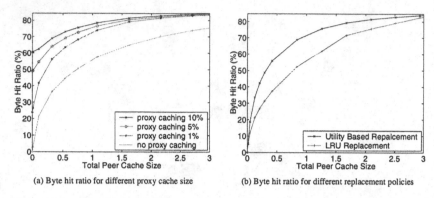

(a) Byte hit ratio for different proxy cache size   (b) Byte hit ratio for different replacement policies

Figure 12.9. The performance of PROP system evaluated on an enterprise media server trace.

where p represents the popularity of the segment, p_{min} and p_{max} estimate the minimum and maximum of segment popularities in the P2P system, respectively. r is the number of replicas of this segment in the system, and $f(p)$ is a monotonic non-decreasing function (in PROP, $f(p) = \log p$ and $\alpha = \beta = 1$). The desired distribution of media data in the system is $r \propto f(p)$. The values of p_{min} and p_{max} can be maintained by the proxy and propagated across the P2P overlay by flooding when necessary. The term $\frac{f(p)-f(p_{min})}{r^{\alpha}}$ captures the segments with small popularities and large numbers of replicas, while $\frac{f(p_{max})-f(p)}{r^{\beta}}$ captures the segments with large popularities and large numbers of replicas. These two kinds of segment replicas should be replaced by the replicas of segments with moderate popularities but a small number of copies. PROP chooses those segments with the smallest utility value as the victims to be replaced when a peer's cache is full. Thus, the data distribution is optimized naturally along with the progress of media accessing, and the efficiency of cache utilization is maximized.

Figure 12.9 shows the performance of PROP, evaluated by using the media server log in an enterprise network. Figure 12.9(a) shows that a dedicated proxy service plays an important role in PROP system. The performance gap between client-based P2P system and the PROP system with a small proxy cache is non-trivial and the QoS and the byte hit ratio are significantly improved with the increase of the proxy cache. Figure 12.9(b) shows that the utility-based replacement policy benefits the workload with low reference locality more than the workload with high reference locality, due to the segment distribution it results in the PROP system. This advantage is very attractive for streaming media delivery systems, since the reference locality in a streaming media workload is much smaller than that in a Web caching workload.

3.4   Streaming Task Dispatch

In PROP, a streaming session is divided into a number of streaming tasks in a moderate granularity determined by the segment size (100-500 KB). These tasks can be served by different peers, and it is the index server's responsibility to dispatch streaming tasks to different streaming servers. Instead of having multiple peers collaboratively serve media steaming for a client [Hefeeda et al., 2003], only one streaming server is needed at a time in PROP. The failure of the streaming server has little impact on the client, and the media player only needs to buffer one segment for a smooth playback. Furthermore, streaming tasks can be dispatched fairly and efficiently based on the information in segment indices and the quality of the streaming server. PROP uses the available bandwidth of the serving peer as the criterion to dispatch streaming tasks for load balancing, and always dispatches streaming tasks to client peers first to reduce the proxy burden.

3.5   Fault Tolerance

When a peer fails, both the media data it caches and the segment indices it maintains are lost. In PROP, each peer periodically checks the validation of the replica location links in the segment indices it maintains and simply removes dead links. The loss of segment indices can be recovered by using the recovery mechanism of distributed hash table, e.g., CAN supports multiple realities to improve fault tolerance of routing [Ratnasamy et al., 2001].

When the proxy fails or is overloaded so that it cannot fetch data for clients, the requesting peer connects to the media server directly, fetches data and caches them locally until the proxy recovers. Since the indices of media segments are distributed in the P2P system, the content locating mechanism still works and system performance degrades gracefully. Compared with the solution of maintaining a central index in the proxy like the browser-aware proxy system [Xiao et al., 2002], PROP not only removes the single point of failure, but also significantly reduces the burdens of index maintenance and segment locating in the proxy.

4.   Conclusion

We have overviewed three existing and representative Internet technologies for delivering streaming media contents. Server-based proxies are cost-effective but not scalable due to the limited proxy capacity and its centralized control. Infrastructure-based CDNs with dedicated network bandwidths and powerful media replicas can provide high quality streaming services but with a high cost. Client-based P2P networks are scalable but do not guarantee high quality streaming service due to the transient nature of peers. To address these limitations, we present a system design called PROP aiming at building a scalable and reliable media proxy supported by its P2P clients. In this system, the proxy and its P2P clients are complementary to each other: the proxy provides a dedicated storage and reliable streaming services when clients are not available or not capable to do so, while clients provide a scalable storage for data caching and significantly reduce the service load of the proxy by carrying some streaming services. We believe this design will be an effective addition and option for Internet multimedia streaming.

References

Akamai Technologies, Inc. (2005). "Delivering a Better Internet". http://www.akamai.com/.

Chen, S., Shen, B., Wee, S., and Zhang, X. (2003). "Adaptive and Lazy Segmentation Based Proxy Caching for Streaming Media Delivery". In *Proceedings of the 13th ACM International Workshop on Network and Operating Systems Support for Digital Audio and Video*, Monterey, California, USA, June, 2003.

Chesire, M., Wolman, A., Voelker, G., and Levy, H. (2001). "Measurement and Analysis of a Streaming Media Workload". In *Proceedings of the 3rd USENIX Symposium on Internet Technologies and Systems*, San Francisco, California, USA, March, 2001.

Cisco Systems, Inc. (2005). http://www.cisco.com/warp/public/cc/so/neso/cxne/.

Cranor, C. D., Green, M., Kalmanek, C., Shur, D., Sibal, S., Van der Merwe, J. E., and Sreenan, C. J. (2001). "Enhanced Streaming Services in a Content Distribution Network". In *IEEE Internet Computing*, July/August, 2001.

Dilley, J., Maggs, B., Parikh, J., Prokop, H., Sitaraman, R., and Weihl, B. (2002). "Globally Distributed Content Delivery". In *IEEE Internet Computing*, September/October, 2002.

Gnutella (2005). http://www.gnutella.com/.

Guo, L., Chen, S., Ren, S., Chen, X., and Jiang, S. (2004a). "PROP: a Scalable and Reliable P2P Assisted Proxy Streaming System". In *Proceedings of the 24th International Conference on Distributed Computing Systems*, Tokyo, Japan, March, 2004.

Guo, L., Jiang, S., Xiao, L., and Zhang, X. (2004b). "Exploiting Content Localities for Efficient Search in P2P Systems". In *Proceedings of 18th International Symposium on Distributed Computing*, Amsterdam, Netherlands, October, 2004.

Hefeeda, M., Habib, A., Botev, B., Xu, D., and Bhargava, B. (2003). "PROMISE: A Peer-to-Peer Media Streaming System". In *Proceedings of the 11th Annual*

ACM International Conference on Multimedia, Berkeley, California, USA, November, 2003.

Jiang, S., Guo, L., and Zhang, X. (2003). "LightFlood: an Efficient Flooding Scheme for File Search in Unstructured Peer-to-Peer System". In *Proceedings of the 2003 International Conference on Parallel Processing*, Kaohsiung, Taiwan, China, October, 2003.

OpenNap (2005). OpenNap: Open Source Napster Server. http://opennap.sourceforge.net/.

Ratnasamy, S., Francis, P., Handley, M., and Karp, R. (2001). "A Scalable Content-Addressable Network". In *Proceedings of ACM SIGCOMM 2001*, pp 161-172, San Diego, California, USA, August, 2001.

Realnetworks, Inc. (2005). http://www.realnetworks.com/resources/contentdelivery/proxy/.

RFC 3174 (2001). RFC 3174 - US Secure Hash Algorithm 1 (SHA1). http://www.ietf.org/rfc.html.

Rowstron, A. and Druschel, P. (2001). "Pastry: Scalable, distributed object location and routing for large-scale peer-to-peer systems". In *Proceedings of IFIP/ACM Middleware 2001*. Heidelberg, Germany, November, 2001.

Stoica, I., Morris, R., Karger, D., Kaashoek,M., and Balakrishnan, H. (2001). "Chord: A Scalable Peer-to-peer Lookup Service for Internet Applications". In *Proceedings of ACM SIGCOMM 2001*, San Deigo, California, USA, August, 2001.

Wu, K., Yu, P. S., and Wolf, J. (2001). "Segment-based proxy caching of multimedia streams". In *Proceedings of the 10th International Conference on World Wide Web*, Hong Kong, China, May, 2001.

Xiao, L., Zhang, X., and Xu, Z. (2002). "On Reliable and Scalable Peer-to-Peer Web Document Sharing". In *Proceedings of 2002 International Parallel and Distributed Processing Symposium*, Fort Lauderdale, Florida, USA, April, 2002.

Zhao, B., Kubiatowicz, J., and Joseph, A. (2001). "Tapestry: An Infrastructure for Fault-tolerant Wide-area Location and Routing". In *Technical Report No. UCB/CSD-01-1141*, Computer Science Division, University of California, Berkeley, April, 2001.

IV

UBIQUITOUS WEB ACCESS

Chapter 13

DISTRIBUTED ARCHITECTURES FOR WEB CONTENT ADAPTATION AND DELIVERY

Michele Colajanni
University of Modena and Reggio Emilia
colajanni.michele@unimo.it

Riccardo Lancellotti
University of Modena and Reggio Emilia
lancellotti.riccardo@unimo.it

Philip S. Yu
IBM T.J. Watson Research center
psyu@us.ibm.com

Abstract   The increased penetration of wired and wireless accesses to the Internet from heterogeneous client devices is a visible reality. The ubiquitous accessibility combined with the dynamic generation of personalized content adds a new dimension to the idea of adaptation and delivery of Web resources. Ubiquitous Web access is deployed by introducing new technologies on the top of pre-existing Internet services. However, the final result is much richer than the sum of the single components. This chapter proposes a taxonomy of the main adaptation services and analyzes the system infrastructures that can provide efficient generation and delivery of transcoded and personalized content.

Keywords: Distributed systems, World Wide Web, Internet services, adaptation, transcoding

1.   Introduction

The success of the Web in the last decade has caused an evolution of the distributed resources. The initial static contents are now enriched by complex contents, with an increasing amount of multimedia resources and of dynamically generated contents. This evolution has shifted the research focus from Web *content delivery* that is, a mature technology, to *service delivery* that introduces new scalability and performance problems to the hardware/software infrastructure that has to generate and distribute content.

In the last years, the overall complexity of the service delivery scenario is further increased by the so called *ubiquitous Web access*. The challenge is to allow access to the Web-based services by any user, from any location through every device, ranging from wired desktop PCs to Internet-enabled mobile phones [Vanderheiden, 1997], [Saha and Mukherjee, 2003]. To enable ubiquitous Web accesses, the software infrastructure must support a new set of *adaptation services*. They include a wide spectrum of services that may require complex interactions with different applications and databases. We find convenient to distinguish two main categories of adaptation services that is,

- *Transcoding*. They are services that tailor Web content to the capabilities of the client device and of the network connection. A typical example is to reduce the definition of an image with the goal of reducing the size of the file to be delivered.

- *Personalization*. They include more sophisticated services that are oriented to adapt the content to (a combination of) user preferences, locations and behaviors. An example of personalization is the insertion of banners tailored to the user gender, country and preferences in the visible pages of a user. The clear difference with the previous services is that the storage and maintenance of an updated archive of user profiles is required.

We will provide a more accurate taxonomy of adaptation services in Section 3.

Adaptation and delivery services enabling ubiquitous Web access are deployed by introducing new technologies on top of pre-existing Internet services. However, the final result aims to be much richer than the simple sum of the individual components.

From a technological point of view, ubiquitous Web access exacerbates the scalability and performance issues that characterize present Web-based services because adaptation services have much higher computing and storage requirements. The heterogeneity and richness of present and future adaptation services increase the complexity of the hardware/software system that must support them, with immediate consequences on the scalability of present infrastructures that support delivery and adaptation services [Canali et al., 2003]. To investigate architectural solutions for efficient content generation, adaptation and delivery through the Internet is the main goal of this chapter that is organized in five sections.

In Section 2, we outline the main services that must be provided by the infrastructure for the ubiquitous Web and some architectural directions that seem more promising. In Section 3, we classify the main adaptation services.

This taxonomy is important to describe the actual distributed infrastructures that can provide an efficient service and that are described in Section 4. In Section 5, we conclude the chapter with some final remarks and notes on open issues.

2. Infrastructures for supporting ubiquitous Web access

The directions to address scalability and performance issues are well known: caching and replication. However, it is important to anticipate how we can apply these possible solutions to the world of content generation and delivery.

- *Replication of system resources.* System resources include hardware resources (i.e., computing power, storage capacity, network bandwidth), and system software, such as operating system and HTTP servers. Hardware and system software replication can be required due to the possible exhaustion of hardware and software resources, such as memory, file descriptors and process identifiers.

- *Replication of content generators.* In this approach, we consider the possibility of completely replicating the sources of the Web resources that is, static contents but also Web applications and databases that are necessary to generate dynamic contents.

- *Replication of Web resources.* This is commonly known as a *caching* technique and includes static resources that is, files that are static in nature or previously generated resources.

Replication of system resources helps addressing performance and scalability issues by augmenting the power of the infrastructure that must perform generation, adaptation and delivery tasks. Replication of content generators allows us to fully exploit the advantages of replication of systems resources by creating independent replicated systems that provide complete functions of adaptation and delivery services. Caching allows to take advantage from already adapted Web resources by leveraging local and temporal locality of client requests. Caching aims to reduce the response time in a twofold way: it limits the amount of adaptations that often are CPU bound operations; when the cache server node is placed in convenient locations, it reduces the delivery time because the distance from the client and the content repository is closer.

In Section 4 we give major details about the ways in which replication of system resources, replication of content generators and caching can improve delivery and adaptation services. By now, it is important to anticipate that we should also consider the space dimension for the previous solutions. The replication scale can go from a LAN to a WAN scale. In a local replication of system resources and content generators the nodes are tightly connected. They are placed on the same LAN and usually share a single upstream link connecting the system to the rest of the Internet. The common term to describe such a system is *cluster*. Nodes within a cluster provide increased computing power because of the replication of system resources. They can interact in a fast and effective way [Cardellini et al., 2002]; and replication tends to improve fault tolerance because a faulty node can be easily bypassed.

WAN-based replication is a geographical replication of system resources that are distributed among multiple Autonomous Systems. These systems address scalability issues related mainly to network congestion in peering points and WAN links. We usually refer to WAN-based replicates systems as *geographically distributed systems*. The replicated resources are typically clusters of nodes. Indeed, building a geographic infrastructure is an expensive task and it would be meaningless to replicate single nodes that have limited computational power, storage capacity and are not fault tolerant.

The combination of replication and caching allows a large set of design options to deploy generation, adaptation and delivery of Web-based services through LAN/WAN distributed architectures. To this purpose, it is important to distinguish the following *servers* that may mapped on the nodes of the infrastructure.

- *Content generators* provide Web contents and services either by storing or by dynamically generating them.

- *Adapters* provide adaptation services that is, they have to classify a client request, to define the necessary adaptation operations to be performed, and to carry out the consequent transcoding and/or personalization function(s).

- *Cache servers* provide partial content repositories. Their main function is to store already generated and possibly adapted contents and to retrieve them. If a client request can be satisfied through a previously adapted and cached content, system performance is improved because the client does not have to wait for the completion of adaptation operations. Even better, if the response can be got from a node that is closer to the client.

In the design of infrastructures for efficient adaptation and delivery services we have multiple choices that depend on how the servers are distributed over the infrastructure for generation, adaptation and delivery. The number of possible combinations is high and we will provide a more detailed discussion on these architectures in Section 4. By now, we can anticipate on outline of the four classes of architectures that we consider most appropriate for providing efficient generation and delivery of Web-based adaptation services. It is worth to anticipate that hybrid architectures may exist as well, but the most important solutions come from these basic *building blocks*.

- *Cluster-based system.*

- *Cluster integrated with geographic replication of cache server nodes.*

- *Cluster integrated with geographic replication of adapters and cache servers.*

- *Geographic replication of clusters* (multi-clusters).

Let us describe the main characteristics of the four basic architectures. In the related four figures (from Figure 13.1 to Figure 13.4), we use the following notation. Each node is represented through a symbol that denotes the server it runs: white diamonds are content generators, black-and white diamonds are cache servers, and circles are adapters. The box enclosing the nodes represents the cluster border. The big dashed circle denotes the Internet edge.

Cluster-based system. In this architecture all servers are mapped within one cluster of nodes. No other function related to generation, adaptation and caching of content for this Web site is delegated to nodes outside the cluster. In most cases, the nodes of the cluster are differentiated according to a multi-tier scheme: a first layer of nodes provides partial content repository (such nodes are also called HTTP accelerators [Cardellini et al., 2002]), a second layer executes adaptation servers, and a third layer (back-end) is devoted to the generation of dynamic contents. Figure 13.1 gives an abstract view of this cluster-based architecture.

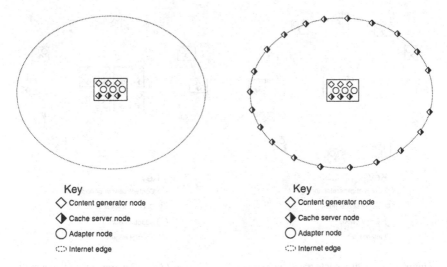

Key
◇ Content generator node
◆ Cache server node
○ Adapter node
⸬ Internet edge

Key
◇ Content generator node
◆ Cache server node
○ Adapter node
⸬ Internet edge

Figure 13.1. Cluster-based architecture

Figure 13.2. Cluster integrated with geographic replication of cache server nodes

Cluster integrated with geographic replication of cache server nodes. This architecture consists of a cluster of nodes, providing all functions content generation, local caching and adaptation, that is enriched by a set of cache server nodes that are distributed in different Autonomous Systems with the purpose of being closer to the clients. (For this reason, they have often been called edge nodes.) Figure 13.2 shows this architecture. The origin cluster is at the center of the infrastructure and is surrounded by a large number of nodes that execute cache servers hopefully in locations that are closer to the clients.

Cluster integrated with geographic replication of adapters and cache servers. This infrastructure is similar to the previously proposed scheme, but the geographically distributed nodes execute both adaptation and caching [Maheshwari et al., 2002]. The goal is to limit the load and the traffic reaching the cluster. The higher scalability of this scheme is obtained by increasing the complexity of the adaptation process. Indeed, as we will see in greater detail in Section 4, complex adaptation services involving personalization can require interaction with content generator servers. Enabling interaction between adapters and content generators while preserving data security and consistency requires considerable additional efforts. Figure 13.3 shows the geographic replication of adapters and cache server. The overall organization of the architecture is similar to Figure 13.2. The difference is the presence of clusters composed by nodes acting as adapters and cache servers.

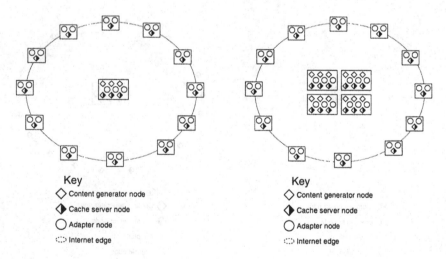

Key
◇ Content generator node
◆ Cache server node
○ Adapter node
⸬ Internet edge

Key
◇ Content generator node
◆ Cache server node
○ Adapter node
⸬ Internet edge

Figure 13.3. Cluster integrated with geographic replication of adapters and cache servers

Figure 13.4. Geographic replication of clusters (multi-clusters)

Geographic replication of clusters (multi-clusters). In this architecture we replicate and distribute geographically the clusters. They are typically mirrors that are organized with a *primary* cluster with a master role and multiple *secondary* clusters. The number of clusters is limited to some units, because of the difficulties of managing complex systems distributed over the world and of preserving consistency of mirrored resources. The issues related to data security and consistency are further increased because of the need to guarantee interactions among the clusters. This architecture offers great scalability and performance because every element that can become a bottleneck is replicated.

Performance of a multi-cluster architecture can be further improved by enriching it through a large set of geographically distributed cache servers and adapters, as illustrated in Figure 13.4.

3.   Adaptation services

The advent of the ubiquitous Web requires on-the-fly transformation of Web-based resources possibly obtained through complex operations, and their delivery to diverse destination devices. The *adaptation service* term spans various types of functionalities, that for the goal of this chapter focused on system infrastructures, we classified in two main categories, each with two sub-categories. *Personalization* services adapt the resources to the user characteristics. We will see that it is quite important also to distinguish whether a personalization function requires some sort of stored information to be completed or not. *Transcoding* services are typically less sophisticated than personalization services. They adapt the content by taking into account the characteristics related to the user device and/or those related to the client interconnection. Figure 13.5 summarizes these categories by considering the implicit/explicit promoter of the adaptation service, i.e., the user or the client device.

Both personalization and transcoding services can be applied to static and dynamically generated content. Hence, a simple response to an explicit query to a database accessible via Web that does not include some additional adaptation

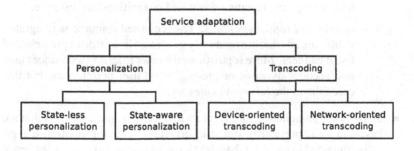

Figure 13.5. Taxonomy of adaptation services

service is not considered in the personalization category, even if the delivered resource is specific for that user.

3.1 Personalization services

A personalized service implies that some additional information is added to the user request for the generation of the resource to be delivered. There are several ways to transfer this information about user preferences. For example, it may be explicitly communicated by the user through a form, or by the client device together with the request (e.g., by means of cookies or HTTP headers). Alternatively, this additional information may be inferred by the present and/or past user behavior or the system infrastructure may implicitly get it from the client request (e.g., user location, connection protocol). We prefer to distinguish personalization services into two subclasses based on the characteristics of the information that is used for personalization, because the two subclasses introduces different issues to be addressed by the infrastructure for content generation, adaptation and delivery.

- *State-less personalization.* It basically refers to the adaptation services that extract user preferences from the user or client request without combining them with previously stored information. Some (not exhaustive) examples of these personalization services include:

  - *Language translation.* It allows the translation of textual information according to user preferences. The user communicates its preferred language and, if the language is not within the set of available texts, the infrastructure executes a run-time translation process.

  - *Virus scanning.* It protects the user against the download of resources (executable files, documents with scripting extensions, and archives) containing harmful viral code, such as viruses or macroviruses. The requested resource is scanned before its delivery. This process looks for known virus signatures and, in case of infected files, it stops the resource download or sanitizes the resource.

  - *Insertion of random banners.* The requested resource is integrated with some ads that are randomly generated links from a pre-selected list of banners. More sophisticated banner insertion techniques take into account dynamic or pre-registered user preferences, but this case falls in the following category.

- *State-aware personalization.* It refers to personalization services that are based on some previously stored information. This information is typically contained in some database(s) and can be extracted as a consequence of explicit information coming from the user request or inferred through the run-time or off-line analysis of the user behavior (e.g., through data mining on log files of a Web site). The use of stored information allows the infrastructure to deploy all the above state-less operations, but also more complex personalization services, such as:

– Personalization based on previously registered user profile. It represents a wide category of personalization services ranging from user filled-in forms to explicit subscription to news feeds (i.e., a personalized portal page is composed by aggregating information from different and heterogeneous sources such as XML-RSS news feeds), to request filtering that protects from harmful or unwanted content. The user profile is typically stored in the infrastructure of the service provider and is used to direct adaptation.

– Cryptographic signature and encoding of multimedia documents. This service can be at the basis of a Digital Right Management service [LaMacchia, 2002].

– Adaptation to the user navigation style. It means that information is dynamically rearranged to help the user reaching the information of interest as soon as possible. Analysis of user click history allows the infrastructure to identify typical behavior patterns such as paths in the navigation graph that leads from a page towards another through a specific sequence of links. Once a known pattern is recognized, the service delivery infrastructure can open directly the target page, thus saving some clicks to the user.

– Adaptation to the user interests. It allows the system to figure out the preferences of the user and to tune services, such as content presentation and ad banner insertion, according to these inferred or specified interests.

– Location and surrounding-based services that achieve personalization on the basis of the user geographic location. The user position is compared with geographic data managed by the service provider and the generation and delivery of static and dynamic content (e.g., queries) is carried out according to the user location and surrounding, possibly combined with user preferences. There are myriads of possible applications for the mobile users ranging from tourist information, commercial information, meetings, blind dates, banner insertion, advertisements. If you do not care much about privacy issues, you can share the opinion that this service may represent the killer application for the ubiquitous Web.

It is worth to observe that the indicated adaptation services are not mutually exclusive. They can be combined to form a chain of adaptation services that must be completed before the resource delivery.

3.2   Transcoding services

The so called pervasive computing devices that characterize the ubiquitous Web show an enormous variability in processing power, storage, display, and connectivity capabilities. The main consequence is that Web resources (including video, image, audio and text) may need to be summarized, translated and converted because of two main requirements related to the client platform, i.e., the features of the physical devices and the characteristics of the connection to Internet. Hence we distinguish the following transcoding services that imply a different dynamic behavior and different architectural needs.

- *Device-oriented transcoding* that is mainly related to the characteristics of the user device interface. The goal is to provide the user with the best quality for content access and Web services that are compatible with the physical capabilities of the device.

- *Network-oriented transcoding* that is mainly due to the medium and protocol characteristics of the connections of the devices to the Internet. As network-oriented transcoding should take into account network link status, the deployment of those services requires the adaptation and delivery service infrastructure to be integrated with a distributed network monitoring system.

It is worth to note that the previous classification does not allow us to partition the transcoding services, because adaptation to device capabilities can impact network resource usage and adaptation to network features may impact the Web resource representation. Due to the heterogeneity of devices, services and network protocols, it is necessary to find techniques and innovative systems that adapts (customizes) the same multimedia content and/or Web service to different client devices, still preserving its semantic attributes.

The conversion task is implemented by software applications, called transcoders, which are able to filter and convert information. A video transcoder can resize, change color palette, format and compression type (e.g., from GIF to JPEG or from AVI to MPEG), transmit only selected spots, single frames or part of them. A text transcoder can summarize the textual content, apply various style sheets to XML documents, and transform HTML objects into WML objects for wireless devices. Intelligent transcoding systems can extract the most meaningful information from a video, and compress data while maintaining its semantic value (for example, by keeping all details on moving objects and limiting background information, according to the MPEG4 and MPEG7 standards). A content filter may discard images or transcode them in textual description if the information has to be delivered to a device that can only visualize text, it may eliminate or compress all the objects larger than a given size for low bandwidth connections and so on.

If we look at the content, we can further distinguish two main classes of transformations for both device- and network-oriented transcoding:

- "within" media types (e.g., changing size and color depth of an image or converting from JPEG to GIF format);

- "between" media types (e.g., from speech to text, from video item to a set of images).

In addition, network-oriented transcoding may be characterized by more dynamic requirements, such as the necessity of

- tunneling/conversion of HTTP protocol over/to different protocol (e.g., to exploit the better characteristics of WAP in the case of wireless links);

- adapting object conversion parameters (e.g., quality factor of JPG images) according to network capability of the device and to the network status [Chandra et al., 2000];

- adapting conversion semantics to the connection characteristics (e.g., changing from a video stream to a sequence of images when an UMTS smartphone switches to a GPRS connection).

4. Distributed architectures for adaptation and delivery services

In section 2 we have identified four basic architectures that can be used to create an efficient infrastructure for content generation, adaptation and delivery services, namely: *cluster-based system, cluster integrated with geographic replication of cache server nodes, cluster integrated with geographic replication of adapters and cache servers, geographic replication of clusters* (multi-clusters).

Although the considered infrastructures are not the only viable solutions, they represent different trends that allow us to discuss a large spectrum of related issues. In particular, the goal of this section is to investigate which adaptation service can be successfully deployed by each of the four architectures.

4.1 Cluster-based system

The first solution to address the performance issues related to adaptation and delivery services is the replication of computing resources over a local area.

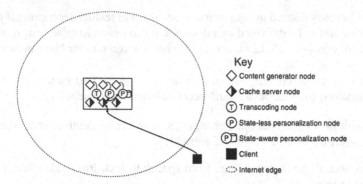

Key
◇ Content generator node
◆ Cache server node
Ⓣ Transcoding node
Ⓟ State-less personalization node
Ⓟ State-aware personalization node
■ Client
◌ Internet edge

Figure 13.6.   Adaptation services implemented in a cluster-based system

A LAN-based system (usually called *cluster*) is a tightly coupled architecture providing a single system interface to the clients. These clusters are typically organized as multi-tier systems, where the front-end tier is often represented by a Web switch that dispatches the client requests among a layer of HTTP servers acting as cache servers that services requests when no adaptation is required. A second layer is composed of adapters that provide transcoding, state-aware and state-less personalization for Web content and services. In the back-end tier, they typically have the content generators that provide the original version of the requested information. These resources may be stored in file systems or dynamically generated through some database servers. Other databases can store information that is useful for some adaptation service and is necessary for state-aware personalization. We reconsider the cluster-based architecture described in Figure 13.1 by highlighting in Figure 13.6 the different types of adaptation: the "T" and the "P" inside the adapter circle denotes transcoding and state-less personalization, respectively. The state-aware personalization that typically requires some previously stored information is evidenced by adding a database symbol near the circle.

   This figure also shows the steps to service a client request through the cluster-based architecture: a solid black line represents the client request, a dashed line is the interaction between an adapter and the back-end tier of the cluster, and the black square represents the client. Client requests received by the cluster are analyzed and classified to determine what adaptation is required, if any. This fist step determines if the request can be satisfied by means of Web resources that are stored in the cache servers or if it is necessary to carry out some adaptation operation(s). The former case occurs when no adaptation is required or when the cache servers store a suitable and already adapted Web resources. If adaptation is required, the request is forwarded to the adapter layers. These servers carry out the adaptation tasks by possibly interacting with content generators and user profile information. It is quite important to observe that the cluster-based architecture allows the deployment of any adaptation task: transcoding and state-less personalization are easily carried out because they only require the information already extracted from the client request. On the other hand, state-aware personalization can be carried out without any problem because user profiles and other sensitive information are stored in the databases of the cluster nodes that are easily accessible by the adapters.

4.2 Clusters integrated with geographically distributed cache servers

LAN-based systems have many pros, but they have scalability problems related to efficient generation, adaptation and delivery of resources when the Web site is highly popular. The first problem that affects replication on a local scale is the so called first mile, i.e., the network link connecting the cluster to the Internet. This link can represent the system bottleneck for the end-to-end performance, moreover it is a potential single point of failure. Traffic on the Web-based cluster zone, failures on an external router, and denial-of-service attacks may cause the service to be unreachable independently of the computational power of the provider platform. When better scalability and performance are needed, it is useful to replicate some elements of the infrastructure over a geographic scale.

The simplest solution towards geographic replication is to distribute the function of cache servers. To improve performance, the nodes hosting cache servers should be placed as close as possible to the clients. The goal is to reduce the response latency and the number of possible bottlenecks between the client and the cache server node. For this reason cache servers are usually located on the *network edge*, for example within the networks of large organizations, such as ISP, providing Internet access to users. Cache servers must also intercept client requests. Multiple techniques are available to this purpose. For example, client devices can be explicitly configured to use cache servers as a proxy, or the cache server layer can rely on traffic redirection mechanisms. When cache servers are on the same network of the Internet access point used by the clients, network-level packet interception is the most popular solution (this approach is called transparent proxy [Wessels, 2001]). When transparent proxies are impracticable, the best alternative is to use DNS-based redirection [Cardellini et al., 2003]. This approach, widely used in CDNs [Rabinovich and Spatscheck, 2002], is based on modified DNS-servers that resolve queries for the site hostname with the IP address of a suitable cache server (the algorithm used to detect the most suitable cache server is usually complex and takes into account geographic and network distance, network link and cache server status).

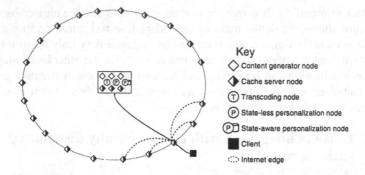

Key
◇ Content generator node
◆ Cache server node
Ⓣ Transcoding node
Ⓟ State-less personalization node
Ⓟ⊐ State-aware personalization node
■ Client
⸬ Internet edge

Figure 13.7. Adaptation services implemented by a cluster integrated with geographically distributed cache servers

Figure 13.7 describes an infrastructure for content generation, adaptation and delivery that is based on a cluster and a geographic replication of cache servers. This figure also shows how client requests are handled by the infrastructure: each request first reaches a cache server node that checks if it holds a valid resource to satisfy that request. In the positive case, it services the request without interacting with the cluster. In the case of miss, the cache server typically acts as a client by issuing a request to the cluster (black arrows in Figure 13.7) that hosts all necessary servers and resources.

As a third alternative, it is possible to implement some sort of cooperation among the cache servers. In this case, a miss does not cause an immediate request to the cluster, but it activates a lookup phase to check whether a (nearby) cache server holds a suitable Web resource (dashed arrows). Several strategies are proposed in the field of cooperative Web caching, such as ICP, Cache Digest, Summary Cache, etc. [Wessels, 2001], [Davison, 2001], but they are out of the scope of this chapter. From the point of view of adaptation services that is the focus of this chapter, there is no difference with the pure cluster-based solution, because all adaptation services are still provided by the cluster.

On the other hand, the geographically distributed nature of this architecture introduces novel management issues. While it is rather easy to think that a cluster is managed by the same content/service provider (if we exclude housing solutions), the deployment and management of architectures distributed over different Autonomous Systems require large investments in structures and technical knowledge. Only a few restricted number of companies may be able to afford this investment. Hence, we can identify three main alternatives that are characterized by the entity that manages the geographically distributed nodes.

- In the *content/service provider-based* solution, the provider deploys and manages this distributed infrastructure of cache servers by using internal resources. In this case, the cache servers are often called *reverse proxies* because the provider can drive the content of its cache servers through some *push-based* mechanism. This allows a high control on which resources are stored in each cache server and also permits the use of cache content invalidation protocols that improve consistency of distributed information.

- On the opposite hand, the provider may refer to a third party entity that has no direct relationship with it. The customers of the third party infrastructure are the Web users. No additional services are offered to the content/service provider. A similar infrastructure of distributed cache servers works for all Web resources, but it does not have any control on the resource location/placement, because a pull-based mechanism populates the cache servers. This *third party independent* infrastructure can be supported by a public organization or by an independent ISP that offers a Web caching service to its customers.

- In the middle between the previous two extremes, it is possible to refer to a third party entity that works in strict relationship with the infrastructure of the service provider. The third party infrastructure provides cache services on behalf of their customer providers. This *third party custom* solution is the core business of CDN companies, such as Akamai [Akamai Inc., 2004] and Speedera [Speedera Networks inc, 2004]. A similar infrastructure has two big advantages with respect to the independent third party: its working set is limited to the resources of its customer providers; it can use some push-based mechanism as in the provider-based solution due to the strict relationship between the provider and the third party operating the distributed infrastructure of cache server nodes.

4.3 Clusters integrated with geographically distributed cache and adaptation servers

The next evolutionary step towards better performance is to replicate also the adapter servers on nodes that are close to the network edge. This architecture is shown in Figure 13.8: it has a central cluster providing all generation, adaptation and caching services, and geographically distributed edge nodes hosting cache and adaptation servers. A client request is processed by cache servers as in the previous architecture with a main difference. In the previous case, the cache server could fulfill a client request only if they held an exact copy of the requested resource. On the other hand, in this case an edge node experiences an hit that does not require an interaction with the cluster even when it has a valid copy that can be adapted locally before its delivery. It is important to observe that a local miss may be due to the absence of some sort of the requested

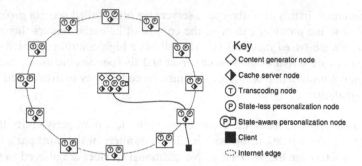

Figure 13.8. Adaptation services implemented by a cluster integrated with geographically distributed cache and adaptation servers

resource or to not being able to adapt the resource on the edge node. To this purpose, we need to consider the three main types of adaptation (transcoding, state-less personalization, state-aware personalization) and to the entity that manages these edge nodes. Typically, transcoding and state-less personalization can be provided even by the edge adapters almost independently of the management organization. The deployment of state-less personalization and transcoding services by an edge node infrastructure managed by the provider or by a custom intermediary is facilitated by the fact that these services do not require previously stored information other than that directly supplied by the client. Hence, they can take full advantage of the highly distributed and replicated nature of the edge nodes. A third party independent infrastructure has some difficulties in providing all types of state-less personalization services because an edge adapter has to figure out in an indirect way the nature and the semantics of Web resources. For example, automated translation requires the identification of resource original language before attempting the translation process. The reduced direct interaction with the service provider can be solved when Web resources are accompanied by metadata providing additional information on the resource content and its semantics. For example, HTML pages may contain explicit meta tags (keywords describing the page content), and XML resources may be even richer about meta information. The use of metadata has been proposed for *server-directed adaptation* [Knutsson et al., 2002], where Web resources are bundled with additional information that describes how to carry out adaptation, especially transcoding-oriented.

The most serious difficulties arise for the state-aware personalization services that require an interaction with some database(s). Clearly, it is difficult, if not impossible, to replicate all state-aware personalization services among replicated adapters. The problems do not derive from the replication of the personalization algorithms, but from the distribution of the information on which these algorithms should operate. The well known problems related to the information replication over some units (e.g., caching [Fan et al., 2000], database management [Gray et al., 1996]) affect the possibility of multiplying services requiring dynamic content generation. Moreover, it seems impracticable to replicate information about users profiles and preferences stored on the content generator of the providers on each adapter node. The user information may be highly volatile, hence it is very difficult to guarantee its consistency among geographically distributed nodes. For third party based solutions an additional problem arises: a user profile database that is necessary to achieve personalized services is often characterized by a commercial value and privacy requirements. Hence, no content/service provider likes its replication over hundreds or thousands of nodes that are not strictly controlled by itself.

All these considerations lead us to conclude that most state-aware personalization services cannot be delegated to a distributed infrastructure consisting of a huge number of nodes. Actually, some solutions exist for personalization like random advertisement banners personalized according to the user language. These adaptation services are oriented to categories of users, and generate dynamic resources on the basis of (portion of) databases containing read-only nonvolatile information. Under these conditions, the databases can be easily replicated over many nodes of the intermediate infrastructure because their information is not affected by the above apparent consistency and privacy problems.

4.4   Geographic replication of clusters

The key feature of this architecture is the geographical replication of the cluster hosting content generators, adapters and cache servers. It is possible to refer to these architectures also as *multi-cluster architectures*. In such an infrastructure, it is possible to distinguish a *primary* cluster and multiple *secondary* clusters. The primary cluster acts as a master, while the secondary clusters are replicas of the primary cluster.

The multi-cluster architecture can be (and usually is) integrated with an infrastructure of edge nodes hosting cache servers and adapters as in the previous architecture. A typical multi-cluster architecture is shown in Figure 13.9, where it can be appreciated that there are few clusters (in terms of some units) providing every function, and a large number of other distributed nodes providing only a subset of the available functions such as caching, transcoding and/or state-less personalization.

The client request service in a multi-cluster architecture is similar to the previously described case of the architecture with one cluster integrated with multiple edge nodes. For this reason, we focus on the primary and secondary clusters. Let us assume that a client request is forwarded to a secondary cluster.

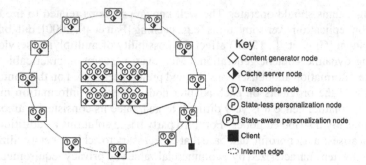

Figure 13.9. Adaptation services implemented by an infrastructure of geographically replicated clusters integrated with cache and adaptation servers on the edge

Multiple dispatching algorithms can be used to select the secondary cluster that should receive the request. Dispatching can take into account multiple factors such as network and geographic distance, network link status, and cluster nodes load (where node load should take into account hardware resources such as CPU and memory and software resources such as file descriptors) [Cardellini et al., 2003].

An alternative approach is to specialize secondary clusters to handle only a specific subset of the global working set [Canali et al., 2005]. Each content generator in secondary clusters handle only a subset of the resources that can be obtained by the content generator of the primary cluster. The dispatching algorithm allows each request to reach the appropriate cluster.

Multi-cluster architectures allow the deployment of any type of adaptation service. Transcoding and state-less personalization can be easily deployed over distributed architectures, as we have seen for the previous architecture. Multi-clusters also allow to provide state-aware personalization. The limited and controlled replication of the clusters addresses the issues of consistency and security in data management: if the number of replicas is reduced, strict data consistency protocols can be used. Moreover guaranteeing the security of few controlled sites is an affordable task [Canali et al., 2005].

5.   Conclusions

The increased penetration of wired and wireless accesses to the Internet from highly heterogeneous client devices is a visible reality. There are major differences among these devices regarding network access methods, computational and memory powers, ability to accept and manage a large variety of data types. The ubiquitous accessibility combined with the dynamic generation of complex services and personalized content adds a new dimension to the problem of efficient generation and delivery of Web resources. The ubiquitous Web includes a huge literature on applications, middleware, protocols, transcoders, programmable proxies, standards, that are considered in other chapters of this book. Here, we focus on the (typically distributed) infrastructures that can provide efficient generation, adaptation and delivery of static and dynamic resources. The motivation is that, independently of the type of adaptation, the ubiquitous Web requires resource intensive operations that place significant overhead on CPU and/or disk if compared to the delivery of traditional Web resources. For example, efficient adaptation and delivery imply several functions, such as replication and caching of resources, client request management, lookup, and adaptation (including transcoding and personalization). Hence, the first question is where to map all these functions on the nodes of the distributed infrastructure. In particular, it seems interesting to solve the trade-off between completely centralized and extremely replicated schemes. Purely centralized architectures show scalability and fault-tolerance limits. On the other hand, replication solutions over a large geographic area are often affected by data consistency problems and management difficulties.

In this chapter, we have demonstrated that any research in the field of systems for the ubiquitous Web must take into account a third dimension of the problem which is the type of adaptation services to be deployed. Due to the heterogeneity of adaptations, an architecture that is optimal for transcoding may result poor for personalization services.

As a final observation, we consider that all analyzed architectures assume a well-known infrastructure of nodes that are typically stable and available most of the time. A radical shift in delivering services for the ubiquitous Web may be inspired to the novel peer-to-peer paradigms. It may be interesting to investigate a non-organized infrastructure of nodes that may join and leave the service infrastructure in a dynamic way, as it usually occurs in overlay peer-to-peer networks. Too many modifications in the infrastructure may degrade absolute performance, but self-organization properties of peer-to-peer networks can improve availability in critical conditions, hence there is space for further investigations.

References

Akamai Inc. (2004). http://www.akamai.com.

Canali, C., Cardellini, V., Colajanni, M., Lancellotti, R., and Yu, P. S. (2003). Cooperative architectures and algorithms for discovery and transcoding of multi-version content. In *Proc. of the 8th Intl. Workshop on Web Content Caching and Distribution (WCW03)*.

Canali, Claudia, Cardellii, Valeria, Colajanni, Michele, Lancellotti, Riccardo, and Yu, Philip S. (2005). A two-level distributed architecture for web content adaptation and delivery. In *Proc. of The IEEE/IPSJ Symposium on Applications and the Internet (SAINT 2005)*.

Cardellini, V., Casalicchio, E., Colajanni, M., and Yu, P. S. (2002). The state of the art in locally distributed web-server systems. *ACM Computing Surveys*, 34(2).

Cardellini, V., Colajanni, M., and Yu, P.S. (2003). Request redirection algorithms for distributed web systems. *IEEE Tran. on Parallel and Distributed Systems*, 14(5).

Chandra, S., Ellis, C. Schaltter, and Vahdat, A. (2000). Application-level differentiated multimedia web services using quality aware transcoding. *IEEE Journal on Selected Areas in Communication*, 18(12).

Davison, B. D. (2001). A Web caching primer. *IEEE Internet Computing*, 5(4).

Fan, L., Cao, P., Almeida, J., and Broder, A. Z. (2000). Summary cache: a scalable wide area web cache sharing protocol. *IEEE/ACM Trans. on Networking*, 8(3).

Gray, J., Helland, P., O'Neil, P. E., and Shasha, D. (1996). The dangers of replication and a solution. In *Proc. of the 1996 ACM SIGMOD International Conference on Management of Data*, volume Jun.

Knutsson, B., Lu, H., and Mogul, J. (2002). Architectures and pragmatics of server-directed transcoding. In *Proc. of 7th Int'l Workshop on Web Content Caching and Distribution*.

LaMacchia, B. (2002). Key challenges in drm: An industry perspective. In *Proc. of 2002 ACM Workshop on Digital Rights Management*.

Maheshwari, A., Sharma, A., Ramamritham, K., and Shenoy, P. (2002). Transsquid: Transcoding and caching proxy for heterogeneous e-commerce environments. In *Proc. of 12th IEEE Int'l Workshop on Research Issues in Data Engineering*.

Rabinovich, M. and Spatscheck, O. (2002). *Web Caching and Replication*. Addison Wesley.

Saha, D. and Mukherjee, A. (2003). Pervasive computing: A paradigm for the 21st century. *IEEE Computer*, 36(3).

Speedera Networks inc (2004). http://www.speedera.com.

Vanderheiden, G. C. (1997). Anywhere, anytime (+ anyone) access to the next-generation www. *Computer Networks and ISDN Systems*, 8(13).

Wessels, D. (2001). *Web caching*. O'Reilly.

Chapter 14

WIRELESS WEB PERFORMANCE ISSUES

Carey Williamson
Department of Computer Science
University of Calgary
carey@cpsc.ucalgary.ca

Abstract   This chapter discusses performance issues that arise for Web content delivery in wireless local area network (WLAN) environments. Two experiments are conducted using IEEE 802.11b WLAN technology. The first experiment considers client-side Web browsing performance for a mobile user with a wireless PDA in an infrastructure-based WLAN. The second experiment considers server-side performance for a wireless Web server delivering Web content in a wireless ad hoc network environment. The results show that the wireless network bottleneck can lead to inefficient HTTP performance, inefficient TCP performance, packet losses, and network thrashing, depending on the characteristics of the Web traffic generated. Solving these issues is important to improve wireless Web performance.

Keywords: Web performance, network traffic measurements, IEEE 802.11b WLAN

1.   Introduction

Wireless technologies have revolutionized the way people think about networks, freeing users from the constraints of physical wires, and bringing closer the "anything, anytime, anywhere" promise of mobile networking. At the same time, the Web has made the Internet available to the masses, through its TCP/IP protocol stack and the principle of layering. The next step in the wireless Internet evolution is the convergence of these technologies to enable the "wireless Web" in the classroom, the office, and the home.

This chapter discusses performance issues that arise for Web content delivery in wireless networks. In particular, we consider both client-side and server-side perspectives in the use of wireless LAN technology. From the client perspective, we study the typical Web browsing performance for a mobile user with a wireless

PDA. From the server perspective, we study the performance of an Apache Web server operating in a wireless ad hoc network.

From both of these perspectives we identify protocol performance issues that limit the achievable Web performance. In most cases, the performance problems arise from the wireless network bottleneck, but the bottleneck manifests itself in subtle ways, because of multi-layer protocol interactions. Examples of these interactions include the inefficiencies of non-persistent HTTP over TCP, the congestion response of TCP to wireless packet losses, and the combination of these two effects.

Our work is carried out using experimental measurements. A wireless network analyzer is used to collect and analyze network packet traces, with traffic analysis spanning from the Medium Access Control (MAC) layer to HTTP at the application layer. Multi-layer protocol analysis is used to identify the performance problems that occur.

The remainder of this chapter is organized as follows. Section 2 provides background information on IEEE 802.11b, TCP, and HTTP. Section 3 presents the client-side results for wireless Web browsing performance. Section 4 presents the server-side results for wireless Web content delivery. Finally, Section 5 summarizes the chapter.

2.   Background and Related Work

2.1   The Web and Web Performance

The Web relies primarily on three communication protocols: IP, TCP, and HTTP. The Internet Protocol (IP) is a connection-less network-layer protocol that provides global addressing and routing on the Internet. The Transmission Control Protocol (TCP) is a connection-oriented transport-layer protocol that provides end-to-end data delivery across the Internet [Stevens, 1994]. Among its many functions, TCP has flow control, congestion control, and error recovery mechanisms to provide reliable data transmission between a source and a destination. The robustness of TCP allows it to operate in many network environments. The Hyper-Text Transfer Protocol (HTTP) is a request-response application-layer protocol layered on top of TCP. HTTP is used to transfer Web documents between Web servers and Web clients. Currently, HTTP/1.0 [RFC1945, 1996] and HTTP/1.1 [RFC2616, 1999] are widely used on the Internet.

Overall Web performance depends on the performance of Web clients, the Web server, and the network in between. The main challenge for Web content delivery in wireless networks is the wireless channel, which has limited bandwidth, high error rates, and interference from other users. The concern is that TCP and HTTP performance may degrade over wireless networks.

2.2   Wireless Internet and IEEE 802.11b WLANs

Wireless technologies are playing an increasingly prominent role in the global Internet infrastructure. One of the popular technologies in the wireless LAN market is the IEEE 802.11b standard. This "WiFi" (Wireless Fidelity) technology provides low-cost wireless Internet capability for end users, with up to 11 Mbps data transmission rate at the physical layer.

IEEE 802.11b is just one member of a growing family of IEEE 802.11 WLAN standards. IEEE 802.11g offers data rates of up to 54 Mbps, using more sophisticated modulation schemes in the same 2.4 GHz frequency band as IEEE 802.11b. IEEE 802.11a offers data rates of up to 54 Mbps, operating in the 5 GHz frequency range. Many commercial WLAN products today support IEEE 802.11a/b/g functionality. The emerging IEEE 802.11e standard offers better Quality of Service (QoS) support for WLAN applications, and the future IEEE 802.11n standard promises much higher data rates.

This chapter focuses solely on IEEE 802.11b as a representative example of the IEEE 802.11 WLAN protocols. The IEEE 802.11b standard defines the channel access protocol used at the MAC layer, namely Carrier Sense Multiple Access with Collision Avoidance (CSMA/CA). It also defines the frame formats used at the data link layer: 128-bit preamble, 16-bit Start-of-Frame delimiter, 48-bit PLCP (Physical Layer Convergence Protocol) header, followed by a 34-byte Logical Link Control (LLC) header and variable size payload, which can be used for carrying IP packets.

The IEEE 802.11b WLAN technology can be operated in either *infrastructure mode* or *ad hoc* mode. In infrastructure mode, an Access Point (AP) is required to provide connectivity to the Internet. The AP relays IP packets between the mobile users in the WLAN and the external wired Internet. The IEEE 802.11b MAC protocol is used for all the datalink layer frames exchanged between a mobile node and the AP.

In ad hoc mode, there is no external Internet involved, and no AP required. Stations within the WLAN communicate with each other directly in a peer-to-peer fashion. All frames are addressed from the sender to the intended receiver using the corresponding MAC address in the frame header. Frames that are correctly received over the shared wireless channel are acknowledged right away by the receiver. Unacknowledged frames are retransmitted by the sender after a short timeout (a few milliseconds), using the same MAC protocol.

2.3   Related Work

There is a growing set of literature on wireless traffic measurement and Internet protocol performance over wireless networks [Balachandran et al., 2002, Bennington et al., 1997, Cheng et al., 1999, Singh et al., 2002, Tang et al. 1999, Tang et al. 2000]. For example, Tang and Baker [Tang et al. 1999, Tang et

al. 2000] discuss wireless network measurements from two different environments: a metropolitan area network, and a local area network. More recently,
Balachandran *et al.* [Balachandran et al., 2002] report on network performance
and user behaviour for general Internet access by several hundred wireless LAN
users during the ACM SIGCOMM conference in San Diego in 2001. They find
that for this set of technology-literate users a wide range of Internet applications
are used, user behaviours are diverse, and overall bandwidth demands are moderate. Kotz and Essien [Kotz et al., 2002, Henderson et al., 2004] characterize
campus-wide wireless network usage at Dartmouth College, for infrastructure
mode using access points. Schwab and Bunt [Schwab et al., 2004] present a
similar study for the University of Saskatchewan.

Our work differs from these in that we consider both wireless Web clients
and a wireless Web server in a WLAN, in either infrastructure mode [Omotayo
et al., 2004] or ad hoc mode [Bai et al., 2003, Bai et al., 2004, Oladosu, 2003].
Our main focus is on the multi-layer protocol interactions that occur, and their
impact on user-perceived Web performance.

3.   Wireless Web Browsing Performance

Today's mobile computing devices offer users unprecedented connectivity
and convenience. Many mobile users rely on a wireless laptop, Personal Digital
Assistant (PDA), or cell phone for Internet access, with Web browsing a primary
application.

Wireless Web access, however, is not without its performance problems.
Wireless channel bandwidth is often limited compared to desktop wired-Internet
access, and the wireless channel is typically shared amongst multiple users. In
addition, the wireless channel quality can vary significantly with time, with an
inherent error rate much higher than that for wired network technologies.

This section presents a detailed analysis of Web browsing performance for a
mobile user with a wireless PDA. Our analysis studies the multi-layer protocol
interactions that occur when HTTP and TCP/IP operate over an IEEE 802.11b
WLAN. A wireless network analyzer is used to collect TCP/IP packet traces of
Web traffic generated by the mobile user's wireless PDA. Trace analysis focuses
on server response time, HTTP transfer time, TCP performance, and wireless
channel quality.

Our results identify several protocol-related issues that affect wireless Web
browsing performance. These results provide insight into performance enhancements for Web content providers, Web servers, HTTP, TCP, and IEEE
802.11b.

3.1   Experimental Setup

Our client-side Web browsing experiments are conducted on an IEEE 802.11b WLAN in the Department of Computer Science at the University of Calgary. The experimental setup is illustrated in Figure 14.1. The network operates in *infrastructure mode*, with the Access Point (AP) providing access to the external Internet. The AP is a NetGear WAB 102. The wireless client is a PDA that communicates directly with the AP. These are the only devices present in the WLAN during our experiments.

The PDA is a Compaq iPAQ 3600 Pocket PC running Windows CE (version 3.09348) as the operating system and Internet Explorer as the Web browser. This device has an ARM SA1110 processor and 64 MB Flash RAM. The PDA has a Proxim wireless network interface card (NIC), and a Maximum Transmission Unit (MTU) size of 1500 bytes.

Our study uses a very simple workload: a single user with a wireless PDA browsing selected sites on the Internet. The client makes requests for Web pages by typing a URL request into the Web browser, or clicking on a hyperlink. Each request generates TCP packets, which are sent across the WLAN as encapsulated IEEE 802.11b data frames. The WLAN traffic generated during our study is captured using a wireless network analyzer.

The trace analyzed in this chapter was collected over a period of 35 minutes on March 3, 2004. During this time, the user browsed Web sites offering news, yellow pages, driving directions, stock quotes, educational resources, and downloadable PDA software. Table 14.1 lists several of the Web sites used in this study.

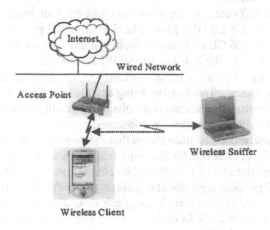

Figure 14.1.   Experimental setup for study

Table 14.1. Partial List of URLs Used in Web Browsing Experiments

Site	URL	Description
1	www.cpsc.ucalgary.ca	University
2	www.cemonster.com	Internet Services
3	www.cnn.com	News
4	www.forecaster.ca	Sports
5	www.cnet.com	Computers
6	www.quickdrive.com	Travel Info
7	www.handmark.com	Software
8	www.ehosting.ca	Domain Hosting
9	mobile.canada.com	Information
10	weather3.cmc.ec.gc.ca	Weather Info

Table 14.2. Statistical Summary of WLAN Web Browsing Trace

Item	Value
Trace Duration (min:sec)	35:33.212
Total TCP Packets	13,705
Total Data Bytes	7,216,491
Total TCP Connections	398
Successful TCP Connections	394

The network traffic measurements were collected using Sniffer Pro 4.60.01, a wireless network analyzer from Sniffer Technologies. This measurement tool passively monitors and records all WLAN traffic, enabling protocol analysis at MAC, IP, TCP, and HTTP layers. Packet timestamps are recorded with microsecond resolution.

The Sniffer software runs on a wireless laptop. Our laptop is a Compaq Armada E500 with a 1.0 GHz Mobile Intel Pentium III processor, 128 MB of 100 MHz RAM, 9.36 GB disk, and a Cisco Systems Aironet 350 wireless NIC. In *promiscuous mode*, the NIC records all WLAN traffic.

Table 14.2 provides a statistical summary of the network trace collected during our experiment. The Web browsing session lasted just over 35 minutes, with 394 successful TCP connections observed. Both persistent (13%) and non-persistent (87%) connections are observed.

Statistical analysis of the trace shows that the network is lightly loaded. The average (user-level) data rate for the entire trace is about 25 Kbps (6.4 pkt/sec), with a peak transfer rate of 1.2 Mbps (180 pkt/sec) on the 11 Mbps WLAN.

Figure 14.2 provides a graphical representation of the network traffic during the trace. The solid vertical lines in the graph show the number of TCP packets transmitted on the WLAN in each 1 second interval of the trace, while the lower horizontal dashed line shows the number of simultaneously active TCP connections from the client.

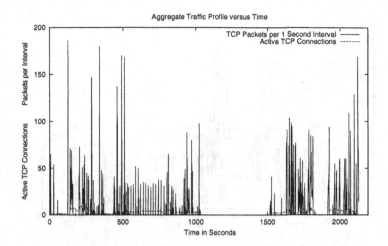

Figure 14.2. Time Series Representation of Web Browsing Traffic

Network usage is clearly bursty, as is typical of Web browsing activity. The browser supports parallel TCP connections, typically with 3-4 connections active at a time, though as many as 10 were observed at one point in the trace. The default socket buffer size was 32 KB for each connection. A total of 56 different IP addresses were seen in the trace, since many commercial Web sites use server clusters, and many Web pages contain advertising banners. About 52% of the TCP packets in the trace were transmitted by the client PDA, which suggests that the TCP implementation in Windows CE does per-packet acknowledgements, rather than the usual TCP Delayed ACKs [Stevens, 1994]. The use of Delayed ACKs or some form of ACK consolidation would economize on wireless network usage, and conserve battery power for the wireless device.

Two idle periods appear in the trace. These occurred when the PDA was rebooted and reassociated with the AP.

3.2   HTTP-layer Analysis

Our first analysis focuses on protocol performance at the HTTP layer. We are interested in issues such as Web server response time, HTTP transfer times for Web objects, and Web object sizes.

Figure 14.3 provides a time series representation of the Web server response time in our experiments. Server response time is defined as the elapsed time between the HTTP "GET" request sent by the client and the first packet of the HTTP response from the server.

Figure 14.3 shows the server response time for each TCP connection initiated in the trace. The graph shows sustained Web browsing to several Web sites,

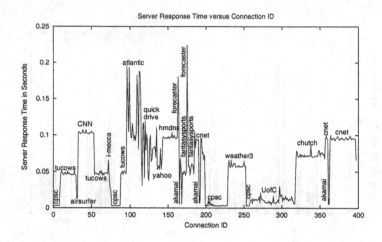

Figure 14.3. Web Server Response Time Results

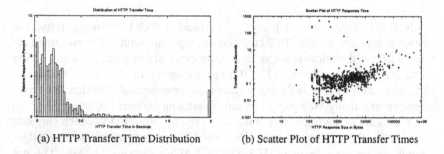

(a) HTTP Transfer Time Distribution   (b) Scatter Plot of HTTP Transfer Times

Figure 14.4. HTTP Transfer Time Analysis

with multiple TCP connections used for most of these sites. Server response time is quite consistent for a given Web site, since the network round trip time (RTT) is a dominant component of this latency. However, server response time can vary a lot from one Web site to another.

The next analysis studies HTTP transfer time: the elapsed time from when a mobile client makes a GET request to when the client has all of the corresponding response data from the Web server (using 1 or more network packets).

Figure 14.4(a) shows the distribution of HTTP transfer times. In general, the HTTP transfer times are low. About 96% of the transfers complete in less than 1 second, and only 2.5% require longer than 2 seconds.

Figure 14.4(b) shows a scatter-plot of the HTTP transfer time versus the Web object size for each transfer. The expected trend is that larger Web objects take longer to download. While this trend is present in the data, the density of points in the graph makes it hard to see. There are also several outliers among the data points. A few small Web objects had excessively long HTTP transfer times.

3.3   TCP-layer Analysis

Figure 14.5 presents results from TCP connection-level analysis. Figure 14.5(a) shows the distribution of packets per connection, while Figure 14.5(b) shows data bytes per connection, and Figure 14.5(c) shows TCP connection durations.

The main observation from Figure 14.5 is that most TCP connections are brief. Approximately 75% of all connections sent fewer than 20 packets, and only 6% sent more than 100 packets. The mean was 35 packets per connection; the fewest sent was 8 packets, and the most was 653 packets. About 80% of the connections sent fewer than 10 KB, and only 8% sent more than 50 KB. Approximately 75% of all connections lasted less than 1 second, and 87% lasted less than 10 seconds. This observation is consistent with the earlier observations that most TCP connections are non-persistent, and most Web object transfers are small. In other words, Web content designed for mobile users is small and usually downloads quickly. While 10% of connections last longer than 30 seconds, over 98% of the connections complete within 100 seconds.

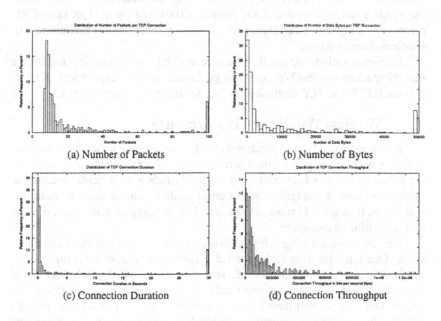

(a) Number of Packets   (b) Number of Bytes

(c) Connection Duration   (d) Connection Throughput

Figure 14.5.   TCP Connection-level Analysis

The final TCP-layer analysis combines HTTP transfer size information with TCP connection duration to study the average throughput for TCP connections. Throughput is expressed in Kilobits per second (Kbps). Higher values reflect more efficient usage of the network.

Figure 14.5(d) shows TCP connection throughput results. About 95% of the connections had throughputs below 400 Kbps. This throughput is low considering the 11 Mbps physical-layer data rate in IEEE 802.11b.

To better understand the low throughput, the mobile client's HTTP requests were studied. Analysis shows that many TCP connections request a single embedded object from a Web page with many embedded objects. The cost of making multiple TCP connections to obtain the embedded objects limits the effective throughput. In other words, the low throughput is a consequence of small HTTP transfer sizes, non-negligible RTTs, TCP slow start effects, and non-persistent TCP connections. Using persistent connections would significantly improve the throughput.

3.4   MAC-layer Analysis

Our final analysis in the Web browsing study focuses on performance anomalies related to the wireless channel quality.

The total number of MAC-layer retransmissions observed was 533. These retries affected 407 packets (3.0%), from 159 connections (40%). In addition, the wireless analyzer reported CRC errors for 0.04% of the total packets. CRC errors are evenly distributed throughout the trace, reflecting the randomness of wireless channel errors.

These observations suggest that the wireless channel quality does not have a major impact on wireless Web browsing performance in our experiment. Rather, it is the HTTP and TCP inefficiencies that limit the Web performance.

4.   Wireless Web Server Performance

The second part of our experimental study focuses on wireless Web servers. Wireless Web servers play a valuable role in *short-lived networks*. A short-lived (or *portable*) network is created in an *ad hoc* fashion at a particular location in response to some event (scheduled or unscheduled). The network operates for some short time period (minutes to hours), before being disassembled, moved, and reconstituted elsewhere.

There are several distinguishing characteristics of a portable short-lived network. Often, the location of the needed network is not known *a priori*. There may not be *any* existing network infrastructure, either wired or wireless, at the needed location. Deployment may need to be spontaneous, with unknown (but often bounded) operating duration. The number of users is typically small (e.g., 10-100), bandwidth requirements are modest, and the geographic coverage area is limited. There is a need for either data dissemination or data collection at the network site, typically involving a "closed" set of specialized content, rather than general Internet content.

Examples of deployment scenarios for short-lived networks are sporting events, press conferences, conventions and trade shows, disaster recovery sites, and classroom area networks. The potential for entertainment applications (e.g., media streaming, home networking, multi-player gaming) is also high. In many of these contexts, an ad hoc wireless network, with a wireless Web server as an information repository, provides a suitable solution.

Our experiments focus on the HTTP transaction rate and end-to-end throughput achievable in an ad hoc wireless network environment, and the impacts of factors such as number of clients, Web object size, and persistent HTTP connections. The results show the impacts of the wireless network bottleneck, either at the client or the server, depending on the Web workload. Persistent HTTP connections dramatically improve the performance for mobile clients accessing content from a wireless Web server.

4.1   Experimental Setup

Our wireless Web server experiments were conducted on an IEEE 802.11b WLAN in our research laboratory. The simple testbed (shown in Figure 14.6) consists of several mobile clients and one Web server. In addition, we use a wireless network analyzer to monitor the wireless channel.

Each of the client and server machines is a Compaq Evo Notebook N600c running RedHat Linux 7.3 and X windows, using a 1.2 GHz Mobile Intel Pentium III. All unnecessary OS processes were disabled prior to conducting measurements, to reduce contention for system resources.

Each laptop has a Cisco Aironet 350 Series Adapter for access to the IEEE 802.11b wireless LAN. The wireless cards are configured in ad hoc mode. During our experiments, these are the only machines operating on the wireless LAN. For simplicity, we do not consider node mobility, multihop, or ad hoc routing issues in our experiments.

The Web server in our experiments is an Apache HTTP server (Version 1.3.23). This version is a process-based implementation of Apache, which is a flexible and powerful HTTP/1.1-compliant Web server [Hu et al., 2001, Nahum et al., 2001]. Apache is currently widely deployed on the Internet, used by approximately 60% of all Web sites [Netcraft, 2005].

Network traffic measurements are collected using a WLAN analyzer. Decoding of the captured traces enables protocol analysis at the MAC, IP, TCP, and HTTP layers.

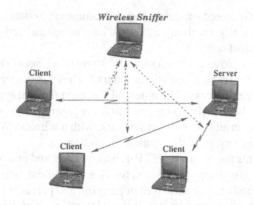

Figure 14.6.   Experimental Setup

The IEEE 802.11b wireless LAN is the performance bottleneck in our experimental environment. The experiments are designed to demonstrate how the wireless bottleneck affects network-level and user-level Web performance.

4.2   Experimental Design

A one-factor-at-a-time experimental design is used to study the impacts of many factors on wireless Web server performance, including HTTP transaction rate, number of clients, transfer size, and HTTP protocol version. The experimental factors are summarized in Table 14.3. The values in bold font show the default levels used.

In our experiments, `httperf` [Mosberger et al., 1998] is used to generate client requests to the Web server. `httperf` is a Web workload generation tool developed at Hewlett-Packard Laboratories for Web performance measurement. It provides a flexible means to generate HTTP workloads and measure server performance. We use synthetic Web workloads that are easy to generate, analyze, and reproduce. Our goals are to determine an upper bound on achievable performance, and to understand behaviour under overload conditions, using the simplest scenarios possible.

Table 14.3.   Experimental Factors and Levels

Factor	Levels
Number of Clients	1, 2, 3, 4
Per-Client TCP Connection Request Rate (per second)	**10**, 20, 30, . . ., 160
HTTP Transfer Size (KB)	**1**, 2, 4, 8, . . ., 64
Persistent Connections	**no**, yes
HTTP Requests per Connection	**1**, 5, 10, 15, . . ., 60

The experiments are conducted using `httperf` as an *open-loop* workload generator. We invoke `httperf` on the client machine, and send requests to the server at a specified rate to retrieve a target Web object repeatedly. Each test lasts 2 minutes, with each TCP connection issuing one or more HTTP requests, depending on the test. The "user abort" timeout in `httperf` is set to 5 seconds.

Performance data are collected using `httperf` and the WLAN analyzer. The `httperf` tool reports application-layer statistics on HTTP behaviours (e.g., reply rate, throughput, response time, error rate), providing a user-level view of performance. Detailed measurements from the WLAN analyzer enable traffic analysis from the MAC layer to the HTTP layer. These traces are used to assess wireless channel contention, TCP protocol behaviours, and HTTP transaction performance.

4.3 Stress-Testing and Overload Performance

The purpose of the first experiment is to determine the sustainable load for a wireless Web server. Initially, only a single Web client machine is used. The client, server, and Sniffer laptops are all on the same desk in the same office, less than 1 meter apart. The wireless channel is assumed to be excellent. The Web object size is 1 KB.

The experiments begin with a request rate of 10 requests per second, using non-persistent connections. That is, there is exactly one HTTP "GET" request per TCP connection; the terms "TCP connection rate" and "HTTP transaction rate" are thus synonymous for this experiment. When one test is complete, the test with the next higher HTTP transaction rate (from 10 to 160 requests per second) begins. The network trace shows that each HTTP transaction generates 10 TCP packets (6 from the client, and 4 from the server). Each TCP packet requires access to the IEEE 802.11b WLAN for the transmission of the frame and its corresponding MAC-layer ACK.

Figure 14.7 shows the application-layer `httperf` results for this experiment. The plots show the successful HTTP transaction rate (Figure 14.7(a)), the achieved user-level throughput (Figure 14.7(b)), the user-perceived response time (Figure 14.7(c)), and the "user abort" error rate (Figure 14.7(d)). In all four graphs, there are two regimes: the "normal" operating regime for feasible loads, and the "overload" regime from the open-loop workload.

Figure 14.7(a) shows the successful HTTP transaction rate as the offered load increases. Initially, the HTTP transaction rate increases linearly with offered load (as expected), up to about 85 requests per second. Beyond this point, there is some instability, and a drop to a lower plateau. Qualitatively similar results are observed in experiments with the same client and server in a 10 Mbps wired-Ethernet LAN, though the peak HTTP transaction rate is 380 requests per second. The peak performance in the WLAN is lower by a factor of 4.5.

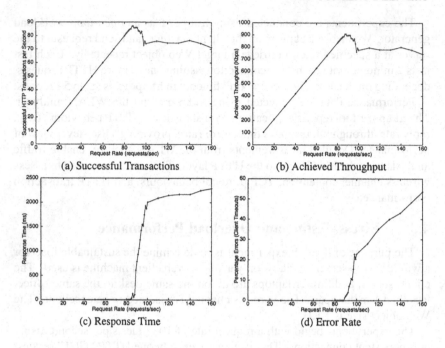

Figure 14.7. `httperf` Results for Experiment 1 (1 client, 1 KB, non-persistent)

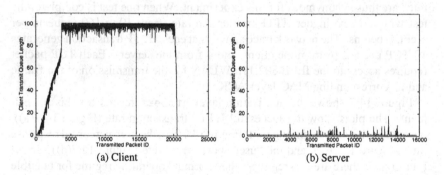

Figure 14.8. Link-Layer Transmit Queue for Experiment 1 (1 client, 1 KB, non-persistent)

The low HTTP transaction rate is explained by the bottleneck at the *client* network interface, where packets wait at the link-layer queue for medium access on the WLAN. Figure 14.8 shows this behaviour for high load on a specially instrumented Linux kernel. With the default Linux queue size of 100, the client queue (Figure 14.8(a)) fills in about 10 seconds. Many packet drops occur from this link-layer queue, *before* the packets make it onto the wireless network.

These packet losses cause the dropoff in HTTP performance. The server does not receive enough requests to keep it busy, so its queue (Figure 14.8(b)) does not fill. Increasing the client queue size is pointless, since there is no back-pressure mechanism to prevent `httperf` from overflowing it; while each TCP connection sends few packets, the sheer number of active TCP connections eventually overwhelms the queue.

With multiple clients, the wireless network bottleneck shifts from the client to the server. Experiments with 2 or more clients show that the server can handle 110 requests per second for 1 KB objects. Beyond this load, the server's link-layer queue fills and overflows, leading to lost packets and erratic TCP performance.

4.4 TCP Protocol Overhead

Figure 14.7(b) shows the application-layer throughput as a function of offered load. The peak throughput achieved is just under 1 Mbps, far from the nominal 11 Mbps capacity of the IEEE 802.11b wireless LAN. Experiments on a 10 Mbps wired-Ethernet LAN achieve 3.8 Mbps.

With non-persistent HTTP connections, most of the WLAN packets are small control packets, and the TCP connection establishment overhead is high relative to the connection lifetime. Each HTTP transaction requires a three-way handshake for TCP connection setup, followed by a 74-byte HTTP request, a 1 KB response, and then a three-way handshake to close the TCP connection. A typical HTTP transaction (10 packets) takes about 9 msec on the wireless LAN. This HTTP transaction time is about 4 times slower than that observed in similar tests of the same client and server on a 10 Mbps Ethernet LAN. Clearly, the wireless MAC protocol overhead limits HTTP transaction performance.

Figure 14.7(c) shows the average response time for the successful HTTP transactions. The response time remains near 9 ms as the offered load increases from 10 to 85 requests per second. At higher loads, the response time increases significantly, eventually exceeding 2 seconds. Figure 14.7(d) shows `httperf` "user abort" errors from client-side timeouts. Under overload, aborts occur frequently.

4.5 Persistent HTTP Connections

The next experiment considers persistent connections, with multiple HTTP transactions sent on the same TCP connection, prior to it being closed [RFC2616, 1999]. This approach amortizes TCP overhead across multiple HTTP transactions, improving HTTP server performance [Nielsen et al., 1997, Padmanabhan et al., 1994, Spero, 2005].

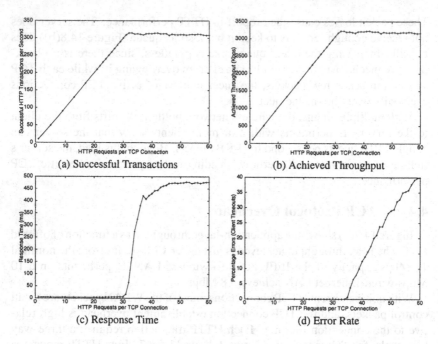

Figure 14.9. httperf Results for Experiment 2 (1 client, 1 KB, 10 conn/sec, persistent)

Figure 14.9 shows the httperf results for this experiment. In all cases, the TCP connection rate is 10 requests per second, and the transfer size is 1 KB. The number of HTTP transactions per TCP connection is varied.

Figure 14.9(a) shows that the successful transaction rate increases with the number of HTTP requests per connection. The highest rate achieved is 320 HTTP transactions per second. User-level throughput (Figure 14.9(b)) reaches a peak of 3.2 Mbps with 32 HTTP transactions per TCP connection. Beyond that point, server throughput is relatively stable, though the average HTTP response time increases sharply (see Figure 14.9(c)).

Compared to the results in Figure 14.7(b), the maximum throughput has increased from 900 Kbps to 3.2 Mbps. These results show that persistent connections offer a 350% improvement in performance over non-persistent connections. These performance improvements are even more dramatic than those reported in the previous literature for HTTP/1.1 [Cheng et al., 1999, Nielsen et al., 1997]. For example, in 10 Mbps wired-Ethernet experiments, persistent connections (merely) double the performance from 380 to 760 HTTP transactions per second. The user-level throughput reaches 7.8 Mbps.

Clearly, persistent connections offer many advantages: fewer control packets (TCP SYN and FIN) on the network, and amortization of the TCP handshakes over many HTTP transactions. These advantages apply to any network environment, wired or wireless, but they are particularly important when the wireless LAN is the bottleneck. With persistent connections, the first HTTP transaction inside the TCP connection requires only 4 TCP packets (GET, ACK, DATA, ACK) instead of 10, while all subsequent HTTP transactions in the same TCP connection require only 2 packets (since TCP can piggyback ACKs on outbound GET and DATA packets). This five-fold reduction in the number of TCP packets per HTTP transaction dramatically reduces the demand on the wireless LAN medium access bottleneck, improving HTTP performance accordingly.

4.6   Network Thrashing Problem

The final experiment studies the impact of HTTP response size on network throughput, for a single client issuing 10 requests per second to the server. The transfer size is 1 KB for the first run, and is then increased to 2 KB, 4 KB, and so on in the subsequent runs.

For space reasons, we discuss the results from this experiment only for two selected transfer sizes: 32 KB and 64 KB. These values represent medium load and overload conditions for the wireless Web server, respectively. The 32 KB transfers complete in about 67 msec, for an average throughput of 3.9 Mbps. A 64 KB transfer, however, takes (on average) well over 100 msec, leading to system overload.

In this experiment, the WLAN bottleneck is at the *server* network interface, since the server transmits more packets than the client, and larger packets as well. The httperf request rate is modest (10 requests per second), placing little stress on the client-side queue. Figure 14.10 illustrates the queue buildup at the server, which increases the HTTP response time by more than an order of magnitude. The large delay is due to the sizes of the queued data packets.

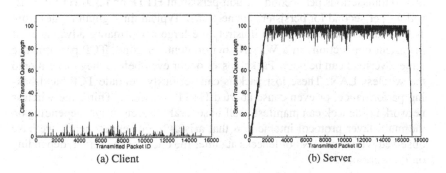

(a) Client   (b) Server

Figure 14.10.   Link-Layer Transmit Queue for Experiment 3 (1 client, 64 KB, non-persistent)

Detailed analysis of the 64 KB scenario shows that about 50% of the TCP connections are aborted with a TCP reset prior to completion. Fewer than 2% of these connections failed during the opening TCP handshake. Most were aborted partially through the transfer. On average, each reset connection sent 68 packets and 47 KB of data.

Network bandwidth is the scarce resource in this experiment. The main concern is "network thrashing": a large portion of the wireless channel bandwidth is consumed by partial TCP transfers that eventually abort. While the average throughput at the network layer exceeds 5 Mbps, the effective user-level *goodput* is less than 2.5 Mbps.

5.   Summary and Conclusions

This chapter studies the performance of Web content delivery in a wireless network environment. Application-layer and network-layer measurements are used to assess performance in an IEEE 802.11b WLAN, both from wireless client and wireless server perspectives. The experiments focus on HTTP performance, TCP performance, and the impacts of the wireless network bottleneck. In many cases, subtle multi-layer protocol interactions occur.

For the client-side Web browsing experiments, two main observations are evident from our results. First, persistent HTTP connections are much more efficient than non-persistent HTTP connections. It is important that Web browser software and Web site developers enable this feature to improve wireless Web browsing performance. Second, the TCP implementations can be further optimized on wireless PDA devices. Simple features such as TCP Delayed ACKs and the caching of TCP connection state parameters could conserve battery power, reduce wireless network bandwidth usage, and reduce the number of network RTTs incurred.

For the wireless Web server experiments, there are three main observations. First, a wireless Web server in an IEEE 802.11b ad hoc WLAN can support up to 110 transactions per second for non-persistent HTTP and 320 HTTP transactions per second for persistent connections. Typical throughput ranges from 1-3 Mbps. These results again illustrate the large performance advantages of persistent connections in a WLAN environment. Second, TCP performance under overload can be poor. Packet losses occur even before they make it onto the wireless LAN. These lost packets can seriously degrade TCP handshaking performance, or even cause aborted HTTP transfers. Third, the wireless network bottleneck can manifest itself in several different ways, depending on the multi-layer protocol interactions that arise. In our experiments, we have observed wireless LAN bottlenecks at either the client or the server, depending on the workload.

Finding practical approaches to improve Web content delivery on wireless networks remains as a high priority on our research agenda.

Acknowledgements

Financial support for this research was provided by iCORE (Informatics Circle of Research Excellence) in the Province of Alberta, as well as NSERC (Natural Sciences and Engineering Research Council) and CFI (Canada Foundation for Innovation). The author is grateful to Adesola Omotayo, Guangwei Bai, and Kehinde Oladosu for carrying out much of the wireless network measurement work described in this chapter, and to Nayden Markatchev for incomparable technical support for this work.

References

G. Bai and C. Williamson (2003). Simulation Evaluation of Wireless Web Performance in an IEEE 802.11b Classroom Area Network. *Proceedings of the Third International Workshop on Wireless Local Networks* (WLN), Bonn, Germany, pp. 663-672, October 2003.

G. Bai, K. Oladosu, and C. Williamson (2004). Performance Issues for Wireless Web Servers. *Proceedings of the International Workshop on Mobile, Wireless, and Adhoc Networks* (MWAN), Las Vegas, NV, pp. 59-65, June 2004.

A. Balachandran, G. Voelker, P. Bahl, and P. Rangan (2002). Characterizing User Behavior and Network Performance in a Public Wireless LAN. *Proceedings of ACM SIGMETRICS Conference*, Marina del Rey, CA, pp. 195-205, June 2002.

B. Bennington and C. Bartel (1997). Wireless Andrew: Experience Building a High Speed, Campus-Wide Wireless Data Network. *Proceedings of ACM MOBICOM Conference*, Budapest, Hungary, pp. 55-65, September 1997.

S. Cheng, K. Lai, and M. Baker (1999). Analysis of HTTP/1.1 Performance on a Wireless Network. Technical Report CSL-TR-99-778, Stanford University, February 1999.

T. Henderson, D. Kotz, and I. Abyzov (2004). The Changing Usage of a Mature Campus-Wide Wireless Network. *Proceedings of ACM MOBICOM Conference*, Philadelphia, PA, pp. 187-201, September 2004.

Y. Hu, A. Nanda, and Q. Yang (2001). Measurement, Analysis, and Performance Improvement of the Apache Web Server. *International Journal of Computers and Their Applications*, Vol. 8, No. 4, December 2001.

D. Kotz and K. Essien (2002). Analysis of a Campus-Wide Wireless Network. *Proceedings of ACM MOBICOM Conference*, Atlanta, GA, September 2002.

D. Mosberger and T. Jin (1998). httperf—A Tool for Measuring Web Server Performance. *ACM Performance Evaluation Review*, Vol. 26, No. 3, pp. 31-37, December 1998.

E. Nahum, M. Rosu, S. Seshan, and J. Almeida (2001). The Effects of Wide-Area Conditions on WWW Server Performance. *Proceedings of ACM SIG-METRICS Conference*, Cambridge, MA, pp. 257-267, June 2001.

Netcraft (2005). http://www.netcraft.com/survey.

H. Nielsen *et al.* (1997). Network Performance Effects of HTTP/1.1, CSS1, and PNG. *Proceedings of ACM SIGCOMM Conference*, Cannes, France, pp. 155-166, September 1997.

A. Omotayo and C. Williamson (2004). Multi-Layer Analysis of Web Browsing Performance for Wireless PDAs. *Proceedings of IEEE Workshop on Wireless Local Networks* (WLN), Tampa Bay, FL, pp. 660-667, November 2004.

V. Padmanabhan and J. Mogul (1994). Improving HTTP Latency. *Computer Networks and ISDN Systems*, Vol. 28, pp. 25-35, December 1995.

K. Oladosu (2003). *Performance and Robustness Testing of Wireless Web Servers*, M.Sc. Thesis, Department of Computer Science, U. of Calgary, August 2003.

RFC 1945: Hypertext Transfer Protocol – HTTP/1.0 (1996). http://www.ietf.org/rfc/rfc1945.txt.

RFC 2616: Hypertext Transfer Protocol – HTTP/1.1 (1999). http://www.ietf.org/rfc/rfc2616.txt.

H. Singh and P. Singh (2002). Energy Consumption of TCP Reno, TCP NewReno, and SACK in Multihop Wireless Networks. *Proceedings of ACM SIGMET-RICS Conference*, Marina Del Rey, CA, pp. 206-216, June 2002.

D. Schwab and R. Bunt (2004). Characterising the Use of a Campus Wireless Network. *Proceedings of IEEE INFOCOMM Conference*, Hong Kong, March 2004.

S. Spero (2005). Analysis of HTTP Performance Problems. http://sunsite.unc.edu/mdma-release/http-prob.html.

W. Stevens (1994). *TCP/IP Illustrated, Volume 1: The Protocols*, Addison-Wesley, 1994.

D. Tang and M. Baker (1999). Analysis of a Metropolitan-Area Wireless Network. *Proceedings of ACM MOBICOM Conference*, Seattle, WA, pp. 13-23, August 1999.

D. Tang and M. Baker (2000). Analysis of a Local-Area Wireless Network. *Proceedings of ACM MOBICOM Conference*, Boston, MA, pp. 1-10, August 2000.

Chapter 15

WEB CONTENT DELIVERY USING THIN-CLIENT COMPUTING

Albert M. Lai
Department of Biomedical Informatics
Columbia University

Jason Nieh
Department of Computer Science
Columbia University

Abstract   Web application access on mobile wireless PDAs is becoming increasingly popular. However, web browsing on these systems can be quite slow. An alternative approach is handheld thin-client computing, in which the web browser and associated application logic run on a server, which then sends simple screen updates to the PDA for display. To assess the viability of this thin-client approach, we compare the web browsing performance of thin clients against fat clients that run the web browser locally on a PDA. Our results show that thin clients can provide better web browsing performance compared to fat clients, both in terms of speed and ability to correctly display web content. Surprisingly, thin clients are faster even when having to send more data over the network. We characterize and analyze different design choices in various thin-client systems and explain why these approaches can yield superior web browsing performance on mobile wireless PDAs.

Keywords: Thin-client computing, web performance, wireless and mobility

1.   Introduction

The increasing ubiquity and decreasing cost of Wi-Fi is fueling a proliferation of wireless PDAs (Personal Digital Assistants). These devices are enabling new forms of mobile computing and communication. Organizations are beginning to use these wireless networks and devices to deliver real-time access to web-

Figure 15.1. Traditional Fat Client

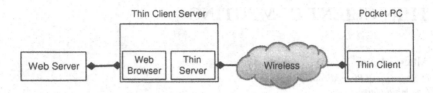

Figure 15.2. Thin Client

enabled information to end users. This is typically done by running a web browser on the PDA to provide access to web applications.

An alternative approach to deliver web-enabled information is using thin-client computing. A thin-client computing system consists of a server and a client that communicate over a network using a remote display protocol. The protocol allows graphical displays to be virtualized and served across a network to a client device, while application logic is executed on the server. Using the remote display protocol, the client transmits user input to the server, and the server returns screen updates of the user interface of the applications from the server to the client. Examples of popular thin-client platforms include Citrix MetaFrame [Citrix Systems, 1998, Mathers and Genoway, 1998], Microsoft Terminal Services [Cumberland et al., 1999, Microsoft Corporation, 1998], AT&T Virtual Network Computing (VNC) [Richardson et al., 1998], and Tarantella [Santa Cruz Operation, 1998, Shaw et al., 2000]. The remote server typically runs a standard server operating system and is used for executing all application logic.

Figure 15.1 shows the traditional web browsing model. We refer to this model with the term fat client because all application logic executes on the web browser on the client device. Figure 15.2 in contrast shows the thin-client computing model. In the thin-client case, the web browser runs on the thin-client server instead of the client device. Only a simple thin-client application for processing user input and screen updates needs to run on the client.

With thin-client computing, because all application processing is done on the server, the client only needs to be able to display and manipulate the user interface. It does not need to run a complex web browser. Clients can then be simpler devices reducing energy consumption and extending battery life, which is often the primary constraint on the benefits of untethered Internet access with wireless PDAs. Thin-client users can access applications with heavy resource requirements that are prohibitive for typical mobile systems with low processing power. Furthermore, because the client in the thin-client model does not run application logic, it does not maintain application state. This provides for much better information security because if an insecure PDA is lost or stolen, no sensitive application state is available on the device.

Despite the potential benefits of thin-client computing, an important issue in the context of web applications is to understand what kind of web browsing performance a thin-client approach provides. The common belief is that web content should be delivered directly to a web browser running locally on the client to achieve the best web browsing performance rather than running the web browser on a remote server and relaying the web browser's display through a thin-client interface via a remote display protocol. In fact, previous work [Yang et al., 2003] in a simulated lossy Wi-Fi environment suggests that while thin clients may perform better than fat clients under very lossy network conditions, they may perform worse when used in near lossless network conditions. However, if a thin-client approach does indeed have inferior performance compared to using a native browser, users will be understandably reluctant to adopt a thin-client computing model despite its other benefits.

We explore the performance of thin clients in both simulated and real Wi-Fi network environments and quantitatively demonstrate that thin-client approaches can provide superior web browsing performance even in lossless Wi-Fi network environments. We compare popular thin-client approaches embodied by Citrix MetaFrame and Microsoft Terminal Services, which represent the dominant commercial thin-client products in the marketplace. We contrast thin-client performance with traditional fat client approaches in combination with a number of different web browsers, including Microsoft Internet Explorer, Mozilla, and NetFront. Our results show that thin clients perform better than fat clients even when they send more data during web browsing. Furthermore, they provide better web browsing functionality, correctly displaying web content on a PDAs that is otherwise not viewable using locally running native web browsers on PDAs. We analyze the differences in the underlying mechanisms used by various thin-client platforms and explain the fundamental characteristics of these approaches that surprisingly result in superior performance.

This chapter is organized as follows. Section 2 details the experimental testbed and application benchmarks we used for our study. Section 3 describes the measurements we obtained on both fat-client and thin-client systems in lossy network environments. Section 4 provides an interpretation of the experimental results and examines how they relate to the use of different remote display mechanisms in thin-client systems. Section 5 discusses related work. Finally, we present some concluding remarks and directions for future work.

2.   Experimental Design

The goal of our research is to compare the web browsing performance of Wi-Fi wireless PDAs using thin-client systems versus fat clients running native web browsers. For our thin-client systems, we compared the performance of Citrix MetaFrame XP and Microsoft Windows 2000 Terminal Services, the two most popular commercial thin-client products in the marketplace. In this chapter, we also refer to the thin-client systems by their remote display protocols, which are Citrix ICA (Independent Computing Architecture) and Microsoft RDP (Remote Desktop Protocol), respectively. To evaluate their performance, we designed an experimental Wi-Fi (IEEE 802.11b) testbed and various experiments to assess both thin-client and native web browsing performance. We focused on the performance of widely deployed commercial solutions in all of our experiments to provide representative and realistic results.

2.1   Experimental Testbed

Figures 15.3 and 15.4 show the simulated and real Wi-Fi isolated experimental testbeds we used for our experiments. Each network testbed consisted of a client machine, a packet monitor, a thin-client server, and a web server. The simulated Wi-Fi network testbed used a desktop PC as the client and a network emulator machine to emulate a Wi-Fi network environment. Both machines were connected using 100 Mbps Ethernet. We used the simulated Wi-Fi network to enable more flexible experimentation with different network characteristics during our study. The real Wi-Fi network testbed used a Pocket PC handheld PDA equipped with a Dell Compact Flash 802.11b card as the client and a Lucent Orinoco AP-2000 wireless access point to provide the Wi-Fi network environment. The packet monitor, thin-client server, and web server were the same for both testbeds. We used two testbeds in part to allow experimentation with different client configurations.

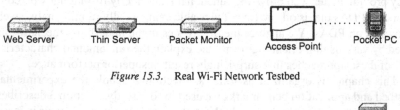

Figure 15.3.   Real Wi-Fi Network Testbed

Figure 15.4.   Simulated Wi-Fi Network Testbed

Table 15.1. Testbed Machine Configurations

Role / Model	Hardware	Operating System	Software
PC Thin Client Micron Client Pro	450 MHz Intel PII 128 MB RAM 10/100BaseT NIC	MS Win XP Pro.	Citrix ICA Win32 Client MS RDP5 Client MS Internet Explorer 6 Mozilla 1.4
Pocket PC Client Dell Axim X5	400 MHz Intel XScale 64 MB RAM Dell 802.11b Wireless CF Card	MS Pocket PC 2003	Citrix ICA Client MS RDP5 Client MS Pocket PC 2003 Internet Explorer Access NetFront 3.0
Packet Monitor IBM Netfinity 4500R	Dual 933 MHz Intel PIII 512 MB RAM 10/100BaseT NIC	Debian Linux Testing (2.4.20 kernel)	Ethereal Network Analyzer 0.9.13
Benchmark Server IBM Netfinity 4500R	Dual 933 MHz Intel PIII 512 MB RAM 10/100BaseT NIC	Debian Linux Testing (2.4.20 kernel)	Apache Web Server 1.3.27
Thin Client Server/ Packet Forwarder IBM Netfinity 4500R	Dual 933 MHz Intel PIII 512 MB RAM 10/100BaseT NIC	MS Win 2000 Server Debian Linux Unstable (2.4.20 kernel)	Citrix MetaFrame XPe MS Win 2000 Terminal Services MS Internet Explorer 6 Mozilla 1.4
Network Emulator IBM Netfinity 4500R	Dual 933 MHz Intel PIII 512 MB RAM 10/100BaseT NIC	MS Win 2000 Server Debian Linux Unstable (2.4.20 kernel)	NISTNet 2.0.12

The features of each system are summarized in Table 15.1. Except for the client machines, all machines are IBM Netfinity PCs, each with dual 933 MHz Pentium III CPUs, 512 MB RAM, 9 GB disk, and 10/100BaseT NICs. The desktop PC client is a Micron Client Pro PC with a 450 MHz Pentium II CPU, 128 MB RAM, and 14.6 GB disk. Although the desktop PC is quite modest by current desktop PC performance standards, the hardware configuration was selected to provide a more even comparison with a modern PDA. The Pocket PC PDA is a Dell Axim X5 with a 400 MHz Intel XScale PXA255 CPU and 64 MB RAM. Because all tests with the wireless network were conducted within ten feet of the access point, we considered the amount of packet loss to be negligible in our experiments. In the simulated Wi-Fi testbed, we used the network emulator to limit available bandwidth to a maximum of 6 Mbps. While the 802.11b specification allows up to 11 Mbps network bandwidth, previous studies have indicated that 6 Mbps network bandwidth is more typical of what is achievable in practice [Heusse et al., 2003, Vasan and Shankar, 2002].

For simplicity and good network performance, both network testbeds were configured using 100BaseT full duplex switched network connections between all wired testbed machines. In this configuration, network traffic was routed through the packet monitor to accurately capture network data. Network packets were timestamped to enable us to measure the performance of the thin-client systems using a non-invasive slow-motion benchmarking technique [Nieh et al., 2003, Lai et al., 2004]. When measuring the performance of fat clients, we reconfigured our thin-client server to simply act as a packet forwarding machine to provide access to the web server directly from the client machine. The added latency of routing through the machines was measured and is negligible.

Whenever possible, we used common system configuration options, common applications, and common thin-client configuration options. When it was not possible to configure all the platforms in the same way, we generally used default settings. Apache 1.3.27 was used as the web server for all of the web benchmarks. All of the fat-client and thin-client systems were run in Microsoft operating system environments. All of the systems were configured with 1024x768 display resolution. Since the Pocket PC PDA only has 240x320 screen resolution, scrolling around the display was necessary to see all of the content displayed.

To account for performance differences due to different web browsers, we experimented with two different web browsers for each platform. For the Pocket PC, we used both Microsoft Pocket PC 2003 Internet Explorer, the latest version Pocket PC browser from Microsoft, and ACCESS' popular NetFront 3.0 web browser. For the desktop PC and thin-client systems, we used both Microsoft Internet Explorer 6 and Mozilla 1.4. The use of Internet Explorer on both platforms provides a common basis for performance comparison. Mozilla was also used with the desktop PC since it represents the next most widely used web browser. However, since no version of Mozilla was available for Pocket PC, we used another popular Pocket PC web browser, NetFront, to compare the performance for different browsers. All of the web browsers used were configured with full screen 1024x768 browser window sizes with default cache settings enabled in each browser. Persistent HTTP 1.1 was used for all experiments to ensure best performance.

2.2   Application Benchmarks

To measure web performance of both thin-client and traditional fat-client systems, we used three web browsing application benchmarks, representative of general consumer web content, clinical image content as would be viewed by medical professionals, and a clinical information system as viewed by medical professionals. We refer to the benchmarks as i-Bench, mammogram, and Web-CIS, respectively. We describe each benchmark and how they were modified to create respective slow-motion versions of each benchmark.

The i-Bench general consumer web content benchmark we used is based on the Web Text Page Load test from the Ziff-Davis i-Bench 1.5 benchmark suite [Ziff-Davis, Inc., 2000]. It consists of a JavaScript controlled load of 54 web pages from the web benchmark server. The pages contain both text and bitmap graphics, with pages varying in the proportions of text and graphics. The graphics are embedded images in GIF and JPEG formats.

The mammogram clinical web content benchmark we used is a multi-page test that downloads a sequence of 20 primarily graphical web pages demonstrating real-time contrast enhancement of mammographic features via multiscale analysis. Each page contains 2 mammographic images. The first mammogram image is a static bitmap. The second is generated by a common gateway interface (CGI) script on the web server which performs a real-time multiscale wavelet enhancement of the first mammogram image. These images are representative of the kinds of image processing activities that are anticipated to become commonplace in the clinical practice of radiological diagnosis in the near future.

The WebCIS clinical information system (CIS) benchmark is a multi-page test that downloads a sequence of 18 web pages from New York Presbyterian Hospital's Web-based clinical information system (WebCIS) [Cimino et al., 1995, Hripcsak et al., 1999]. WebCIS displays data from a variety of clinical data sources including results from laboratory, radiology, and cardiology departments. These pages contain primarily textual data in free text and in tabular form. Navigation and forms submission is JavaScript driven. The pages selected for the benchmark were based upon common page sequences derived through CIS log analysis [Chen and Cimino, 2003], a pattern discovery method based on data mining and Web usage mining. We used typical sequences in the WebCIS benchmark, determined from a year's worth of WebCIS logs, in order to reflect the usage patterns of actual clinical users of WebCIS.

3.   Measurements

We ran the three web benchmarks on both fat-client and thin-client systems running on both the desktop PC and handheld PDA with the three different web browsers and measured their resulting performance. We report results for the twelve different combinations shown in Table 15.2. The primary performance measurements for running each web benchmark are presented in terms of average web page download latencies for each system. For each benchmark, we present data showing both the average web page download latency, and the average amount of data transferred per web page when all web data is downloaded properly. These measurements provide quantitative performance comparisons of handheld thin-client systems in Wi-Fi network environments. They also provide some useful data about the performance of different web browsers in different system configurations.

Figures 15.5 and 15.6 show the measurements for running the i-Bench web benchmark on each of the twelve platform configurations. Figure 15.5 shows the average web page latency for running the i-Bench benchmark on each platform.

Table 15.2.   Platform Configurations Used

Name	Description
PC FAT IE	PC running native Internet Explorer
PC FAT MOZ	PC running native Mozilla
PC ICA IE	PC running Citrix ICA client w/ Internet Explorer
PC ICA MOZ	PC running Citrix ICA client w/ Mozilla
PC RDP IE	PC running Microsoft RDP client w/ Internet Explorer
PC RDP MOZ	PC running Microsoft RDP client w/ Mozilla
PDA FAT IE	PDA running native Internet Explorer
PDA FAT NF	PDA running native NetFront
PDA ICA IE	PDA running Citrix ICA client w/ Internet Explorer
PDA ICA MOZ	PDA running Citrix ICA client w/ Mozilla
PDA RDP IE	PDA running Microsoft RDP client w/ Internet Explorer
PDA RDP MOZ	PDA running Microsoft RDP client w/ Mozilla

Some usability studies have shown that web pages should take less than one second to download for the user to experience an uninterrupted browsing process [Nielsen, 2000], while others indicate that the current ad hoc industry quality goal for download times is six seconds [Keeley, 2000]. All of the platforms provide average web page latencies of less than six seconds and all of the PC platforms provide average web page latencies of less than one second. However, on the PDA, only the thin-client platforms provide average web page latencies of less than one second. On the PDA, ICA MOZ, RDP IE, and RDP MOZ all provide average web page latencies of a second or less.

More importantly, on both the PC and the PDA, Figure 15.5 shows that the thin-client systems provide lower web browsing latencies than the fat-client systems when using the same browser. On the PC, ICA IE and RDP IE are 20 to 40 percent faster than FAT IE while ICA MOZ and RDP MOZ are roughly three times faster than FAT MOZ. The performance difference between the thin-client and fat-client approaches are even more substantial on the PDA. On the PDA, ICA IE is almost three times faster than FAT IE while RDP IE is more than seven times faster than FAT IE. While the Mozilla-based systems are slower than their Internet Explorer counterparts on the PC, even the Mozilla-based thin-client configurations significantly outperform FAT IE on the PDA. On the PDA, while FAT NF provides better fat-client performance than FAT IE, FAT NF is still much slower than all of the thin clients, with the Mozilla-based thin clients still more than twice as fast as FAT NF.

Figure 15.5 also shows some performance inversions between the PC and PDA platforms. On the PC, Internet Explorer performs better than Mozilla on all platforms. On the PDA, the non-Microsoft NetFront browser used in FAT NF outperforms the Internet Explorer-based FAT IE. On the PC, ICA performs better than RDP but on the PDA, RDP performs better than ICA.

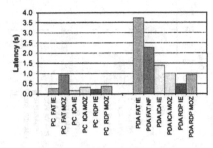

Figure 15.5. i-Bench Page Latency

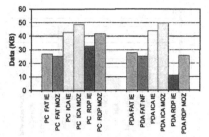

Figure 15.6. i-Bench Page Data Transfer

Figure 15.6 shows the data transferred for running the i-Bench benchmark. For each platform, the data transferred is generally similar for both the PC and the PDA. As would be expected, all of the fat clients running native web browsers transfer roughly the same amount of data on both the PC and PDA. ICA IE on PC and PDA also send roughly the same amount of data, and ICA MOZ on PC and PDA also send roughly the same amount of data. However, RDP transfers very different amounts of data on PC versus PDA, with the data transferred when running on the PDA being much less than running on the PC. RDP IE on PDA transfers almost three times less data than RDP IE on PC.

Figure 15.6 also shows that there are also large differences in the amount of data transferred across different platforms. On the PC, all of the fat clients transfer less data than all of the thin clients, with ICA transferring the most amounts of data, almost twice as much data as the fat clients. However, on the PDA, RDP sends the least amount of data among all of the platforms. RDP IE transfers less than half the amount of data as the fat clients. ICA still sends the most amounts of data on the PDA, sending almost twice as much data as the fat clients. Among the thin clients, there are also differences in the amount of data transferred depending on the web browser used. For a given thin client, using Internet Explorer resulted in less data transferred than using Mozilla. For instance, ICA MOZ transfers roughly ten percent more data than ICA IE on both PC and PDA.

Figures 15.5 and 15.6 taken together show that there is generally little correlation between the latency and the amount of data transferred for each platform. The fat clients had the worst latency performance for both PC and PDA yet generally sent less data, sending the least amount of data for the PC. ICA transferred the most amounts of data but had better performance than the fat clients. Only in the case of RDP on the PDA did a platform both have the small latencies and the least amount of data transferred. However, RDP still outperformed the fat clients on the PC even though it transferred more data in that case.

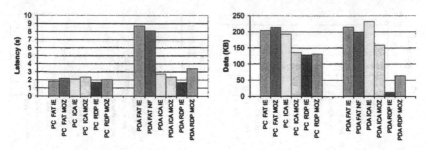

Figure 15.7.   Mammogram Page Latency   *Figure 15.8.*   Mammogram Page Data Transfer

Figures 15.7 and 15.8 show the measurements for running the mammogram benchmark on each of the twelve platform configurations. Figure 15.7 shows the average web page latency for running the mammogram benchmark on each platform. All of the PC platforms and all of the thin-client systems on the PDA provide average web page latencies well under six seconds. However, none of the platforms provided average web page latencies less than one second. On the PDA, FAT IE and FAT MOZ provided web page latencies over eight seconds.

More importantly, on both the PC and the PDA, Figure 15.7 shows that the thin-client systems overall provide lower web browsing latencies than the fat-client systems when using the same browser. On the PC, RDP IE had the lowest latencies of all of the platforms and RDP MOZ had the lowest latencies of all of the Mozilla-based platforms. However, while there are some differences in latencies among different platforms on the PC, these differences are relatively small. On the PDA, the latency differences among different platforms were much more substantial. The PDA fat clients were generally more than two times slower than the thin clients and in the worst case, more than five times slower than the fastest thin client. On the PDA, RDP IE provided the fastest performance. However, RDP MOZ was roughly fifty percent slower than the ICA-based platforms. Based on the industry quality goal of download times of less than six seconds, only the thin clients provided acceptable web browsing performance on PDAs.

Figure 15.7 also shows some performance inversions between the PC and PDA platforms. On the PC, Internet Explorer performs better than Mozilla on all platforms. On the PDA, the non-Microsoft NetFront browser used in FAT NF outperforms the Internet Explorer-based FAT IE. On the PC, ICA performs worse than RDP but on the PDA, RDP has higher variance in performance when used with different web browsers and does noticeably worse than ICA when using Mozilla.

Figure 15.8 shows the data transferred for running the mammogram benchmark. For each platform, there is some variability in the amount of data trans-

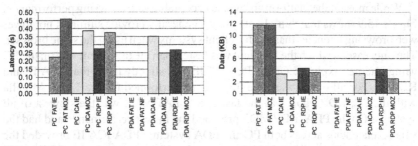

Figure 15.9. WebCIS Page Latency   *Figure 15.10.* WebCIS Page Data Transfer

ferred using PC versus PDA. Figure 15.8 shows that ICA IE transfers approximately the same amount of data as the fat-client systems. However, ICA MOZ transfers significantly less data. RDP on both the PC and the PDA also transfer less data than their fat client counterparts.

This difference in data transfer between fat and thin clients may seem surprising. However, in the mammogram benchmark, the images transferred to the fat clients were sent as uncompressed GIFs. When these same images were sent to the thin clients through the remote display protocol, these images were automatically losslessly compressed. One might assume that this difference in data transfer would account for the performance difference of the fat and thin clients.

However, Figures 15.7 and 15.8 taken together show that there is generally little correlation between the latency and the amount of data transferred for each platform. For the PC, all of the platforms had similar latencies but there is a factor of two difference in the amount of data transferred between FAT MOZ, which sent the most data, and RDP IE, which sent the least data. The fat clients had slightly better performance than ICA on the PC but sent more data. Only in the case of RDP IE on the PDA and the PC did a platform both have the small latencies and the least amount of data transferred. However, RDP MOZ sent the second least amount of data on the PDA and performed worse than both ICA IE and ICA MOZ.

Figures 15.9 and 15.10 show the measurements for running the WebCIS benchmark on each of the twelve platform configurations. Figure 15.9 shows the average web page latency for running the WebCIS benchmark on each platform. All of the platforms except for FAT IE and FAT NF on the PDA provided average web page latencies well under one second. On the PDA, data for FAT IE and FAT NF are not shown because the browsers were unable to complete the benchmark. For this benchmark, the platforms that completed the benchmark all provided acceptable web browsing performance based on the one-second download metric for providing an uninterrupted browsing experience.

While most of the platforms provided acceptable web browsing performance, Figure 15.9 shows that thin-client systems generally provide similar if not lower web browsing latencies than the fat-client systems when using the same browser. The only case in which the fat client was faster than the thin client was on the PC using Internet Explorer. On the PC, FAT IE was slightly faster than ICA IE and RDP IE. For all other cases, the thin clients performed better. Using Mozilla with the PC, RDP MOZ was the fastest and FAT MOZ was the slowest of all systems. On the PDA, RDP MOZ provided the fastest performance and had the smallest latencies across both PC and PDA systems. PDA ICA IE provided the worst performance among the thin clients, roughly twice as slow as RDP MOZ. However, even the slowest PDA thin client performed better than any of the PDA fat client approaches, since none of those systems could even complete the benchmark.

Figure 15.9 also shows some performance inversions between the PC and PDA platforms. On the PC, Internet Explorer performs better than Mozilla on all platforms. On the PDA, the thin clients using Mozilla performed better than those using Internet Explorer. In particular, the Microsoft RDP thin client performed better than any other system on the PDA using Mozilla, not Microsoft's own Internet Explorer. Similarly on the PC, ICA performed better than RDP using Internet Explorer, even though RDP and Internet Explorer are both from Microsoft. In contrast, RDP performed better than ICA using Mozilla.

Figure 15.10 shows the data transferred for running the WebCIS benchmark. For each platform, the data transferred is generally similar for the PC and PDA. As would be expected, all of the fat clients running native web browsers transfer roughly the same amount of data on both the PC and PDA. ICA IE on PC and PDA also send roughly the same amount of data, and ICA MOZ on PC and PDA also send roughly the same amount of data. RDP transfers slightly different amounts of data on PC versus PDA, with the data transferred when running on the PDA being much less than running on the PC. Figure 15.10 shows that there are also large differences in the amount of data transferred across different platforms. On the PC, all of the fat clients transfer approximately three times as much data as the thin clients. On the PC and PDA, ICA transfers the least amount of data among all of the platforms. RDP transfers slightly more data than ICA for both web browsers on both PC and PDA.

This large difference in data transfer between fat and thin clients is a particularly surprising result with WebCIS. Because WebCIS is a text rich application, one would likely come to the conclusion that a fat client should transfer less data than the graphical representation used by thin clients to represent the web page. However, like many modern web applications, WebCIS makes extensive use of JavaScript and other code that is executed in the browser. This code accounts for the surprisingly large amount of the data transferred to the fat clients. With thin clients, this code does not need to be transferred to the client and only the end results of the execution of the JavaScript need to be transmitted to the client. As a result, thin clients can transfer less data than fat clients even when primarily textual data is being displayed.

Figures 15.9 and 15.10 taken together show that there is generally little correlation between the latency and the amount of data transferred for each platform. The fat clients varied widely in performance, yet transferred similar amounts of data. On the PC, FAT IE and FAT MOZ transfer the same amount of data yet FAT IE is more than twice as fast as FAT MOZ. On the PC, RDP IE is faster than RDP MOZ although RDP IE sends more data. On the other hand on the PDA, RDP IE is slower than RDP MOZ and RDP IE still sends more data. The results with the WebCIS benchmark are consistent with those for the i-Bench and mammogram benchmarks in that there is not much correlation in any of the results between the latency and the amount of data transferred for each platform.

4. Interpretation of Results

Our measurements show that thin-client systems can provide functionally better web browsing and faster web page download latencies than fat-client systems, especially in the case of PDAs. These results are counterintuitive given that thin clients add an extra layer of software between client and web server, which it would seem should add extra latency to processing web pages. These results are also counterintuitive given that our measurements show that these thin-client systems provide faster web page download latencies even when transferring more data than their fat-client counterparts. To explain the reasons for the behavior shown in our measurements, we discuss four reasons that account for the performance differences between these systems and point to the benefits of the thin-client approach: limitations of PDA web browsers, distribution of client and server processing, and display size web browsing costs.

4.1 Limitations of PDA Browsers

One important reason why our measurements show that thin clients can provide better performance on PDAs is that web browsers that run natively on PDAs simply do not work well. Measurements shown in Figures 15.5 and 15.7 not only show that thin clients provide better performance than fat clients on PDAs, but that native web browsing on a PDA gives much worse perform than native web browsing on a desktop PC.

The fat-client model is inherently harder to support from a software development perspective. First, the model requires that each platform needs to be able to run its own web browser, which means that browsers must be developed for each platform. Supporting multiple browser versions for different platforms is certainly harder than supporting just one. This is exacerbated by the fact that a web browser is a complicated piece of software to start with. Second, getting a complicated web browser to work effectively on a PDA is a doubly challenging problem. Not only must complex browser functionality be stripped down enough to run in a PDA environment, but it must also be optimized to run in a much more resource constrained environment as well. Furthermore, as earlier PDAs were even more resource constrained than the relatively powerful Pocket PC model we used for our experiments, PDA web browser developers are also faced with the challenge of having to somehow evolve the web browser from an even more resource constrained environment while at the same time optimizing it for best performance.

The problem of developing effective PDA web browsers was evident by the poor functionality of these browsers in our experiments. We discuss two examples from our study. A first egregious example of poor PDA web browser functionality is shown in Figure 15.9, which demonstrates the inability of Pocket PC Internet Explorer and NetFront to work with the WebCIS benchmark. This problem was again due to poor support for JavaScript by these PDA browsers. The JavaScript used in this benchmark is the same code used in the WebCIS web-based clinical information system [Cimino et al., 1995], which is widely deployed and used at New York Presbyterian Hospital. The lack of browser functionality in PDA browsers means that these devices could simply not be used to access a production web-based information system.

A second example is that the Pocket PC Internet Explorer browser advertises its ability to a web server that it can use HTTP 1.1 and persistent connections. However, the behavior it exhibits is completely nonstandard and is in fact more like that of using non-persistent connections. In our experiments, for each request for a page of HTML or an image, Pocket PC Internet Explorer opened a new connection. After the data for the object is received, it closed the connection using a TCP reset, forcing the connection to close abnormally, resulting in a separate connection for each web object.

In contrast to the fat-client model, thin clients do not require the development and maintenance of complex software on multiple platforms. Only a simple thin-client application needs to run on each client platform. Since all application logic resides on the server, only a web browser that runs on the server is required, despite having a plurality of different client devices. Thin clients can then leverage substantial existing investments in PC web browser technology. These investments provide for a more optimized web browser with a more highly tuned rendering engine, which can be effectively used via a thin-client system on any client. This results in much better performance on PDAs than running native PDA web browsers that may not function well in the first place. More importantly, there are production web applications such as WebCIS with a significant investment in their development that do not run on web browsers designed for PDAs and would require significant modification in order to support those browsers. These applications are also often not tested on PDA browsers. In contrast, thin clients leverage desktop web browsers to work seamlessly with such production systems without any modifications.

4.2   Distribution of Client and Server Processing

Another important reason why our measurements show that thin clients can provide better performance than fat clients on both PCs and PDAs is how each approach distributes client and server processing. A fat client places all of the web browsing processing on the client. This places complex browser processing on a client, which is often slower than typical servers. In particular, PDAs are necessarily resource constrained devices given their size and power requirements. Servers on the other hand do not have these limitations and can be larger and more powerful machines.

In contrast, a thin client runs its web browser application logic on the more powerful server while only running a simple thin-client application for processing display updates on the client. The thin-client model provides a better distribution of web browsing processing requirements by putting the complex, more resource intensive processing on the server. Our measurements showed that the thin clients outperformed the fat clients when using the PC client. This performance difference was largely due to the fact that the web browser was running on a faster server when using the thin client. For example, for the i-Bench benchmark, Internet Explorer running on the server was twice as fast as the same browser running on the slower PC client. This difference in performance more than compensates for the extra processing involved with the extra layer of software introduced with the thin-client systems.

The difference in processing power between server and client was not simply an issue of CPU speed, but it was also an issue of CPU architecture functionality. The Pentium III CPU in the server was designed as a powerful server CPU. In contrast, the Dell Axim PDA used for our study is based on the Intel XScale PXA255 CPU. The Dell Axim PDA is considered one of the more high performance PDAs available today, but its XScale CPU was designed as a lower cost, low power, integrated CPU to work in the context of mobile devices. These are different design goals and result in different functionality. In particular, the Pentium CPU in the server provides MMX instructions, which can be used to provide very fast image processing operations. The XScale CPU does not provide this functionality. Internet Explorer takes advantage of MMX instructions when available to dramatically improve the speed of GIF and JPEG decoding and processing. As a result, GIF and JPEG decoding and processing on the server was well more than an order of magnitude faster than such processing on the PDA, even though the difference in CPU clock rate of the server CPU and

PDA CPU was only a factor of two. The thin-client approach takes advantage of this speed difference since its web browser processing occurs on the server. In contrast, the fat-client approach is limited by the client and cannot take advantage of the special CPU instructions available on the server to optimize GIF and JPEG processing. Thin clients provide a model of distributing client and server processing and functionality that matches well with the underlying client and server hardware resources.

4.3   Display Size Web Browsing Costs

Another reason why our measurements show that thin clients can provide better performance than fat clients on PDAs is how each approaches display updates. When accessing a web page, a fat client sends all of the data related to that web page, regardless of whether or not the entire page is viewed. This aspect is particularly important when considering the limited display sizes on PDAs. Because screen sizes are so limited on PDAs, frequently a large portion of a web page is never viewed by the user, but is sent to the client web browser anyways. This limitation is fundamental to the model of HTTP.

In contrast, with thin clients, the model is based upon display updates. The server does not need to send to the client what is not being displayed. Because of the small display size of PDAs, this gives an opportunity to optimize what information is sent from server to client for each display update. In particular, a thin-client system can avoid sending display updates that are not actually viewed and only send data associated with display updates that are visible on the client. This server-side clipping optimization not only reduces the amount of data that needs to be sent, it also reduces the amount of display update processing required on a client. Both of these benefits can result in improved performance for thin clients.

As shown in Figures 15.5, 15.7, and 15.9, RDP provides the best performance on the PDAs for all three benchmarks, in part because it uses this display clipping optimization. The impact of the optimization can be seen by comparing the amount of data transferred using RDP on the PC versus the PDA in Figures 15.6, 15.8, and 15.10. For all of the benchmarks, RDP sends less data when used from the PDA versus the PC because of the PDA's much smaller display size. This effect is most pronounced with the mammogram benchmark, where PDA RDP IE transfers eight times less data than PC RDP IE.

Not all thin clients provide this display clipping optimization. Figures 15.6, 15.8, and 15.10 show that ICA transfers roughly the same amount of data on both the PC and the PDA. ICA sends the entire display to the client even though the viewable region is smaller than the display. ICA then pans around the desktop through clipping the viewable region on the client side. As a result,

ICA sends more data than RDP since it performs the clipping after transmission to the client.

5.   Related Work

In addition to the systems discussed in this chapter, several other thin-client and remote display systems have been developed. These include Sun Ray [Schmidt et al., 1999, Sun Microsystems, 2001], Tarantella [Santa Cruz Operation, 1998, Shaw et al., 2000], VNC [AT&T Laboratories Cambridge, 2001, Richardson et al., 1998], X [Scheifler and Gettys, 1986] and extensions such as low-bandwidth X (LBX) [broadwayinfo.com, 1997] and Kaplinsk's VNC tight encoding [Kaplinsk, 2002], as well as remote PC solutions such as Laplink [LapLink, 1999] and PC Anywhere [Symantec Corporation, 2002]. Several studies have examined the performance of thin-client systems [Lai and Nieh, 2002, Schmidt et al., 1999, Tolly Research, 2000, Microsoft Corporation, 2000, Wong and Seltzer, 2000, Nieh and Yang, 2000, Nieh et al., 2000, Nieh et al., 2003, Yang and Nieh, 2000, Yang et al., 2002]. These studies have focused on measuring the performance of thin clients in network environments with different network bandwidths and latencies, but have not considered the performance of thin-clients in wireless networks or PDAs. More recently, another study co-authored by one of the authors of this chapter demonstrated that thin clients can outperform fat clients in lossy wireless networks [Yang et al., 2003] due to several factors, including lower connection setup costs and the ability to ignore previous display updates that may have been lost. That study did not consider using PDAs and the resulting performance and functionality impact.

Other approaches to improving the performance of mobile wireless web browsing have focused on using transcoding and caching proxies in conjunction with the fat client model [Maheshwari et al., 2002, Kangasharju et al., 1998]. Top Gun Wingman was a proxy-based system that pushed some of the application complexity to a back end proxy server [Fox et al., 1998]. The proxy transcoded images into scaled reduced fidelity images and translated HTML into a simplified markup language. The system effectively requires a web browser reimplementation by introducing a HTML parser in the proxy and a specialized application for display and layout at the client. Another approach used a combination of a transcoding proxy and a content negotiation scheme to optimize the content transmitted to the client based on client advertised capabilities [Joshi, 2000]. Our thin client approach differs fundamentally from these fat client approaches by pushing all web browser logic to the server, leveraging existing investments in desktop web browsers to work seamlessly with production systems without any web proxy configuration or web browser modifications.

6.   Conclusions and Future Work

We have presented the first experimental study to quantitatively compare the web browsing performance of thin-client systems versus traditional fat clients running native web browsers on wireless PDAs. To make this study possible, we used a variation of slow-motion benchmarking that effectively accounts for end-to-end web browsing latencies in a non-invasive manner. This technique accounts for client processing time during web browsing, which can be significant when using PDAs.

Our measurements demonstrate that thin clients provide better web browsing performance than fat clients across a wide variety of web content, including general consumer content, medical imaging content, and text-based clinical information content widely used in a major academic medical center. Our results show that thin clients can, in some cases, require less bandwidth to achieve superior web browsing performance than fat clients. Our results also show that thin clients can in other cases achieve superior web browsing performance even when they send more data during web browsing. More importantly, our results demonstrate that thin clients provide better web browsing functionality than fat clients running native web browsers on PDAs. While all web page content was viewable using thin clients, several of our experiments demonstrated that PDA web browsers were not able to properly display web page content with any significant JavaScript functionality.

Our results show that thin clients provide faster and more functional web browsing by leveraging existing investments in widely used desktop web browsers and by pushing complex web browsing application logic from less powerful mobile devices to more powerful servers. Our results also show that thin clients can provide faster web browsing than fat clients by clipping the display region on the server before it is sent to the PDA, reducing both client processing time and network bandwidth requirements.

Our study explores two important dimensions of web browsing performance on wireless PDAs, speed and functionality. Another important dimension of performance in the context of PDAs is energy consumption. We have conducted some preliminary studies of energy consumption which indicate that thin clients can extend the battery life of a PDA to last significantly longer than with fat clients. However, the cause of this needs further investigation. Given that battery life is a dominant factor in the performance of PDAs, the benefits of thin clients for energy consumption is an important area that merits future work.

Acknowledgments

This research was supported in part by NSF grant CCR-0219943 and an IBM Sur Award. Albert Lai is supported by a National Library of Medicine training grant NO1-LM07079. Klaus Schauser initially suggested that thin clients may outperform fat clients on PDAs, motivating this study. Bhagyashree Bohra, Vijayarka Nandikonda, Madhuri Shinde, Abhishek P. Surana, and Suchita Varshneya assisted with running the benchmark experiments. Andrew Laine, Yinpeng Jin, and Elizabeth S. Chen provided the application data for creating some of the benchmarks used in this study.

References

AT&T Laboratories Cambridge (2001). Virtual Network Computing. http://www.uk.research.att.com/vnc.

broadwayinfo.com (1997). Broadway / X Web FAQ. http://www.broadwayinfo.com/bwfaq.htm.

Chen, E S and Cimino, J J (2003). Automated Discovery of Patient-Specific Clinician Information Needs Using Clinical Information System Log Files. In *Proc. AMIA Symp.*, pages 145–149.

Cimino, J J, Socratous, S A, and Clayton, P D (1995). Internet as clinical information system: application development using the world wide web. *J. Am. Med. Inform. Assoc.*, 2(5):273–284.

Citrix Systems (1998). Citrix MetaFrame 1.8 Backgrounder. Citrix White Paper, Citrix Systems.

Cumberland, B. C., Carius, G., and Muir, A. (1999). *Microsoft Windows NT Server 4.0, Terminal Server Edition: Technical Reference.* Microsoft Press, Redmond, WA.

Fox, Armando, Goldberg, Ian, Gribble, Steven D., and Lee, David C. (1998). Experience with top gun wingman: A proxy-based graphical web browser for the 3com palmpilot. In *Proceedings of Middleware '98, Lake District, England, September 1998.*

Heusse, Martin, Rousseau, Franck, Berger-Sabbatel, Gilles, and Duda, Andrzej (2003). Performance anomaly of 802.11b. In *Twenty-Second Annual Joint Conference of the IEEE Computer and Communications Societies (INFOCOM 2003)*, volume 2, pages 844–852, San Francisco, CA, USA. IEEE.

Hripcsak, G, Cimino, J J, and Sengupta, S (1999). WebCIS: large scale deployment of a Web-based clinical information system. In *Proc. AMIA Symp.*, pages 804–808.

Joshi, Anupam (2000). On proxy agents, mobility, and web access. *Mobile Networks and Applications*, 5(4):233–241.

Kangasharju, Jussi, Kwon, Young Gap, and Ortega, Antonio (1998). Design and implementation of a soft caching proxy. *Computer Networks and ISDN Systems*, 30(22–23):2113–2121.

Kaplinsk, C. (2002). Tight Encoding. http://www.tightvnc.com/compare.html.

Keeley, Terry (2000). Thin, High Performance Computing over the Internet. In *Proceedings of the 8th International Symposium on Modeling, Analysis and Simulation of Computer and Telecommunication Systems*, page 407, San Francisco, CA. IEEE Computer Society.

Lai, Albert and Nieh, Jason (2002). Limits of Wide-Area Thin-Client Computing. In *Proceedings of the 2002 ACM SIGMETRICS International Conference on Measurement and Modeling of Computer Systems*, pages 228–239, Marina del Rey, CA, USA. ACM Press.

Lai, Albert M., Nieh, Jason, Bohra, Bhagyashree, Nandikonda, Vijayarka, Surana, Abhishek P., and Varshneya, Suchita (2004). Improving web browsing performance on wireless pdas using thin-client computing. In *Proceedings of the 13th International Conference on World Wide Web*, pages 143–154. ACM Press.

LapLink (1999). *LapLink 2000 User's Guide*. LapLink, Bothell, WA.

Maheshwari, A., Sharma, A., Ramamritham, K., and Shenoy, P. (2002). Transquid: Transcoding and caching proxy for heterogenous ecommerce environments.

Mathers, T. W. and Genoway, S. P. (1998). *Windows NT Thin Client Solutions: Implementing Terminal Server and Citrix MetaFrame*. Macmillan Technical Publishing, Indianapolis, IN.

Microsoft Corporation (1998). Microsoft Windows NT Server 4.0, Terminal Server Edition: An Architectural Overview. Technical White Paper.

Microsoft Corporation (2000). Windows 2000 Terminal Services Capacity Planning. Technical White Paper.

Nieh, Jason, Yang, S. Jae, and Novik, Naomi (2003). Measuring Thin-Client Performance Using Slow-Motion Benchmarking. *ACM Trans. Computer Systems*, 21(1):87–115.

Nieh, Jason and Yang, Seung Jae (2000). Measuring the Multimedia Performance of Server-Based Computing. In *Proceedings of the 10th International Workshop on Network and Operating System Support for Digital Audio and Video*, pages 55–64, Chapel Hill, NC.

Nieh, Jason, Yang, Seung Jae, and Novik, Naomi (2000). A Comparison of Thin-Client Computing Architectures. Technical Report CUCS-022-00, Department of Computer Science, Columbia University.

Nielsen, J. (2000). *Designing Web Usability: The Practice of Simplicity*. New Riders Publishing, Indianapolis, Indiana.

Richardson, Tristan, Stafford-Fraser, Quentin, Wood, Kenneth R., and Hopper, Andy (1998). Virtual Network Computing. *IEEE Internet Computing*, 2(1).

Santa Cruz Operation (1998). Tarantella Web-Enabling Software: The Adaptive Internet Protocol. SCO Technical White Paper.

Scheifler, R. W. and Gettys, J. (1986). The X Window System. *ACM Transactions on Graphics*, 5(2):79–106.

Schmidt, Brian K., Lam, Monica S., and Northcutt, J. Duane (1999). The Interactive Performance of SLIM: A Stateless, Thin-Client Architecture. In *Proceedings of the 17th ACM Symposium on Operating Systems Principles (SOSP)*, volume 34, pages 32–47, Kiawah Island Resort, SC.

Shaw, A., Burgess, K. R., Pullan, J. M., and Cartwright, P. C. (2000). Method of Displaying an Application on a Variety of Client Devices in a Client/Server Network. US Patent No. 6,104,392.

Sun Microsystems (2001). Sun Ray 1 Enterprise Appliance. http://www.sun.com/products/sunray1.

Symantec Corporation (2002). PC Anywhere. http://www.symantec.com/pcanywhere.

Tolly Research (2000). Thin-Client Networking: Bandwidth Consumption Using Citrix ICA. *IT clarity*.

Vasan, Arunchandar and Shankar, A. Udaya (2002). An empirical characterization of instantaneous throughput in 802.11b wlans. Technical Report CS-TR-4389, University of Maryland. http://www.cs.umd.edu/Library/TRs/CS-TR-4395/CS-TR-4395.ps.zip.

Wong, A. Y. and Seltzer, M. (2000). Operating System Support for Multi-User, Remote, Graphical Interaction. In *Proceedings of the USENIX 2000 Annual Technical Conference*, pages 183–196, San Diego, CA.

Yang, S. Jae, Nieh, Jason, Selsky, Matt, and Tiwari, Nikhil (2002). The Performance of Remote Display Mechanisms for Thin-Client Computing. In *Proceedings of the 2002 USENIX Annual Technical Conference*, Monterey, CA, USA.

Yang, Seung Jae and Nieh, Jason (2000). Thin Is In. *PC Magazine*, 19(13):68.

Yang, Seung Jae, Nieh, Jason, Krishnappa, Shilpa, Mohla, Aparna, and Sajjadpour, Mahdi (2003). Web Browsing Performance of Wireless Thin-Client Computing. In *Proceedings of the Twelfth International World Wide Web Conference (WWW 2003)*, Budapest, Hungary.

Ziff-Davis, Inc. (2000). i-Bench version 1.5. http://etestinglabs.com/benchmarks/i-bench/i-bench.asp.

Chapter 16

OPTIMIZING CONTENT DELIVERY IN WIRELESS NETWORKS

Pablo Rodriguez Rodriguez

Microsoft Research
Cambridge, UK

Abstract   Wireless networks all over the world are being upgraded to support 2.5 and 3G mobile data services. GPRS and UMTS networks in Europe, and CDMA 1xRTT and CDMA 2000 networks in the USA and Asia are currently being deployed and tested to provide Wireless data services that enable ubiquitous mobile access to IP-based applications. During recent years a lot of attention has been paid to improving the physical and the MAC Wireless layers. Thus, advances in coding mechanisms, FEC, and scheduling algorithms have been critical for the success of these technologies. However, despite of the advances in layer-2 techniques and the momentum behind these networks, surprisingly little attention has been paid to evaluating how efficient content delivery can be achieved over cellular networks and how the different protocol stacks interact with the Wireless bearer.

In this chapter we consider how to provide efficient content delivery in wireless networks. To this extend, we examine the main performance problems suffered by transport-level, session-level and application-level protocols in wireless networks. We present several practical experience results, and study how Wireless Performance Enhancing Proxies can improve content delivery over such networks.

Keywords: Cellular wireless networks, PEPs, content delivery, optimizations

1.   Introduction

Wireless cellular networks are being upgraded world-wide to support 2.5G and 3G mobile data services. For example, GPRS and UMTS networks in Europe, and CDMA 1xRTT and CDMA 2000 networks in the USA and Asia are currently being deployed and tested to provide wireless data services that enable ubiquitous mobile access to IP-based applications.

We next examine the performance of these IP-based applications running over such Wireless Wide-Area Networks (WWANs). WWAN links are severely plagued with problems like high round trip times (RTT), fluctuating and relatively low bandwidths, frequent link outages and burst losses. As a consequence the end-user experience in the WWAN environment is significantly different from the relatively stable indoor wireless environments, e.g. 802.11b based Wireless LANs (WLANs).

During the last years important advances have been made in the lowest layers of the Wireless protocol stack. As a result new modulation protocols were depicted, smarter schedulers, optimized error correction techniques, etc. However, despite the advances in the wireless MAC layers, little attention has been paid to evaluate the performance of the higher layers in the protocol stack, e.g. TCP, HTTP, etc. Optimized wireless networking is one of the major hurdles that Mobile Computing must solve if it is to enable ubiquitous access to networking resources. However, current data networking protocols have been optimized primarily for wired networks and do not work in Wireless networks. Wireless environments have very different characteristics in terms of latency, jitter, and error rate as compared to wired networks. As a result applications experience unnecessary losses, bursty behaviour, slow response times, and sudden losses of connectivity. This mismatch between traditional wireline protocols and the wireless bearer can significantly reduce the benefits provided by link layer protocols. Accordingly, traditional protocols have to be adjusted and tuned to this medium.

Some of the performance problems observed in WWAN networks have also been observed to some extent in other long-thin or long-fat networks (e.g. Satellite, WLANs, Metricon Ricochet). However, little in depth analysis has been done about the real underlying problems that impact content delivery over WWANs. In this chapter we investigate the performance of layers 4-7 of the protocol stack over Wide-Area wireless networks. We first analyze the characteristics of a GPRS network as a representative WWAN network and then we study the performance issues of TCP, DNS and HTTP to enable an efficient content delivery system.

To overcome the problems posed by Wireless links we will study a **Wireless Performance Enhancing Proxy** (W-PEP) architecture that attempts to handle the underlying characteristics of WWAN wireless links. The W-PEP sits at the edge of the wireline network, facing the wireless link, and monitors, modifies, and shapes traffic going to the wireless interface to accommodate the wireless link peculiarities. W-PEP implements a number of optimizations at the transport, the session and the application layer that overall provide a significant improvement to the end user experience. It also includes caching and advanced logging and billing systems. Some of these W-PEP proxies have been recently deployed in wireless commercial networks over the world to enable remote Web access to business users using their laptops. In this chapter we present some results of the real benefits that these proxies provide in WWAN networks.

2. Overview of Cellular Networks

WWAN networks consist of a number of standards and solutions that greatly vary around the world. For instance, GPRS networks represent an evolution of GSM networks and are considered to be an intermediate step towards 3G networks, e.g., UMTS. That is why GPRS networks are given the name of 2.5G. While GSM networks are mostly a European phenomenon, similar efforts are under way in the USA and in Asia. For instance, CDMA 1xRTT is the equivalent of GPRS in the USA market. CDMA 1xRTT is supposed to evolve to the equivalent 3G standard, CDMA 1xEDVD, at about the same time when GPRS is expected to evolve to UMTS. Despite the difference in the cellular wireless standards in different countries, all these networks share a similar set of problems. To better understand the problems posed by these networks we next show the result of a set of pings through a live commercial GPRS network in Europe. Similar results were obtained in other networks both in Europe and the USA.

```
Pinging www.microsoft.com [192.11.229.2] (32 bytes):
Reply from 192.11.229.2: bytes=32 time=885ms TTL=109
Reply from 192.11.229.2: bytes=32 time=908ms TTL=109
Reply from 192.11.229.2: bytes=32 time=4154ms TTL=109
Reply from 192.11.229.2: bytes=32 time=870ms TTL=109
Reply from 192.11.229.2: bytes=32 time=795ms TTL=109
Ping statistics for 192.11.229.2:
Packets: Sent = 80, Received = 80, Lost = 0 (0\% loss),
Approximate round trip times in milliseconds: Min = 761ms, Max = 4154ms, Avrg = 1001ms
```

As we can see the average RTT delay measured by a ping request is equal to one second. Moreover, the variability in the delay is quite extreme, ranging from 761 msec to 4 sec. An important point to note is that there were *zero losses*. A deeper analysis using tcpdump also revealed *zero out of order* packets. The main reason for this is the strong link-layer reliability implemented by cellular wireless networks. Cellular wireless networks implement ARQ retransmissions, FEC, and other related techniques to ensure that packets are not lost or disordered by the air interface. As an example, link-layer GPRS protocols provide 10^{-9} packet loss rates and similar values for out-of-order packet reception. The fact that reliability is implemented at the link layer ensures that higher layers see practically no losses or packets out of order. However, the drawback is that the variability and value of the wireless RTTs increases drastically. This is an inherent problem of cellular wireless links that will not go away with the arrival of 3G wireless networks.

Another problem is the fact that these wireless networks have a very low throughput. For instance GPRS networks provide a throughput of 15-25 Kbps while CDMA 1xRTT provide a throughput of 50-70 kbps for HTTP traffic.

These problems require an in-depth study of their impact on the higher layer protocols. As we will see in this chapter, a careful study of these problems and a set of intelligent content distribution optimizations techniques can overcome many of the problems that plague WWAN links.

3.   Wireless PEP

Wireless Performance Enhancing Proxies (W-PEP) are required to minimize the big performance mismatch between terrestrial and wireless links. By splitting the connection between the terrestrial and the wireless side into two different connections, W-PEPs can significantly improve end-to-end protocol performance. Wireless performance enhancing proxies have traditionally been used to alleviate the problems that occur due to high losses over the wireless links. However, 2.5 and 3G links provide reliable and orderly delivery by implementing link-layer reliability. As a result we will now revisit the concept of W-PEPs, taking into account the peculiarities of 2.5 and 3G wireless networks and seeing how they can be used to optimize content delivery.

In a GPRS/UMTS architecture [Bettstetter et al., 1999], two new nodes have been added to the traditional GSM network: Serving GPRS Support Node (SGSN) and Gateway GPRS Service Node (GGSN). The SGSN acts as a packet switch that performs signalling, along with cell selection, routing, and handovers between different Base Station Systems (BSS). It also controls the Mobile Terminal (MT)'s access to the GPRS network and routes packets to the appropriate BSC. The GGSN is the gateway between the mobile packet routing of GPRS and the fixed IP routing of the Internet. A similar architecture exists in CDMA networks.

The W-PEP can be located in multiple places in the network. The most natural place is to collocate the W-PEP with the GGSN since this the first IP node where all IP traffic is anchored from the BSS (Figure 16.1). Other locations could also provide interesting benefits and a more distributed architecture (e.g., at the SGSN, at the Base Station). However, deploying the W-PEP at these locations would need substantial work since it requires accommodating a layer 3-7 proxy between layer-2 nodes. The W-PEP can be deployed using an explicit proxy configuration or a transparent proxy configuration plus a layer-4 switch. W-PEPs provide a number of enhancements that improve the overall end-to-end user experience. These optimizations cover transport layer optimizations, session level optimizations and application level optimizations.

One important characteristic of W-PEP is that it does not require any modifications to the client or server stacks and performs all the optimizations transparently. This makes it very easy to deploy and avoids the hassle of having to provide and maintain new purpose build client software. However, we point

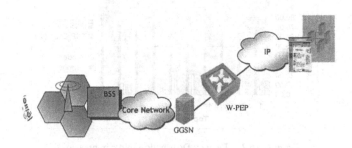

Figure 16.1. W-PEP network architecture

out those optimizations that would benefit more from having a special client-software.

In the rest of the chapter we will show the performance benefits of a commercial W-PEP implementation. This implementation runs on Solaris 8 and enables TCP and session optimizations, application-level optimizations, and caching. The W-PEP was tested on a typical GPRS cell with the following parameters: 18 dB of SNR, GPRS phone with four downlink slots and 2 uplink slots, background traffic of voice calls with 60 seconds of active time and 15 seconds of inter-arrival time exponentially distributed, 10 background users, and no data slots being reserved exclusively for GPRS traffic.

4. Latency Components

To have a better understanding of the different factors that determine the overall latency to download a document, we have disaggregated the total download time of a document into various components. We try to determine the impact of: a) the time to resolve DNS names; b) the time to establish TCP connections; c) the idle times between the end of the reception of an embedded object and the beginning of the reception of the next one; and d) the transmission time of the data payload. We do not explicitly consider the processing time of the server since we assume that in a wireless link, the server processing time is negligible compared to the other latency components. Figure 16.2 shows the GPRS latency components for the top-level page of the 10 most popular web sites. These Top 10 pages are described in Table 16.4. From this Figure we see that time to deliver the payload accounts for most of the latency (about 65%). This is an expected result since the throughput of the GPRS link is quite low. The idle RTTs in between GET requests for embedded objects account for

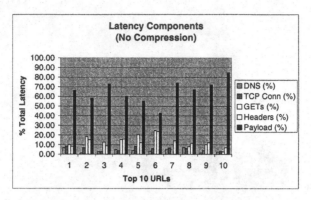

Figure 16.2.   Latency Distribution (No compression)

the second largest latency component, especially in pages with many objects. These idle times represent a significant overhead since the RTT through wireless links can be quite high. HTTP headers also account for a large overhead since many objects in Web pages tend to be quite small and the Header sizes could potentially be on the same order as the size of the object itself.

At the transport and session layer, DNS queries and TCP connection setups account for the smallest portion of the overhead. Most of these overheads are barely noticeable in terrestrial links with quite small RTTs. However, in GPRS links where RTTs are in the order of seconds, these overheads can significantly affect the end-user experience. In the next sections we describe in more detail these overheads and identify solutions for some of these problems.

5.   Transport/Session Optimizations

TCP faces several problems in GPRS links. Given the Radio Link Protocol (RLP) link-layer retransmissions, TCP sees very large and variable delays. On top of this, the throughput of the wireless link is very small. The two possible options to deal with these problems are to tune/alter the TCP/IP networking stack at an intermediate node only (i.e., W-PEP), or to change/replace the networking stack at the mobile host and intermediate node. The latter approach may be based on a completely new transport protocol (e.g., based on UDP) that handles the particularities of wireless links and replaces TCP. This new transport protocol should provide reliability, congestion control, flow control, and fairness. However, TCP has proven to be a very flexible and robust protocol that can be adapted to many types of networks. Creating a completely new transport protocol may not prove to be the most efficient solution since one may end up re-implementing most of the TCP features. Therefore, in this chapter we consider solutions that do not replace TCP but instead optimize it for cellular wireless links. These type of solutions can be implemented in an intermediate proxy such as the W-PEP and do not require any modifications to TCP/IP stack on either end of connection (servers or mobile clients).

Before describing in detail the problems and solutions for TCP performance in wireless links, we would like to have a rough estimate of how much improvement we should expect from TCP optimizations. From Figure 16.2 we can estimate the best case scenario for TCP and session-level optimizations. By eliminating TCP setup, and removing DNS lookups, the best improvement possible is about 18%. As we will see later, this number goes up to 30% once the content is compressed since the relative impact of TCP setup and DNS queries increases (See Figure 16.5). Next we will consider how to deal with specific TCP problems in more detail.

5.1   TCP Tuning

To better understand the problems of the TCP performance in wireless links we run the following experiment. We first calculate the FTP throughput obtained when downloading a large file. Then we compare it with the throughput obtained when downloading a Web page of the same size using HTTP (the page had 10 embedded objects). The results can be seen in Table 16.1.

Table 16.1 shows that the throughput provided by an FTP transfer of a large file is quite close to the maximum TCP throughput than can be achieved through the wireless link. The main reason for this is that FTP uses a single connection and therefore TCP connection setup overhead is very small. This result also shows that the long-term TCP throughput is very good.

When we compare the FTP throughput of a large file with the HTTP throughput of a size-equivalent Web page, we noticed see that the HTTP throughput drastically drops from 37 − 39 Kbps to 21 − 28 Kbps. This is due to the large number of TCP connections opened by the browser and the DNS lookups needed to resolve the domain names of embedded objects. In addition to the TCP and DNS problems, HTTP also suffers from the fact that there are multiple idle RTTs in between object requests since pipelining is not enabled. We will later discuss in more depth the impact of pipelining.

Table 16.1.   TCP Throughput

	Throughput (Kbps)
Maximum Airlink GPRS Rate	53.6
Maximum TCP Throughput Rate	43-45
FTP Rate	37-39
HTTP Rate	20-28

As discussed earlier in the chapter, one can use a standard TCP/IP stack and tune it to optimize TCP performance in GPRS networks. Different stacks require different levels of tuning, however, the optimal combination of TCP parameters should be the quite similar for different OS implementations. In order to tune a given TCP stack we consider critical parameters that could potentially impact the TCP wireless performance. These parameters include the maximum transfer unit size, the slow start window, and several timers that determined the retransmission timeouts calculation:

- a) A careful selection of the MTU allows for efficient link utilization. Selecting a small MTU increases the chance of a successful transmission through a lossy link; however, it also increases the overhead of header to data. Selecting a large MTU, on the other hand, increases the probability of error and the delay to transmit one segment. However, wireless links such as GPRS and CDMA provide low-level techniques that strongly reduce the probability of loss. Having large MTU has several benefits, such as a smaller ratio of header overhead to data and a rapid increase of TCP's congestion window (TCP's congestion window increases in units of segments). As a result, a large MTU (*tcp_mss_def* about 1460 bytes) may prove to be quite beneficial to optimize TCP in GPRS networks.

- b) Traditional slow start, with an initial window of one segment, is too slow over wireless networks. Slow start is particularly harmful for short data transmissions [Padmanabhan, 1998], which is commonly the case for web traffic. Increasing the initial slow start window (*tcp_slow_start*) to three to four segments may improve the transfer time significantly and therefore it is highly recommended as a possible TCP optimization.

- c) A correct estimation of a connection timeout (RTO) is very important since it may lead to unnecessary segment retransmissions and a sharp decrease in TCP throughput. To estimate RTO, the sender uses periodic measurements of the RTT between the client and the server. However, it takes several RTTs before the sender can efficiently estimate the actual delay of the connection. In between, many packets can be retransmitted inefficiently. One way to minimize spurious retransmission due to incorrect RTT estimation is to set the initial values of the RTT closer to its real values in the wireless link. Thus, parameters such as *tcp_rtx_interval_initial* and *tcp_rtx_min* can play an important role in optimizing TCP performance.

To have a better understanding of the impact of a wrong estimation of the retransmission timer, in Figure 16.3(a) we can see a TCP trace for a page download from a standard Web server which parameters have not been tuned for GPRS links. Let us focus on the number of retransmissions that were received

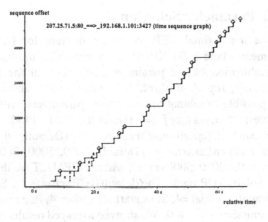

(a) W-PEP disabled

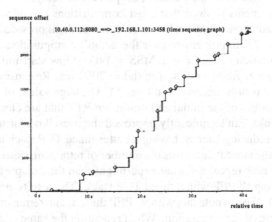

(b) W-PEP enabled

Figure 16.3. TCP Behavior.

at the client (marked by an R). The results in Figure 16.3(a) show that at the beginning of the download the Web server has a completely wrong (too short) estimation of the RTT, thus, it generates many unnecessary retransmissions. As the download progresses the retransmissions disappears since the RTT estimation improves. However, it takes about 30 seconds for the Web server to properly estimate the parameters of the wireless connection and stop sending unnecessary retransmissions. This overhead can be catastrophic for short Web transfers. Similar results can be obtained with other pages, showing that in many situations the number of retransmissions account for up to 50% of the packets. As we will see later, W-PEP solves this problem.

5.2   TCP Parameter Selection

To determine the optimal TCP parameter mixture for GPRS links we run an experiment where a 50 KB file is downloaded multiple times with a different combination of the parameters described in the previous section (tcp_mss_def, tcp_slow_start, $tcp\_rtx\_interval$, and tcp_rtx_min). We used all possible combinations of these parameters with the following input values: tcp_mss_def = (Default, 1500, 1400, 1200) Bytes, $tcp\_slow\_start\_initial$, $tcp\_slow\_start\_idle$ = (Default, 4, 3, 2) segments, $tcp\_rtx\_interval\_initial$ = (Default, 7000, 5000, 3000) msec, and tcp_rtx_min = (400, 3000, 5000) msec, where DEFAULT are the default TCP settings of the Solaris TCP stack. The default TCP settings for Solaris 8.2 are: MSS = 536, Slow start initial =4, Slow start after idle= 4, Retransmission initial =3000, Retransmission min =400. We showed averaged results compared with the results obtained using the default TCP parameter setup.

The measurements showed that most combinations provided little benefit versus the default configuration, however, some of them provided an improvement of up to 17% improvement over the default configuration. The optimal tuning configuration consisted on: MSS = 1400, Slow start initial = 4, Slow start after idle =4, Retransmission initial = 7000 ms, Retransmission min = 3000ms. These results indicates that large MTUs, large values of the slow start window, and values of the initial and minimum RTT that are closer to those in the wireless links, can significantly improved the overall performance of TCP. In addition to reducing latency, having a better tuned TCP stack also improves bandwidth usage since it decreases the number of retransmissions. To illustrate this point, we now repeat a similar experiment than the one presented in Figure 16.3(a) using W-PEP with a tuned TCP stack. The results are presented in Figure 16.3(b). We can note that with W-PEP there are no retransmissions, even at the beginning of the connection. When repeating the same experiment with many other Web sites, one can consistently see a significant reduction in the number of retransmissions. Without W-PEP, the number of retransmissions for certain Web sites sometimes accounted for half of the data delivered, therefore, significantly reducing the available bandwidth and download rates. Using W-PEP, on the other hand, the number of retransmissions due to spurious timeouts was negligible. As a result, a well-tuned TCP stack can drastically improve the wireless link efficiency.

5.3   TCP Connection Sharing

In standard TCP/IP implementations each new TCP connection independently estimates the connection parameters to match an end to end bandwidth and round trip time of the network. The two critical connection parameters that require estimation are RTT and congestion window size. For each connection the estimation process normally starts with the same default values, set in the stack configuration. This estimation process takes several RTTs to converge. In wireless links with very large and highly variable RTTs, estimation process converges very slowly. For short connections typical for Web access, it is common to have most of the traffic flow over connections with sub optimal parameters, therefore underutilizing the available capacity. It can be observed however that RTT and congestion parameters for connections to the same mobile host are likely to have very similar values, primarily determined by device and network capabilities (e.g., number of uplink and downlink time slots), and by current network load and conditions (e.g., current link error rate).

To minimize the amount of time required for TCP to converge to the right connection parameters, we instrumented W-PEP TCP stack to cache RTT and congestion window parameters of currently running or recently expired connections, and to reuse them as a starting values for the new connections *to the same mobile host*. A second advantage of this approach is that connection parameters are effectively estimated over considerably longer period of time, spanning several connections to the same mobile host. This provides for much better estimates of link parameters. We set a timeout before the cached values expire to 2 minutes. If there are no new connections to the same mobile host over this period of time, the cached values are cleared. We found this value to be a good heuristic timeout.

Whenever a new connection is initiated, W-PEP re-uses previously cached connection parameters. The new connection immediately starts sending data at the same rate at which a previous connection had been sending just before it finished. Therefore, we virtually eliminate the overhead of the slow start phase of most connections, the convergence process happens much faster, and estimated connection parameters are more precise.

One drawback of this approach is that at the beginning of a given connection W-PEP may produce bursts of data that are higher than it would otherwise be the case; however, current GPRS networks provide large buffers that can easily absorb it.

To evaluate the performance of this TCP connection state sharing technique we downloaded the Top 10 pages with and without this feature enabled, and averaged the results over multiple rounds. We used HTTP1.1 persistent connections. The results showed an average improvement of 12% over all pages. This is a significant improvement that can clearly have an effect on end-user experience, and it does not require any modification of the client or server TCP stacks.

5.4   Number of TCP connections

One of the main factors that impacts the performance of TCP through GPRS networks is the number connections opened and closed. Each time a new connection is opened, there is a corresponding connection setup overhead which includes several idle RTTs before TCP is able to fully utilize the available link capacity. Next we study how standard browsers such as Netscape or IE use/reuse TCP connections and what their impact is on GPRS networks. To study this, we considered a page with 25 embedded objects and 142 KB of data that was downloaded by the browser. While the download was happening we collected TCP traces using tcpdump to study the dynamics of TCP. The traces where captured on a Windows 2000 laptop. The address of the laptop was 192.168.1.101. Version of IE used was 5.50. The IE was set to use an explicit HTTP proxy at the address 10.40.0.112 port 8080. "Use HTTP1.1 through proxy connection" (in IE Options) was turned on. The collected traces cover the period time between the initial page request and when all its embedded objects are received in full.

Figure 16.4 shows a time graph of the TCP connections opened and closed by the browser. From this figure we see that the total number of connections used to retrieve the page by the browser is equal to 10 connections (the first connection coincide with the beginning of X axis on the graph, and can only be seen with appropriate magnification of this corner). All connections were closed by the browser and not by the proxy or the server. The number of connections used is very large. According to HTTP1.1 specifications, browsers are supposed to use only two connections to a proxy. In the same Figure we can also note that IE never uses more then 2 connections in parallel, however, it routinely opens new connections, just to close an "older" connection in lieu of newly opened one.

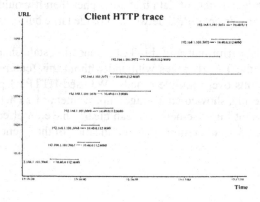

Figure 16.4.   TCP Connection Behavior

By examining the breakdown of number of URLs served per connection, we noticed that the bulk of objects is retrieved using 2 or 3 connections, however the rest of the connections are only used to retrieve 1 or 2 objects per connection. In fact, in this experiment, 6 out of 10 connections were used to retrieve only 1 object.

To better understand this behaviour we analyzed the source code of TCP connection scheduler of a popular browser. Next we describe the algorithm used when a new object request is received. We assume that the browser is explicitly connected to the proxy, thus, all connections opened to the proxy can be potentially reused to retrieve any object from any Web site.

```
if (num_conn_open < max_conn){
  if (idle_conn & !conn_expired()){
    reuse_conn();
  }
  elseif{
    open_new_conn();
    close_expired_conn();
  }
}
elseif{
  open_new_conn();
  close_oldest_idle_conn();
}
```

The main motivation behind this algorithm is the following. Browsers open multiple connections in parallel to fetch embedded objects as fast as possible. The browser first opens a TCP connection to fetch the home page (i.e., index.html file). If embedded objects need to be fetched, the browser will try to re-use any existing connections that have finished previous downloads (i.e., idle connections) and that have not yet expired (as determined by the keep-alive timeout). If no connections are idle, the browser will open new connections until it reaches the maximum number of connections allowed. For an HTTP 1.1 browser in explicit proxy mode this limit is usually two. Once the browser has reached its maximum number of connections, if a new object request arrives, the browser still creates a new connection. At this point, the browser is exceeding its maximum connection allowance. To balance the number of connections, the browser closes the first connection that becomes idle or any connection that has been active for more than the maximum allowed delay.

This is an aggressive behaviour that prevents browsers from getting slowed down by connections that are stalled. In a wireless network, however, connections take a long time to complete. The browser frequently thinks that the connection is stalled and opens a new connection to try to get the download going as fast as possible. At the same time it closes other pending active connections that according to the browser's algorithm are not progressing at a fast enough rate. This can lead to a behaviour where many connections are frequently opened and closed and a single object can take a very long time to complete download since it never gets to progress. This is counter productive in wireless networks since opening and closing many connections creates and extremely high overhead that significantly increases the download times. One way to overcome these problems is to ensure that browsers for wireless networks try to keep a constant number of connections that they re-use them as much as possible, and use connection timers that are in accordance with the delays/throughputs of wireless links. These modifications require slight changes or re-configuration of the client browsers.

Even though the number of connections should be kept constant as much as possible, the number of connections should not be very small to prevent stalled connections from delaying the overall download. In the next experiment we try to provide some intuition of why using a very small number of connections may not be very efficient. To this end, we calculate the performance of a file download using one single connection vs. four connections. We consider a large 1 MB file. When using four connections, the file is divided into four equal pieces and all of them are fetched in parallel. The results show that the throughput obtained with four connections is about 11% higher than with a single connection. One reason for this higher throughput is that multiple asynchronous connections can better utilize the wireless link capacity since some connections are able to grab additional bandwidth while others are idle or slow.

5.5   Temporal Block Flow Release

Wireless Base Station Controllers (BSC) and SGSNs allocate wireless link resources to a particular mobile host only for a certain period of time. After a mobile host is idle for more than a preconfigured period of time, the wireless link resources are released. The logical resource in question is called TBF (temporary block flow) and we will refer to this behaviour as TBF release. This improves the utilization of a given GPRS channel since the period of channel inactivity is limited. However, when the mobile host comes back and starts requesting data again it goes through the acquisition of a new TBF and associated time slot. Acquiring a new TBF and time slot is an expensive process that adds an initial latency before data transfer can be initiated. In the next experiment we try to determine the TBF release timeout, i.e., the idle period of time before the mobile host's GPRS channel is released. To this end we periodically ping the W-PEP from the mobile host with increasing pinging intervals. Table 16.2 shows that there is a jump in the value of RTT when the time between pings

Table 16.2. Ping times for different inter-ping intervals

Ping Interval (sec)	Avrg. Ping Time (msec)
1	1667
2	1726
3	1664
4	1778
5	1726
6	2110
7	2551
8	2345
9	2123
10	2314

increases from 5 seconds to 6 seconds. This indicates a TBF release timeout of around 6 seconds. This empirical experiment to determine the TBF value was later confirmed by a number of GPRS vendors.

A TBF equal to 6 sec can create very frequent wireless channel releases and acquisitions, especially given that user think times in between page downloads are frequently higher than 6 seconds. As a result when the think time between requests is higher than the TBF value, the mobile host suffers an extra delay to acquire a new GRPS channel before any data can be transmitted. In order to determine the impact of the TBF release in a page download, we consider the following experiment. Let us download the Top 10 pages repeatedly, with a new page request happening 10 seconds after the end of the previous page download finished. We then repeat the same experiment while having a background ping from the W-PEP to the mobile host every 5 seconds. This background ping happens before the TBF is released, thus, the mobile host gets to keep the channel and does not need to re-acquire on each page. Only one ping request is required per mobile host to keep the wireless GPRS channel active. The results show that keeping the GPRS channel and not releasing it in between page requests provides a 15% latency improvement. In a real implementation this background ping should stop after the mobile host inactivity period goes over a given threshold, e.g., 20 sec, to avoid flooding the wireless link with unnecessary packets and to release the GPRS channel.

5.6 Session-level overheads: DNS

DNS is a session-level protocol that is used to resolve the server names associated with all objects in a Web page. However, DNS queries can have a significant impact in the GPRS performance. For example, we observed that www.britannica.com has 14 different domain names used by objects embedded on its home page, or www.cnn.com has 6 different embedded domain names. Performing DNS queries through the wireless interface can drastically increase the overall download time of this and similar pages. The way of overcoming DNS delays is by caching DNS responses and re-using them for a certain Time-to-live without having to re-contact the DNS server each time a given domain is accessed. However, popular domains names are frequently served by content distribution networks, which set very small TTLs in their DNS responses. When TTL response is very small, the browser has to repeat the same DNS query over and over again to resolve a given domain name. Performing repeated DNS queries through terrestrial links may not have a significant performance impact; however, in wireless links this can be a source of major overhead.

In order to estimate the impact of DNS queries we can conduct the following experiment. We download the main CNN page with all its embedded objects. First we download it ensuring that all DNS lookups required resolving the embedded domain names happen through the GPRS link. Then we repeat the same experiment with all DNS lookups being satisfied from the local DNS cache, thus avoiding the GPRS link. To make sure that in the first experiment DNS lookups were not satisfied from a local client DNS cache, the DNS Time To Live key value was set to 0 in the Windows registry, and IE was restarted after every run (IE keeps its own DNS cache). The results obtained show that avoiding DNS lookups over the wireless interface reduces the response time by 16%. This is a significant time reduction that requires special attention. There are several ways to fix this problem by having the proxy do the lookups over a terrestrial link in a transparent way. However, due to its lengthy considerations we refer the reader to the following paper [Rodriguez et al., 2004].

6.   Application Level Optimizations

Application level optimizations are intended to minimize the overhead of the application level protocol (e.g., HTTP) and to minimize the time to delivery the payload. Figure 16.2 showed that payload transmission time accounts for the major portion of the delay since the bandwidth of the GPRS link is quite low. The idle time in between object requests (GETs) as well as the HTTP headers also account for a large portion of the total delay, however, its significance depends on the number of objects in a given page. Pages with a large number of small objects have a higher number of idle RTTs and higher proportion of HTTP headers to content, while pages with a low number of large objects barely experience these kinds of overhead.

Given that the time to deliver the payload accounts for most of the transmission time, minimizing the amount of data delivered will significantly reduce the total download time. To this end we have instrumented the W-PEP to intercept all Web requests and process the responses before passing them to the mobile host. Once W-PEP downloads the Web document requested, it performs the following actions: a) *transform* the page format into a suitable page format readable in the mobile host. If the mobile host is a laptop then there is no page transformation; b) *lossless content compression*, e.g., compresses text/html files; c) *lossy compression* of images. Regarding lossy compression, W-PEP has several adjustable levels of compression which can be configured by the W-PEP administrator, the content provider, or the end-user. The parameters that can be adjusted include: number of colours in a GIF, level of quality degradation in JPEGs, and whether animated GIFs should be converted into static ones or not.

6.1   Compression Results

Next, we present the compression factors attained by W-PEP on different types of Web pages. We focus on optimizing the downlink channel since it carries most of the data in WEB applications. We assume that the page is already pre-formatted to fit the device screen, and therefore, we do not consider the impact of content transformation. Instead, we measure the compression achieved by W-PEP through lossy or lossless compression. For lossless compression, W-PEP used gzip on all possible content-types. Some servers already support gzipping of text/html content, however, we found that most pages were uncompressed, and therefore, W-PEP had to compress them. Recent versions of most browsers support the reception of compressed content, which is uncompressed on the fly. For lossy compression we selected 16 colours for GIFs, no animated GIFs (in banners), and a level of JPEG quality degradation that was barely perceived by the human eye. W-PEP caches all transformed content, thus, it only needs to compress it or transcode it once and then multiple requests for the same object can be served from the cache, substantially increasing scalability.

We considered an experiment using the Top 100 pages to understand how W-PEP would behave in a real scenario. The average compression factor for the Top 100 pages is 2.83, however, some specific pages with large portions of text and highly compressible images can be compressed by a factor close to 6.

Table 16.3 presents the compression factor for each content type individually as well as the percentage of a page corresponding to each type. We can see that GIFs as well as HTML content amount for a large portion of all files and can be highly compressed, which helps achieving a high overall compression factor.

6.2   Acceleration Results

Given the compression factors calculated in the previous section we would like to determine how this data compression factors translate into a latency reduction experienced by the end user. To this end we calculated the compression factors and the latency reduction seen by the end user for the Top 10 Web pages

Table 16.3.   Compression Factors by Content Type.

Content Type	% of Content	Compression Factor
Octetstream	0.45	x2.3
Xjavascript	4.50	x2.73
Xpotplus	0.60	x2.5
Xshockwaveflash	0.68	x3.1
GIF	77.33	x2.44
JPEG	4.80	x1.93
PNG	0.38	x1.92
CSS	0.23	x4.94
HTML	8.41	x3.84
Text/PLA	0.60	x3.45

Table 16.4.   Top 10 Web sites. Impact of Compression, Acceleration, and Pipelining.

Name	Objects	Domains	Size (KB)	Compression	Speedup	Pipelining
1-Altavista	6.00	3	25.4	2.15	1.51	1.87
2-Chek	14.00	1	37.7	2.77	1.67	2.42
3-CNN	36.00	8	185	2.72	2.8	4.42
4-Excite	16.00	5	55.4	3.46	2.43	4.13
5-Fortunecity	36.00	7	142	3.46	1.97	3.57
6-Go	16.00	2	33.7	3.66	1.72	2.96
7-Google	2.00	1	10.3	3.96	1.76	2.00
8-Lycos	5.00	3	30.3	4.09	1.76	2.36
9-MS	16.00	2	87	3.95	2.37	3.25
10-Yahoo	4.00	2	37.4	3.53	3.18	3.59

(see Table 16.4). The latency reduction is calculated as the ratio between the total page download time with W-PEP and without W-PEP. We can see that the average latency reduction for these pages is 2.12, and the average compression factor is 3.18. The average ratio between latency/compression is 0.64, thus, the compression factor for most pages is higher than the latency reduction achieved. This indicates that there is not a perfect direct translation between compressing data and reducing latency, though, the correlation is quite high. This is caused by other overheads that are not affected by compressing data (e.g., idle RTTs, TCP connection setup, DNS lookups, etc.) and that still accounts for a significant portion of the total download latency as we will see later.

To better understand how different factors affect the overall latency after compression has been applied, we re-calculated the results of Figure 16.2. The new latency distribution with compressed data is presented in Figure 16.5.

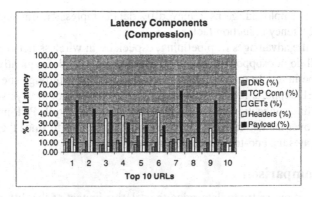

Figure 16.5. Latency Distribution (Compression).

From this Figure we see that payload's transmission time has been reduced substantially and accounts for a much smaller portion (about 40%) of the total latency. This causes other latency factors such as idle RTTs, or HTTP headers to account for a much higher portion of the delay, sometimes equal or more than the actual payload delivery.

6.3   Impact of Pipelining

We will now consider the impact of pipelining. Pipelining is required to avoid the idle RTTs that occur when browsers wait until an embedded object is fully received before requesting the next object. This overhead can be quite important for GPRS links since the RTT delays through a GPRS link are usually over one second. One way to avoid these idle RTTs is by requesting a given embedded object before the previous one has been fully downloaded. This is known as *request pipelining* and its benefits have been well studied in the past on wireline and satellite networks. To estimate the benefits associated with pipelining in a cellular network, we compare the latency obtained when downloading the Top 10 Web pages with and without request pipelining. The results obtained are presented in Table 16.4. This table shows that the speedup factor obtained when pipelining is turned on is 3.06, which is a 42% improvement versus not having pipelining (Table 16.4). Similar results have been presented in [Chakravorty and Pratt, 2002].

Assuming that pipelining was turn on, we now attempt to determine whether the relationship between compression and latency reduction improved. To this end we compare the latency reduction obtained with pipelining vs. the compression factors. (We do not show the individual results for each page.) The results obtained show a new average ratio between latency reduction and compression of 0.90 versus 0.64 without request pipelining. This indicates that when request pipelining is employed, gains achieved by data compression translate almost fully into a latency reduction factor.

Despite the advantages of pipelining, especially in wireless networks, most servers still do not support it. Browsers, on the other hand, frequently support request pipelining. In order to enable request pipelining through the wireless link, W-PEP supports request pipelining. Pipelining is not always supported in the wireline connection to the origin servers. But having W-PEP implement pipelining over the wireless link provides most of the benefit since the wireless link dominates the end-to-end latency.

7.   Comparison

In this section we try to determine the relative impact of the different optimizations presented in this chapter. We compare transport-level optimizations with application-level optimizations. To do this, we measured the latency of downloading certain Web objects when W-PEP performs only transport-level optimizations, and when W-PEP performs both transport-level and application-level optimizations. The application-level optimizations included pipelining and compression of Web objects (lossless and lossy). The transport-level optimizations considered were TCP tuning, TCP connection sharing, TBF release avoidance, use of two persistent TCP connections, and no DNS lookups.

We first compared both sets of optimizations for a large object, a 400 KB image, and then we repeated the same experiment with a Web page. In Figure 16.6 we show the speedup obtained when downloading this large image for the cases of no W-PEP, W-PEP with transport-level optimizations only, and W-PEP with transport-level and application-level optimizations. From this figure we see that relative benefits obtained from optimizing long-term TCP behaviour are quite small (about 6%). Compressing the large image, on the other hand, provides a compression factor over 800% with very small visual perception impact. It is clear from this example that application-level optimizations are much more important than transport-level optimizations when considering a large single object that is highly compressible.

In Figure 16.7 we repeated the same experiments for a typical Web page. Given that this page has multiple objects and it is hosted in several different domain names, the overhead of DNS lookups and TCP connection setup is much higher. Using the previously mentioned transport-level optimizations, the speedup obtained equals 30% instead 6% obtained with a single large object. Transport-level optimizations provide better results in this case since the complexity of the page is higher, with many objects hosted in multiple domains, which is the case of many popular Web sites. Regarding application-level optimizations, we note that they do not work that well with the tested Web page since the objects were quite small and not very compressible. The actual speedup

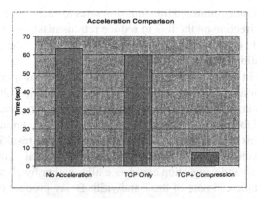

Figure 16.6. Comparison between application-level and transport-level optimizations. 400 KB image.

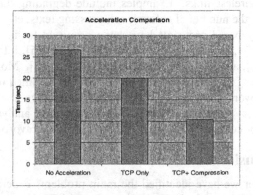

Figure 16.7. Comparison between application-level and transport-level optimizations. 100 KB image.

obtained when compressing text and images on the tested Web page was close to 250%, which is a much lower number than the 800% obtained previously with a single large image. Still this factor is much higher number than the 30% provided by the transport-level optimizations alone. Therefore, application-level optimizations amount for a larger portion of the overall latency reduction, although their relative impact highly depends on the type of pages and their complexity.

8. Further Reading

In the literature, physical/link/MAC layer enhancements have been proposed that aim to provide improved scheduling algorithms over wireless links to increase the total system throughput, provide fairness or priorities between the different users, assure minimum transmission rates to each user and incorporate forward error correction on the link to reduce retransmissions. The scheduling algorithms aim to control the system or user throughput at the physical layer. For data applications, it is equally important to consider the data performance at higher layers in the protocol stack, especially at the transport (TCP) layer. Techniques such as the ACK Regulator [Chan and Ramjee, 2002] has been proposed to monitor and control the flow of acknowledgment packets in the up-link channel and therefore regulate the traffic flow in the downlink channel of a wireless link. This solution avoids buffer overflow and the resulting congestion avoidance mechanism of TCP. Similarly [Chakravorty et al., 2003b] proposes to avoid slow-start and congestion avoidance all together by clamping the TCP window to an static estimate of the Bandwidth Delay product of the link. At the application layer several data compression techniques have been proposed [Forelle Systems Inc., 2005, Bytemobile Inc., 2005] to increase the effective throughput of wireless links. Examples include degrading the quality of an image, reducing the number of colours, compressing texts, etc.

Several proxy based protocols have been proposed to fix TCP problems over wireless links, e.g. Snoop [Balakrishnan et al., 1995], I-TCP [Bakre and Badrinath, 1995], and W-TCP [Ratnam and Matta, 1998]. More recent work suggests the use of a small proxy at the mobile host combined with a proxy on the wireline network to implement a new transport protocol that replaces TCP [Chakravorty et al., 2003a]. An extensive comparative analysis of wireless optimizations for content delivery can be found in [Chakravorty et al., 2004].

9.   Conclusions

In this chapter we have identified the main problems experienced by providing efficient Web content delivery in 2.5G and 3G wireless networks. We have considered the problems at each layer of protocol stack separately, e.g., transport, session, and application. Given the peculiarities of these wireless networks with very large and highly variable latencies and low throughputs, we have studied the performance of a Wireless Performance Enhancing Proxy (W-PEP), which is deployed completely transparently at the border between the wireline and the wireless network. We showed that the suite of optimizations implemented at the W-PEP can provide significant latency reduction to the end user, thus, significantly improving the content delivery experience over such links.

Other problems in wireless links that are not covered in this chapter but that require a careful consideration relate to the loss of efficiency under temporary loss of connectivity, (e.g., when users go inside a tunnel) or to the impact when a mobile user switches access networks, e.g., GPRS to WiFi.

References

Bakre, Ajay and Badrinath, B. R. (1995). Indirect TCP for mobile hosts. In *ICDCS*.

Balakrishnan, H., Seshan, S., Amir, E., and Katz, R. (1995). Improving TCP/IP performance over Wireless Networks. In *Proceedings of ACM MOBICOM*.

Bettstetter, C., Vögel, H., and Eberspächer, J. (1999). GSM Phase 2+ General Packet Radio Service GPRS: Architecture, Protocols, and Air Interface. In *IEEE Communications*.

Bytemobile Inc. (2005). The Macara Optimization Service Node.

Chakravorty, R., Clark, A., and Pratt, I. (2003a). GPRSWeb: Optimizing the Web for GPRS Links. In *ACM/USENIX First International Conference on Mobile Systems, Applications and Services*.

Chakravorty, R., Katti, S., Crowcroft, J., and Pratt, I. (2003b). Flow aggregation for enhanced tcp over wide-area wireless. In *IEEE INFOCOM*.

Chakravorty, R., Banerjee, S., Rodriguez, P., Chesterfield, J., and Pratt, I. (2004). Performance Optimizations for Wireless Wide-Area Networks: Comparative Study and Experimental Evaluation. In *ACM MOBICOM, Philadelphia. Sep 2004*.

Chakravorty, R. and Pratt, I. (2002). WWW Performance over GPRS. In *IEEE MWCN*.

Chan, M.C. and Ramjee, R. (2002). TCP/IP Performance over 3G Wireless Links with Rate and Delay Variation. In *Proc. of ACM Mobicom*.

Forelle Systems Inc. (2005). The Venturi Server.

Padmanabhan, V. (1998). *Addressing the challenges of web data transport*. PhD thesis.

Ratnam, K. and Matta, I. (1998). W-TCP: An Efficient Transmission Control Protocol for Networks with Wireless Links. In *In Proceedings of Third IEEE Symposium on Computer and Communications*.

Rodriguez, P., Mukherjee, Sarit, and Rangarajan, Sampath (2004). Session level techniques for improving web browsing performance on wireless links. In *WWW Conference, New York, 2004*.

Chapter 17

MULTIMEDIA ADAPTATION AND BROWSING ON SMALL DISPLAYS

Xing Xie
Microsoft Research Asia
xingx@microsoft.com

Wei-Ying Ma
Microsoft Research Asia
wyma@microsoft.com

> *Guan Zhong Kui Bao, Shi Jian Yi Ban - a famous Chinese saying. It is usually used to mean understanding the whole picture by only seeing parts of it, similar to the English saying "seeing the forest through the trees "*
>
> —Yiqin Liu, 420AD-480AD

Abstract   As a great many of new devices with diverse capabilities are making a population boom, their limited display sizes are becoming the major obstacle that undermines the usefulness of these devices for information access. In this chapter, we introduce our recent research on adapting multimedia content including images, videos and web pages for browsing on small-form-factor devices. A theoretical framework as well as a set of novel methods for presenting and rendering multimedia under limited screen sizes is introduced to improve the user experience. A system framework has also been proposed to provide the content modelling and processing as subscription-based web services on the Internet.

Keywords: Small display, content adaptation, attention model, mobile device, edge computing, content delivery networks

1.   Introduction

In the PC+ era, a variety of new computing devices, such as SPOT watch, smart phone, Pocket PC, Tablet PC, etc, are making a population boom. These devices are becoming more and more powerful in both numerical computing and data storage. However, low bandwidth connections and small displays remain two serious obstacles that undermine the usefulness of these devices in people's everyday lives. With the rapid and successful development of 2.5G and 3G wireless networks, the bandwidth factor is expected to be less constrained in the near future. However, the limitation on display size is likely to remain unchanged in the foreseeable future.

Since most of the information on the Internet is presented by multimedia, improving the experience of multimedia access and browsing on small displays is critical for unleashing the power of these mobile devices. Existing research directions to address this problem can be classified into following four categories:

- *Trivial methods.* For example, direct down-sampling of image or video in the spatial domain. This approach often decreases the user experience since the results may be unreadable or unacceptable.

- *Authoring multiple versions.* For example, building separate, dedicated mobile web sites for small devices. This approach results in additional burdens on content management. Also, it is hard to predict what devices will emerge in the market and the solution could be transient.

- *Re-authoring the content offline or on-the-fly.* This approach depends on the extraction of the original semantic structure of the content. Certain success has been achieved in certain areas but generally it is a hard problem because of the nature of reverse engineering.

- *New formats which are scalable by themselves.* This is the most promising direction and has been adopted in many areas, such as scalable image and video coding. However, current research efforts are less focused on the problem of diverse and small displays, and there is much space for improvement on multimedia browsing techniques.

In this chapter, we focus on the latter two approaches since they are more preferred by content authors or consumers. In fact, these two schemes are related to each other. The intermediate representation used in content re-authoring should be flexible and adaptive to the display size. Therefore, it will be referential when standardizing a new scalable format.

2. Related Work

So far only a few efforts have addressed the problem of browsing large web pages on small terminals and little has been done for images or videos. In the following, we will give a brief introduction to the prior art based on the media type that the content adaptation technique is designed for.

2.1 Web Page Adaptation

Typical web pages are designed for desktop PCs with large displays. When they are browsed on small devices, the user experience is unacceptable. Current approaches for adapting web pages can be divided into two categories: the first one is to transform existing web pages such as [Buyukkokten et al., 2002] [BickMore and Schilit, 1997][Chen et al., 2001][Chen et al., 2005][Gu et al., 2000][Wobbrock et al., 2002][Milic-Frayling and Sommerer, 2002], while the other attempts to introduce new formats and mechanisms [Badros et al., 1999] [Borning et al., 2000] which make web pages themselves adaptive to different display sizes.

Among the first category, there are two different approaches for transforming web pages. The first one, which originated from the user interface community, only changes the presentation of page contents without any structure modification. For example, the most straightforward approach is eliminating the annoying horizontal scrolling requirement, i.e. present all the contents into a single narrow column, such as Opera Small Screen Rendering (http://www.opera.com) . Fast and simple though it is in implementation, this method greatly increases the page height and forces the user to scroll up and down excessively. Other UI-based approaches try to use thumbnails or keywords as well as zooming techniques to aid browsing [Wobbrock et al., 2002]. However, this kind of aid tends to work only on pages that users are very familiar with, because thumbnails are often scaled down too much to give much information beyond a rough overview. The other way to do web page transformation is to retrieve the semantic structure from original contents and rewrite the page according to user's context. The basic idea is to partition the web page into a set of sub-pages and generate a Table-of-Content with/without hierarchy as the index page, such as [BickMore and Schilit, 1997][Buyukkokten et al., 2002]. Our previous work [Chen et al., 2001][Gu et al., 2000] belongs to this category. A promising direction is to combine these two techniques together to provide a better user experience, for example, [Chen et al., 2005][Milic-Frayling and Sommerer, 2002] uses the whole page thumbnail as the Table-of-Content.

Although many efforts have been put on automatic extraction of document structure, it is still hard for computers to fully understand the semantic structure of web pages. Moreover, most of them did not address the layout problem which is very essential because the representation of contents directly affects the user's perception. A CSS compatible mechanism is proposed in [Badros et al., 1999] [Borning et al., 2000] which allowed web page designers or editors to designate layout constraints explicitly in mathematic equalities or inequalities, and then turned the display problem into a constraint solving problem. Although constraints for interactive graphical applications have been researched since the early 1980's, there are still a number of unsolved problems with constraint-based layout. For instance, it is difficult to specify proper mathematical formulas for different layouts. In addition, the constraint solving procedure is computationally expensive for the browser of thin clients. There are also some interesting solutions for specific problems such as [Gonzalez et al., 2002] for web newspaper layout and [Fuchs, 2000] for optimizing picture placement in a web page.

As we notice, few of current approaches considered the priorities of different parts in a page. What's more, none of them let authors control the final layout conveniently. That is to say, the final presentation is usually unpredictable during the designing phase.

2.2   Image Adaptation

Current digital cameras usually can take photos with more than 3M pixels. These photos should be down-sampled in order to be viewed on small devices like smart phones. However, people might not recognize crucial details such as the human faces and texts in these down-sampled versions.

Quite a few efforts have been put on image adaptation including JPEG and MPEG standards. The ROI coding scheme and Spatial/SNR scalability in JPEG 2000 [Christopoulos et al., 2000] have provided a functionality of progressive encoding and display. It is useful for fast database access as well as for delivering different resolutions to terminals with different capabilities. In MPEG-7 Multimedia Description Schemes, Media Profile Descriptor was proposed to refer to the different variations that can be produced from an original or master media depending on the values chosen for the coding, storage format, etc. Currently, MPEG-21 has started to define an adaptation framework named Digital Item Adaptation for multimedia content including images.

The image adaptation problem has also been studied in proxy-based transcoding to perform on-demand datatype-specific content adaptation [Fox et al., 1996]. In particular, the authors have made image distillation to illustrate that adaptation is beneficial in saving data transmission time. Smith J. R. et al. [Mohan et al., 1999][Smith et al., 1998] present an image transcoding system based on the classification of image type and purpose. The authors of [Han et al., 1998] proposed a framework for determining when/whether/how to transcode images in a HTTP proxy while focusing their research on saving response time by JPEG/GIF compression, which is determined by bandwidth, file size and transcoding delay.

Although there have been so many approaches for adapting images, most of them focused on compressing and caching content on the Internet in order to reduce the data transmission time and speed up the delivery. Hence, the results are often not consistent with human perception because of excessive resolution reduction or quality compression.

2.3   Video Adaptation

More and more mobile devices are capable of playing videos, though the limited bandwidth and small window sizes remain two critical obstacles. Currently, most of the video adaptation efforts focus on bandwidth constraints. Among them, caching and rate adaptation are the two dominating approaches.

Rate adaptation solutions can be classified into three categories: single-layer based solutions, discrete scalability based solutions, and fine-granular scalability solutions. The most straightforward single-layer solution is to encode and distribute video sequences at multiple discrete rates that correspond to typical connection speeds. Certain aspects of discrete scalability video coding schemes, such as the spatial, temporal, and SNR scalability structures, are supported in MPEG-2 and MPEG-4. The bit-rates of the base and enhancement layers in discrete scalability video coding schemes are predetermined at encoding time, and therefore cannot be adjusted easily at transmission time. Fine-granular scalability is provided by the MPEG-4 FGS coding scheme, which has become a part of the MPEG-4 standard. It differs from previous layered video encoding schemes in that the bit-rate can be adjusted at transmission time with a much finer granularity and with very little complexity.

Though the size of video sequences is usually too large to cache on proxies, caching parts of the video can be also very useful in reducing the bandwidth consumption and the load on streaming servers. Proxy caching for video has been explored by researchers for several years. Many caching techniques have been proposed in the literature, e.g., layered caching [Rejaie et al., 1999], prefix caching [Sen et al., 1999], video staging [Zhang et al., 2000] and selective caching [Miao and Ortega, 2002].

3.   The Theoretical Framework

The following two observations are important to the development of our framework for optimizing viewer's browsing experience on small displays:

Information Asymmetry: Different parts of content have different importance values. Thus, there exists an optimal set of content blocks when a screen constraint is given. This observation has its origins in the psychology community. It has become clear that not all but only a small part of incoming visual information can reach short-term human memory for further processing, i.e., the Attention as Filter Metaphor [Desimone and Duncan, 1995]. Attentional selection allows only the attention-getting parts to be presented to the user without unduly affecting the user experience. For example, human faces in a home photo are usually more important than the other parts. Generally, most perceptible information can be located inside a small number of objects and at the same time these objects catch most of the attention of the user. As a result, the rendering of content can be treated as manipulating objects to provide as much information as possible under resource constraints.

Flexible Rendering: The content layout should not be fixed to a specific display size. In other words, the layout should be optimized for each specified screen size. Therefore, we need not design multiple versions for the same content. In addition, we should not restrict us to have exactly the same browsing experience as on desktop PCs. More advanced user interface technologies can be employed to improve the usability.

In summary, a scalable content model and a flexible rendering algorithm are two essential issues that we would like to address in this framework. Though different media types may need some customization, it is possible to develop a common content model to provide the basic operations for the optimization process.

3.1   A Content Model for Small Screen

A piece of media content P usually consists of several information objects B_i. An information object is an information carrier that delivers the author's intention and catches part of the user's attention as a whole. For example, it may be a human face, a flower or a text sentence.

Since each information object has different importance values, we introduce property *IMP* as a quantified value of author's subjective evaluation of an information object. It is also an indicator of the weight of each object in contribution to all of the information. This value is used when choosing less important objects for summarization under small displays. The importance values in the same content should be normalized so that their sum is 1.

As mentioned before, the information delivery of an object relies significantly on its area of presentation. If an information object is scaled down too much, it may not be perceptible enough to let users catch the information that authors intend to deliver. Therefore, we introduce *minimal perceptible size (MPS)* to denote the minimal allowable spatial area of an information object. They are used as thresholds to determine whether an information object should be shrunken or summarized when rendering the adapted view.

As regards to those information objects of less importance, it is desirable to summarize them in order to save display space for more important objects.

Instead of deleting content or showing imperceptible adapted version, we introduce *alternative (ALT)* as a substitute for the original content. It should occupy less space than the original information object.

Our proposed content model for small screen presentation is defined as below.

Definition 1: The basic content representation model for a piece of media content P is defined as an unordered set of information objects:

$$P = \{B_i\}, 1 \le i \le N \tag{17.1}$$

and

$$B_i = (IMP_i, MPS_i, ALT_i) \tag{17.2}$$

where

B_i, the ith information object in P
IMP_i, importance value of B_i
MPS_i, minimal perceptible size of B_i
ALT_i, alternative of B_i

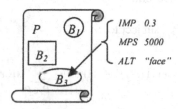

Figure 17.1. An example of the content representation model.

The representation can be in a form of XML descriptions and saved as metadata within original content. An example of the content representation model is shown in Figure 17.1. In the example, three information object, B_1, B_2 and B_3 are contained in the media content P. Each information object has three properties, *IMP*, *MPS* and *ALT*. For object B_3, they are 0.3, 5000 and "face", respectively.

3.2   Presentation Optimization

We introduce *Information Fidelity (IF)* as an objective comparison of a modified version of media content with the original version. The value of information fidelity is confined between 0 (lowest, all information lost) and 1 (highest, all information kept). It is defined as a sum of importance values of existing objects in the adapted version. If an object is replaced by its alternative, its importance value will not be included. Suppose P' is the set of existing information objects in the adapted version, $P' \subset P = \{B_1, B_2, \ldots, B_N\}$. Thus, the mission of the rendering phase is to find the set P' that carries the largest information fidelity which meets the display constraints.

In order to ensure that all the information objects are possible to include in the final presentation, the following space constraint should be satisfied.

$$\sum_{B_i \notin P'} size(ALT_i) + \sum_{B_i \in P'} MPS_i \leq Area \qquad (17.3)$$

where $Area$ is the size of target area and $size()$ is a function which returns the size of display area needed by ALT_i. It says that the space occupied by the information objects or their alternatives should be smaller than the target display area.

If Equation 17.3 is transformed to

$$\sum_{B_i \in P'} (MPS_i - size(ALT_i)) \leq Area - \sum_{B_i \in P} size(ALT_i) \qquad (17.4)$$

the rendering problem becomes:

$\max_{P'}(\sum_{B_i \in P'} IMP_i)$, subject to

$$\sum_{B_i \in P'} (MPS_i - size(ALT_i)) \leq Area - \sum_{B_i \in P} size(ALT_i) \qquad (17.5)$$

We can see that Equation 17.5 is equivalent to a traditional NP-complete problem, 0-1 knapsack. It can be efficiently solved by a branch and bound algorithm. As shown in Figure 17.2, we build a binary tree for object set selection in which the root node is a null set $\emptyset$ implying all the objects are not included and

- Each node denotes a set of included objects.

- Each level presents the inclusion of an information block.

- Each bifurcation means the choice of including the block in the next level or not.

Thus, the height of this tree is N, the total number of objects, and each leaf node in this tree corresponds a different possible object set P'.

For each node in the binary tree, there is a boundary on the possible *IF* value it can achieve among all of its sub-trees. Obviously, the lower boundary is just the *IF* value currently achieved when none of the unchecked objects can be added, that is, the sum of *IF* values of objects included in the current configuration.

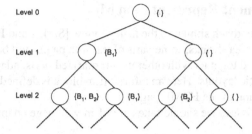

Figure 17.2. The binary tree used in presentation optimization.

And the upper boundary is the addition of all *IF* values of those unchecked blocks after the current level, in other words, the sum of IF values of all blocks in *P* except those discarded before the current level. We perform a depth-first traversal on this tree according to following constraints:

- Whenever the upper bound of a node is smaller than the best *IF* value currently achieved, the whole sub-tree of that node including itself will be truncated.

- At the same time, for each node we check Equation 17.3 to verify its validity. If the constraint is broken, the node and its whole sub-tree will be truncated, because including a new block will increase the sum of *MPS* values.

- If we arrive at a block set with an *IF* value larger than the current best *IF* value, we will replace the current best *IF* value by this one.

By checking the bounds on possible *IF* value, the computation cost is greatly reduced. We can also use some other techniques to reduce the time of traversal such as arranging all the objects in a decreasing order of their importance values at the beginning of search, since in many cases only a few objects contribute the majority of *IF* value.

The complexity of this algorithm is exponential with the number of information objects in the worst case. However, our approach can be conducted efficiently, because the number of information objects is often less than a few dozens and the importance values are always distributed quite unevenly among information objects.

4. Adapting Web Pages for Small Displays

In this section, we show how we apply the previous content model to define a web page representation that is scalable to various display sizes.

4.1   Document Representation Model

We adopt an approach similar to the fisheye view [Sarkar and Brown, 1994]: when the display area shrinks, some parts of the web pages will be summarized and then, presented together with other unsummarized parts, adaptively to end users with aesthetic layouts. Here an information block is defined as a logically independent portion of the HTML page.

There are two issues we should take care of in web page adaptation:

- Web authors usually do not want their content to be randomly shuffled after adaptation. Therefore, we'd better keep the relative position of information blocks.

- For information blocks like texts, they usually require a minimal height and width to be properly displayed. In addition, some information blocks like text blocks can be reflowed while others can not.

Based on the content representation model described in Definition 1, we introduce a scalable web page representation, as shown in Definition 2. The extensions to the original representation model are mainly twofold:

- In order to let authors have controls on the final page layout, we leverage binary slicing trees, a data structure widely used in computer aided design community [Cohoon and Paris, 1987], instead of an unordered set to organize the information blocks.

- We add three additional properties to each information object in order to characterize their special display constraints.

Definition 2: The resulting web page representation is a binary slicing tree with N leaf nodes. Each inner node is labelled with either v or h denoting vertical or horizontal split, and each leaf node is an information block defined as follows:

$$B_i = (IMP_i, MPS_i, ALT_i, MPH_i, MPW_i, ADJ_i) \qquad (17.6)$$

where $1 \leq i \leq N$,
MPH_i, minimal perceptible height of B_i
MPW_i, minimal perceptible width of B_i
ADJ_i, whether the aspect ratio of B_i is adjustable
Other symbols are defined as same as Definition 1.

The label on each inner node determines how the display area is recursively subdivided into sub-rectangles by slicing vertically (v) or horizontally (h). An information block will be placed in the sub-rectangle held by the leaf node. Our

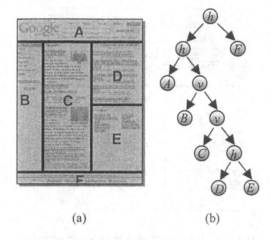

Figure 17.3. (a) An example Web page. (b) The slicing tree.

definition of slicing tree template does not cover where to split, i.e. the ratio of each split, which is often referred to as the slicing number. In our approach, all the slicing numbers will be adjusted adaptively to the display size. A benefit of using slicing trees is that it usually reflects both the intended logical structure and layout structure of the content. An example web page and its corresponding slicing tree are shown in Figure 17.3 (a) and (b) respectively.

For display constraints, we introduce *minimal perceptible height* (*MPH*) and *minimal perceptible width* (*MPW*) to denote the minimal allowable height and width of an information block. *Adjustability* (*ADJ*) denotes whether the aspect ratio of an information block is adjustable. For example, if the content block is a pure text block or a mixture of images and texts, e.g. a news paragraph, it can be wrapped and adapted to fit into the aspect ratio of final display region. However, when the information block is a table like navigation bar, or a large image, the aspect ratio is usually fixed.

4.2 Adaptive Web Page Rendering

In order to ensure that all the content blocks are possible to include in the final presentation, Equation 17.3 should be satisfied. However, Equation 17.3 does not ensure that *MPH* or *MPW* will be satisfied. We solve the problem by a two-level approach. First we use the previous proposed branch and bound algorithm to enumerate all possible block set P'. Then for each block set, we use a capacity ratio based slicing algorithm to test whether a valid layout can be found. By this process, we search among all possible block set P' to select the

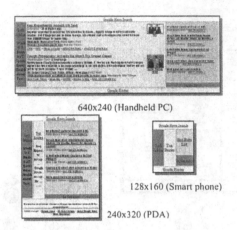

640x240 (Handheld PC)

128x160 (Smart phone)

240x320 (PDA)

Figure 17.4.   Example of adaptive web page rendering.

optimal one, i.e. the scheme that achieves the largest *IF* value while presenting an aesthetic view.

The capacity ratio based slicing method includes two steps. First, we go through the slicing tree in a bottom-up way to calculate the capacity, height and width constraints for each node. The second step compares the capacities of two sub-trees of each inner node and let the slicing number of that node be proportional to them.

After layout optimization, each block, whether summarized or not, has been assigned a rectangle region for display. We use the *ADJ* attribute of each information block to aid the content accommodation process. If a block is indicated to be adjustable, we will fit it into the target rectangle by zooming and wrapping. Otherwise, we will only zoom the block while maintaining its aspect ratio. Figure 17.4 shows the rendering results on three typical screen sizes for the example web page in Figure 17.3. More details of these algorithms can be found in [Chen et al., 2002].

5.   Adapting Images for Small Displays

We have developed an attention model based image adaptation approach in [Chen et al., 2003][Fan et al., 2003a][Liu et al., 2003]. In this section, we will show how the content representation model introduced in Section 3 can be extended to incorporate the image attention model. With the image attention model and the corresponding adaptation algorithm, the image browser down-samples the resolution and relocates the viewing region to achieve the largest information fidelity while preserving satisfying perceptibility.

5.1   Image Attention Model

In [Chen et al., 2003], we give the definition of image attention model as following:

Definition 3: The visual attention model for an image is defined as a set of attention objects:

$$\{AO_i\} = \{(ROI_i, AV_i, MPS_i)\}, 1 \le i \le N \qquad (17.7)$$

where
AO_i, the ith attention object within the image
ROI_i, Region-Of-Interest of AO_i
AV_i, attention value of AO_i
MPS_i, minimal perceptible size of AO_i

Besides that the notion of attention object is just equivalent to information object, the differences between Definition 3 and Definition 1 are:

- The image attention model adds a *ROI* property to each information object. It is borrowed from JPEG 2000 [Christopoulos et al., 2000] and is referred in this model as a spatial region or segment that corresponds to an information object.

- We suppose the alternative of an object in images to be null since the information object will be cropped if it can not be put on the display.

We have also developed a set of algorithms in [Chen et al., 2003][Ma and Zhang, 2003] to generate the content model automatically.

5.2   Attention Model Based Image Rendering

In [Chen et al., 2003], we propose a technique to transform the problem into integer programming and a branch-and-bound algorithm to find the optimal adaptation result. This algorithm is just a variant of our previous algorithm in Section 3 where a few problem-specific display constraints have been taken into consideration.

As shown in Figure 17.5, the most important part of a large image is identified and cropped to fit the limited display size. However, much other information which a user cares may be lost by this approach. In [Fan et al., 2003a][Liu et al., 2003], we further propose to employ a widely-used presentation technique, Rapid Serial Visual Presentation (RSVP), in which space is traded for time [Bruijn and Spence, 2000]. In RSVP, amounts of content are displayed serially, each for a brief period of time, to aid users' browsing or searching through the whole content.

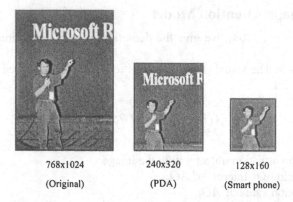

768x1024   240x320   128x160

(Original)   (PDA)   (Smart phone)

Figure 17.5.   Example of attention based image adaptation.

We depict the attention movement as two states: the fixation state and the saccade state. The iterations of these two states compose the whole simulation of the shifting process in a similar way with RSVP. The acquirement of the fixated region depends on the algorithm in [Chen et al., 2003]. The saccade state can be described as a shifting process from the most informative region to the second one, then the third and so on. A motivation of this process comes from a psychophysical phenomenon called "inhibition-of-return" [Itti and Koch, 2001], which demonstrates that current attention focus will be suppressed while selecting the next focus. We have implemented it by removing the information objects contained in the current display area and applying the same algorithm to the rest objects when selecting the next fixating area. The trace of the saccade is defined as the shortest path between centers of the two fixation areas.

6.   Adapting Videos for Small Displays

Video adaptation is another natural application of our content model for small displays. In this section, we will only focus on real-time programs or spontaneous video clips such as home videos and surveillance videos. For this kind of video, it is more possible and also in greater demand to optimize the content for different display conditions. Previous results on image adaptation can be easily extended to video adaptation if we simply consider each video frame as an image [Shimoga, 2002]. However, this naive approach will cause jitters in the video sequences since the frames will be discontinuous after cropping.

To solve this problem, virtual camera control [Sun et al., 2001] is applied to improve the quality of output stream. Suppose there is a virtual camera which can pan and zoom in the original video frames, it can be steered to focus on the most important regions and only deliver those focused regions.

Two types of focuses are introduced here: *Camera Focus (CF)* and *Target Focus (TF)*. *CF* stands for the focus displayed to the users and *TF* is the destination focus either manually assigned or automatically determined. Corresponding display ratios of the two types of focus regions are defined as *Camera Ratio (CR)* and *Target Ratio (TR)*, respectively. The Euclidean distance between *CF* and *TF* is denoted as Δd and the difference of *CR* and *TR* is defined as Δr. The direct focus shifting is substituted for a smooth following process from the current focus region to the target focus region, with a set of pan and zoom operations. In our system, the virtual camera is in one of following three states:

- *Fixation state*: If both Δd and Δr are very small, the virtual camera will be fixed in order to avoid unpleasant dithers in the video stream.

- *Following state*: When either Δd or Δr is larger than a predefined threshold, we will let the virtual camera smoothly follow the new target focus. In moving object tracking, *Infinite Impulse Response (IIR)* filtering is often used to smooth temporally the spatial derivatives. In our algorithm, a recursive implementation of the second order filter is adopted:

$$C(k) = \alpha_1 C(k-1) + \alpha_2 (T(k) + T(k-1)) \qquad (17.8)$$

where $\alpha_1 + \alpha_2/2 = 1, \alpha_1, \alpha_2 > 0$, $C(k)$ is either the position of *CF* or *CR* at time k and $T(k)$ is the corresponding position of *TF* or *TR*.

- *Shifting state*: When either Δd or Δr is less than a threshold, we will directly steer the virtual camera to the new target region in order to eliminate the lag as a result of the *IIR* filter:

$$C(k) = T(k) \qquad (17.9)$$

In addition, the virtual camera will also come to shifting state when a shot boundary occurs, which is mainly because that we consider the content is not related between two different shots.

For videos, motion will catch more attention than any other stationary objects. Therefore, we add a new motion attention model to the original image attention model. We extract the *motion vector field (MVF)* directly from MPEG streams and employ a detection approach similar to [Ma et al., 2002] to find the motion attention objects. The importance value of a motion object will be set to be much larger than other stationary objects.

This kind of video adaptation is very useful in video conferencing scenarios. For instance, a mobile worker with only a handheld device wants to chat with his friends from a desktop. The attention based video adaptation can detect the

Figure 17.6.   Example of attention based video adaptation.

human faces in the video stream and only deliver those regions to the client device. Therefore, he/she can see a clearer face image on the small screen and the bandwidth cost can also be reduced. Figure 17.6 shows an example of the attention based video adaptation.

7.   Content Services Networks

As the Internet is moving towards a service-centric model, more and more storage and computational resources are being plugged into the Internet infrastructure and provided as services to customers. In the content networking world, for instance, this trend can be seen on the development of *content delivery networks* (*CDNs*) which make content distribution a network infrastructure service available to content providers and network access providers. On the other hand, the progress on standardization and development of web services has marked the beginning of a new era that every computational resource and service on the Internet can be connected to provide new user experiences on accessing, sharing, and using information anytime, anywhere, from any device.

In this section, we propose to provide content modelling and adaptation functions as subscription-based web services. It is based on our previous work named *content services networks* (*CSNs*) [Ma et al., 2001] which aim to make *content delivery networks* (*CDNs*) capable of delivering content adaptation services.

Figure 17.7 shows the overall system, which constitutes two layers of network infrastructures: content delivery overlay (i.e. *CDNs*) and service delivery overlay. The content delivery overlay is constituted of a network of service-enabled web caches which extend the functionalities of traditional web caches for performing value-added processing. The service delivery overlay consists of a large number of application servers which act as remote call-out servers for service-enabled web caches. These two overlays work together to provide content-oriented web services.

Before the content modelling and adaptation service becomes available, it needs to be registered in the *UDDI* (*Universal Description and Discovery Inte-*

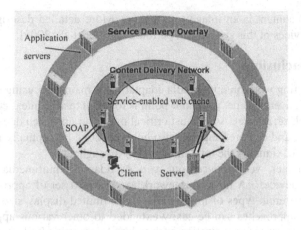

Figure 17.7. The architecture of content services network.

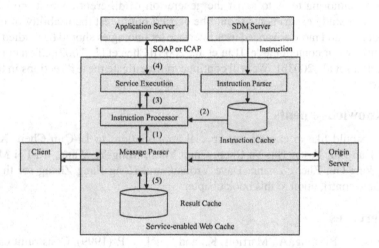

Figure 17.8. The service-enabled web cache.

gration) registry first. The received components such as service specifications and binaries from service providers are stored in the service database. In order to use the service, a mobile client needs to first find and subscribe to the service via *UDDI* registries. Then the service instructions are generated and transferred from the management servers to the service-enabled web caches that the subscriber is associated with. As shown in Figure 17.8, the service-enabled web cache determines if a message needs services according to the service instructions. In our case, the instructions may simply be type comparison, i.e., whether the content is an image or a video. More detailed description and example services of this system can be found in [Ma et al., 2003].

8.   Conclusions

Most existing work on multimedia adaptation is mainly focusing on saving file size or delivering time, while our point is to adapt to all context constraints among which screen size is the most critical one. Our approach does not only using scaling and compressing, but also helps locating perceptually important regions and maximizing the total information throughput.

In this chapter, we introduced our work on adapting multimedia to small-form-factor devices. A novel framework as well as a set of approaches for presenting different types of multimedia under limited display size was proposed. Our approaches can be easily extended to other various applications such as information summarization or thumbnail generation [Suh et al., 2003], since space limit is also the critical issue there. We are currently developing a set of authoring tools to assist the generation of different content models. More user study experiments should be carried out to test the usability of our approaches and more advanced user interface technologies should be studied to best utilize our content model [Liu et al., 2003][Chen et al., 2003][Chen et al., 2005][Fan et al., 2003b]. We will continue to investigate these directions in the future.

Acknowledgements

We would like to express our special appreciations to Li-Qun Chen, Xin Fan, Hao Liu, Yusuo Hu, Yu Chen, Chun Yuan, Ming-Yu Wang, Yu-Fei Ma, Xiaodong Gu, Zheng Zhang, Dave Vronay, and Hong-Jiang Zhang for their valuable contribution to this book chapter.

References

Badros, G., Borning, A., Marriott, K., and Stuckey, P. (1999). Constraint cascading style sheets for the web. In *UIST '99 Proc.*, pages 73–82, Asheville, USA.

BickMore, T.W. and Schilit, B.N. (1997). Digestor: device-independent access to the world wide web. In *WWW '97 Proc.*, pages 655–663, Santa Clara, USA.

Borning, A., Lin, R.K., and Marriott, K. (2000). Constraint-based document layout for the web. *ACM Multimedia Systems Journal*, 8(3):177–189.

Bruijn, O. and Spence, R. (2000). Rapid serial visual presentation: a space-time trade-off in information presentation. In *AVI '00 Proc.*, pages 189–192, Palermo, Italy.

Buyukkokten, O., Kaljuvee, O., Garcia-Molina, H., Paepcke, A., and Winograd, T. (2002). Efficient web browsing on handheld devices using page and form summarization. *ACM Trans. on Info. Syst.*, 20(1):82–115.

Chen, J.L., Zhou, B.Y., Shi, J., Zhang, H.J., and Wu, Q.F. (2001). Function-based object model towards website adaptation. In *WWW '01 Proc.*, pages 587–596, Hong Kong.

Chen, L.Q., Xie, X., Fan, X., Ma, W.Y., Zhang, H.J., and Zhou, H.Q. (2003). A visual attention model for adapting images on small displays. *ACM Multimedia Systems Journal*, 9(4):353–364.

Chen, L.Q., Xie, X., Ma, W.Y., Zhang, H.J., Zhou, H.Q., and Feng, H.Q. (2002). Dress: A slicing tree based web representation for various display sizes. Technical Report MSR-TR-2002-126, Microsoft Research, Redmond, WA, USA.

Chen, Y., Xie, X., Ma, W.Y., and Zhang, H.J. (2005). Adapting web pages for small-screen devices. *IEEE Internet Computing*, 9(1):50–56.

Christopoulos, C., Skodras, A., and Ebrahimi, T. (2000). The jpeg2000 still image coding system: an overview. *IEEE Trans. on Consumer Electronics*, 46(4):1103–1127.

Cohoon, J.P. and Paris, W.D. (1987). Genetic placement. *IEEE Trans. on Computer-Aided Design*, 6(6):956–964.

Desimone, R. and Duncan, J. (1995). Neural mechanisms of selective visual attention. *Annual Review of Neuroscience*, 18:193–222.

Fan, X., Xie, X., Ma, W.Y., Zhang, H.J., and Zhou, H.Q. (2003a). Visual attention based image browsing on mobile devices. In *ICME '03 Proc. Vol. 1*, pages 53–56, Baltimore, MD, USA.

Fan, X., Xie, X., Zhou, H.Q., and Ma, W.Y. (2003b). Looking into video frames on small displays. In *ACM multimedia '03 Proc.*, pages 247–250, Berkeley, CA, USA.

Fox, A., Gribble, S., Brewer, E.A., and Amir, E. (1996). Adapting to network and client variability via on-demand dynamic distillation. In *Proc. of 7th Int. Conf. on Architectural Support for Programming Languages and Operating Systems*, pages 160–170, Cambridge, USA.

Fuchs, M. (2000). An evolutionary approach to support web page design. In *Proc. of 2000 Congress on Evolutionary Computation*, pages 1312–1319, Piscataway, USA.

Gonzalez, J., Rojas, I., Pomares, H., Salmeron, M., and Merelo, J.J. (2002). Web newspaper layout optimization using simulated annealing. *IEEE Trans. on Systems, Man, and Cybernetics - Part B: Cybernetics*, 32(5):686–691.

Gu, X.D., Chen, J.L., Ma, W.Y., and Chen, G.L. (2000). Visual based content understanding towards web adaptation. In *Proc. of 2nd Intl. Conf. on Adaptive Hypermedia and Adaptive Web Based Systems*, pages 164–173, Malaga, Spain.

Han, R., Bhagwat, P., Lamaire, R., Mummert, T., Perret, V., and Rubas, J. (1998). Dynamic adaptation in an image transcoding proxy for mobile web access. *IEEE Personal Communications*, 5(6):8–17.

Itti, L. and Koch, C. (2001). Computational modeling of visual attention. *Nature Reviews Neuroscience*, 2(3):194–203.

Liu, H., Xie, X., Ma, W.Y., and Zhang, H.J. (2003). Automatic browsing of large pictures on mobile devices. In *ACM multimedia '03 Proc.*, pages 148–155, Berkeley, CA, USA.

Ma, W.Y., Shen, B., and Brassil, J. (2001). Content services network: the architecture and protocols. In *WCW '01 Proc.*, pages 83–101, Boston, USA.

Ma, W.Y., Xie, X., Yuan, C., Chen, Y., Zhang, Z., and Zhang, H.J. (2003). Enabling multimedia adaptation services in content delivery networks. In *Proc. of 3rd International Workshop on Intelligent Multimedia Computing and Networking*, pages 1321–1324, Cary, North Carolina, USA.

Ma, Y.F., Lu, L., Zhang, H.J., and Li, M.J. (2002). A user attention model for video summarization. In *ACM multimedia '02 Proc.*, pages 533–542, Juan-les-Pins, France.

Ma, Y.F. and Zhang, H.J. (2003). Contrast-based image attention analysis by using fuzzy growing. In *ACM multimedia '03 Proc.*, pages 374–381, Berkeley, CA, USA.

Miao, Z. and Ortega, A. (2002). Scalable proxy caching of video under storage constraints. *IEEE Journal on Selected Areas in Communications*, 20(7):1315–1327.

Milic-Frayling, N. and Sommerer, R. (2002). Smartview: flexible viewing of web page contents. In *WWW '02 Proc.*, Honolulu, USA.

Mohan, R., Smith, J.R., and Li, C.S. (1999). Adapting multimedia internet content for universal access. *IEEE Trans. on Multimedia*, 1(1):104–114.

Rejaie, R., Handley, M., Yu, H., and Estrin, D. (1999). Proxy caching mechanism for multimedia playback streams in the internet. In *Proc. of the 4th International Web Caching Workshop*, San Diego, CA, USA.

Sarkar, M. and Brown, M.H. (1994). Graphical fisheye views. *Communications of the ACM*, 37(12):73–84.

Sen, S., Rexford, J., and Towsley, D. (1999). Proxy prefix caching for multimedia streams. In *Infocom '99 Proc.*, pages 1310–1319, New York, USA.

Shimoga, K.B. (2002). Region of interest based video image transcoding for heterogeneous client displays. In *Proc. of 12th International PacketVideo Workshop*, Pittsburgh, USA.

Smith, J.R., Mohan, R., and Li, C.S. (1998). Content-based transcoding of images in the internet. In *ICIP '98 Proc., Vol. 3*, pages 7–11, Chicago, USA.

Suh, B., Ling, H., Bederson, B.B., and Jacobs, D.W. (2003). Automatic thumbnail cropping and its effectiveness. In *UIST '03 Proc.*, pages 95–104, Vancouver, Canada.

Sun, X., Foote, J., Kimber, D., and Manjunath, B.S. (2001). Panoramic video capturing and compressed domain virtual camera control. In *ACM multimedia '01 Proc.*, pages 329–347, Ottawa, Canada.

Wobbrock, O.J., Forlizzi, J., Hudson, S.E., and Myers, B.A. (2002). Webthumb: interaction techniques for small-screen browsers. In *UIST '02 Proc.*, pages 205–208, Paris, France.

Zhang, Z.L., Wang, Y., Du, D.H.C., and Su, D. (2000). Video staging: a proxy-server-based approach to end-to-end video delivery over wide-area networks. *IEEE Trans. on Networking*, 8(4):429–442.

Index